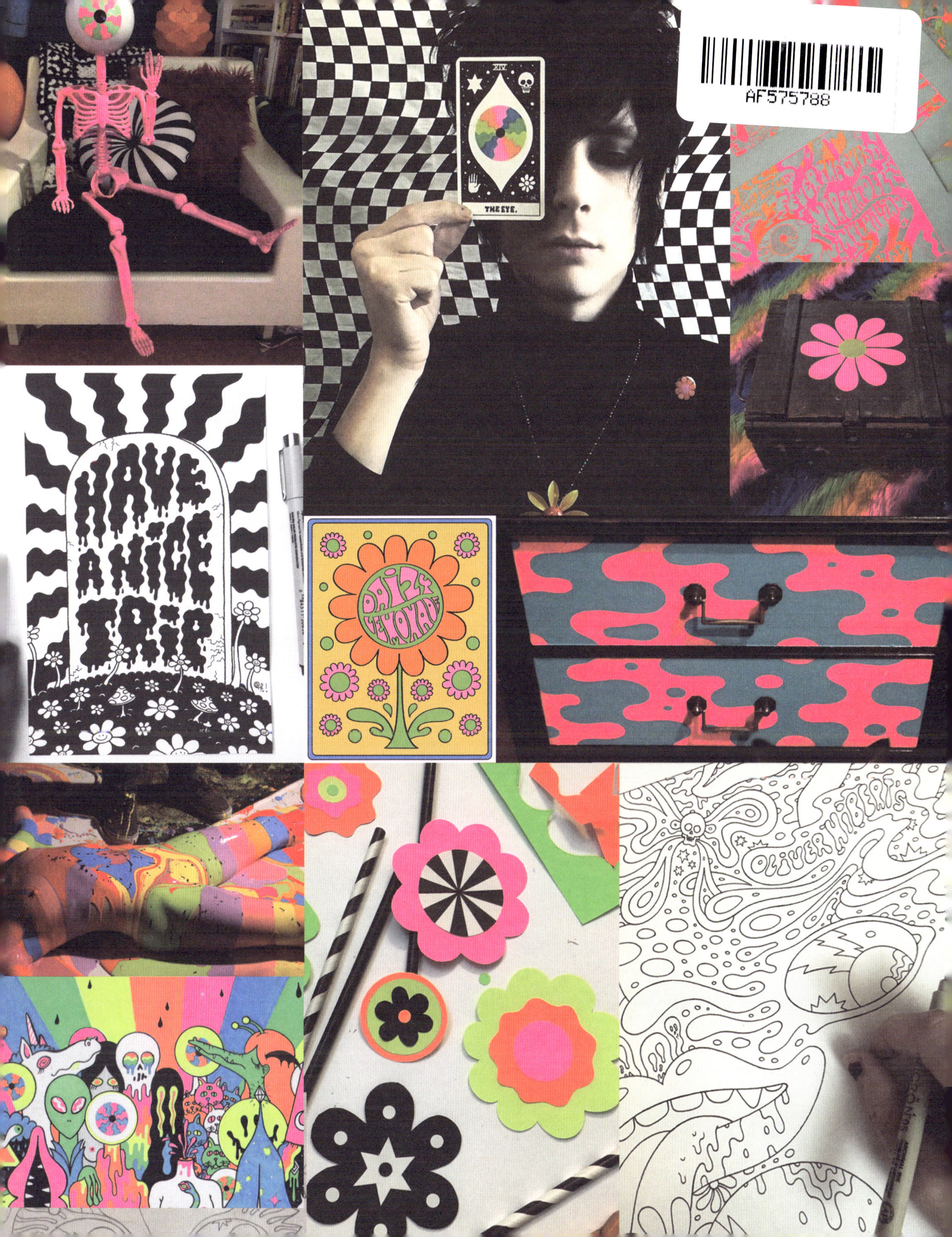
XIV
THE EYE.
HAVE A NICE TRIP
OLIVER HIBERT'S

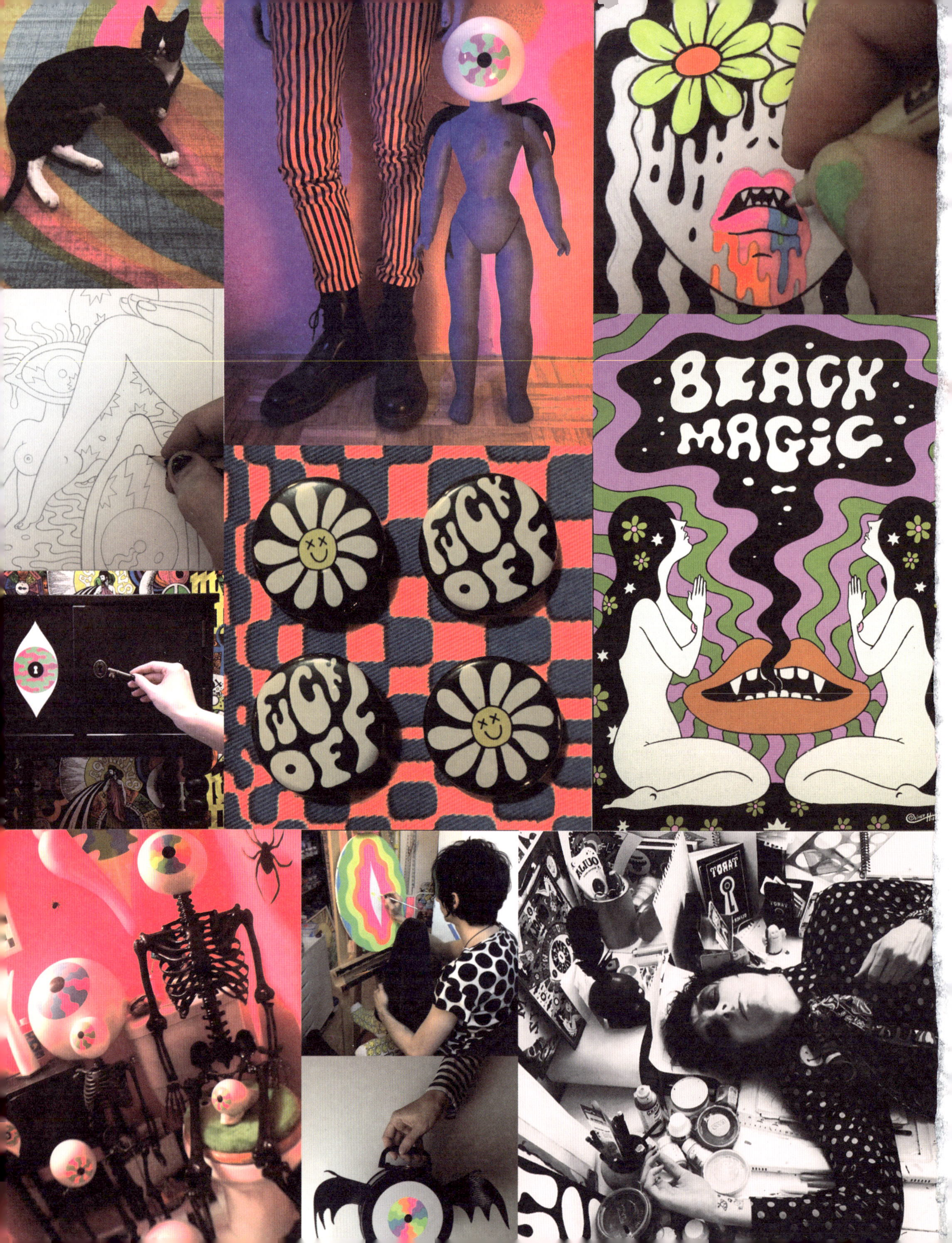
FUCK OFF
FUCK OFF
BLACK MAGIC

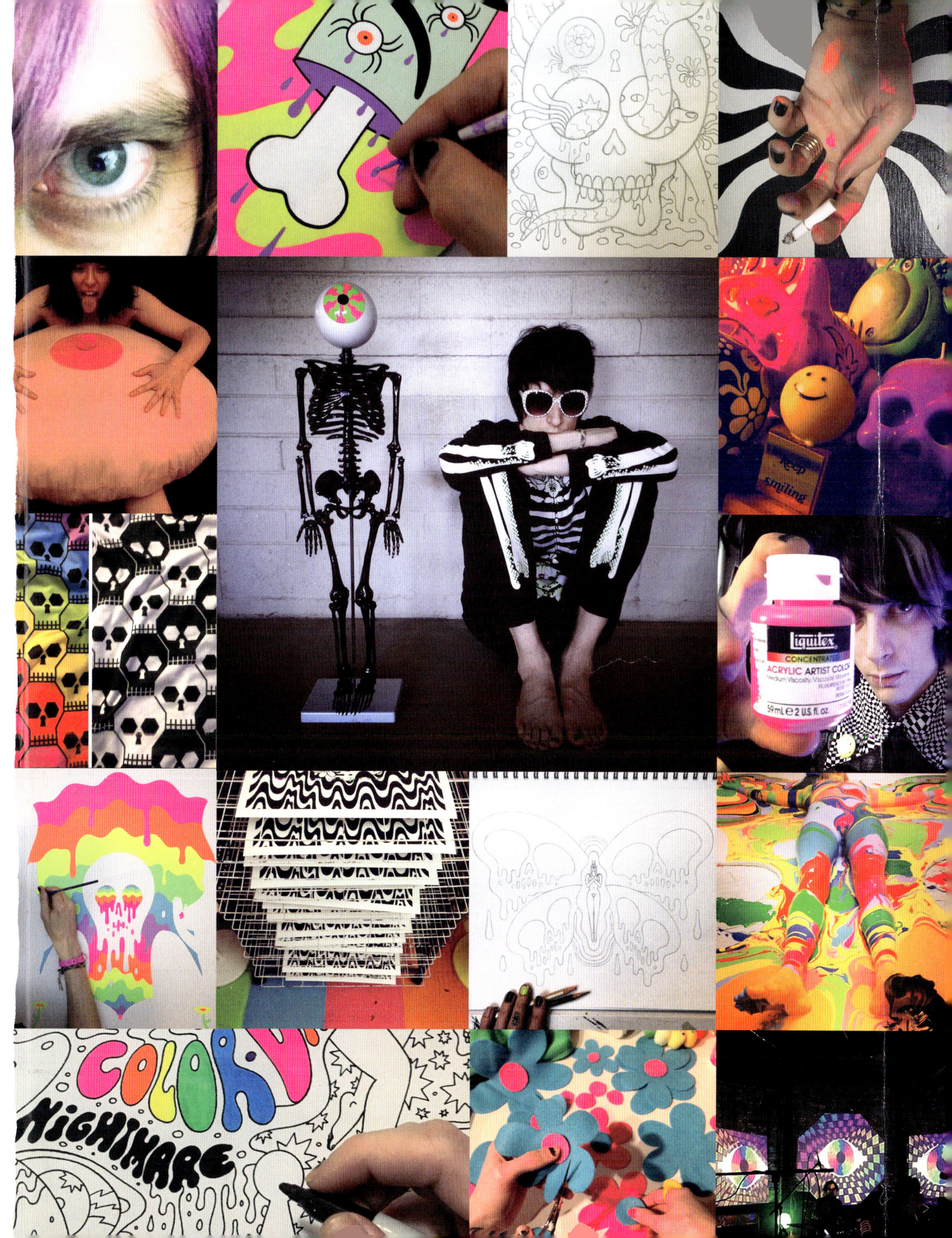
Keep
smiling
Liquitex
CONCENTRATED
59 mL ℮ 2 U.S. fl. oz.
COLOR
NIGHTMARE

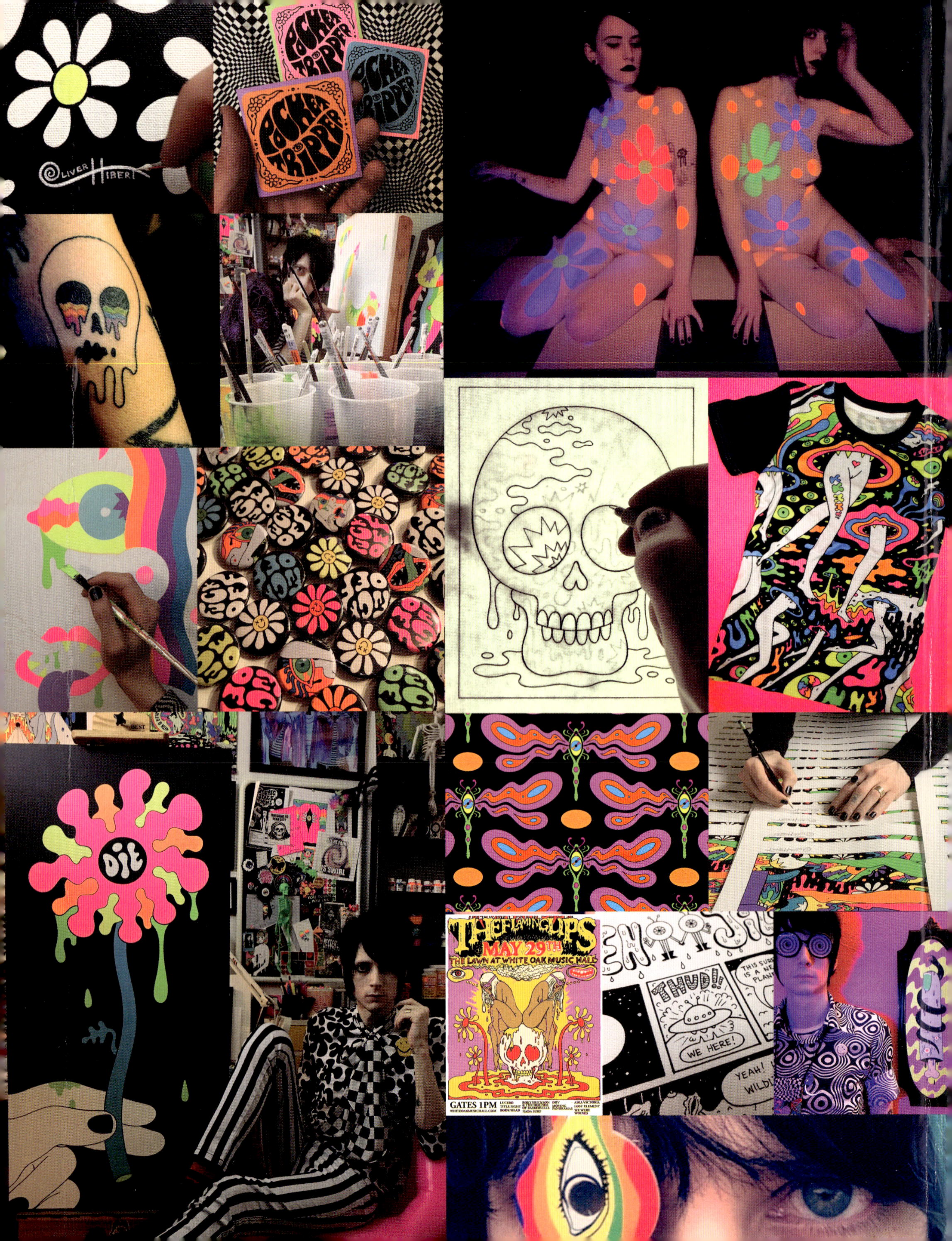
OLIVER HIBERT
POCKET TRIPPER
THE FLAMING LIPS
MAY 29TH
THE LAWN AT WHITE OAK MUSIC HALL
GATES 1PM
THUD!!
WE HERE!

EYE SEE YOU

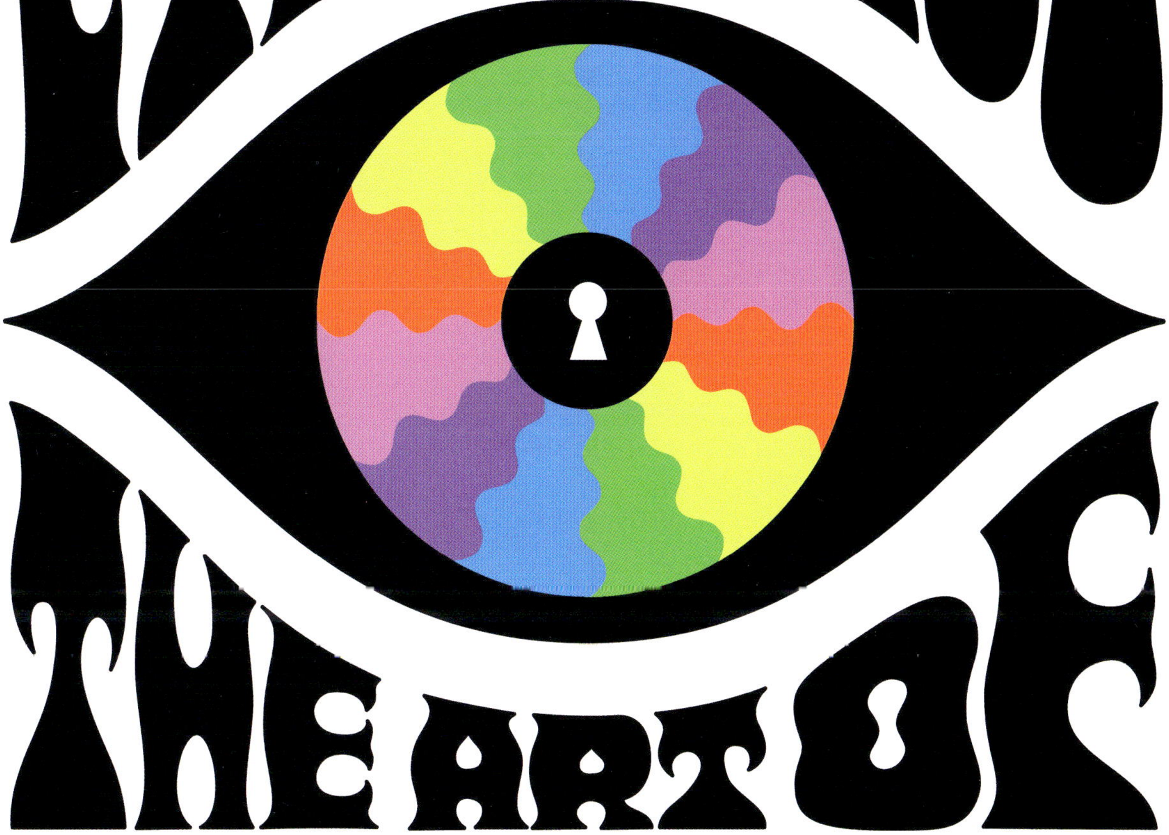

THE ART OF OLIVER HIBERT

Angelo [illegible] & Oliver Hibert, Foreword by Wayne Coyne

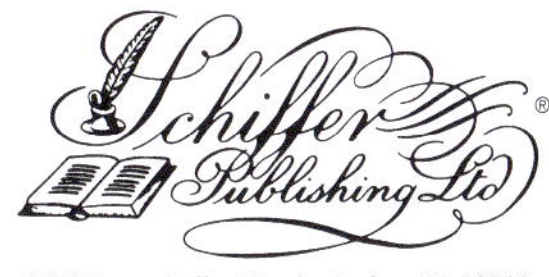

4880 Lower Valley Road • Atglen, PA 19310

I dedicate this book to a few very special humans that have always believed, supported, and stuck by my side through the thick, the thin, the beauty, and the madness of my life and art. It is because of you that this book and all the art it holds even exists. You know exactly who you are. I love you more than I could ever express. Thank you from the bottom of my heart to the top of the stars.

–Oliver Hibert

Library of Congress Control Number: 2017935741

Cover design by Oliver Hibert
Interior designed by Matthew Goodman

Credits: We would like to thank Nike, Lush Ltd, The Flaming Lips, Salomon Snowboards, Fender, *Beautiful Decay* Magazine, House Ghosts, *Fondle* Magazine, Creature Skateboards, The Moon Life, DSL55, *Tribe* Magazine, Haunted Rainbow, and Warner Bros. for usage of Oliver's design work in this book.

Type set in Century Gothic

ISBN: 978-0-7643-5443-4
Printed in China

Published by Schiffer Publishing, Ltd.
4880 Lower Valley Road
Atglen, PA 19310
Phone: (610) 593-1777; Fax: (610) 593-2002
E-mail: Info@schifferbooks.com
Web: www.schifferbooks.com

For our complete selection of fine books on this and related subjects, please visit our website at www.schifferbooks.com. You may also write for a free catalog.

Schiffer Publishing's titles are available at special discounts for bulk purchases for sales promotions or premiums. Special editions, including personalized covers, corporate imprints, and excerpts, can be created in large quantities for special needs. For more information, contact the publisher.

Contents

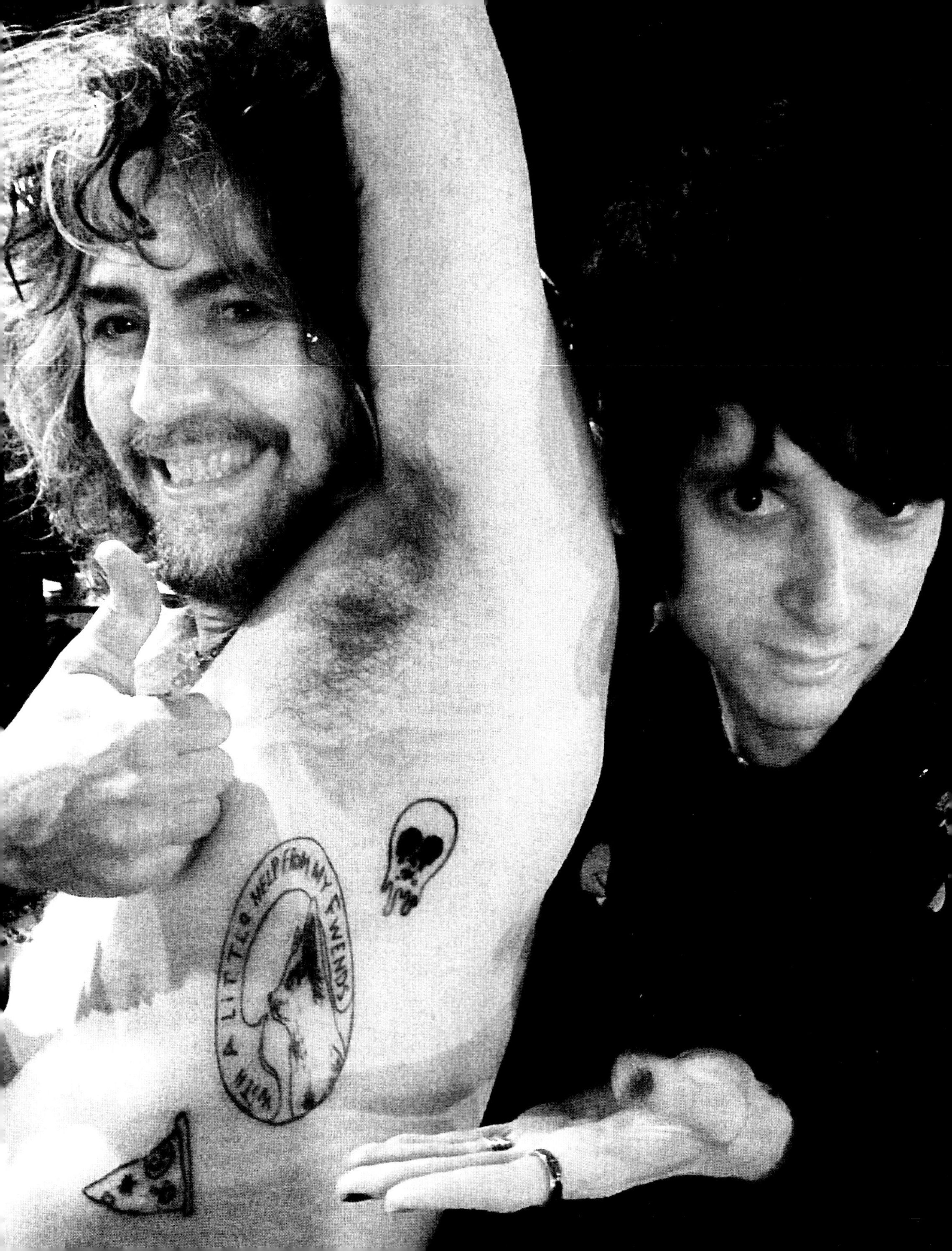
WITH A LITTLE HELP FROM MY FWENDS

Foreword

Oliver Hibert is . . . well . . . he's like an insect. A praying mantis . . . . Yeah. If you see photos of him (with his big oval sunglasses on) you'll see what I mean. And . . . he's skinny as fuck. Like Nosferatu if he was alive in 1969. So yeah . . . he is a praying mantis, Nosferatu guy who lives perpetually in a counterculture freak-out fantasy world of 1969. But not to stop any war. And not to "hate the pigs." And not to riot in the streets. He lives there only to paint. When he is NOT painting he has a nervous energy about him which is like a drug addict (and kind of like a praying mantis) that's in need of his fix or in need of eating another insect's head . . . and luckily for us (and the world and the universe), painting is his fix. His insect head. And he is full of love . . . you can see it in his saturated sexed up color palette. His purples are kind of pink. His yellows are kind of pink. His pinks are kind of fleshy. His reds are kind of bloody. His oranges are a kind of piss color. His green is pus. And you can see it in his characters. His characters are from a cartoon bible, and upon seeing his paintings, we immediately understand their meaning . . . (I don't know why, maybe it's a subconscious thing, like the giant drawings the UFOs made on the mountainside in Sri Lanka). They squirt and spit and bleed and piss . . . their eyes are popped out. Their heads are cut off . . . but not for gore. For sheer joy. There is a blobby-ness, a roundness, a voluptuousness in his style and design that lets you know he is a very nice person and that he has no darkness or problem to unload on you . . . he just loves to paint what he paints. He is not complaining about the world . . . he just loves to paint what he paints. He is not saying, "Fuck You!" to the world . . . he just loves to paint what he paints. His paintings are everything about religious paintings that you like without any of the judgment and authority that you don't like. I think he takes a lot of acid . . . but it hasn't damaged him like it does most artists. Most acid-damaged artists want to show you all the wonders of the hidden universe that they have discovered while they are tripping and, like someone telling you about an endless weird dream they had last night, it is exhausting to pay attention to. With Oliver, you never get preached at, you never get put down, there is no science you should learn, or no reference you are missing. Oliver is all impact . . . soft, gentle, impact. Like sucking on your mother's nipple. She wants you to do it and you want to do it. That's as deep as it gets. There is no pain waiting for you at the end of the story. There is no lesson to be learned. With Oliver, life ends when you are sixteen. Full of life. Full of love. Full of sperm. Full of energy. Full of hope. Full of a dream that still seems like it will come true.

Wayne Coyne

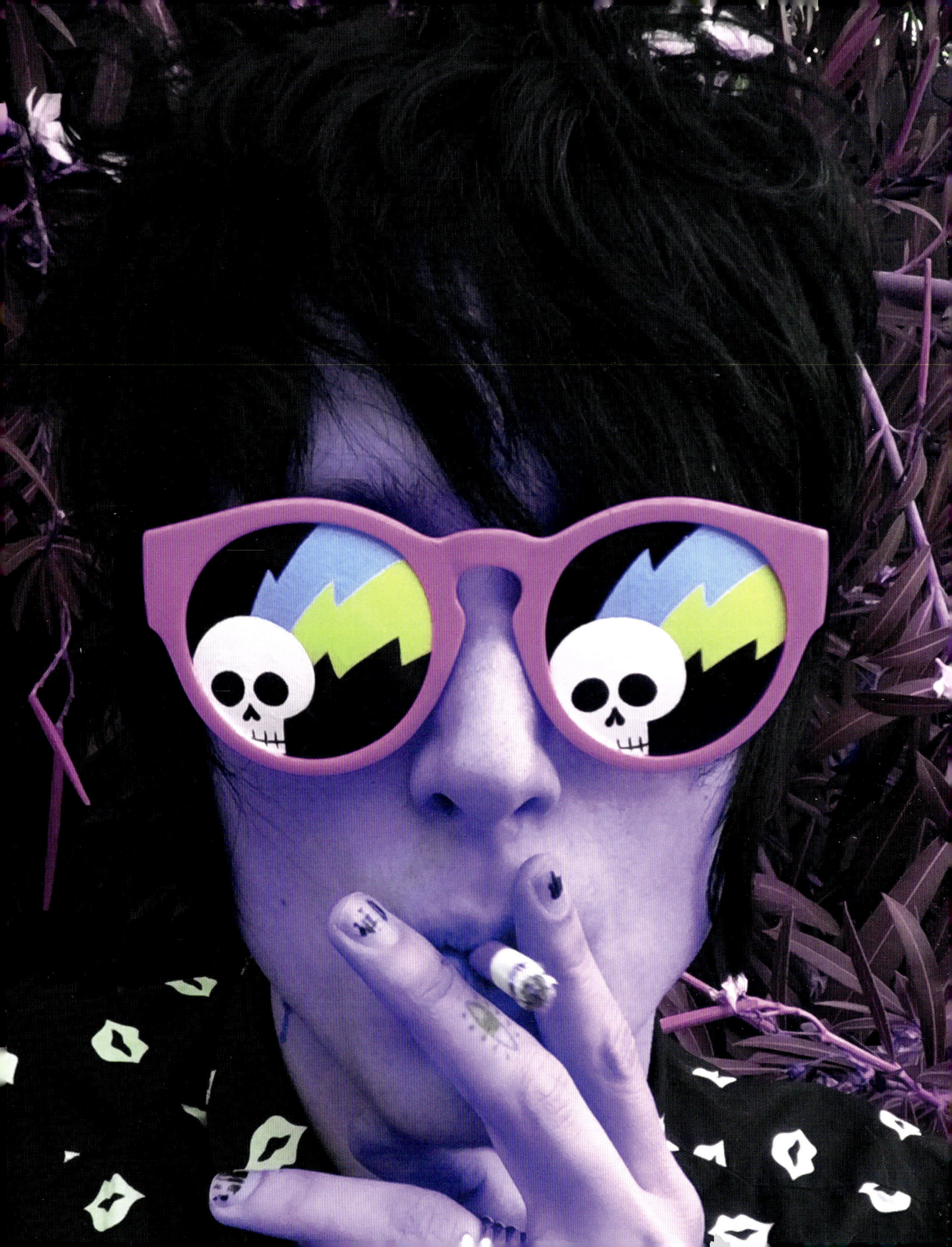

Introduction

There was a brief, bizarre time in the early 2000s where prototypical social media websites like Myspace offered a platform for discovery, an odd and largely imperfect way to stumble upon new young artists. And in this auspicious manner, my wife and I came upon the art of Oliver Hibert. Even as tiny thumbnail images, his work resonated. We saw in his art something new and different from many other young painters at the time, and we fell in love with the effortless way Oliver could approximate 60s pop and psychedelia and make it fresh and fun again, without being shameless or redundant. Being that we were both heavily influenced by *Juxtapoz* Magazine and artists like Robert Williams, Shag, and Coop, Oliver's work appealed to us for his ability to embrace nostalgia while innovating and nodding vigorously to the past while pushing forward and exploring new ideas. Fast-forward to our solo show of his work. The reaction was instant and overwhelming—people fought over pieces already sold, parents bought stickers and prints for their kids while buying paintings for themselves. A retired mailman, discreetly "growing his own" on a remote farm outside of town, covered his walls with as much of Oliver's art as he could carry. We felt his would be a fitting home. The gallery itself resembled some sort of alternate-universe, Haight-Ashbury head shop/space station, the heavy radiating colors knocking people out from across the street. And while we of course prided ourselves on showing artists we loved, more than ever, the idea of parting with any of Oliver's paintings felt like giving away newborns. Though our existence may have been hand-to-mouth at times, we found a way to keep a half-dozen paintings for ourselves.

In getting to know Oliver, it was incredibly exciting to find that he lived these paintings—what I mean is that his artwork could just as well be photographs of his daily existence. He dresses like his art, he looks like his art; his tripped-out, Kool-Aid acid tab Arizona compound is a work of art in and of itself. So, while Clement Greenberg talked about kitsch being the opposite of art way back in 1939, we've now come to know how Frank Frazetta, Ed "Big Daddy" Roth, and Jack Kirby are just as responsible for the art of the twentieth century as Pollock or de Kooning. Plus, whether you think Greenberg is right or wrong, I'm sure we can agree he's simply not much fun. And fun is what Oliver's art is about. Even when it's ugly or creepy or confrontational, it's fun like a haunted house or a rubber Halloween mask. We do have to live with these paintings—we have to share our homes with the art we own every day, so why not keep it fun?

It's incredibly important and special for me to bring you the first survey of Oliver Hibert's art. If this is your first time seeing what he does, I'm excited for you. If you're already among the initiated, I'm confident that this book contains all the things you love about what he does. When you turn the pages, hopefully you get the feelings you got the first time you read a comic book, watched H.R. Pufnstuf, dug the prize out of the bottom of a box of Lucky Charms, or maybe even the first time you made out with somebody. I know it does for me.

Angelo Madrigale

Chapter One:

Paintings & Sculptures

Disembodied eyeballs, floating lips. Amoebic shapes hang in the background as clouds, sometimes masquerading as a snake's stripes. Hallucinogenic rainbows act as borders, walkways, and portals. Oliver Hibert's paintings seemingly tick all the boxes necessary to be labeled psychedelic art, yet there are major differences between his work and that of his psych predecessors. The LSD-fueled, swinging London-influenced works by "Yellow Submarine" cartoonist Heinz Edelman may be the closest predecessor to Oliver's own, yet British pop art legend Peter Blake may have more in common with the illustrative flatness of Oliver's paintings.

Working almost exclusively in acrylic allows Oliver to achieve the goal of the "Superflat" ideal first articulated and championed by Takashi Murakami, a kindred spirit who himself looked back to the cartoons and cereal boxes of his youth for inspiration. Painting in this style can be illusory, drawing another art historical line to the op-art movement and works by artists like Victor Vasarely, who reconsidered trompe l'oeil as a perceptual effect ages before his work was unfairly relegated to the stuff of black light posters. But again, while Vasarely and others may have been dealt art intellectual short shrift by being merchandised for the masses, Oliver's work knows no separation between highbrow and lowbrow. The work of the Old Masters is every bit as valid as that of the psychedelic rock poster/ underground comix artists such as Moscoso, Griffin, and Mouse—it's all on an even playing field, recontextualized and reborn in new art bereft of compartmentalization. Hibert's art history book ranks Walt Disney alongside Pablo Picasso; his paintings equal parts technical prowess and culture fanaticism.

According to Hibert, "I believe as my paintings have progressed through time—and keep progressing, that color is the most concrete connection with my work and the 60s."

From Vermeer through Bridget Riley to Ellsworth Kelly, color is an undeniable connecting force in art. Hibert's use of color plays on our memory. Whether it recalls Screaming Yellow Zonkers, a Philip K. Dick paperback cover, or the packaging of a Dungeons and Dragons game, his colors are encoded with our memories and gut-level interpretation of graphic design. Who knew by the time we went to our first museum that our minds had already been blown by the little-known toy makers and animators of our youth? That our perception of art didn't begin with our first art history course, but at birth, inhaling every visual stimulant that crossed our path? In Oliver Hibert's work, nostalgia is a misnomer, and time is a construct. What we see and have seen exists simultaneously and our interpretation is more about who we are than what we think.

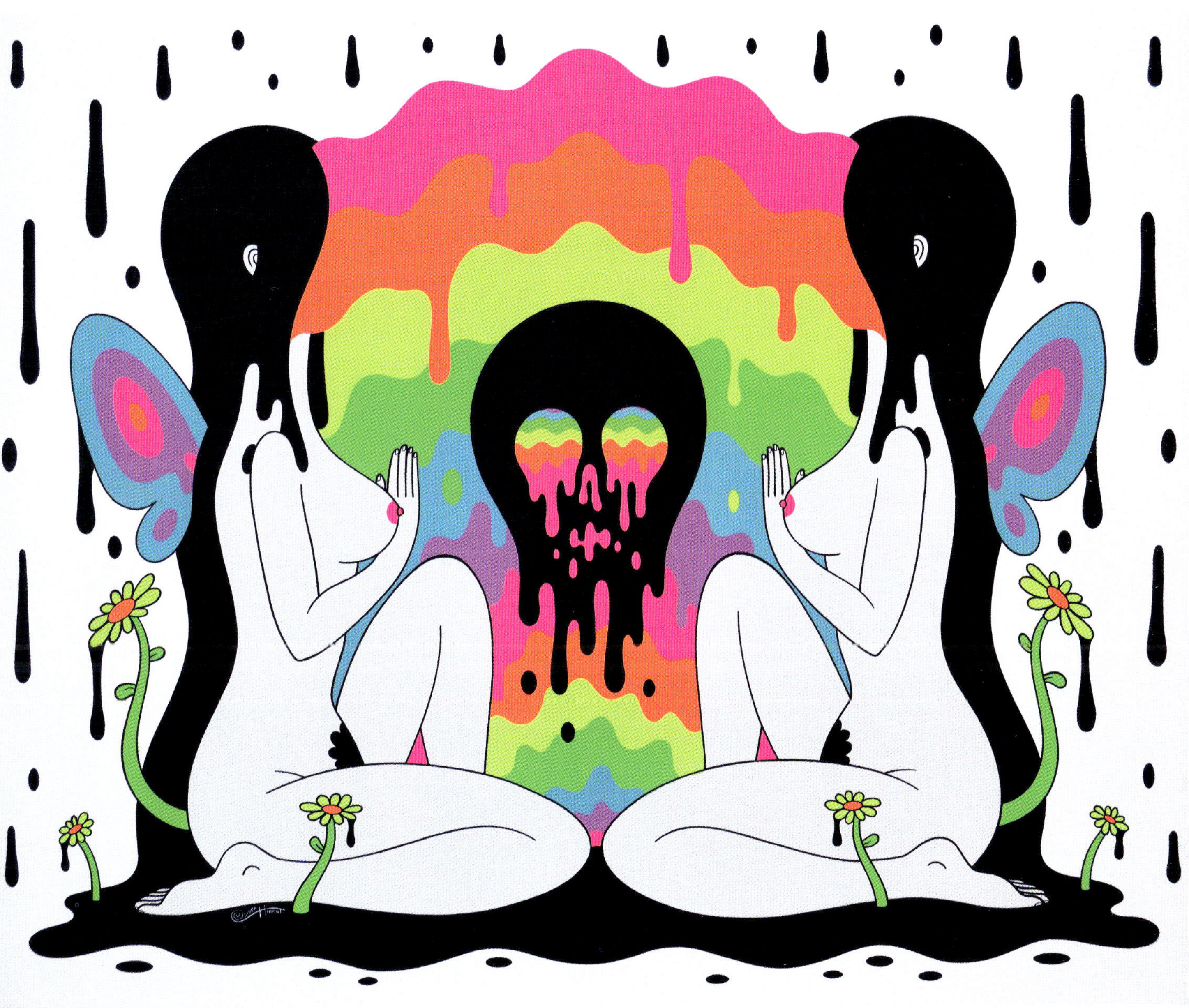

Psychic Rainbow of Doom

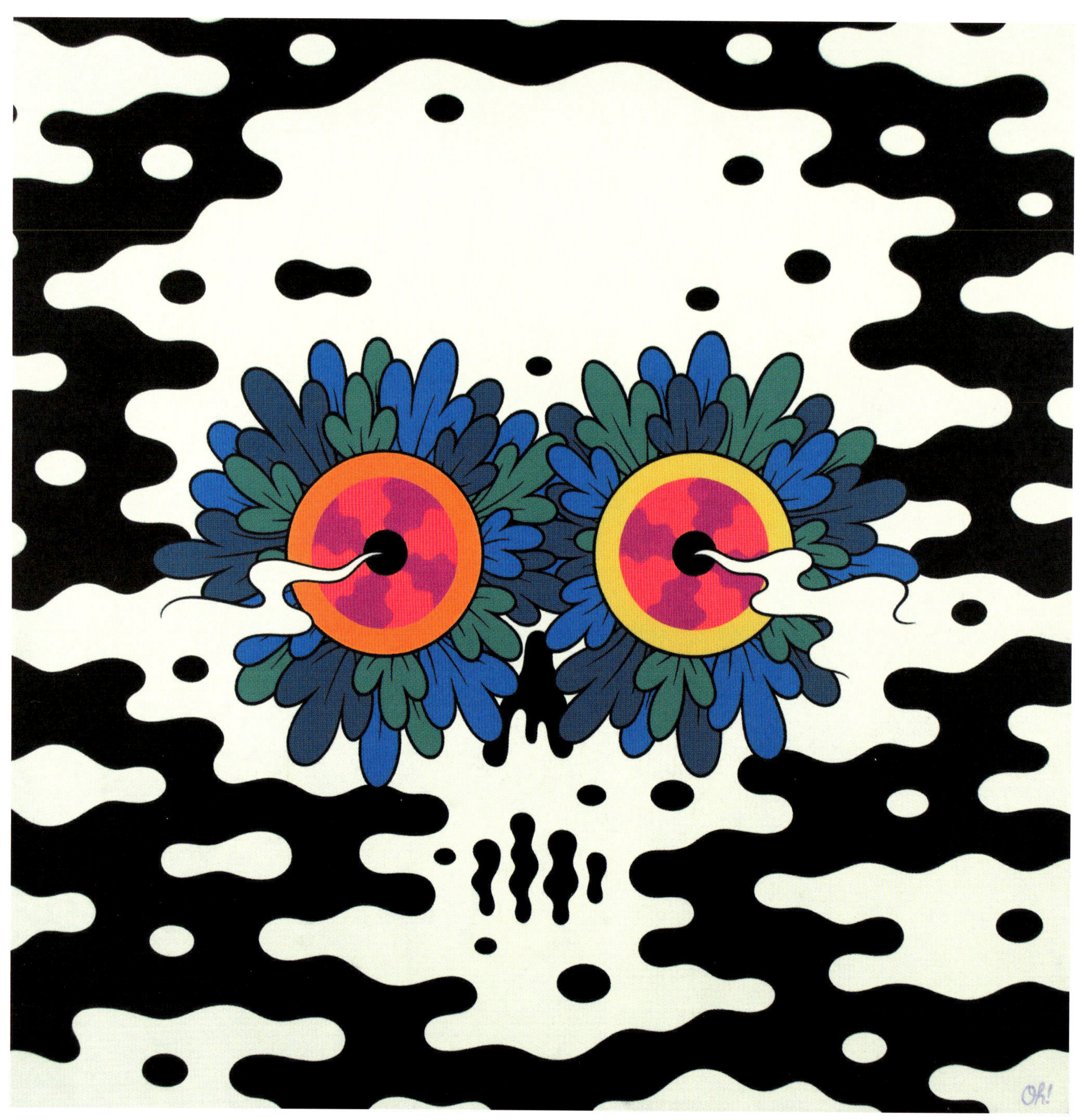

The Mellossofossor

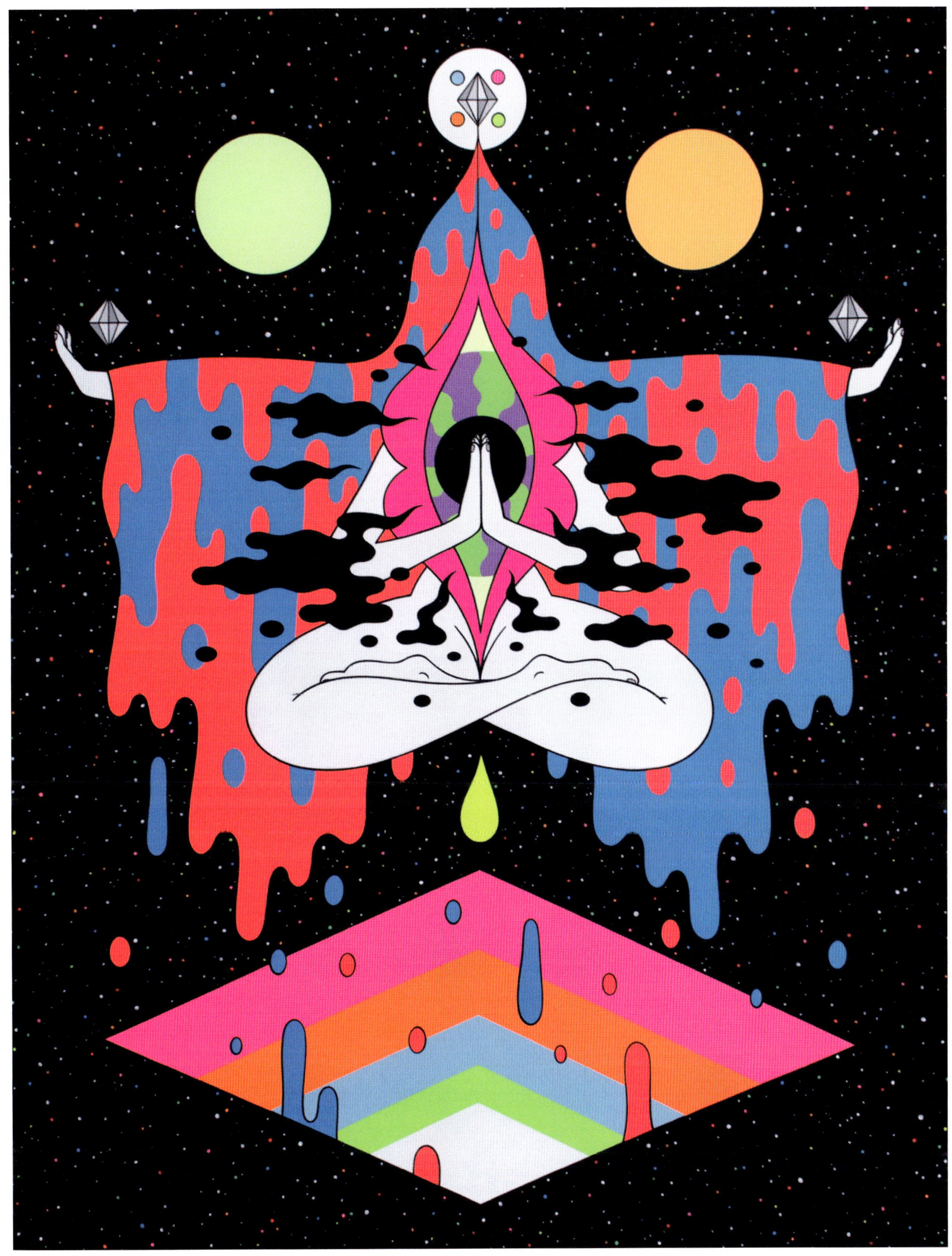

Magic Sun Magic Moon
"It is all in us. We are gods."

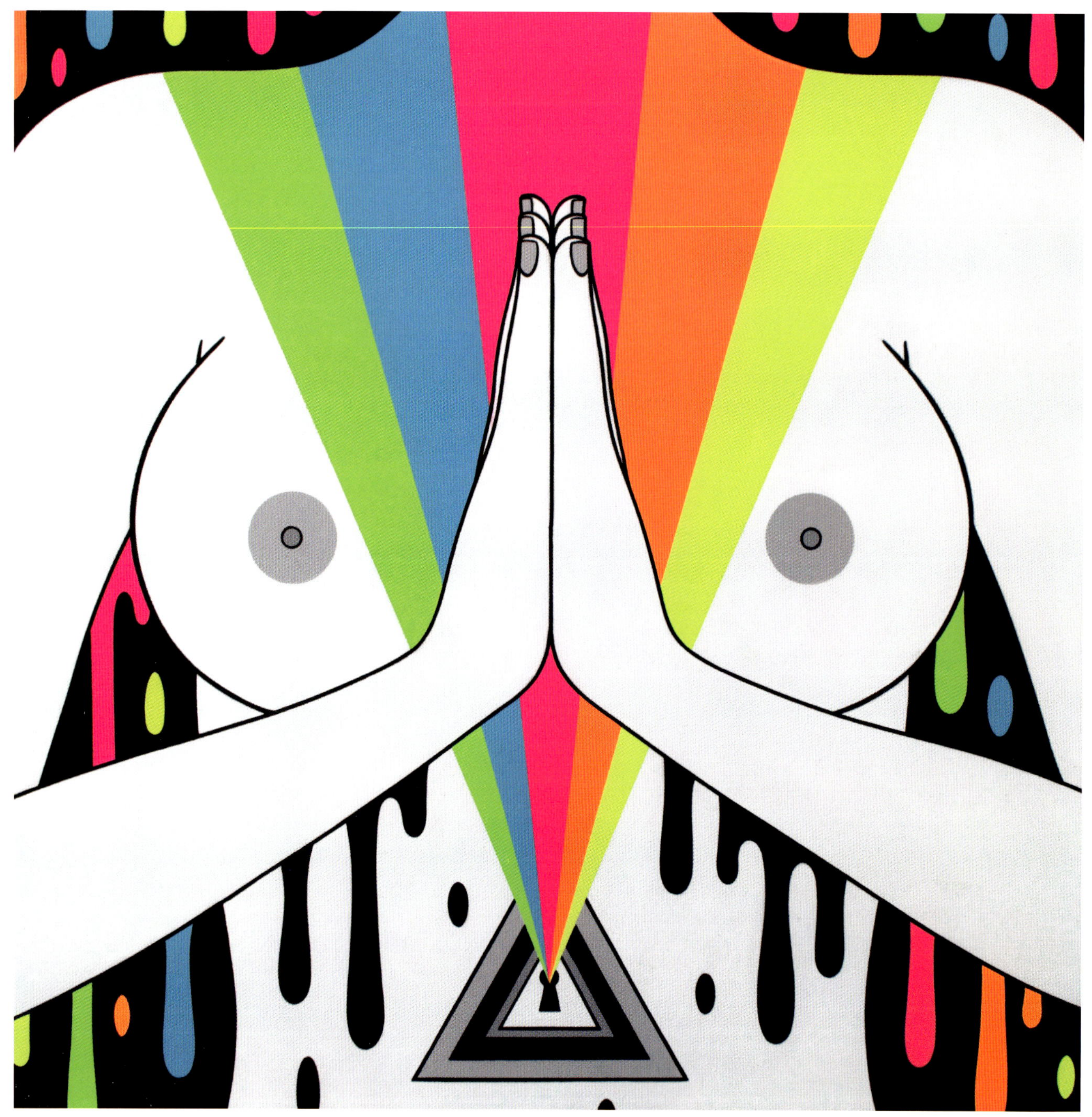

Gateway to Gold
"The key, the door, the beauty, the fear."

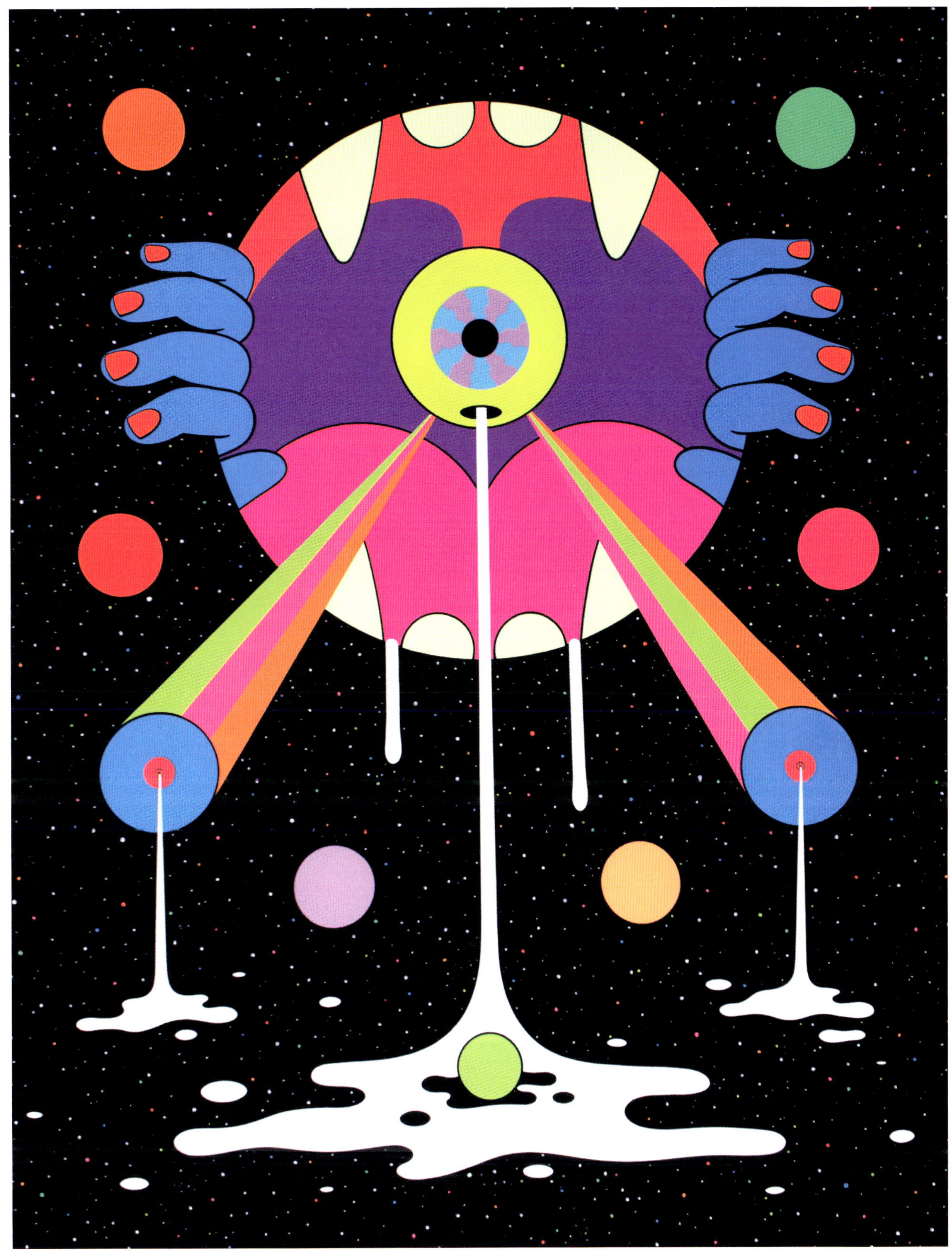

Sailing into Oblivion
"It's all in us. We are devils."

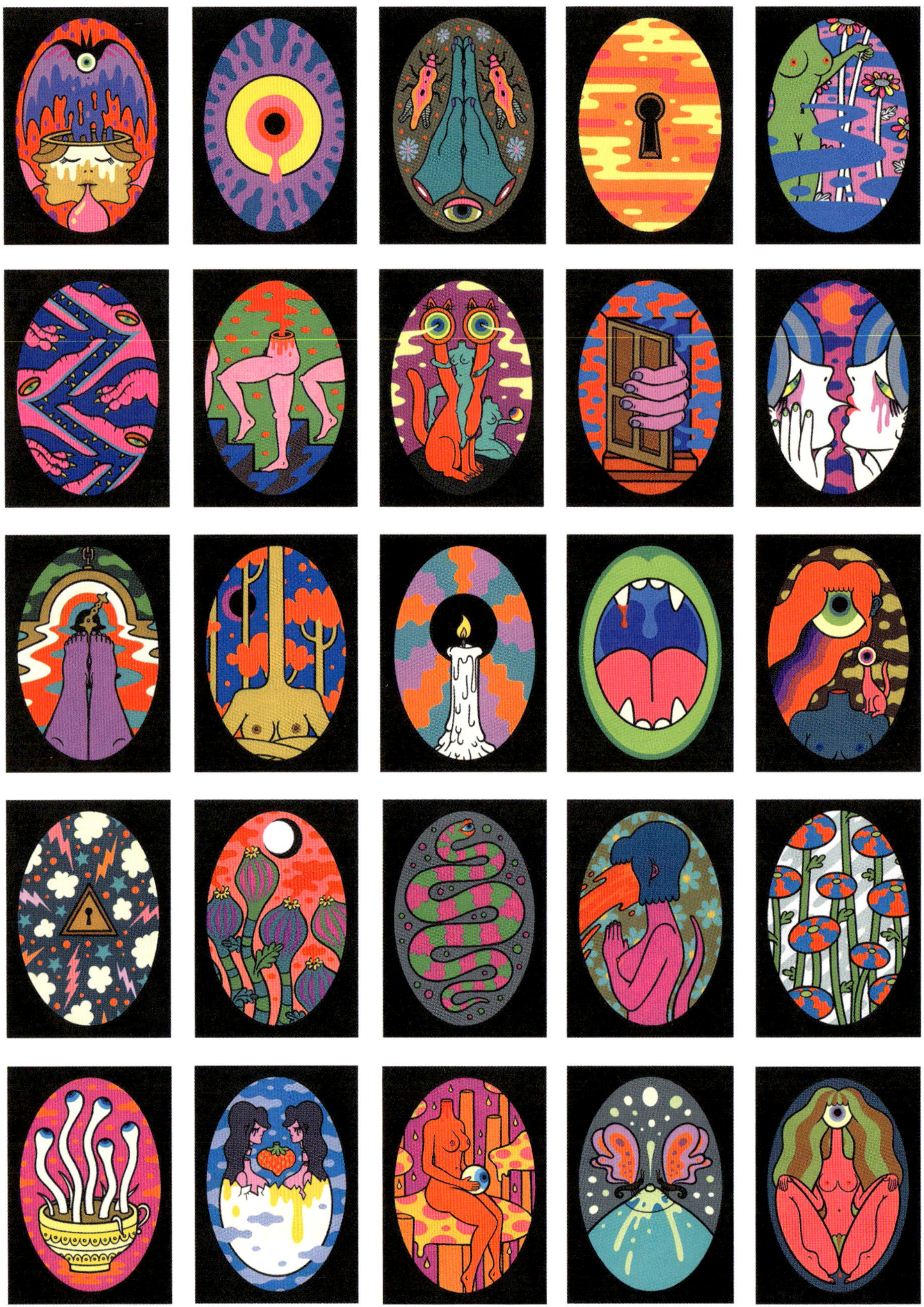

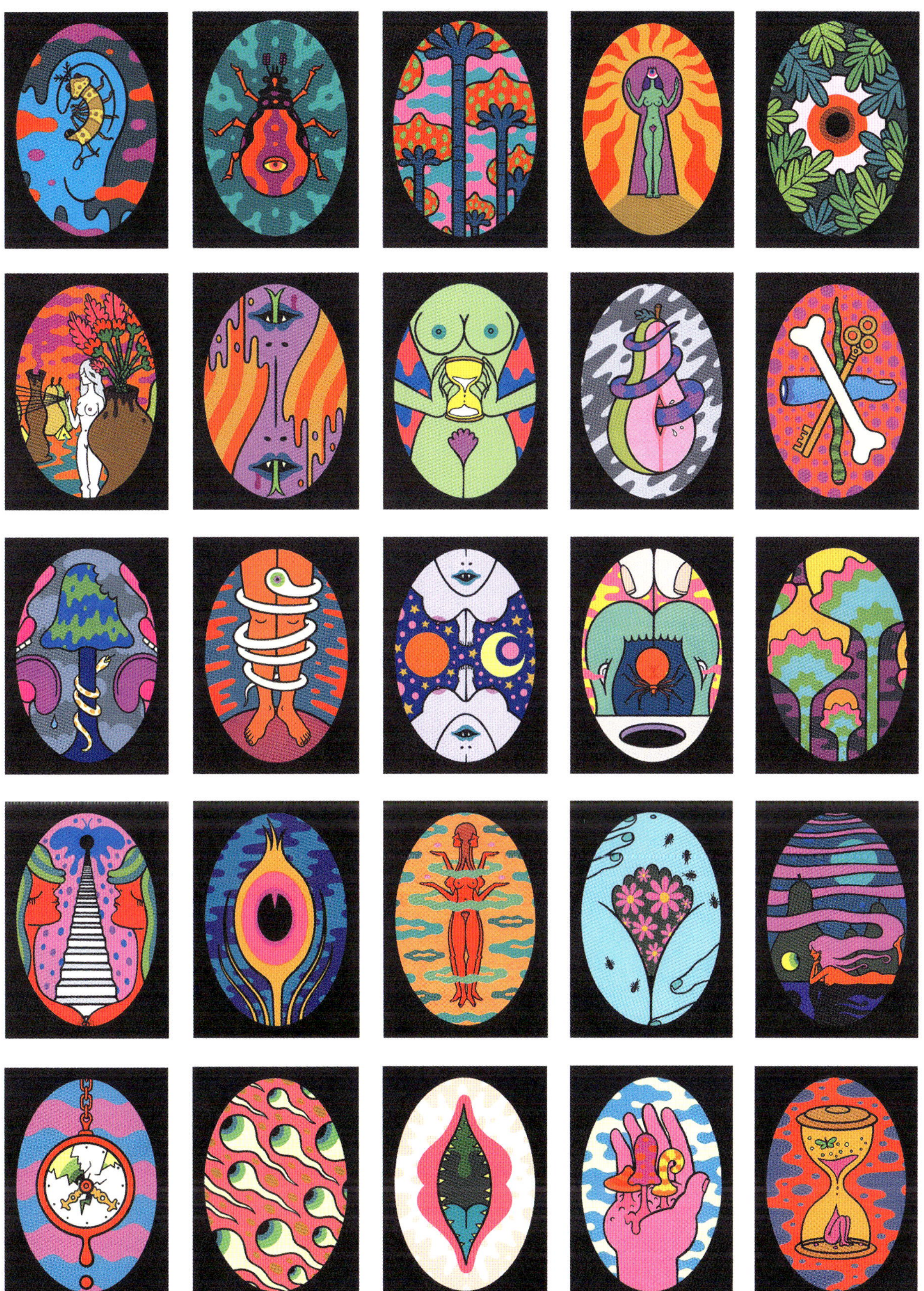

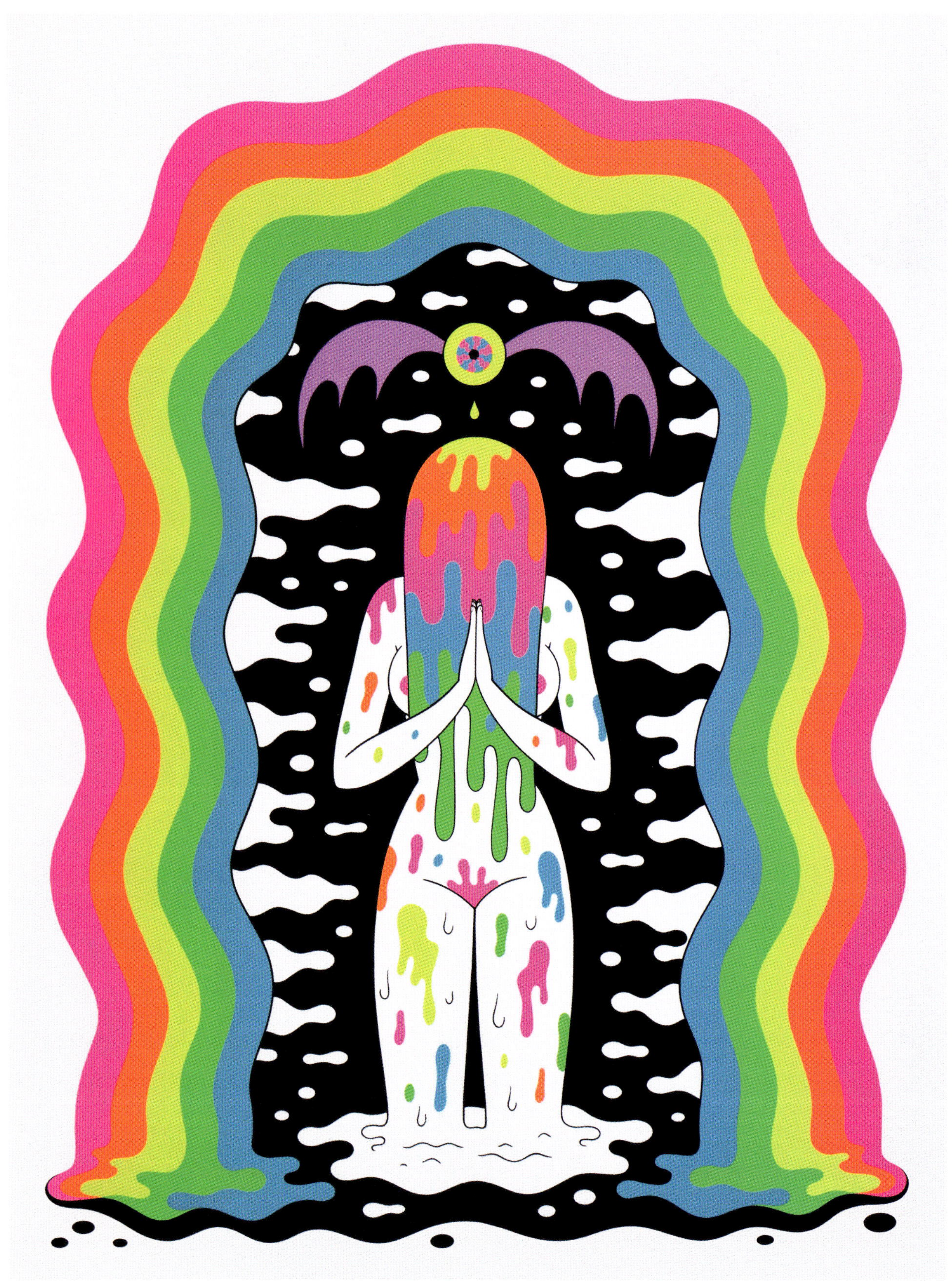

Safe in Her Rainbow of Doom
"Whether we like it or not, we are always alone in the end."

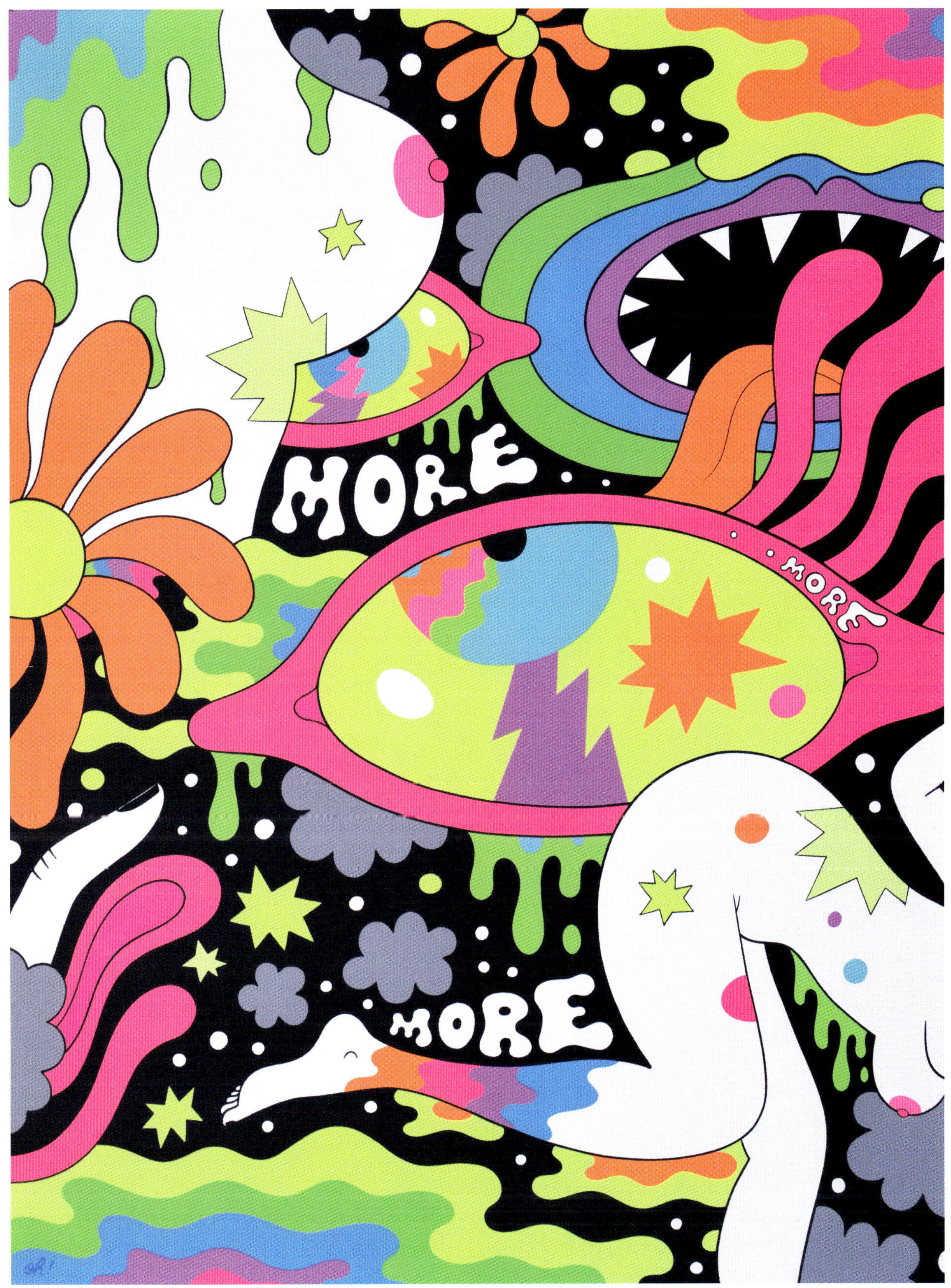

More

"An experimental painting within an experimental series of paintings and drawings created with the aid of experimental substances . . . "

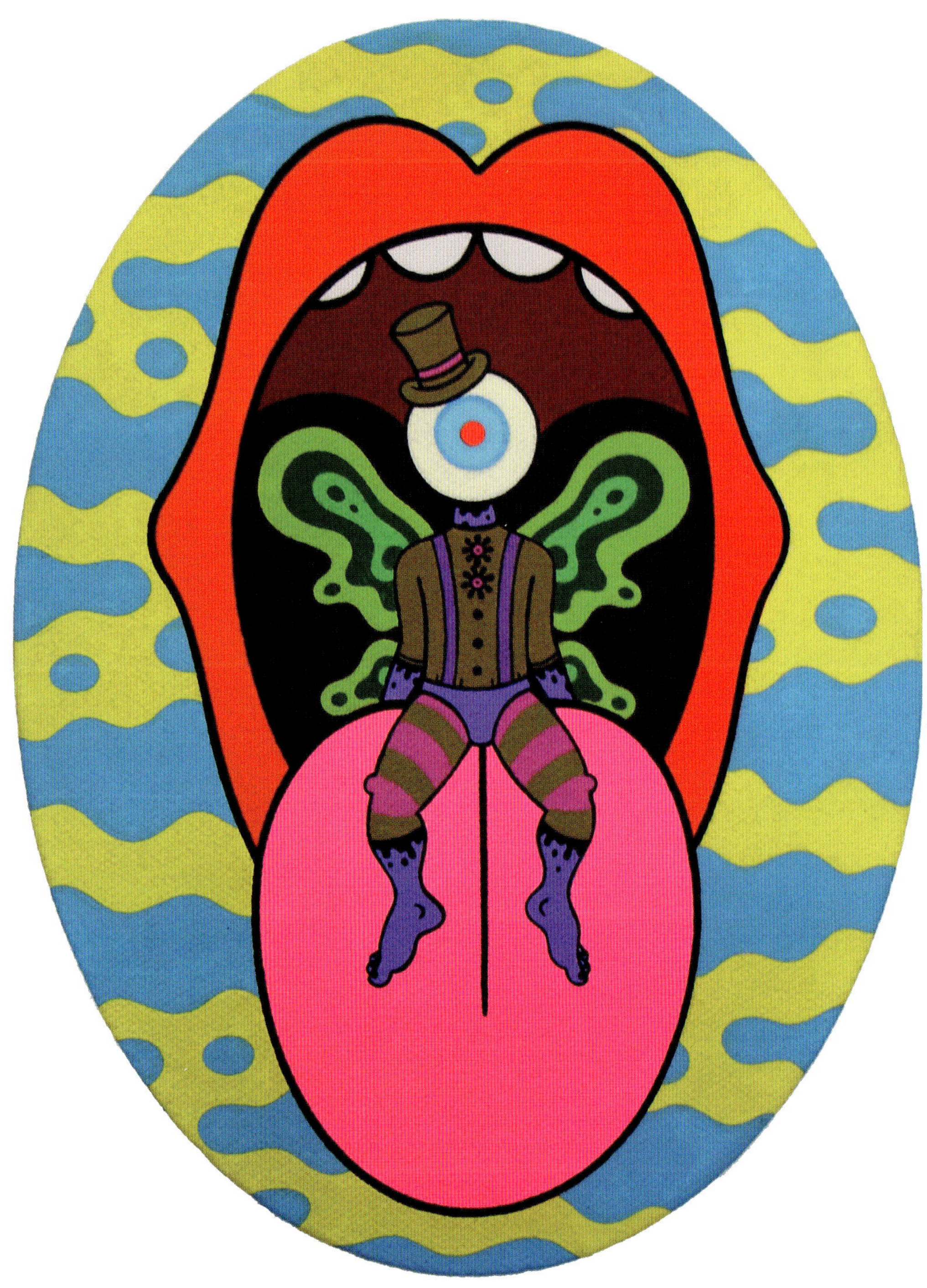

Eddy the Eye

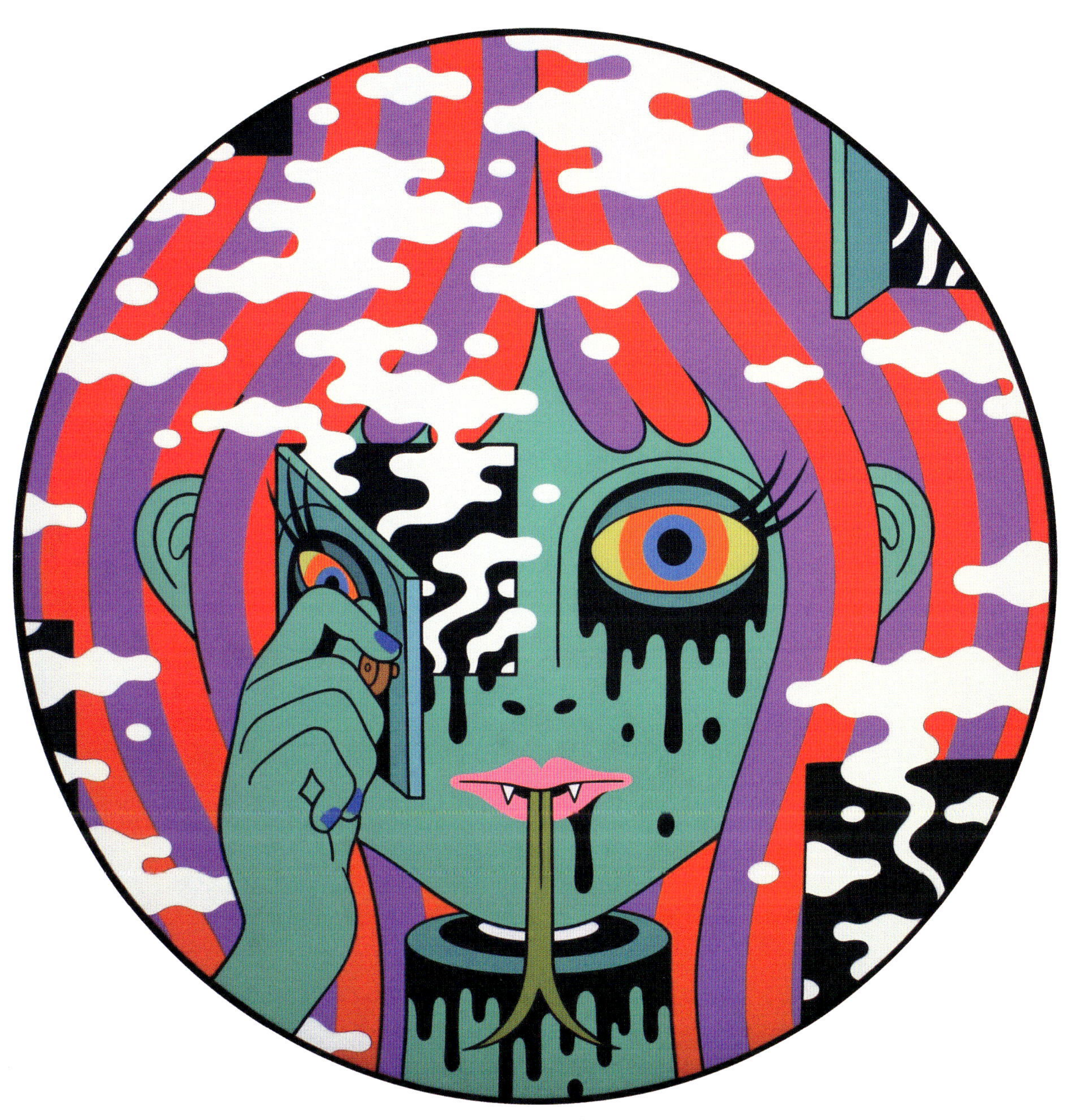

Coma Cometissa

"Look within or look without."

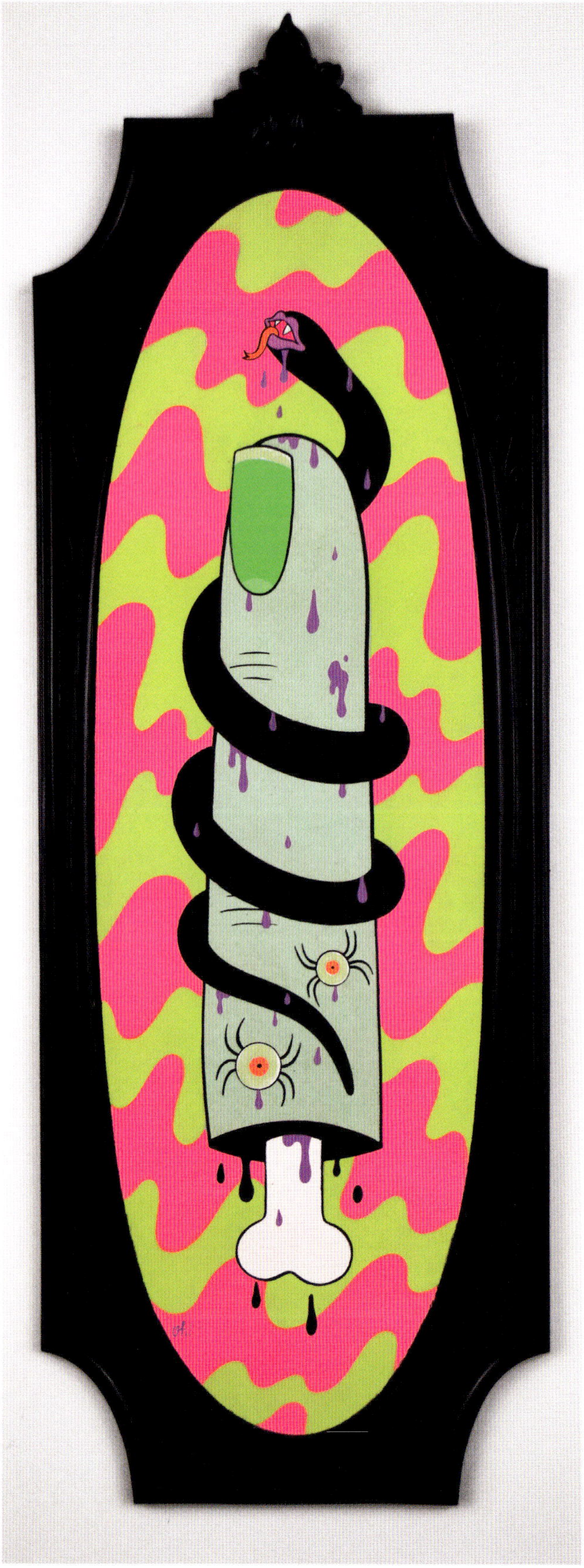

Cursed

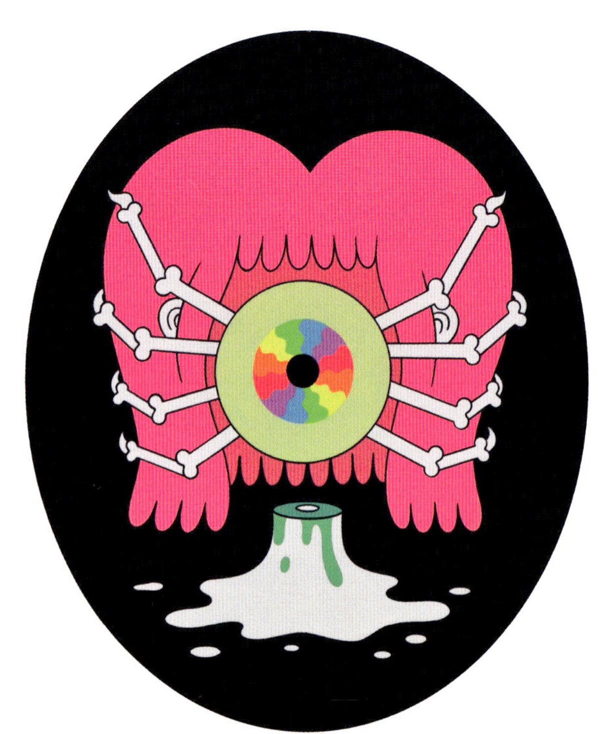

Spider Eyed Girl

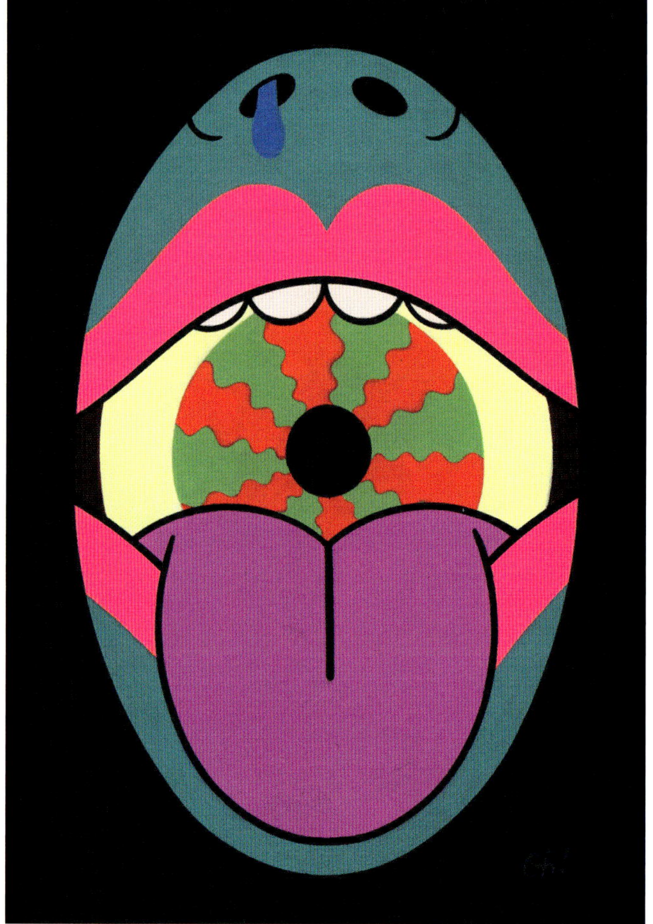

I Love Japan

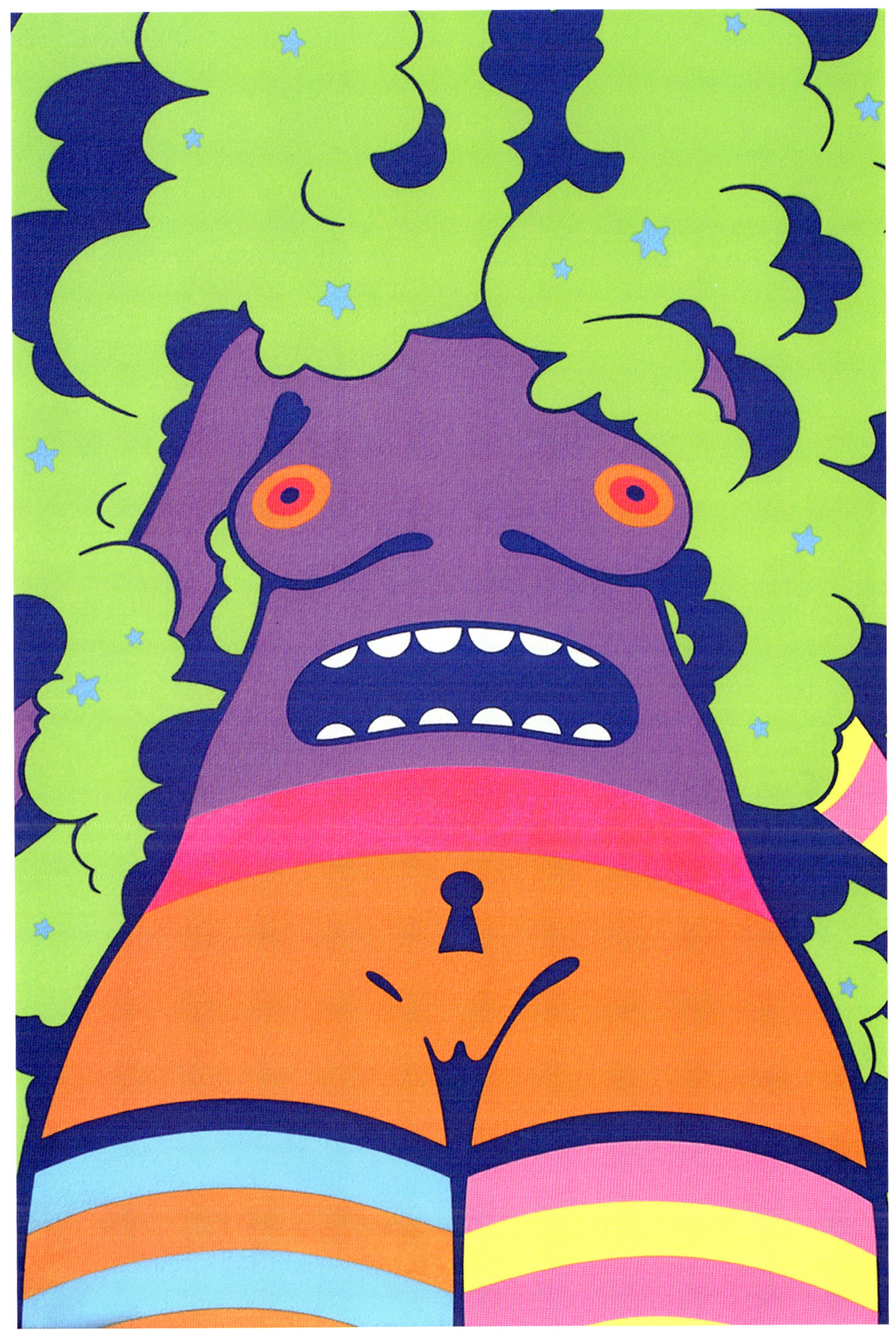

Venus Garden Girl

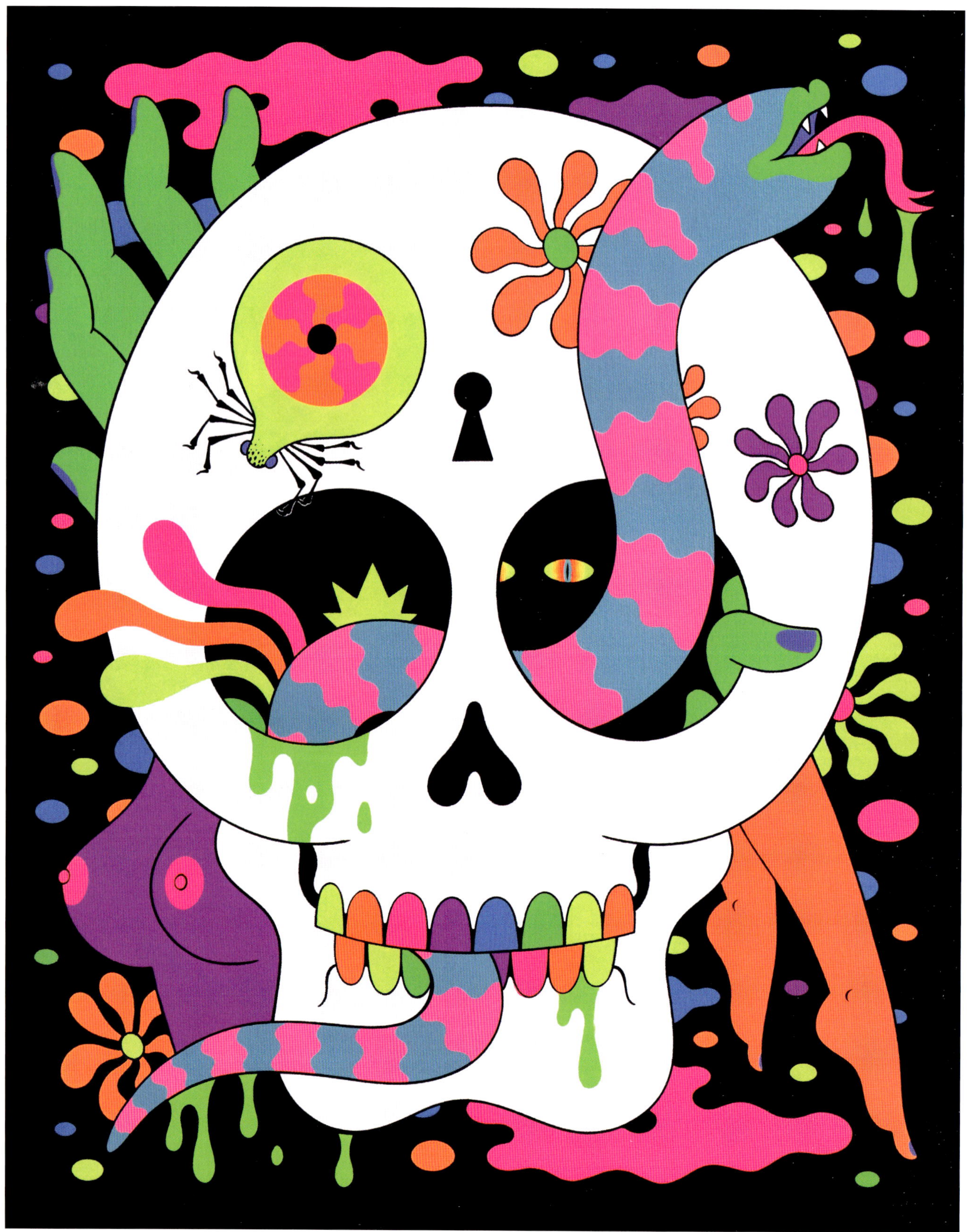

Secrets Inside

"They will kill you. But you are going to die regardless."

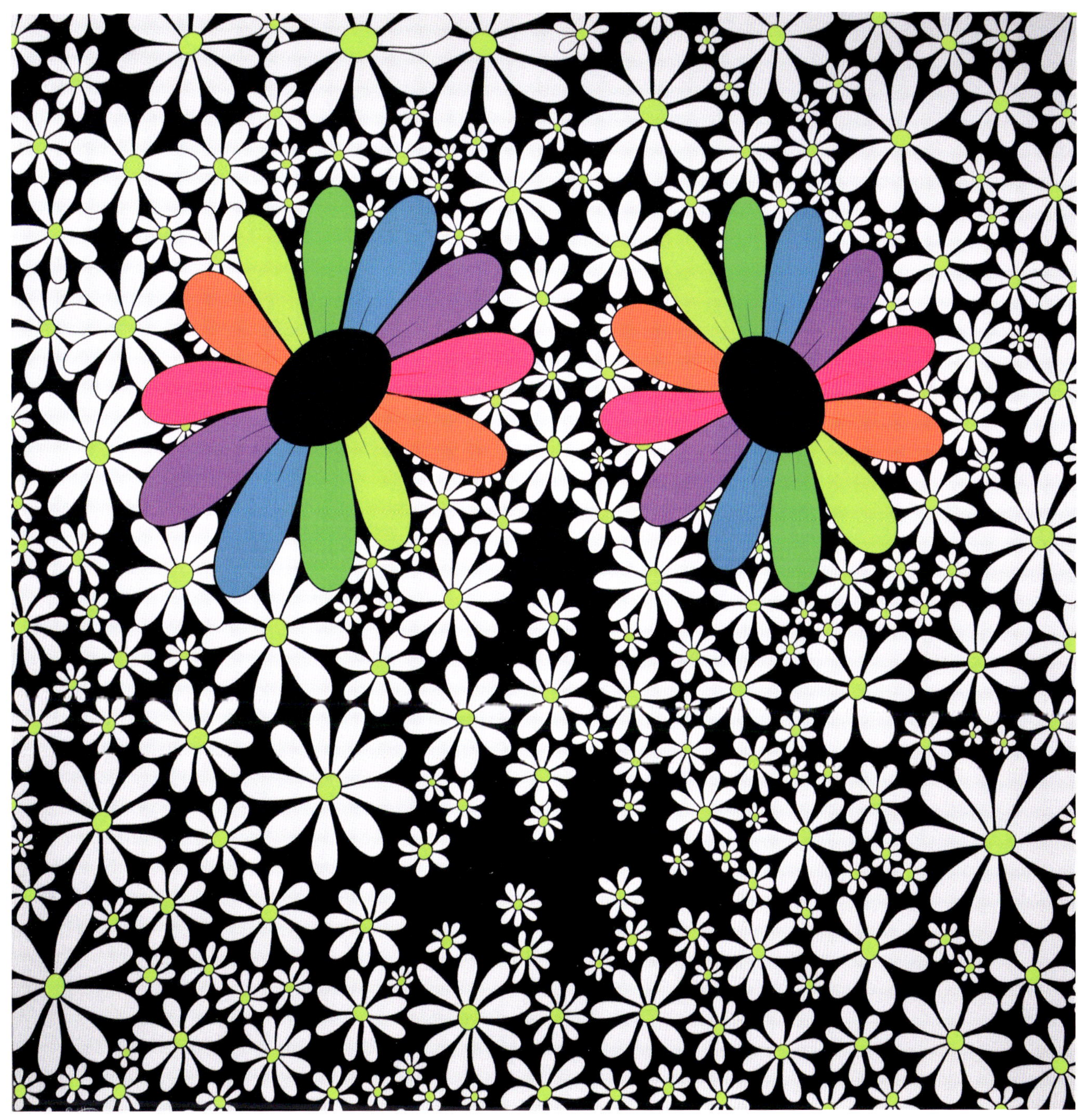

Scream Thy Last Scream

"The beauty of death is the death of beauty. But nothing fully dies. Everything evolves. Even death."

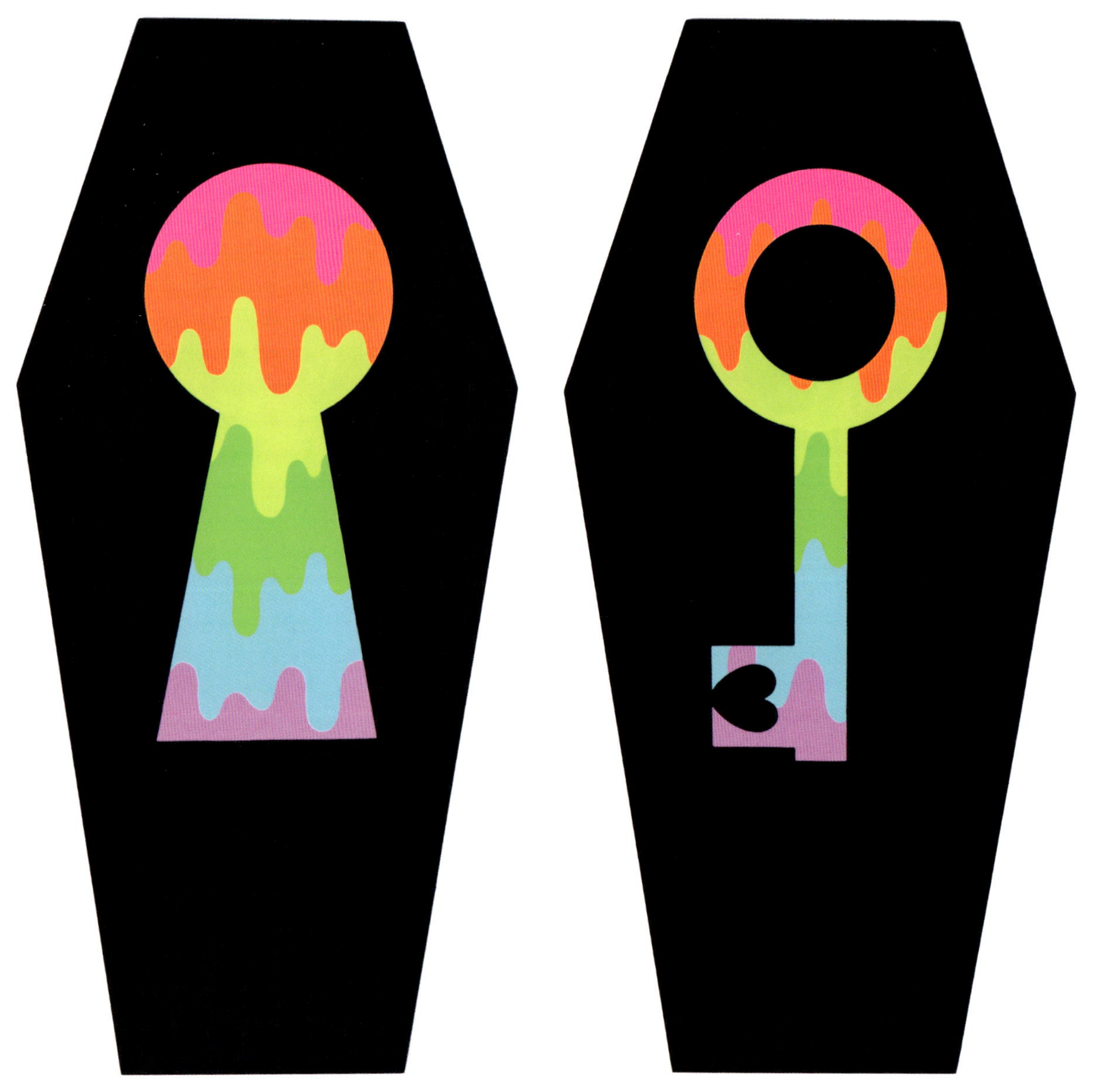

His and Hers

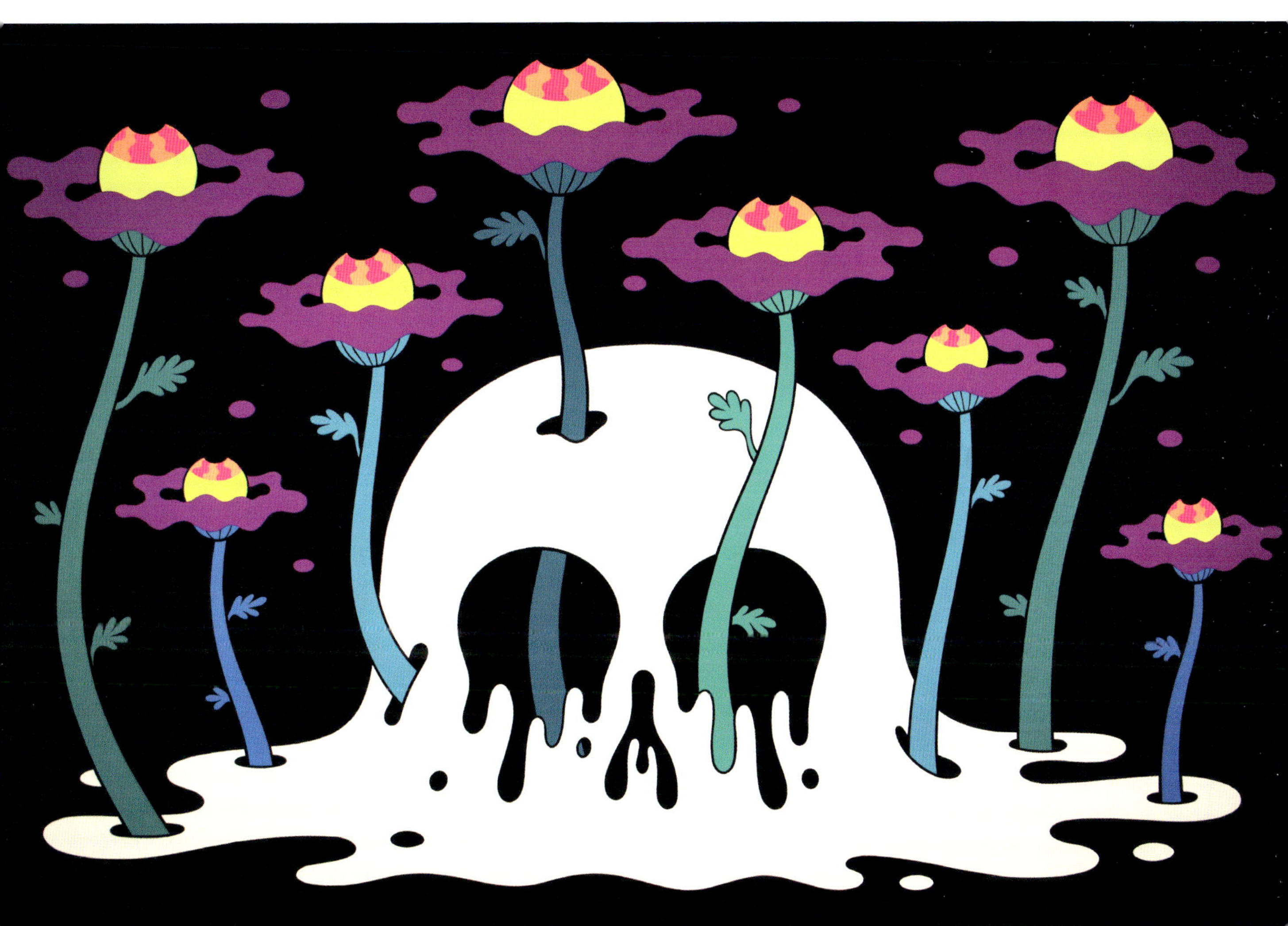

I Love You

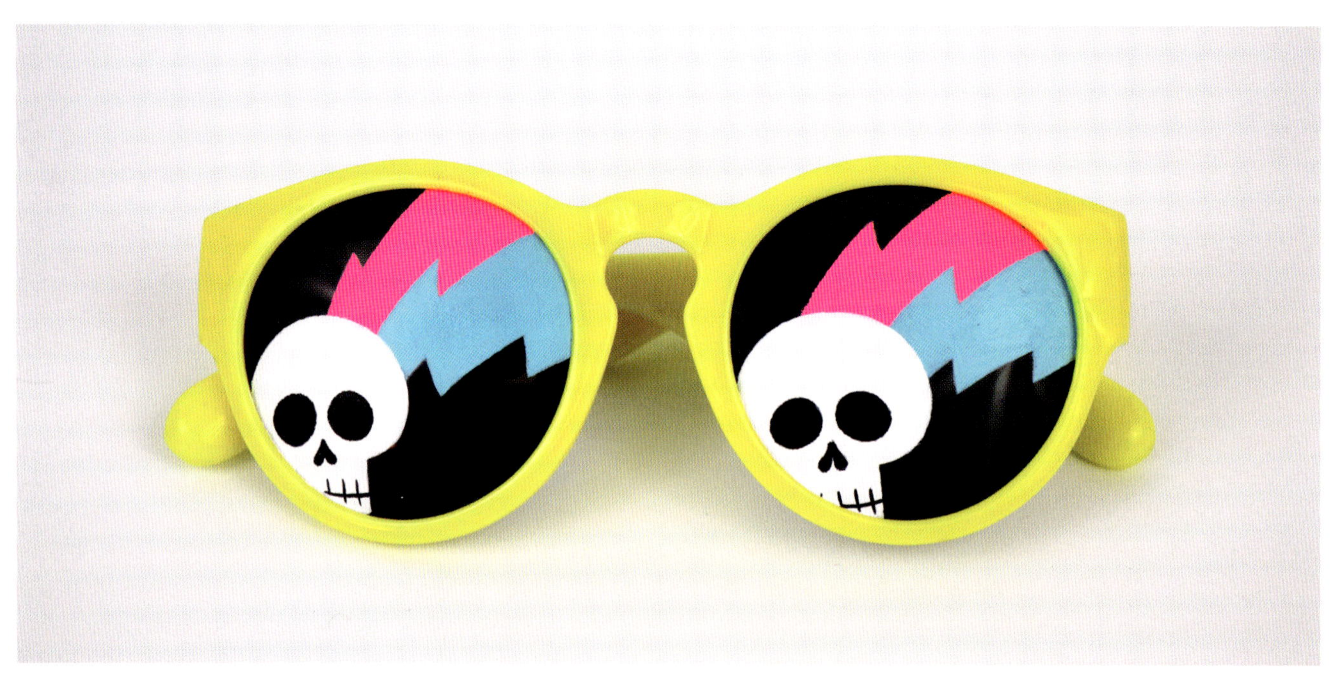

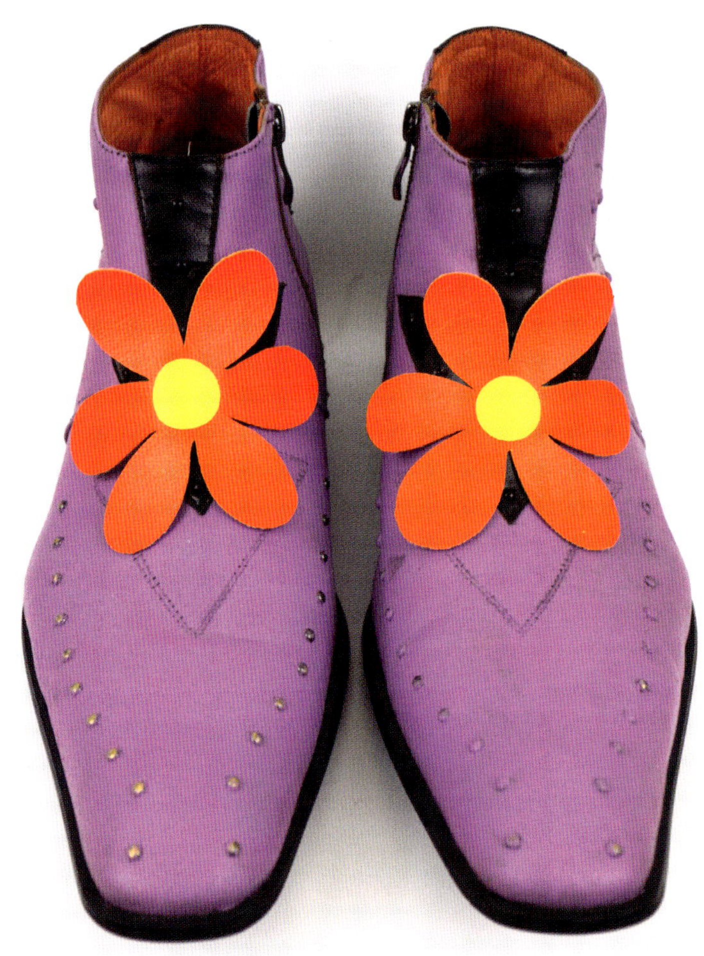

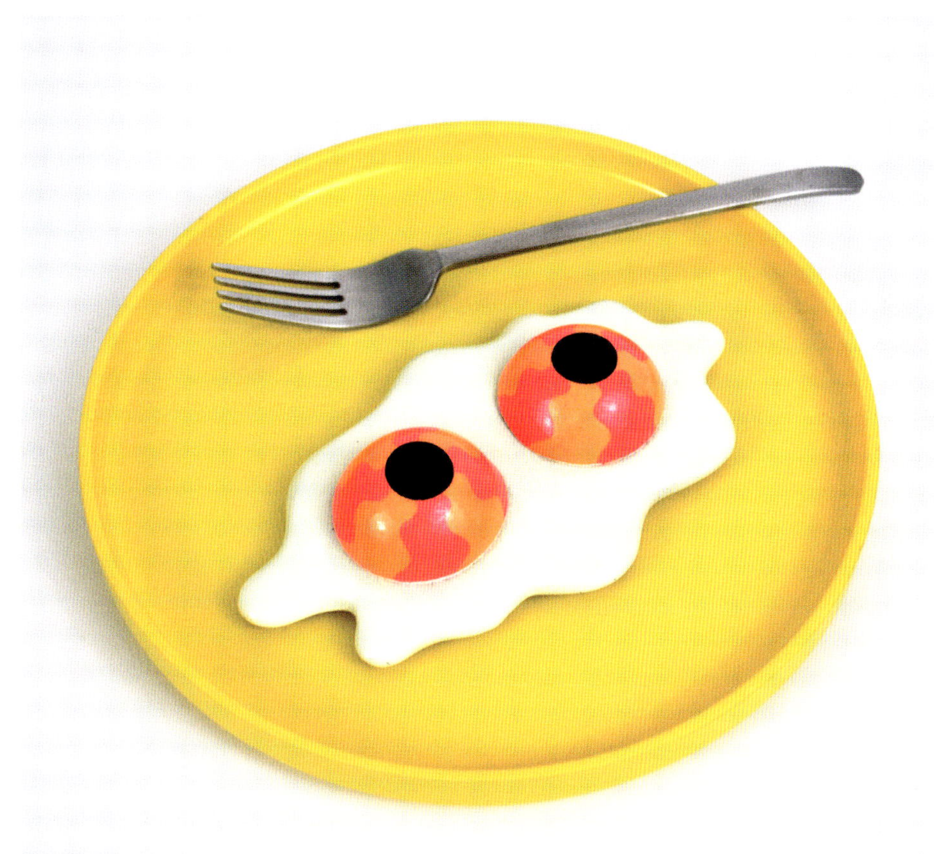

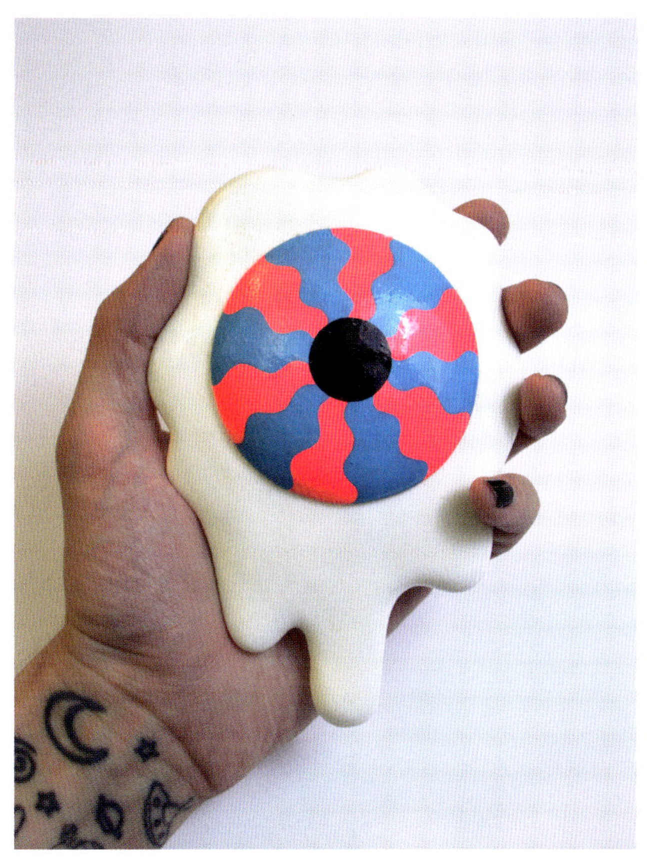

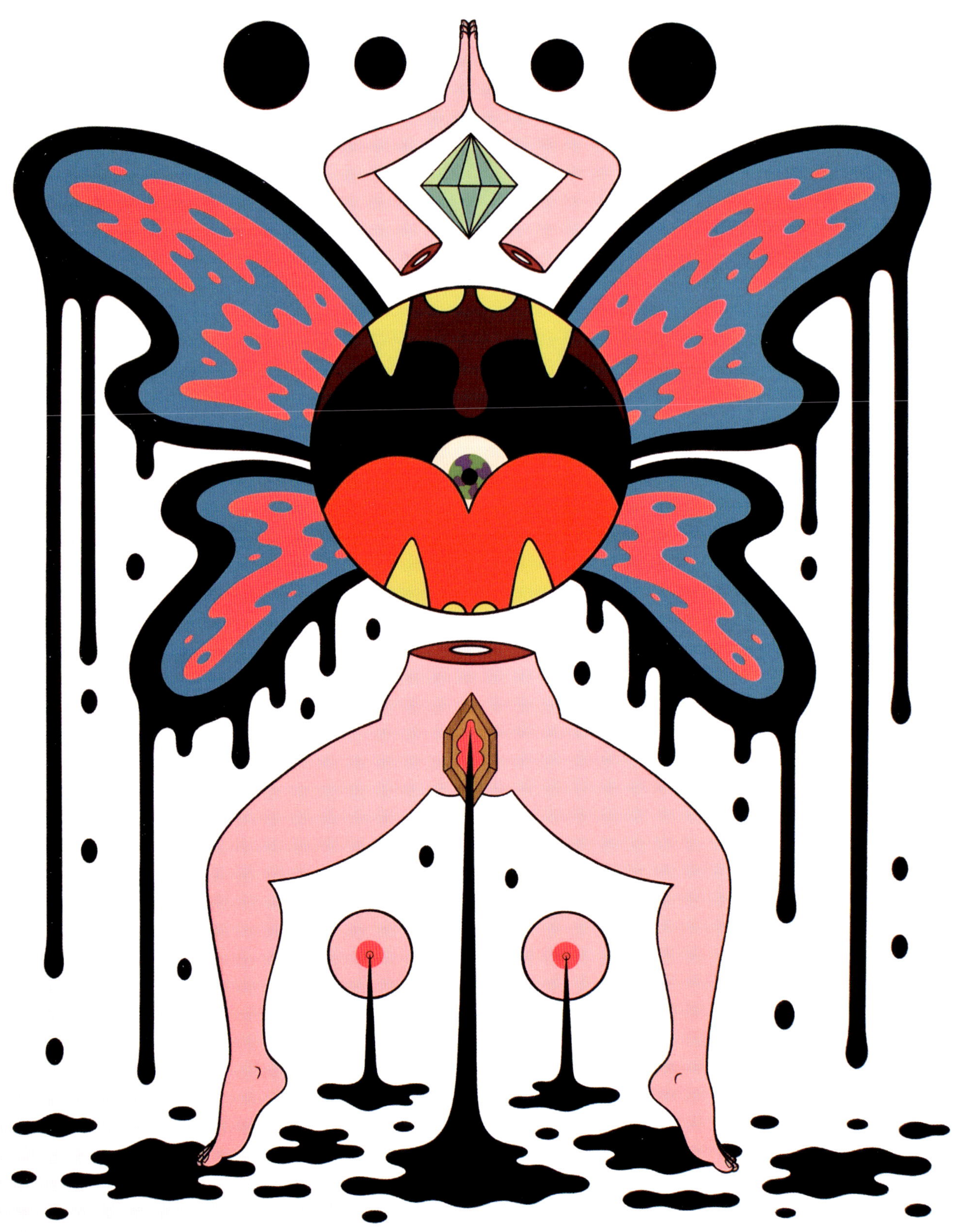

Reverse Alchemy
"Your material love is complete shit. But it's nice to have things to love."

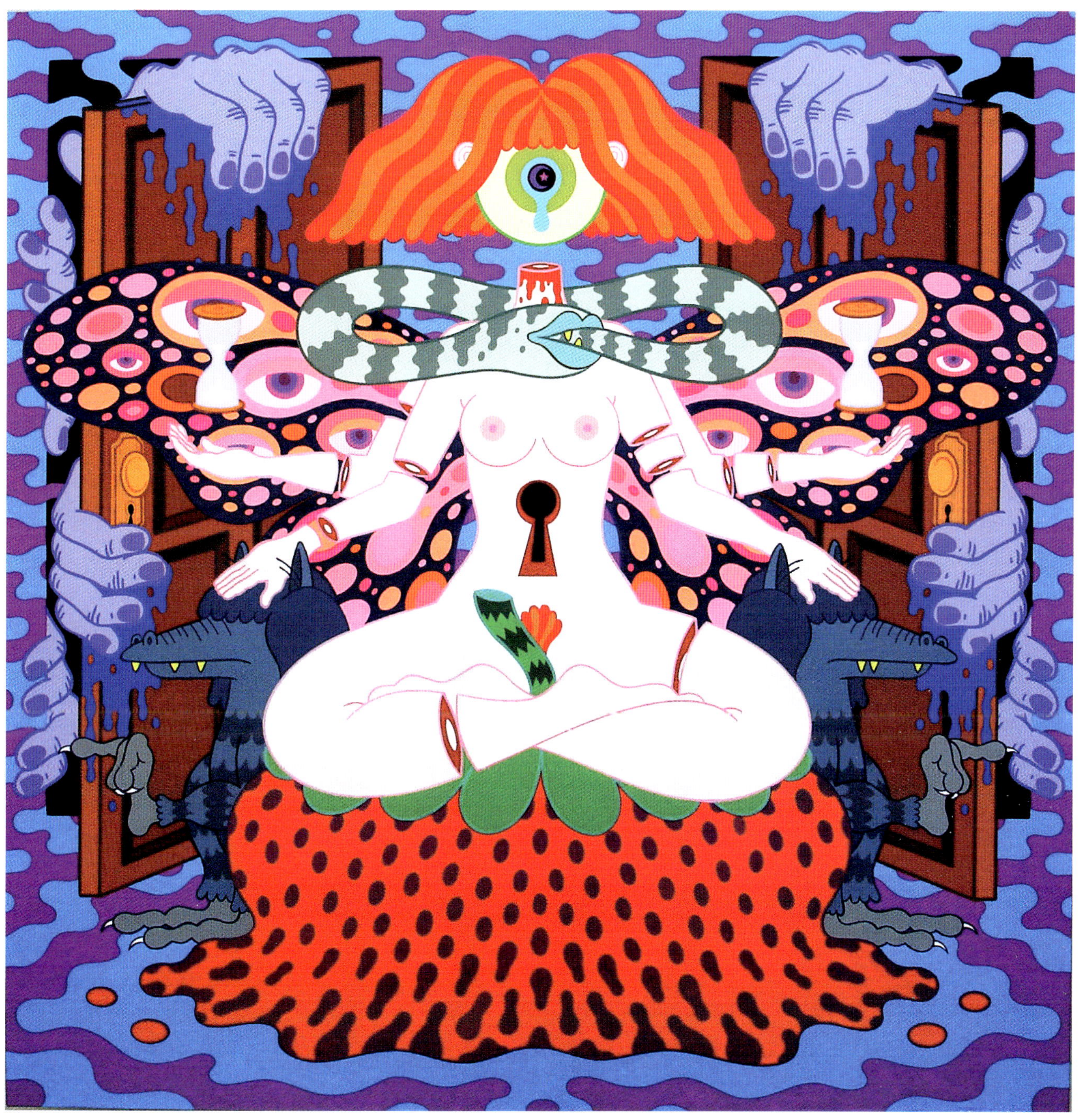

Akgistrodon Piscivorus

"Another early and important experimental painting in symmetry and secrets."

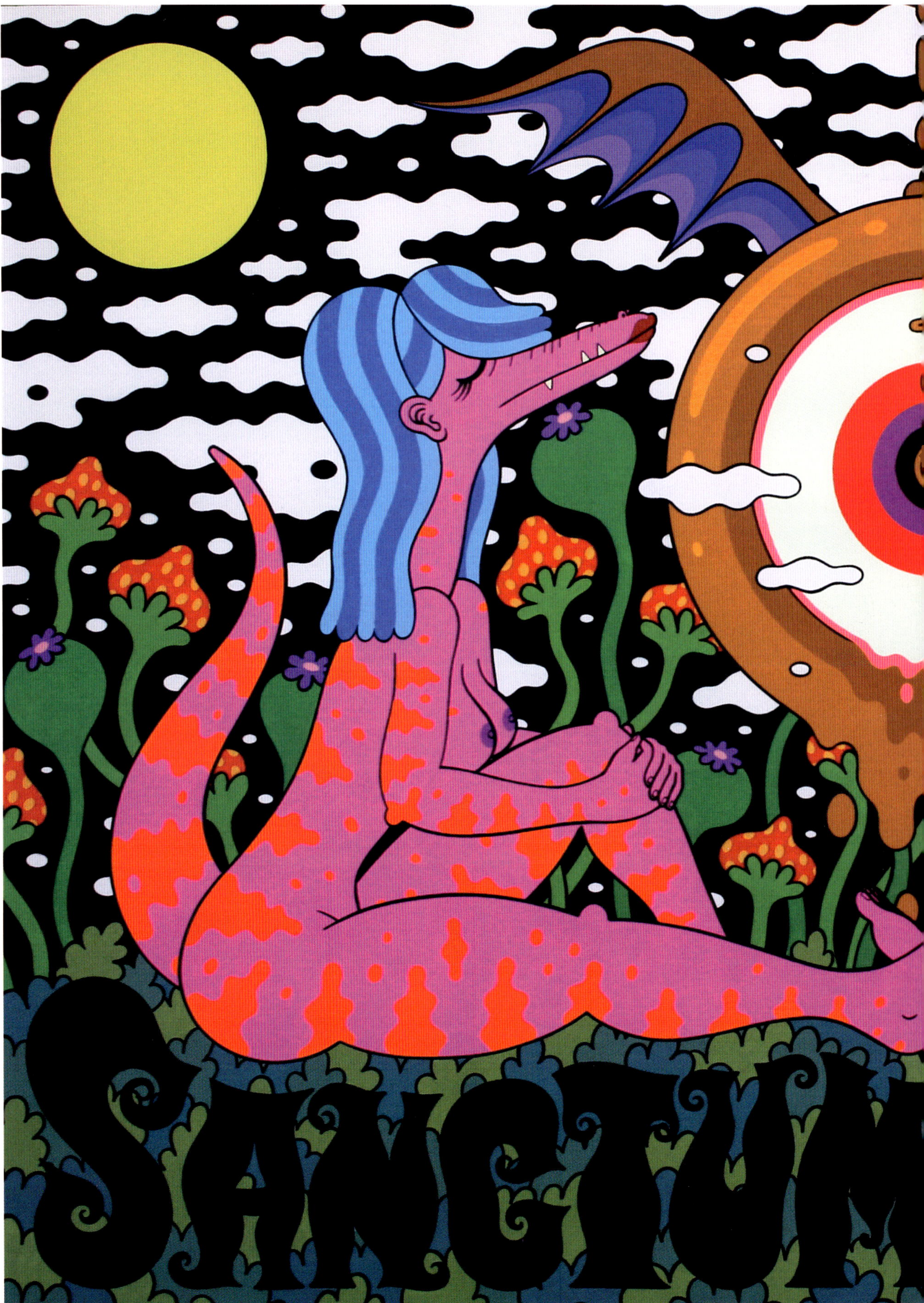
SANCTU

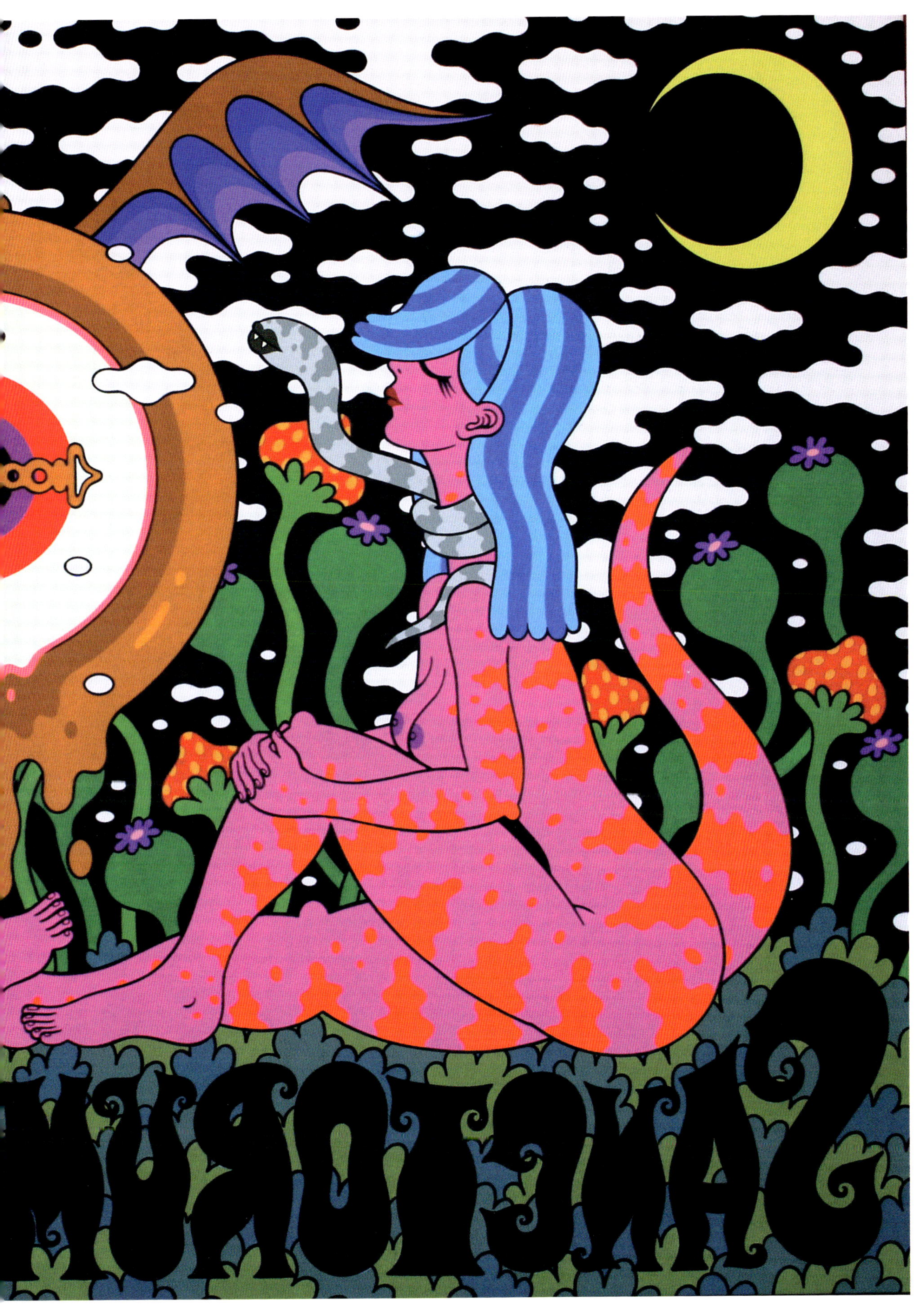

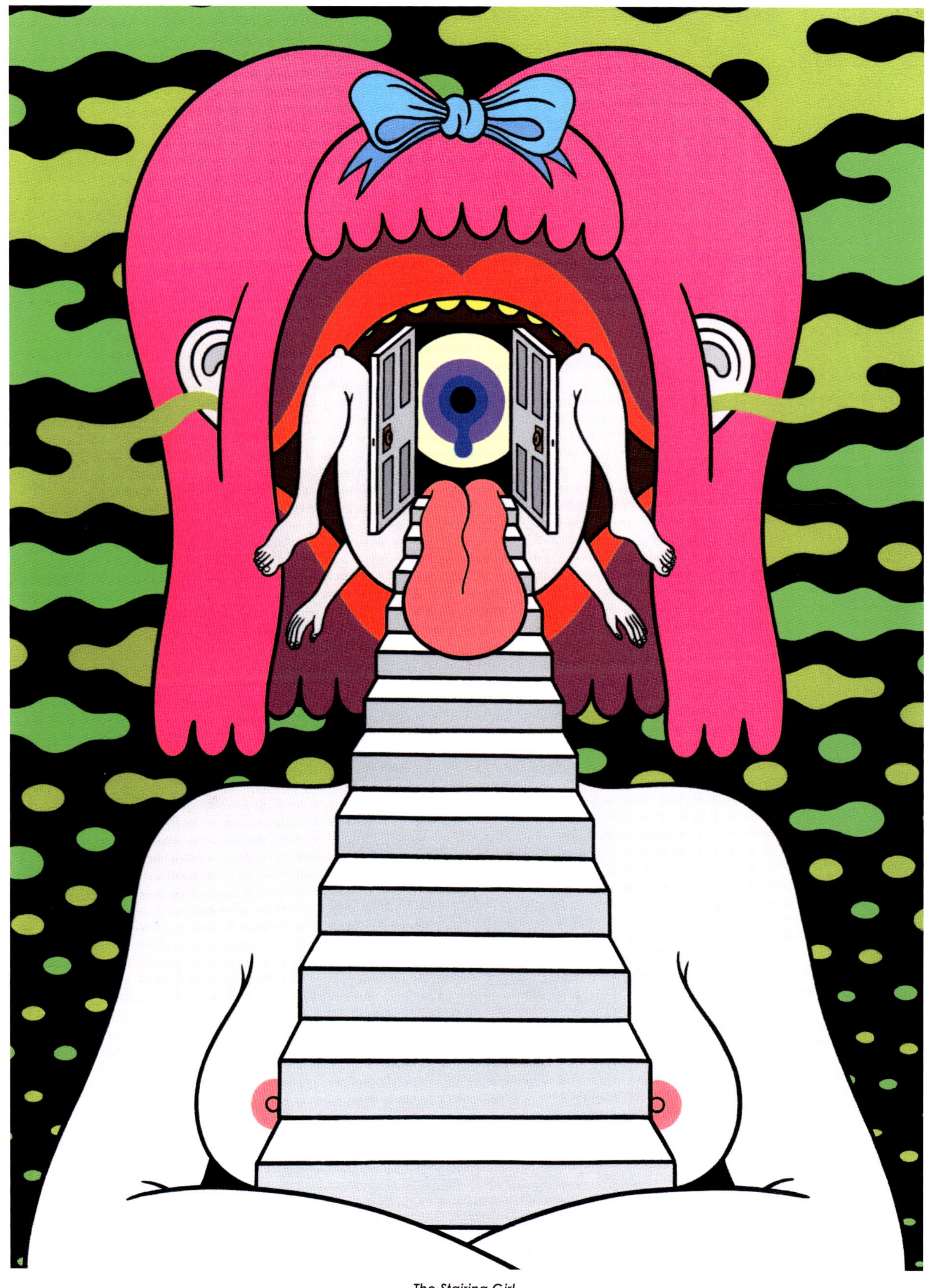

The Stairing Girl

"What do you find? What is in You? Do you know?"

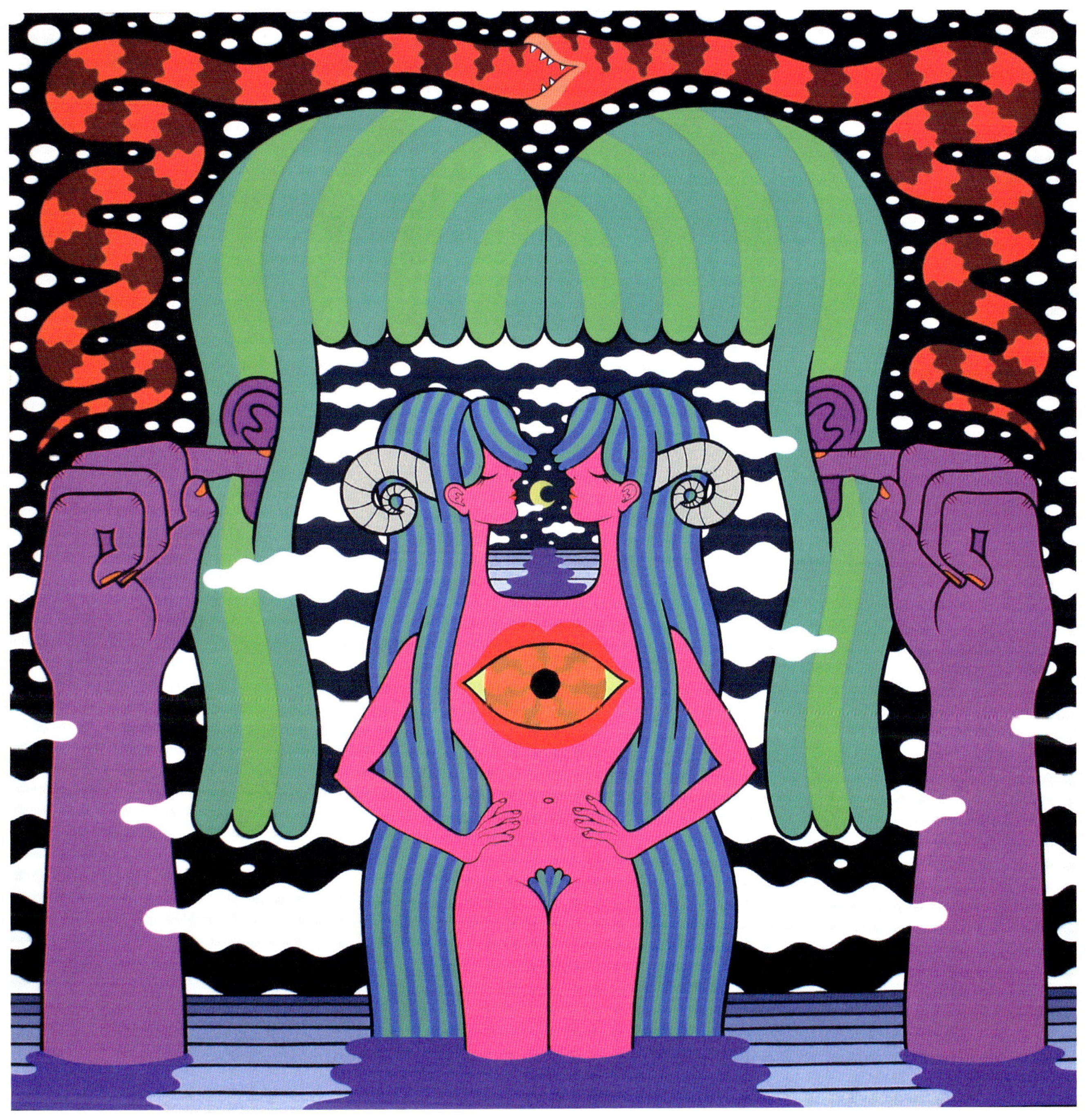

The Sapphic Sleep
"A certain sex. A certain feel."

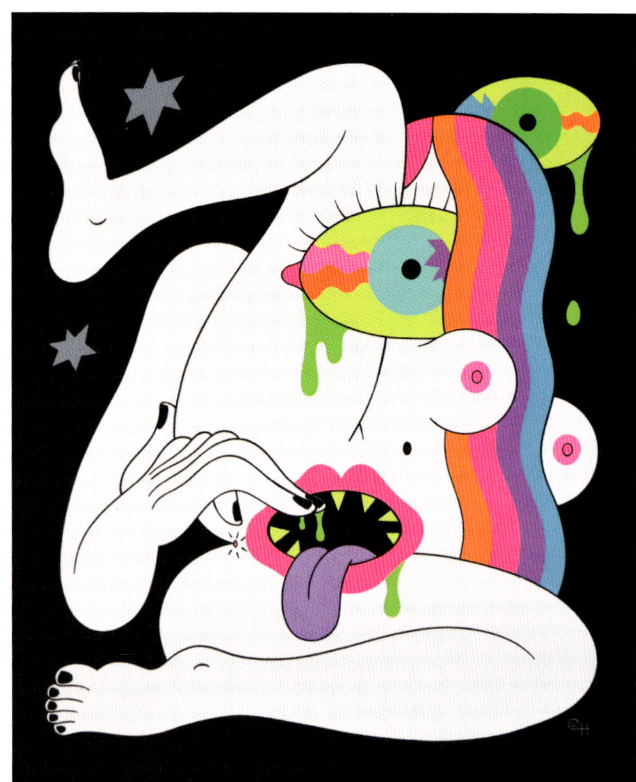
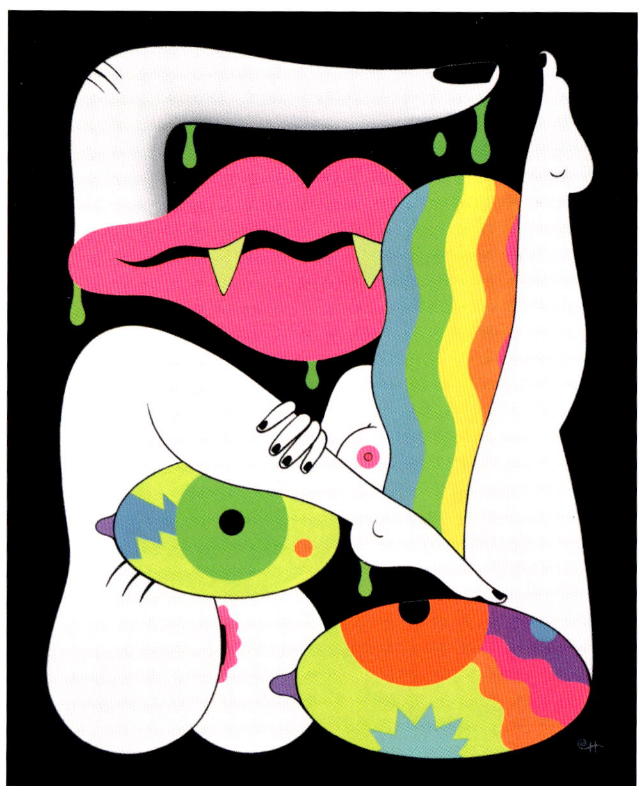
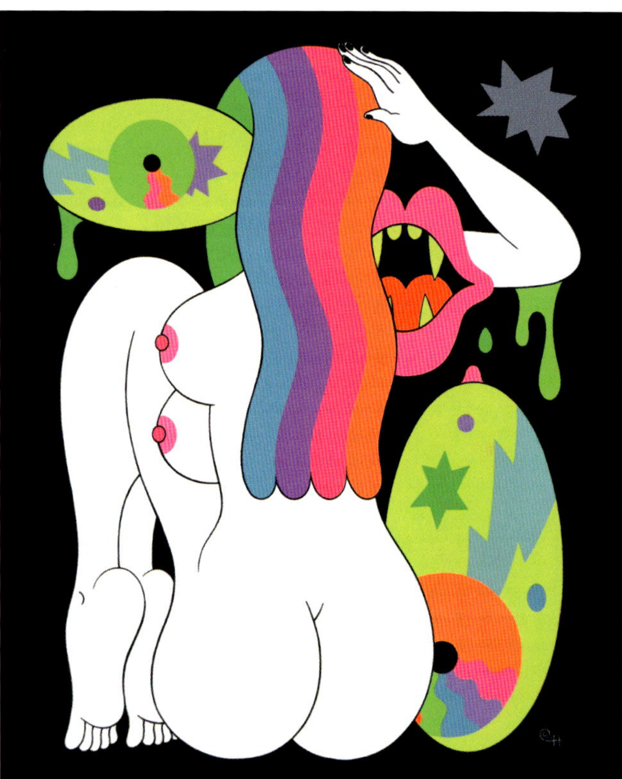
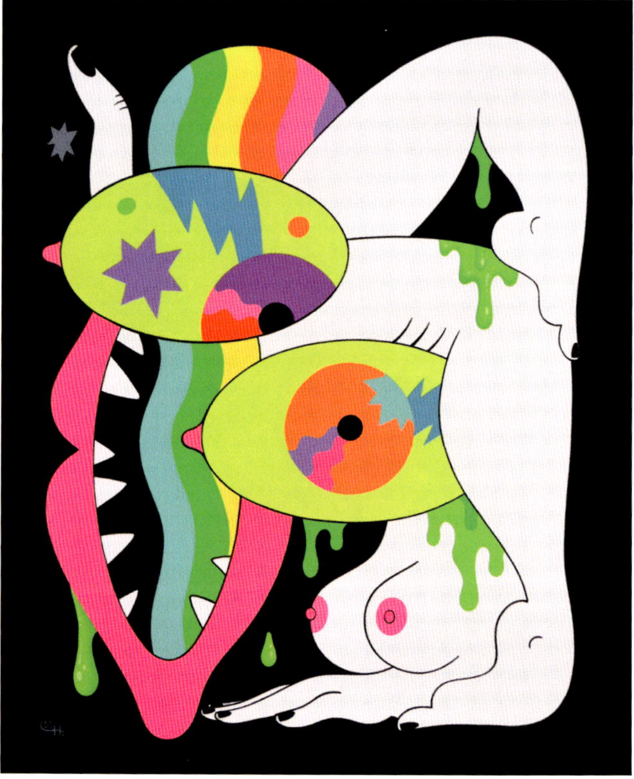

"This was a very important series for me. Breaking my own rules of years of living within a sturdy and very comfortable world of symmetry and structure. It's essential to make your own rules in life but at times it's just as important to break them."

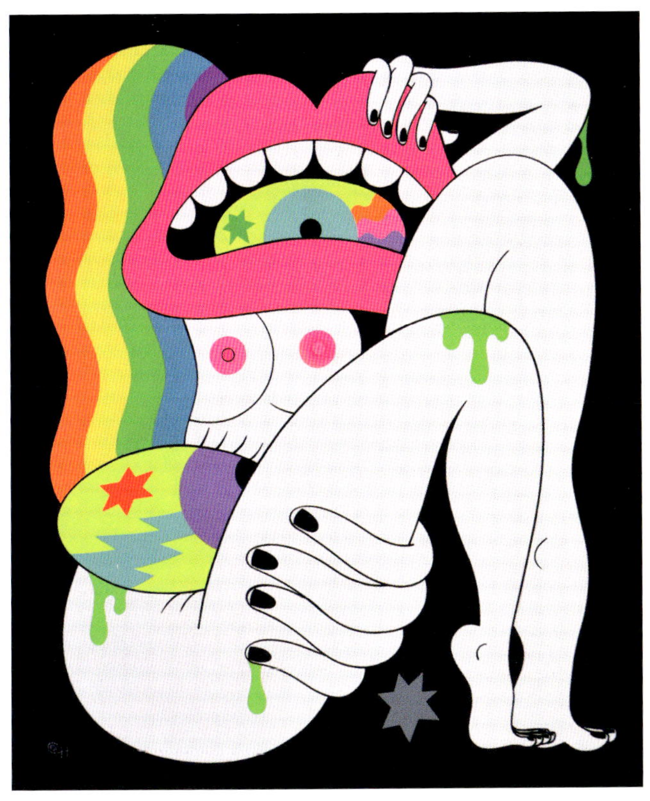
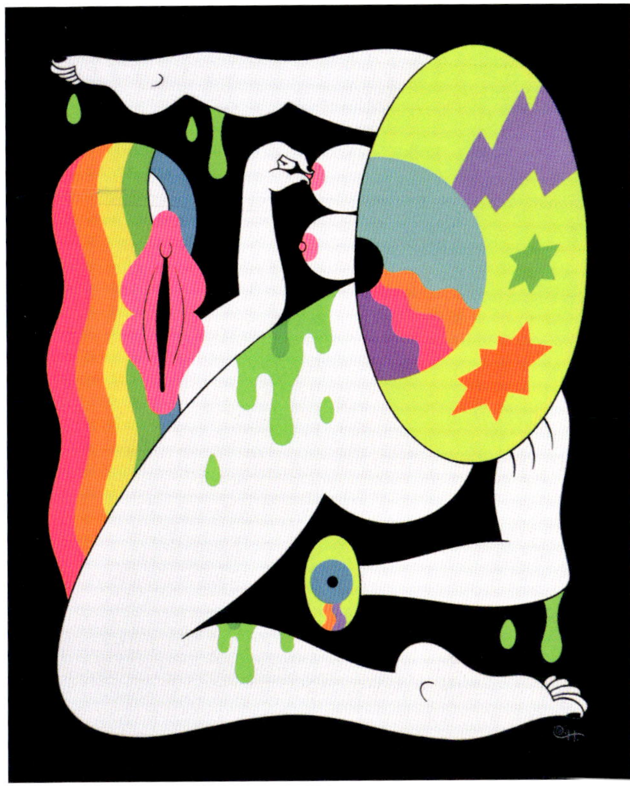
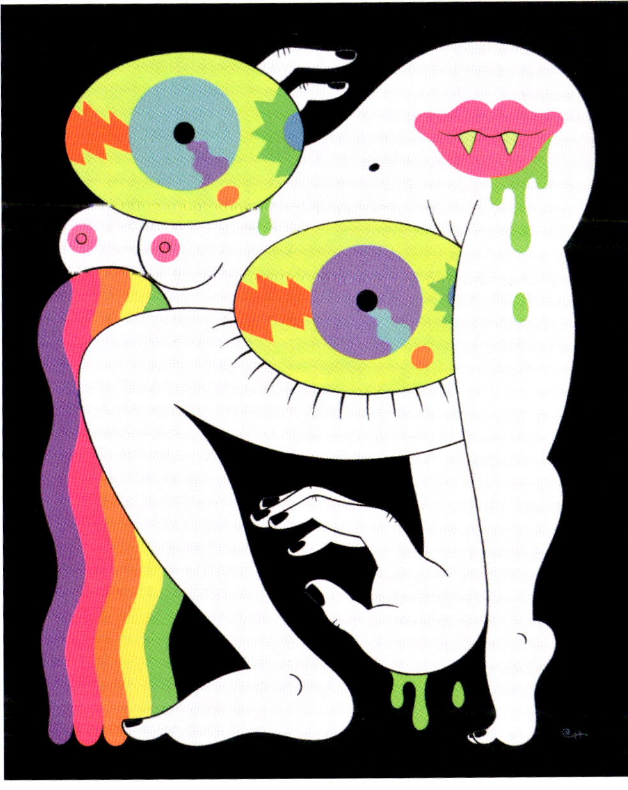
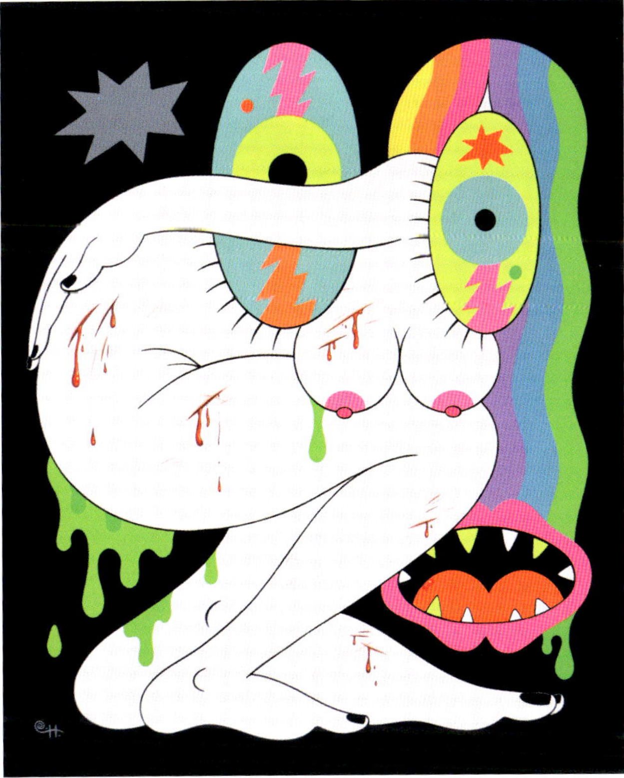

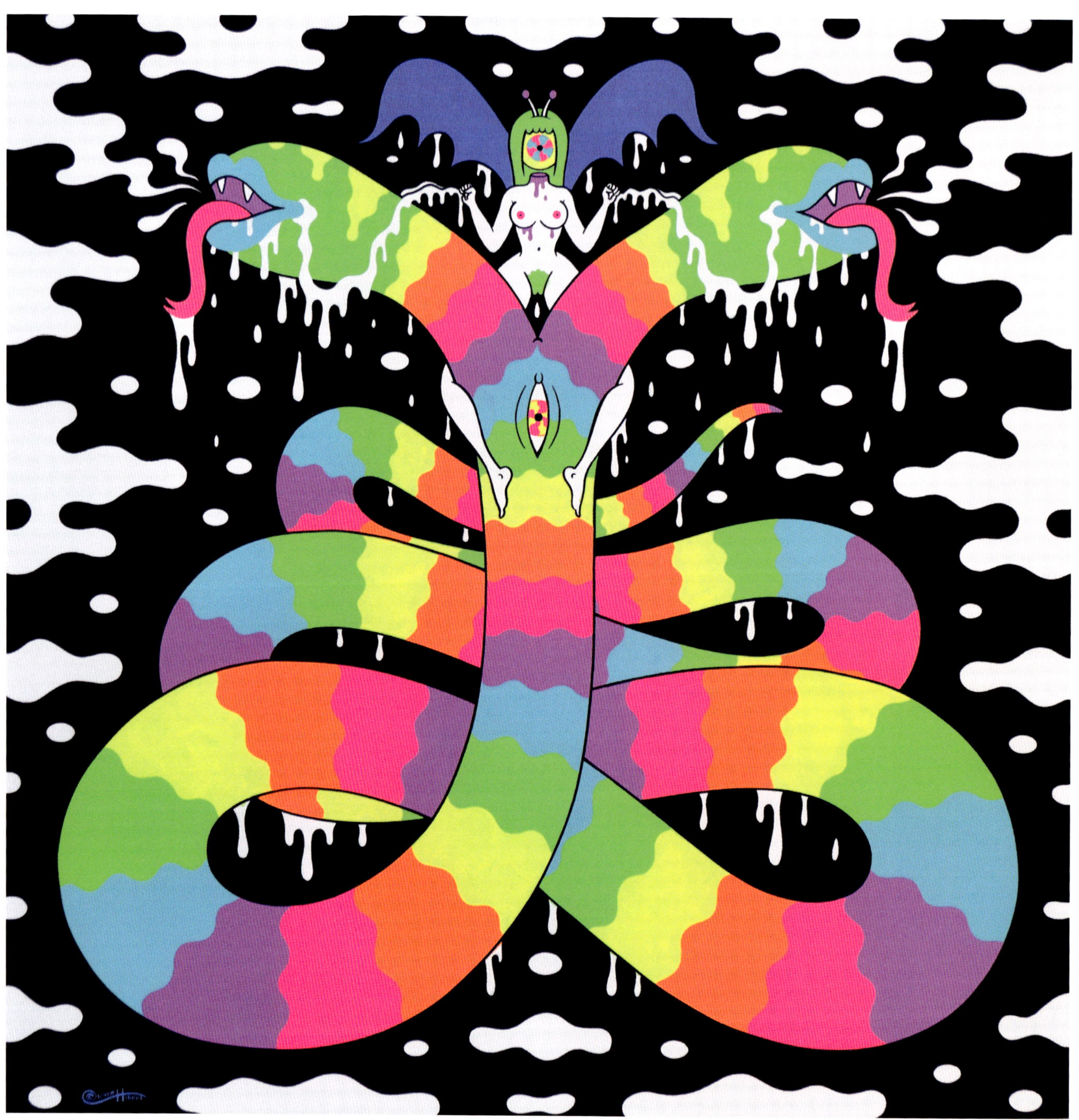

The Cumming of the Rainbow Serpent
"Tame it, ride it."

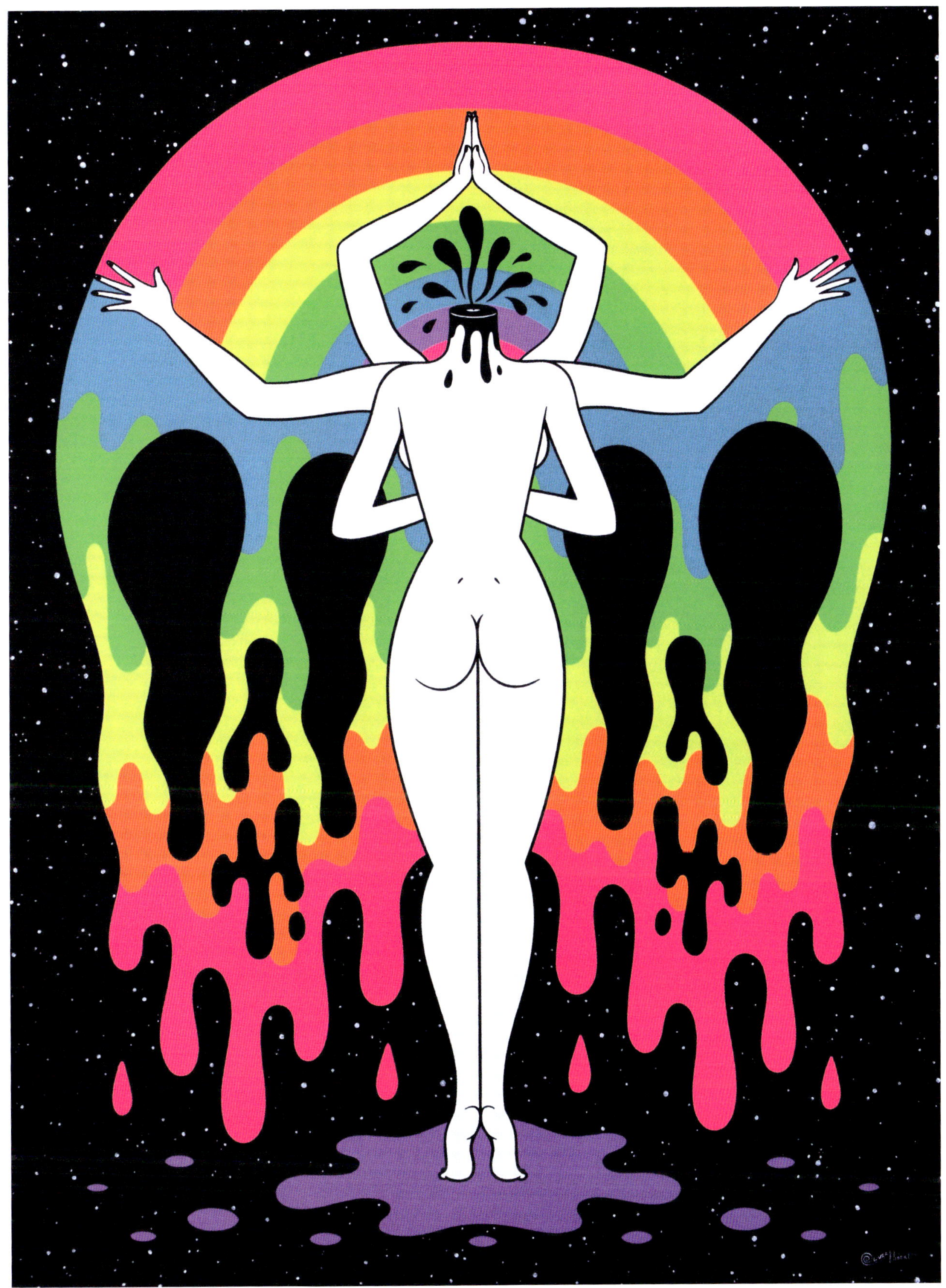

Darrier of Doom

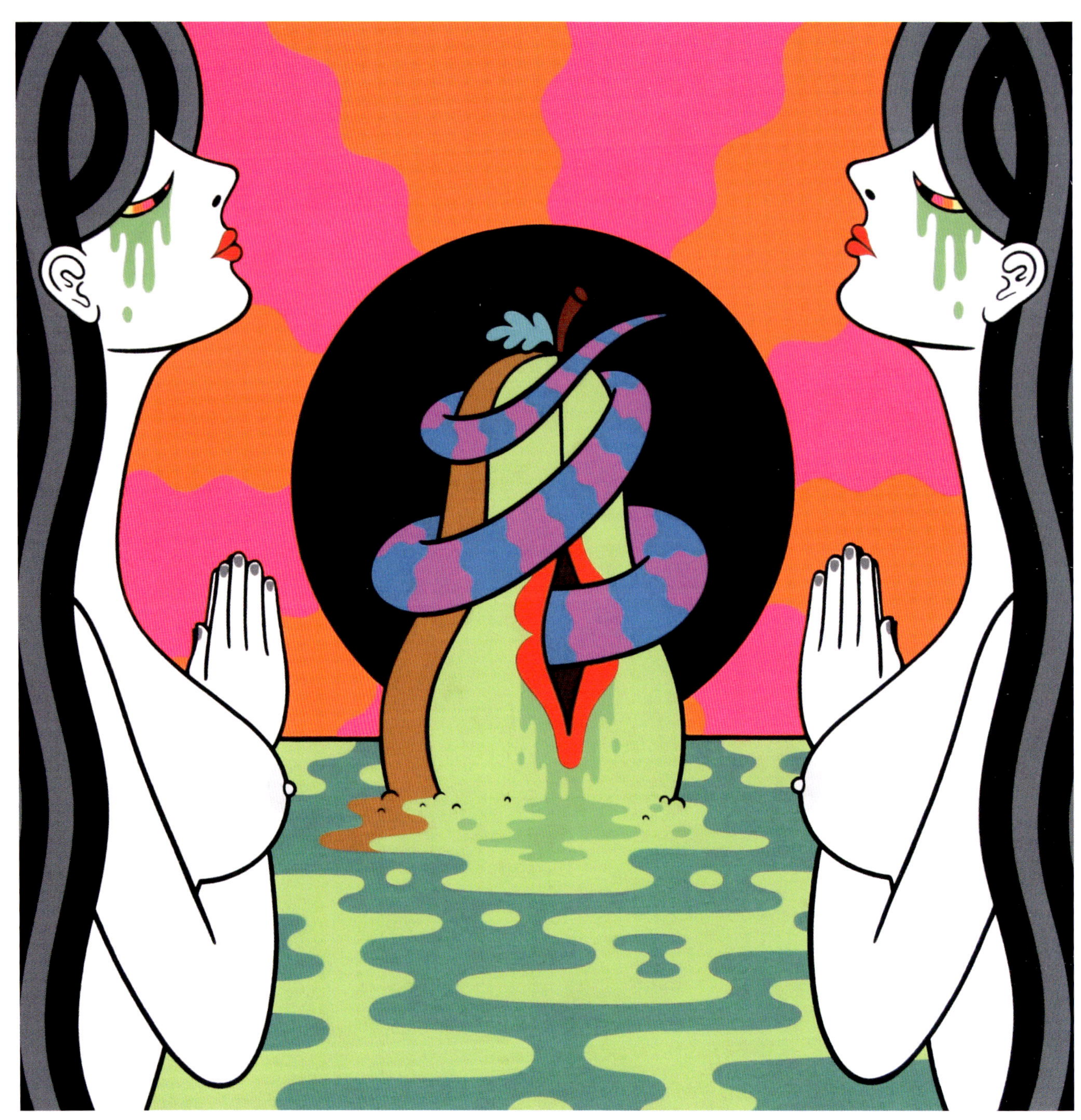

Hollow Son

"It's gone."

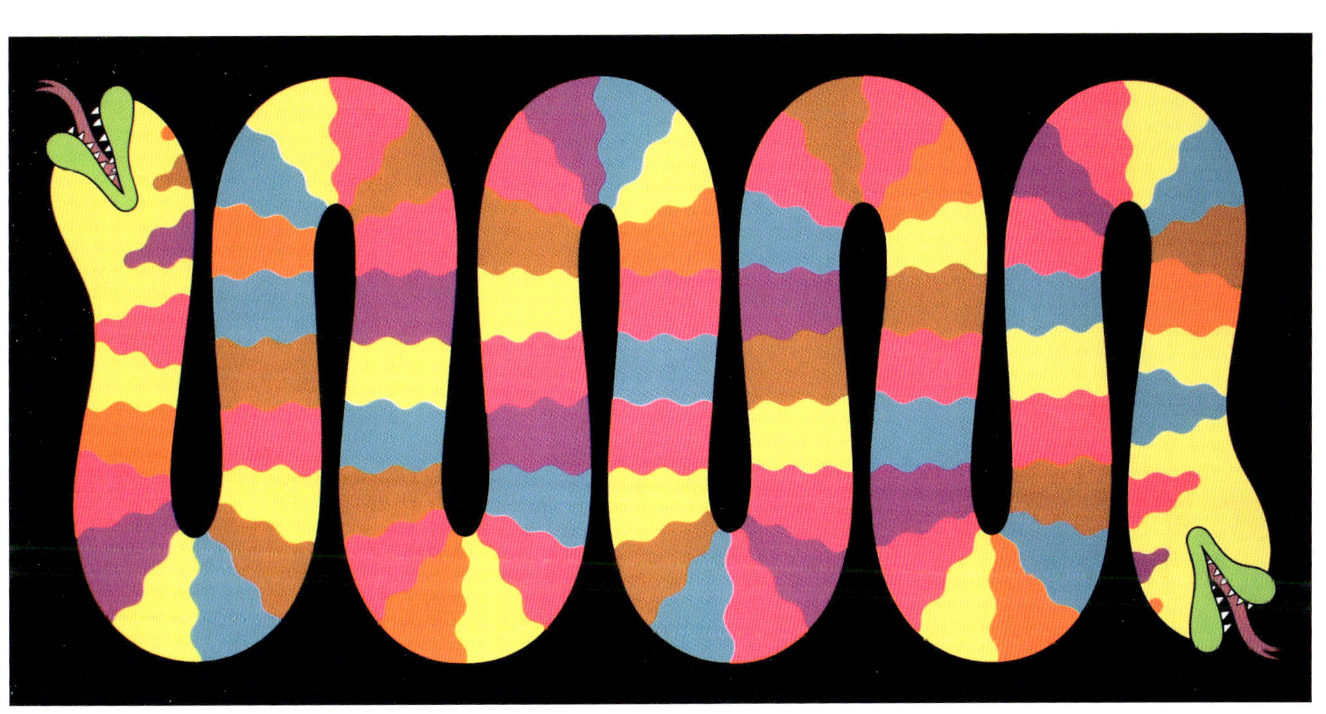

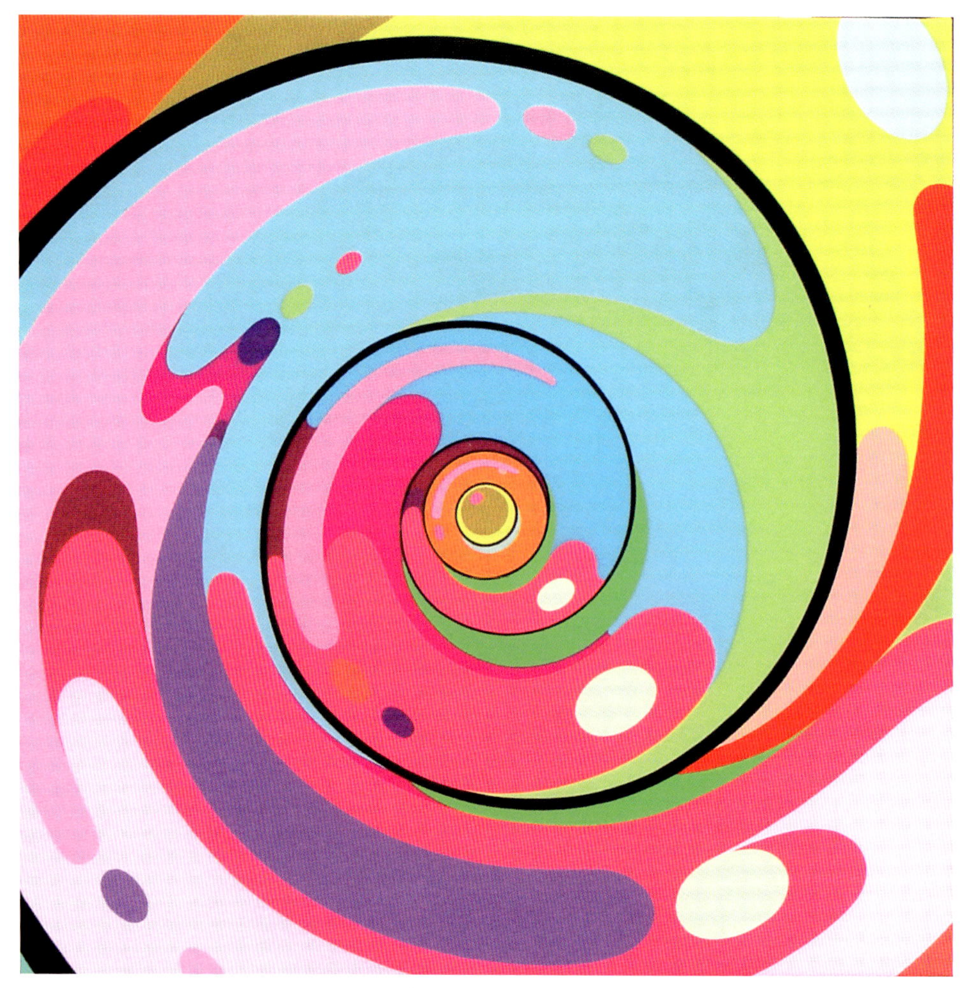

I Lost My Last Brain Cell at the Bottom of the Ocean

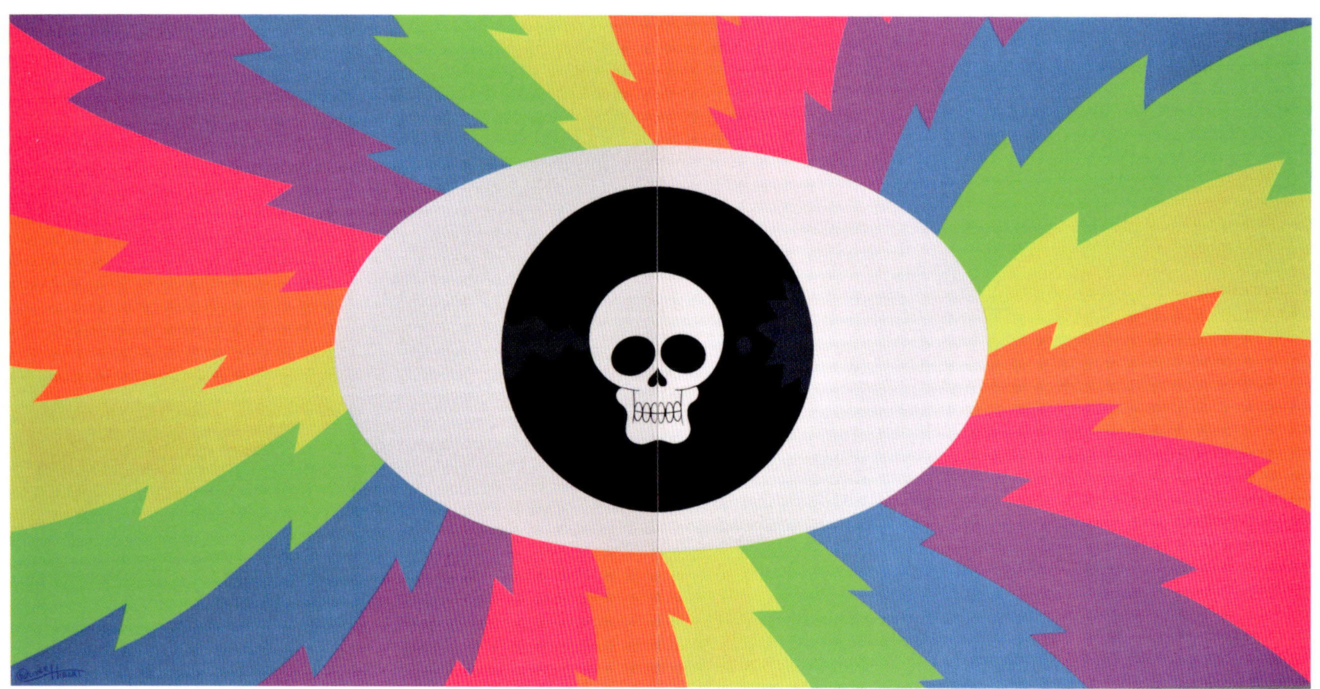

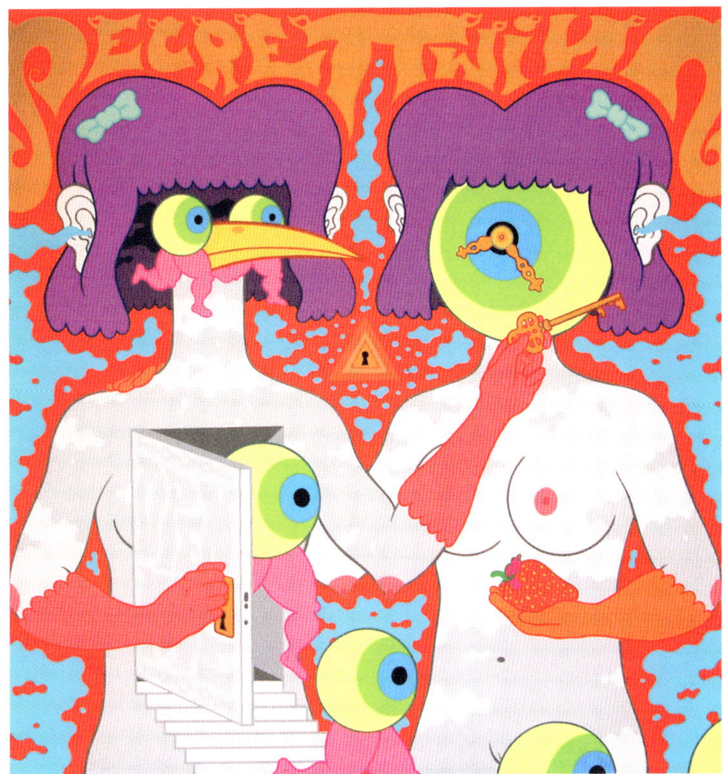

Secret Twins

"A turning point for me as a painter. My most prized piece that opened my eyes to things I could not and will not unsee. A true personal epiphany and one of the first steps in a long journey through symmetry and secrets."

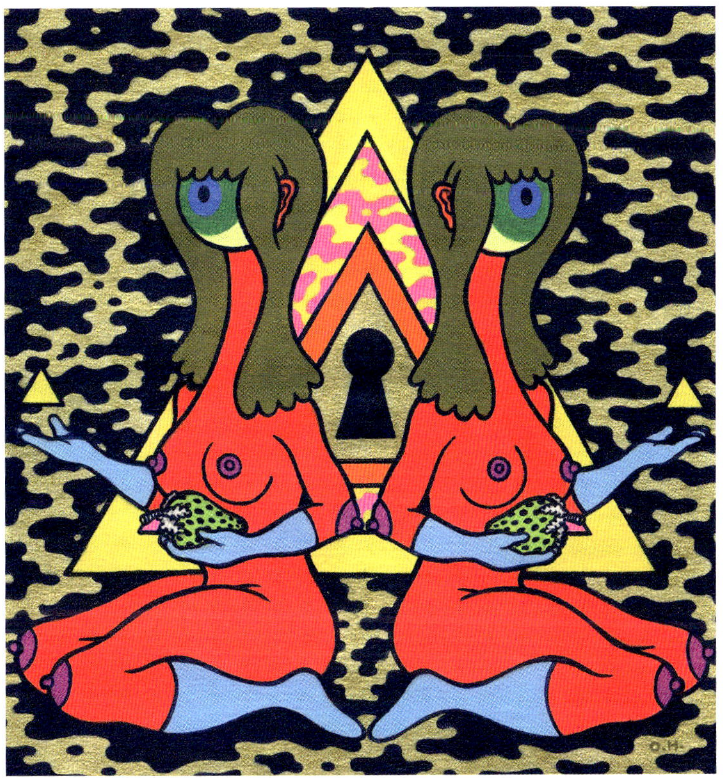

Secret Daydream

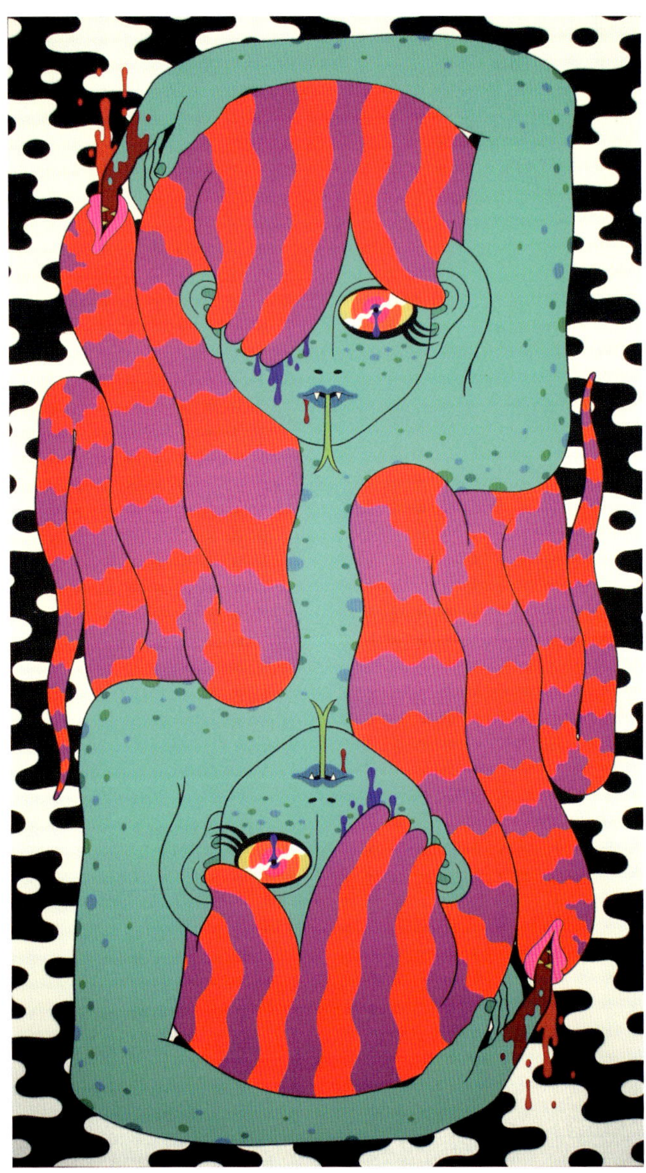

Invisible Mirror

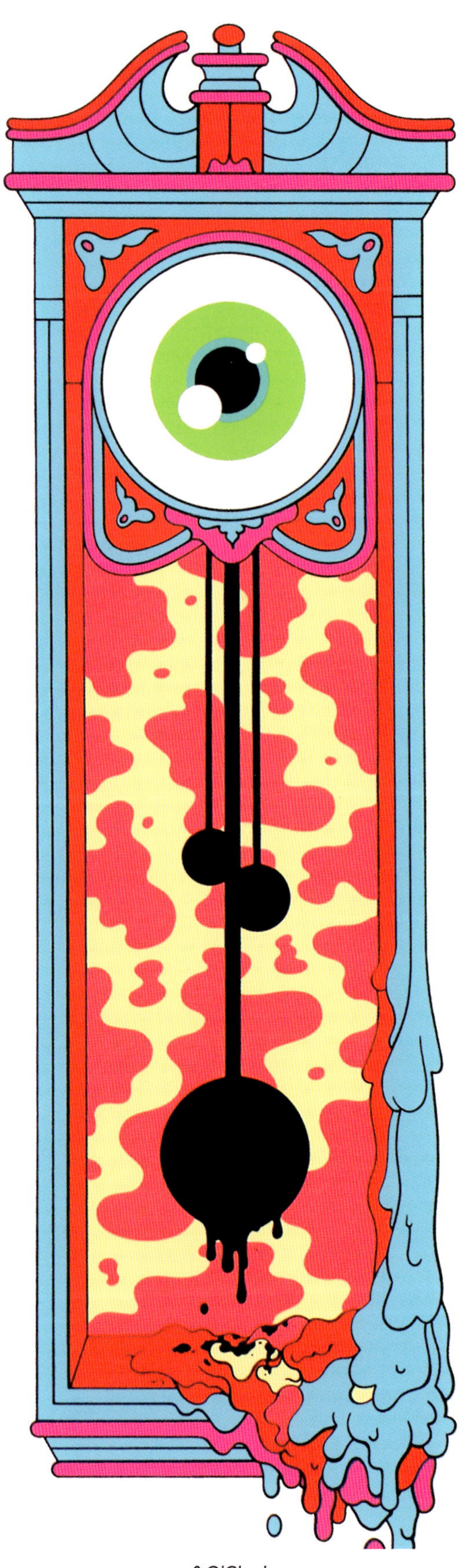

0 O'Clock

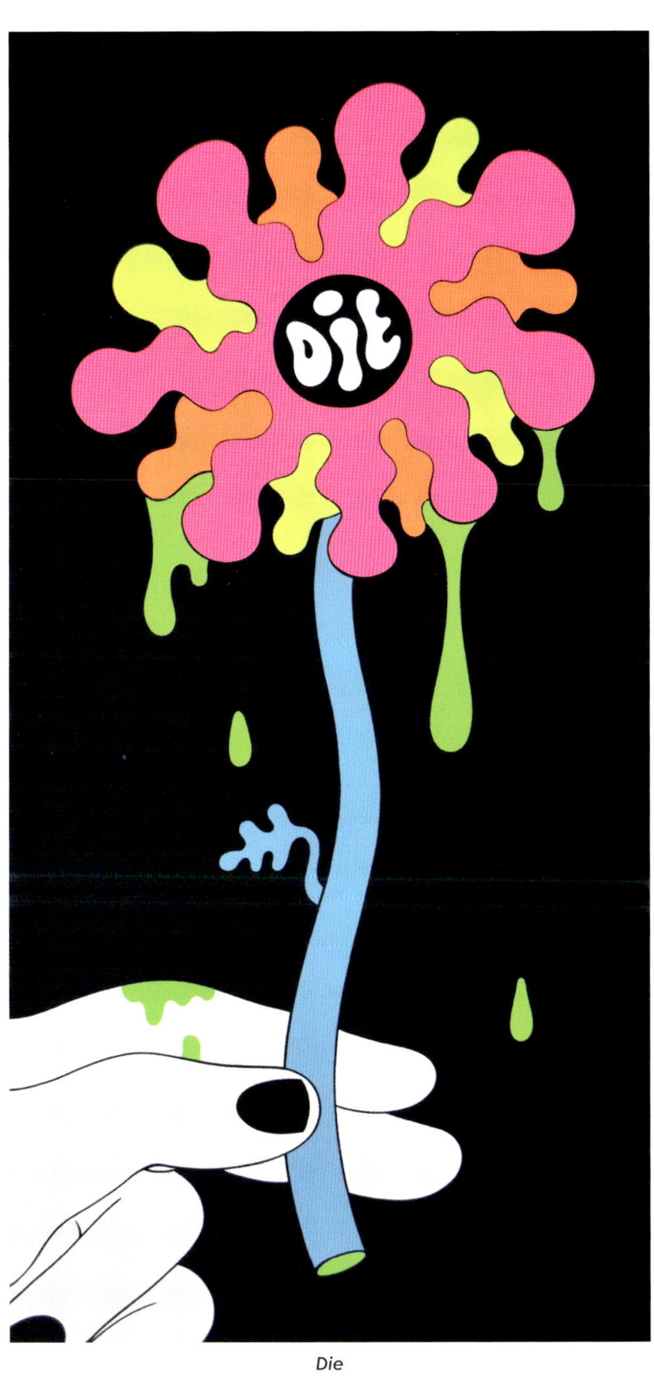

Die

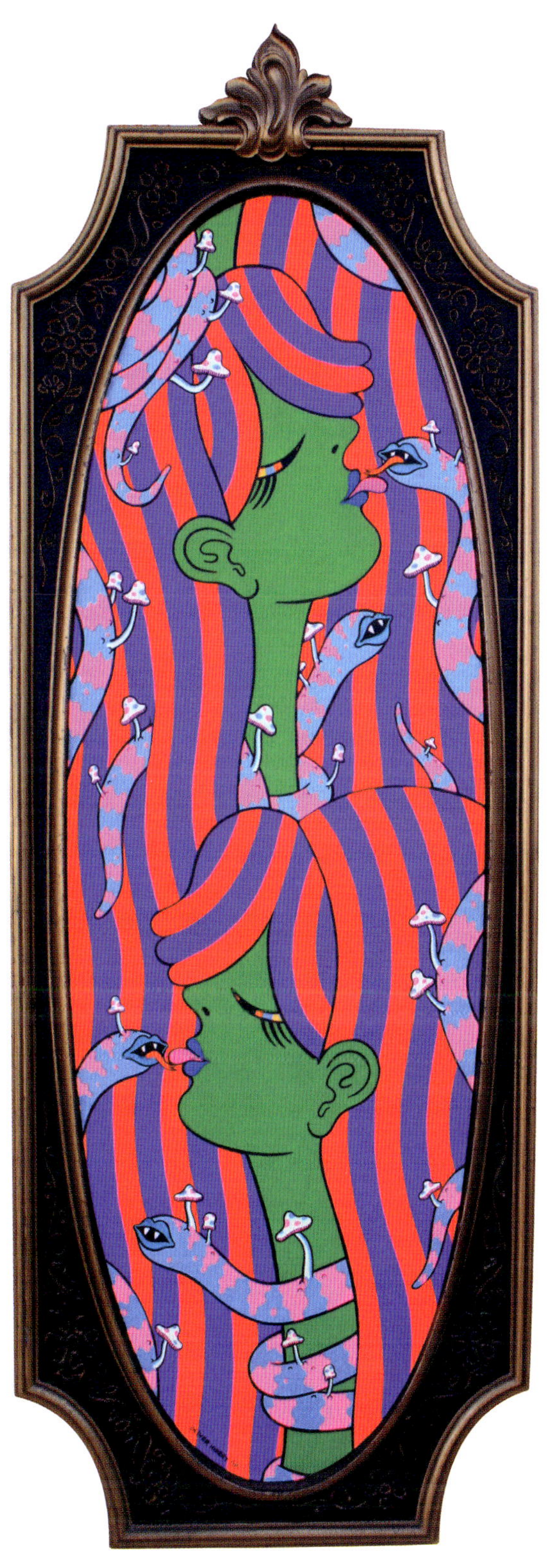

Serve the Serpents

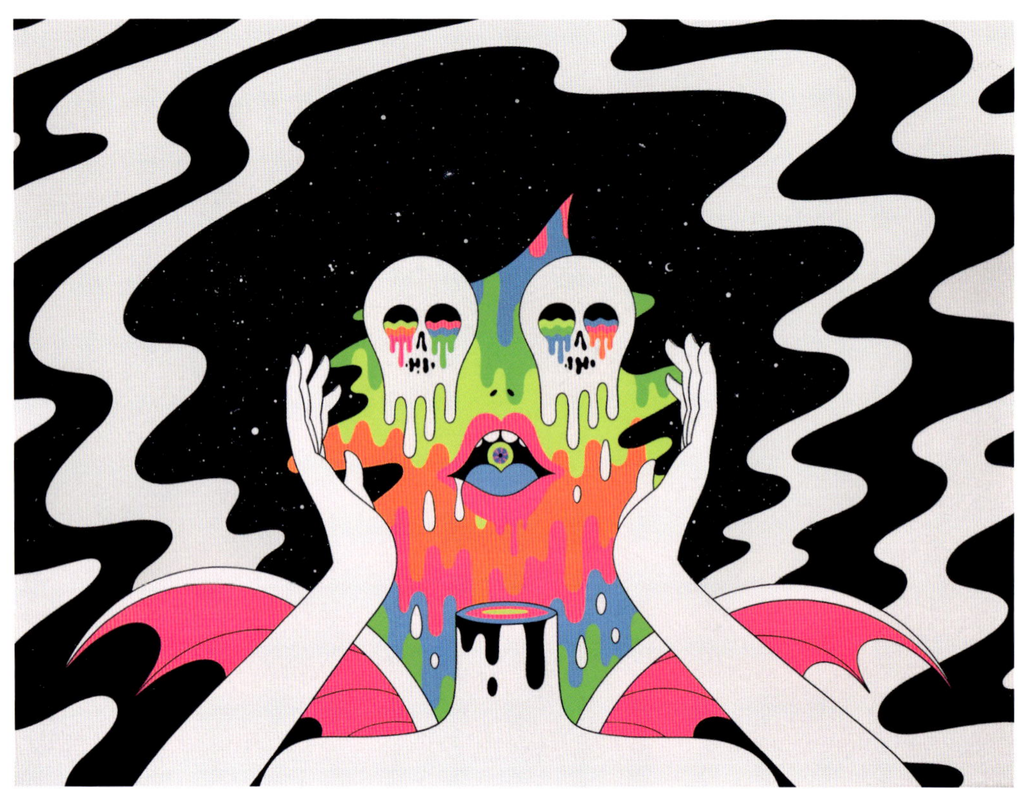

Death at First Sight

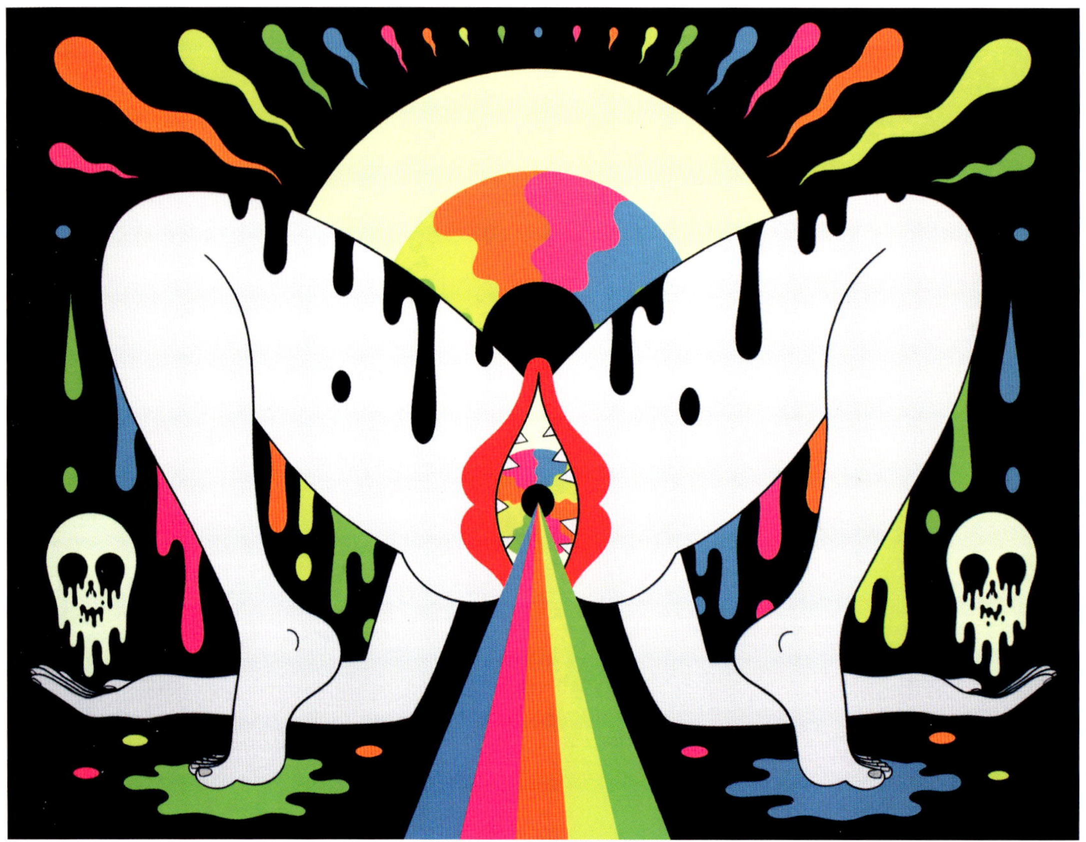

Birth of Death

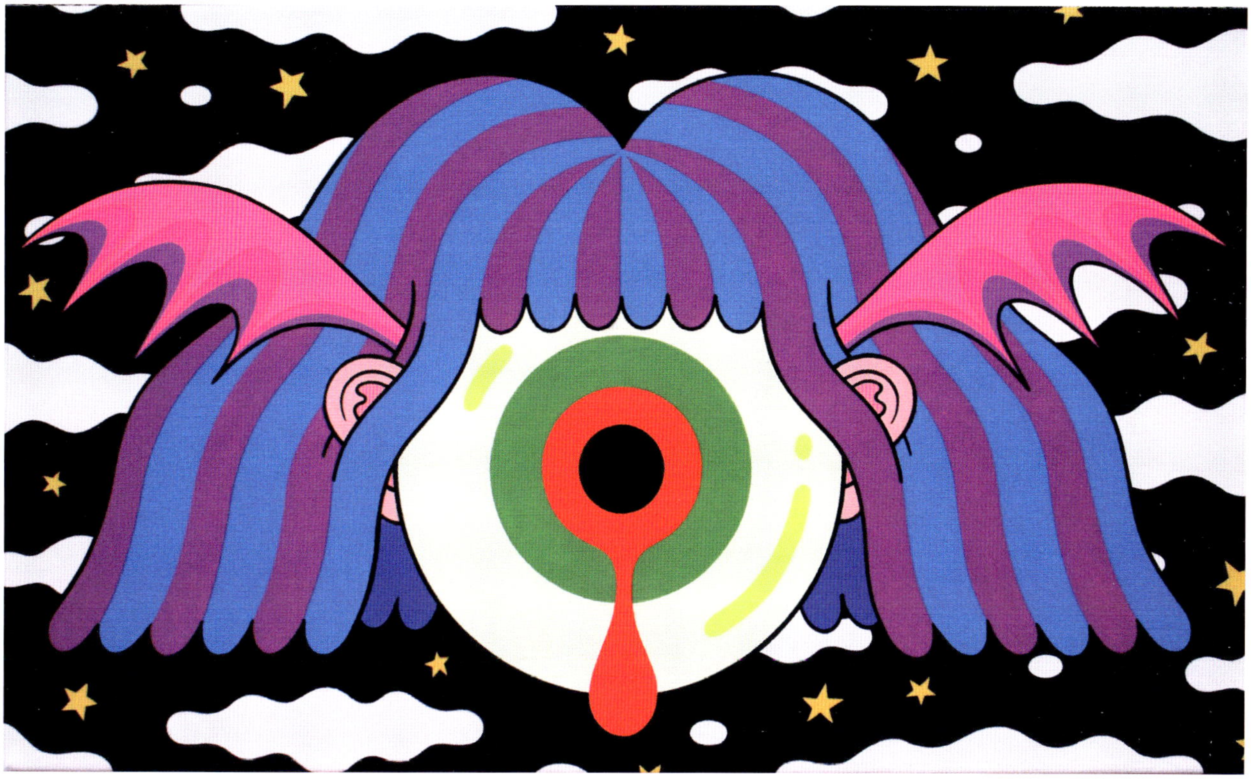

In Vesper Verum

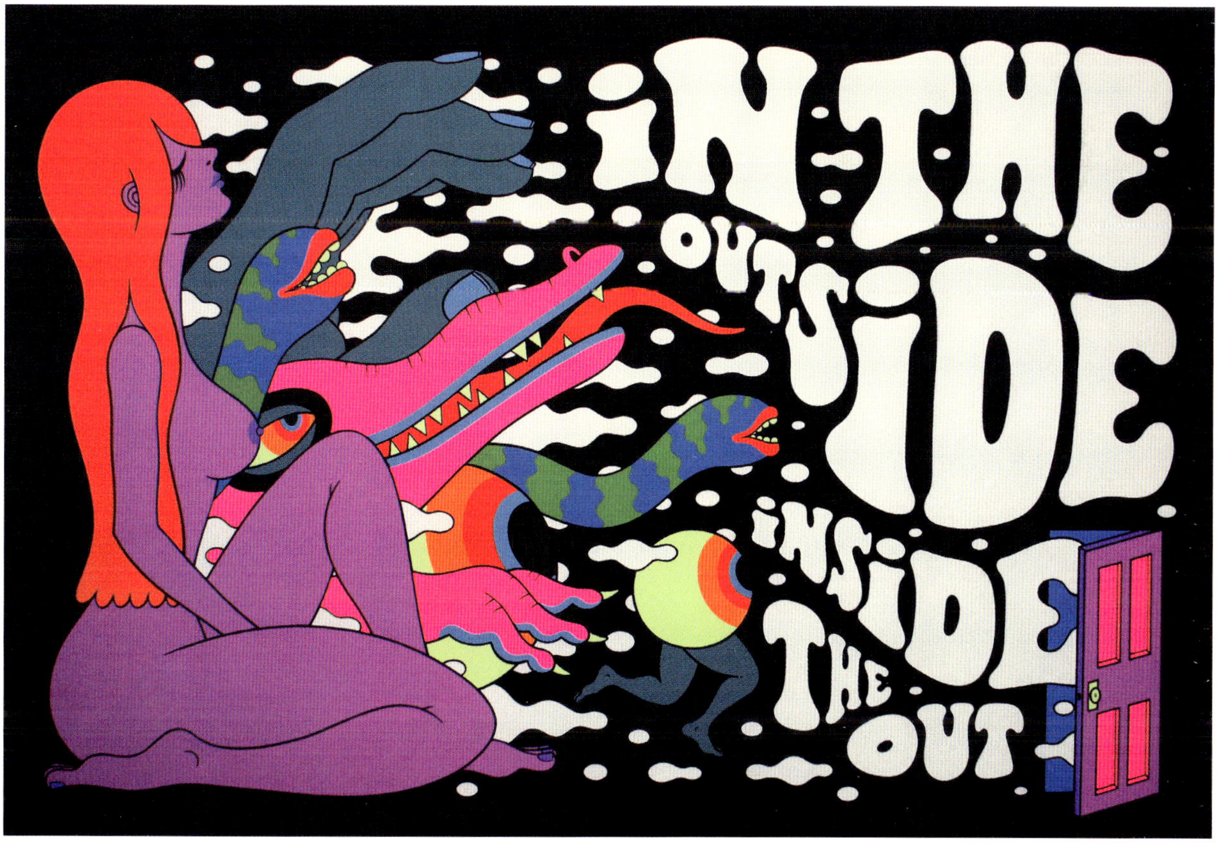

Inside Out

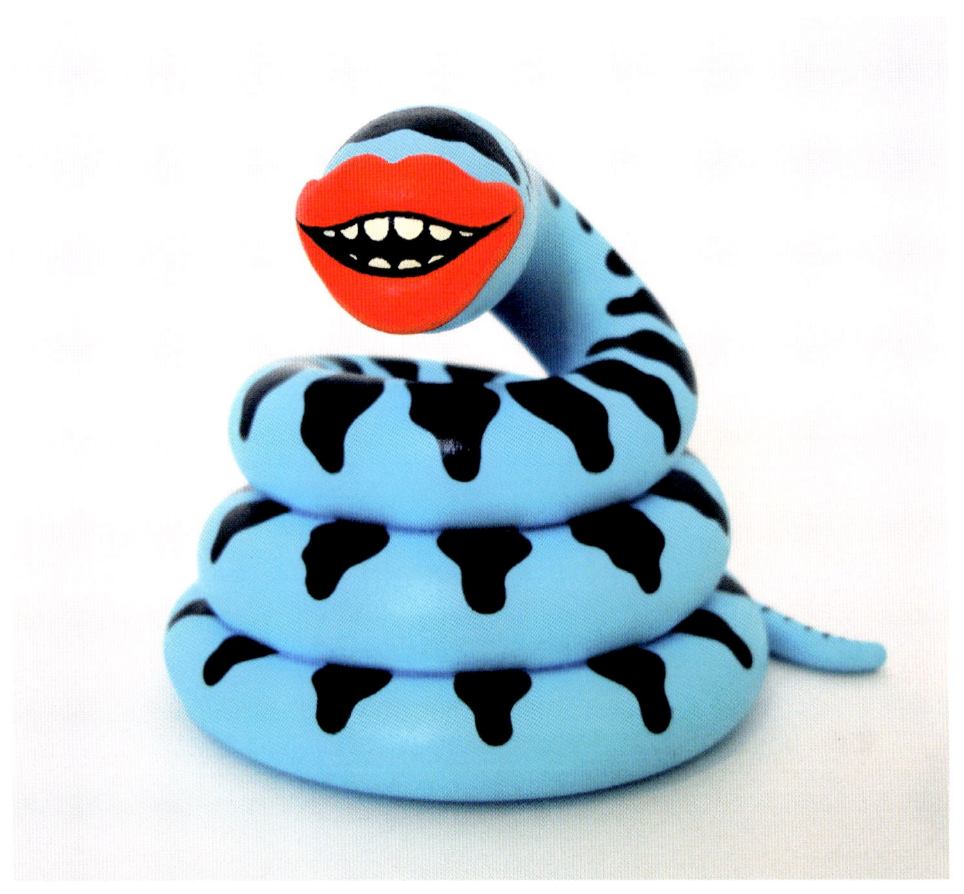

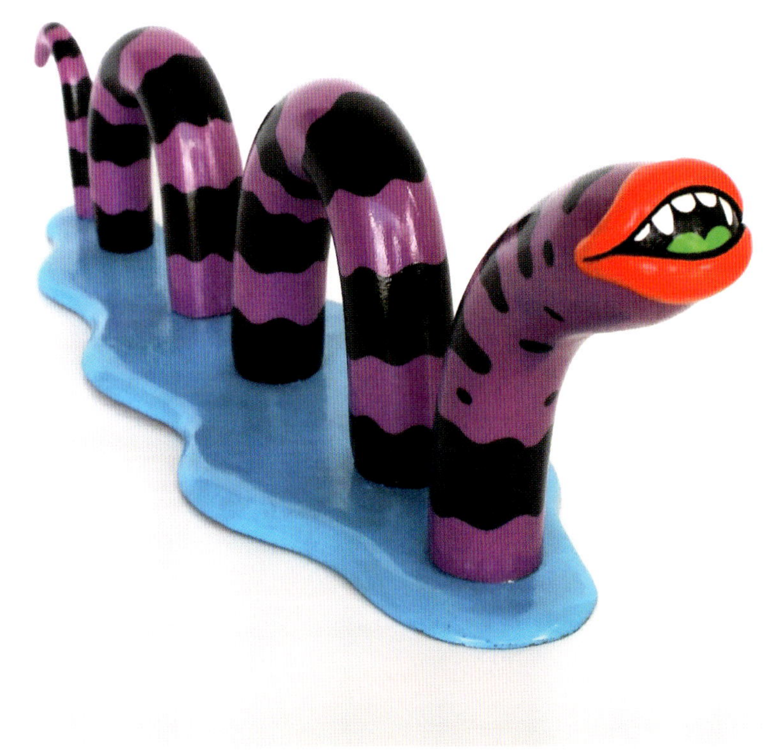

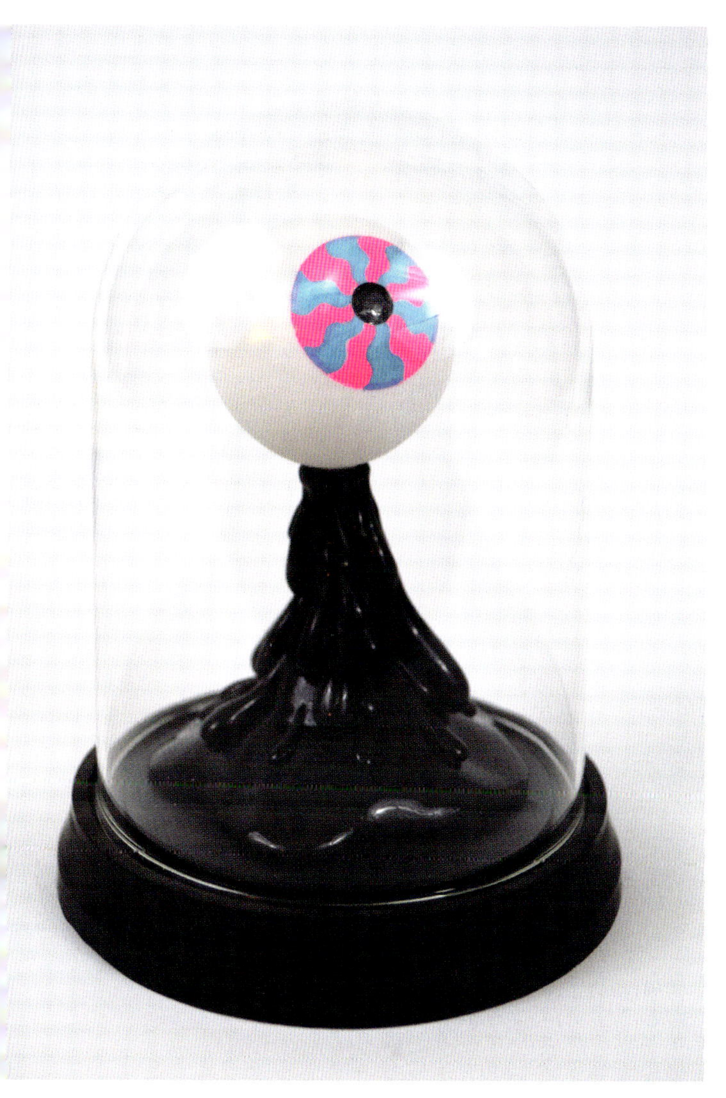

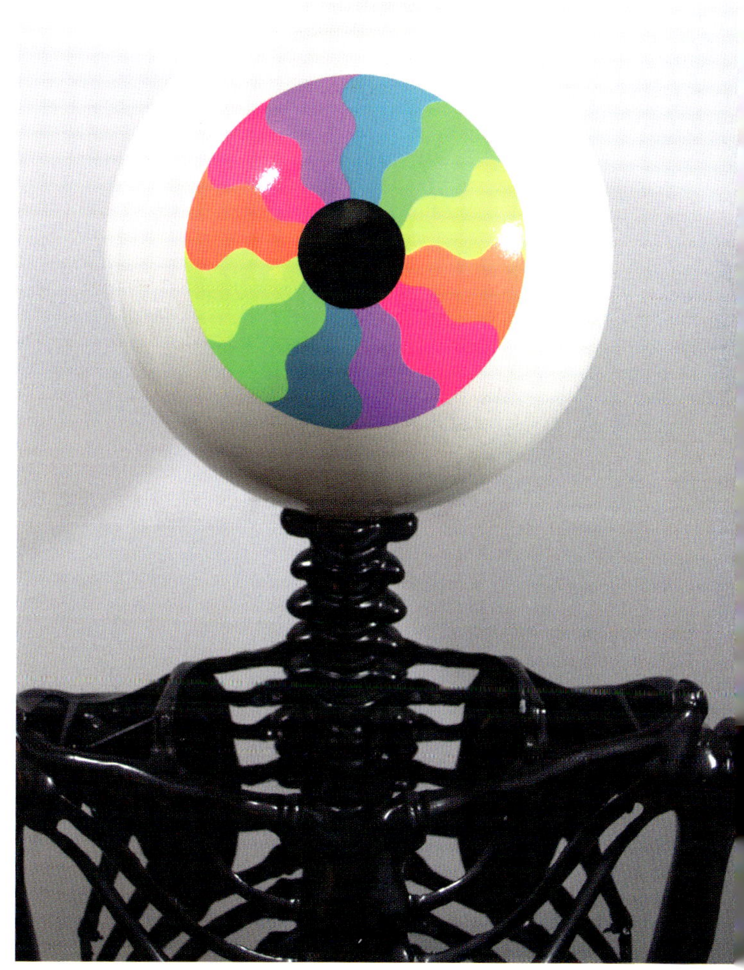

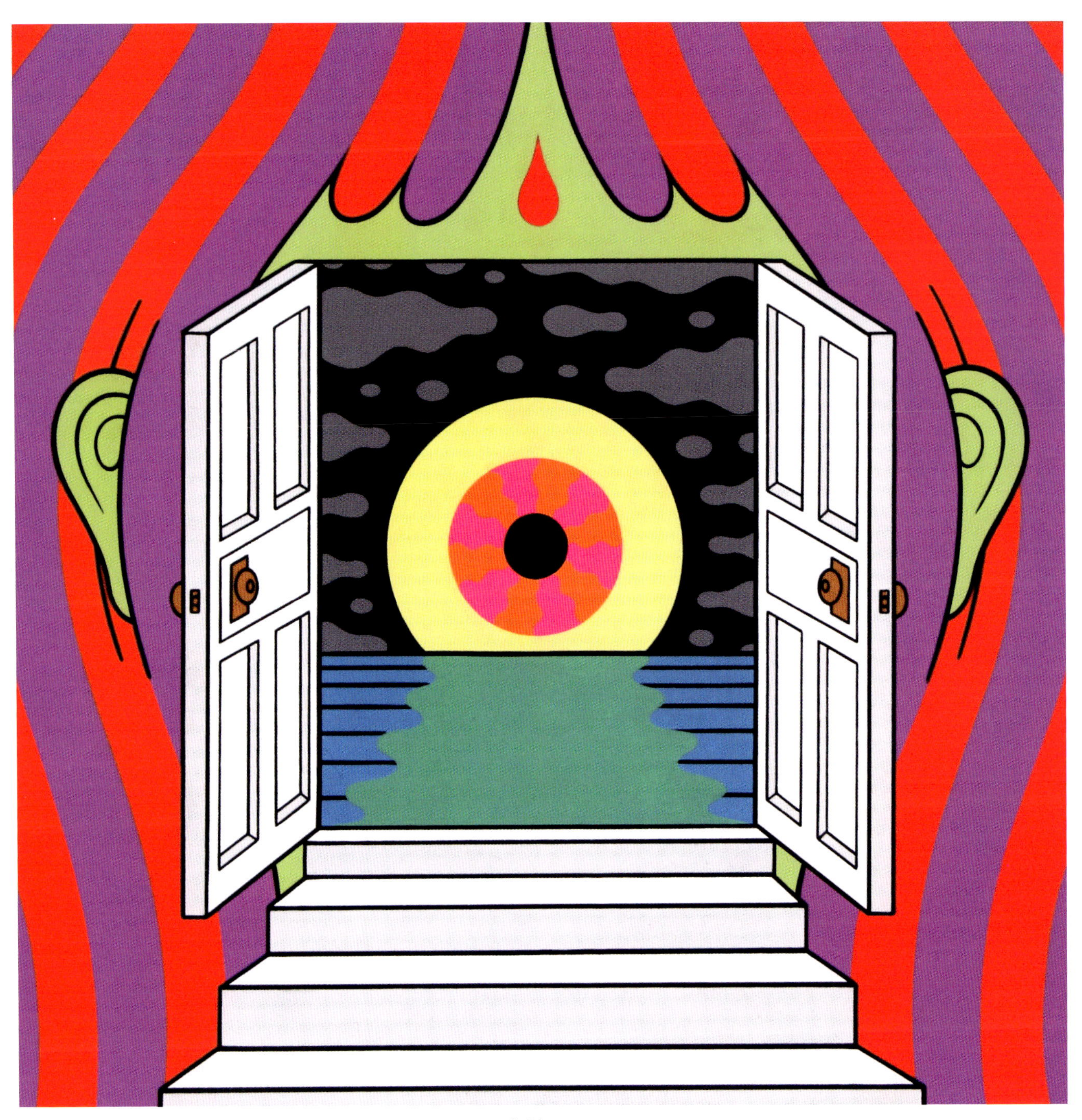

Full Loon

" . . . because of you."

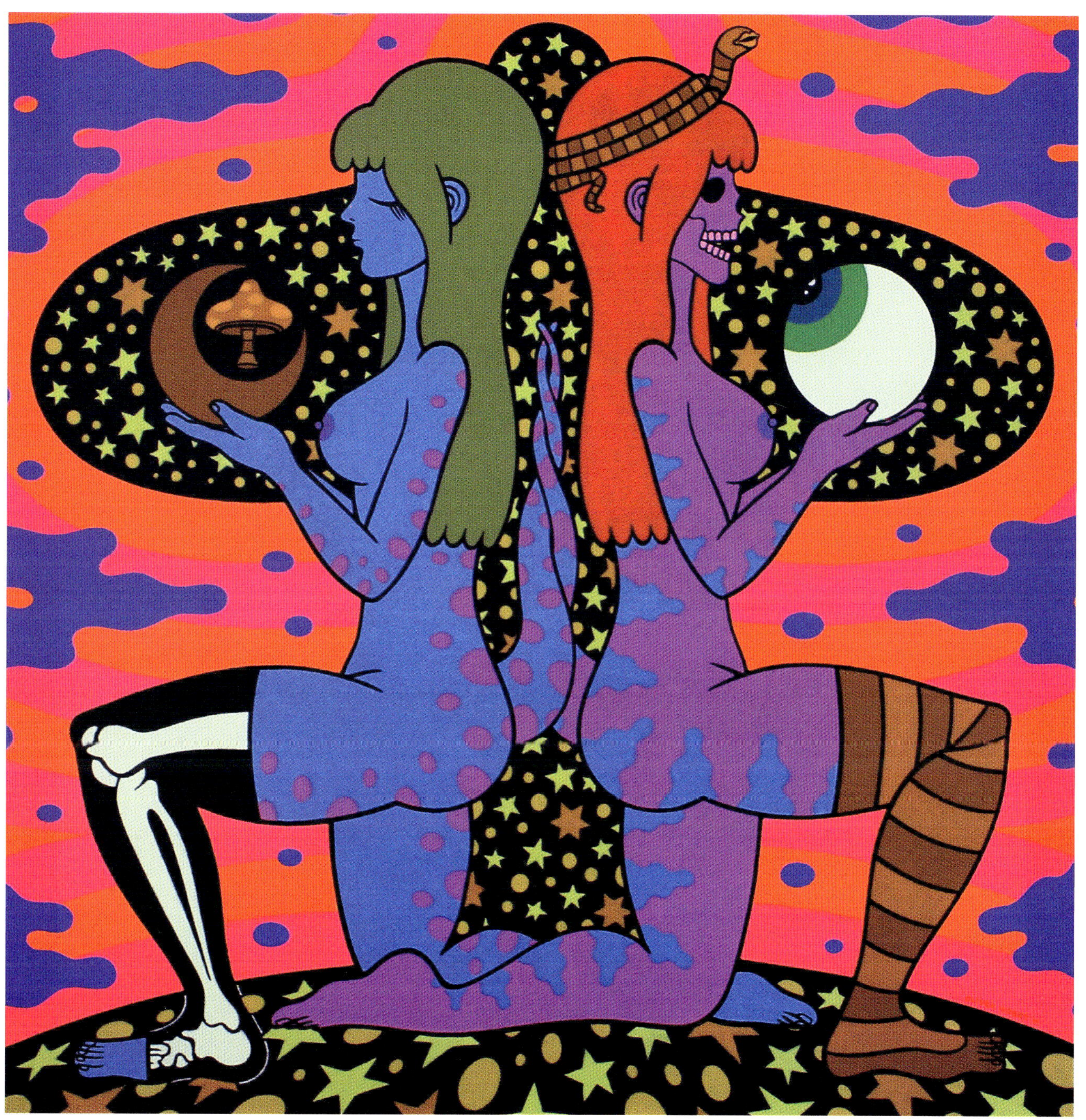

Death Shroom Gloom

"This was painted for a mushroom-themed show . . . mush mush fun."

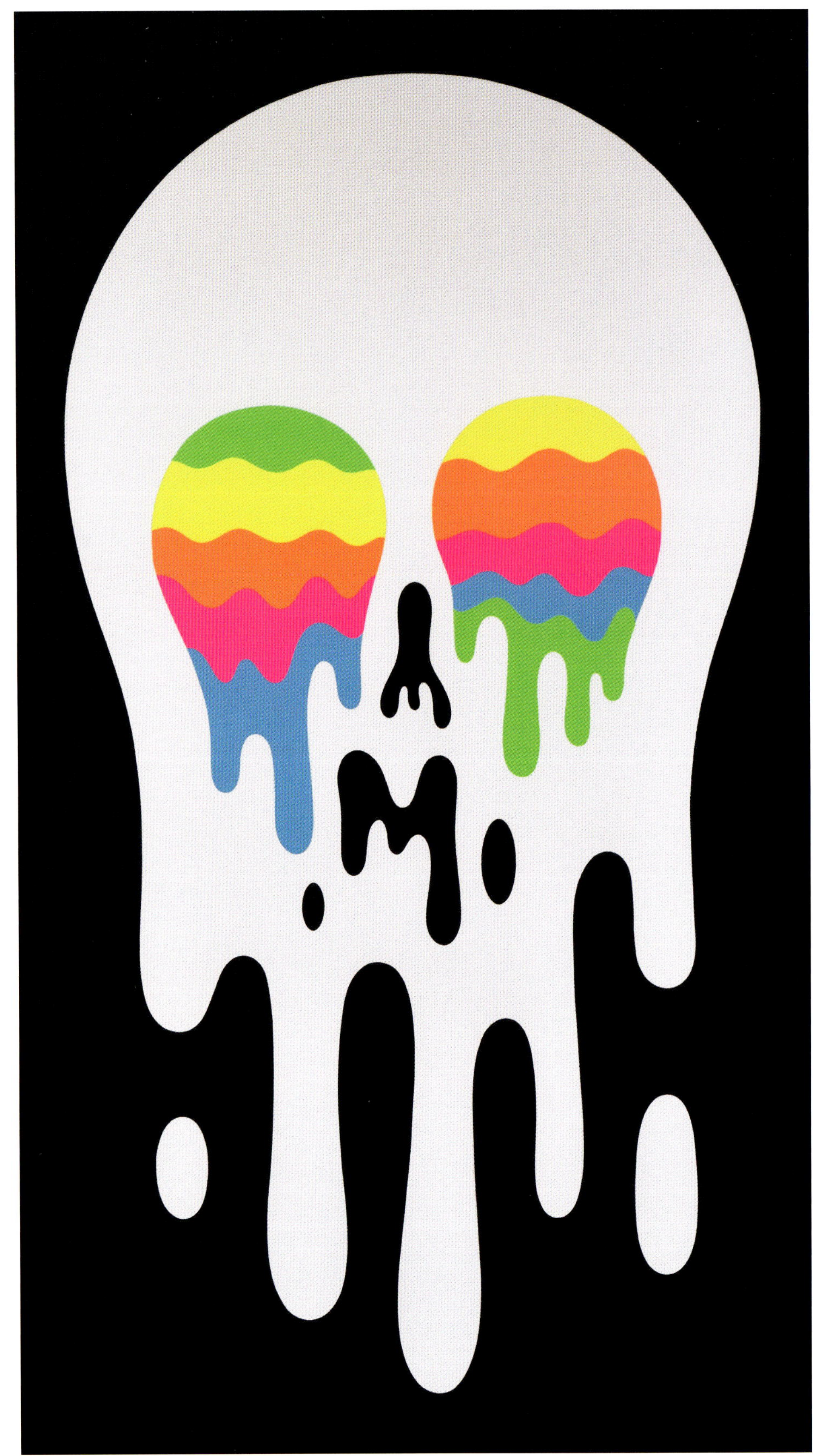

The Doom Skull

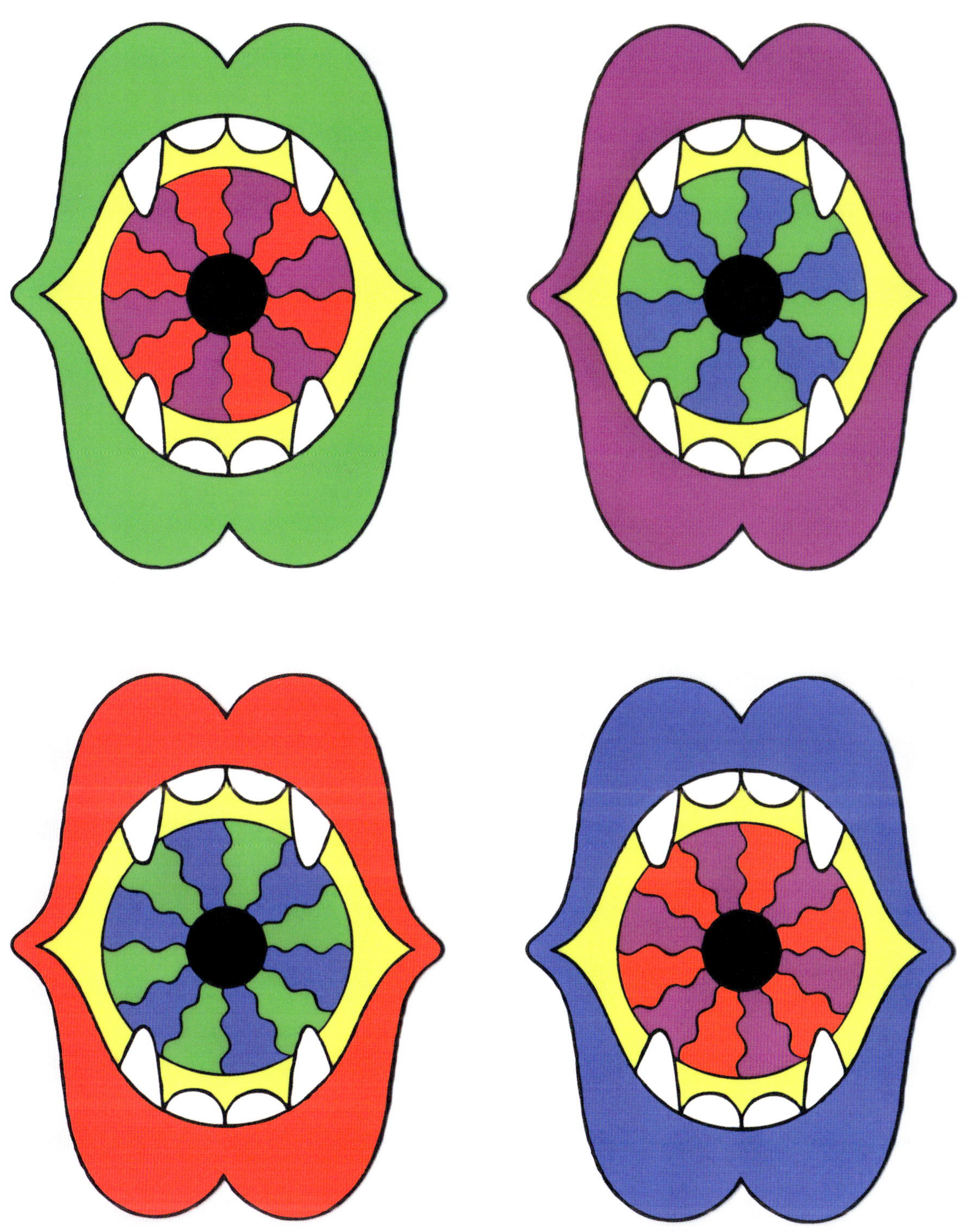

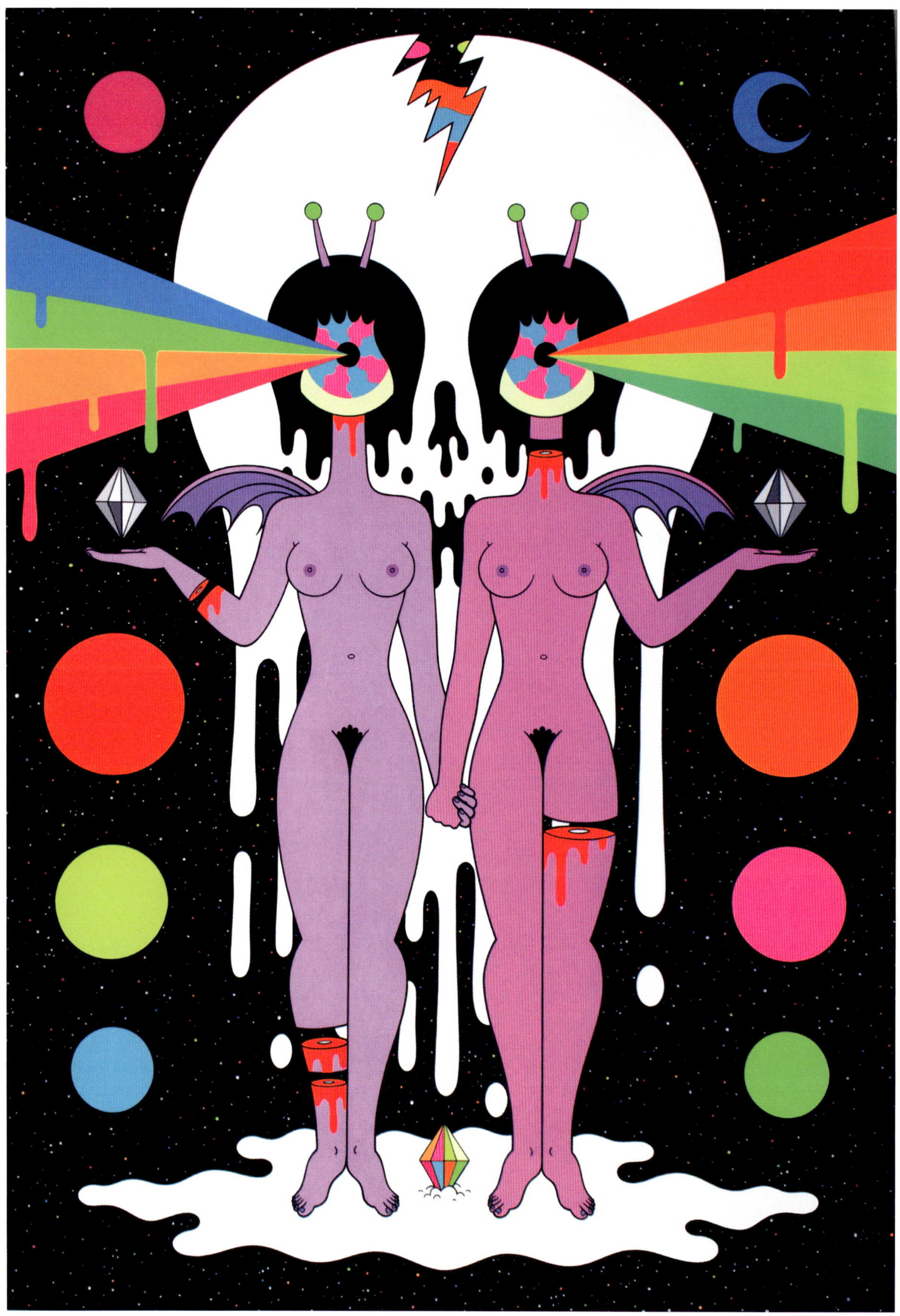

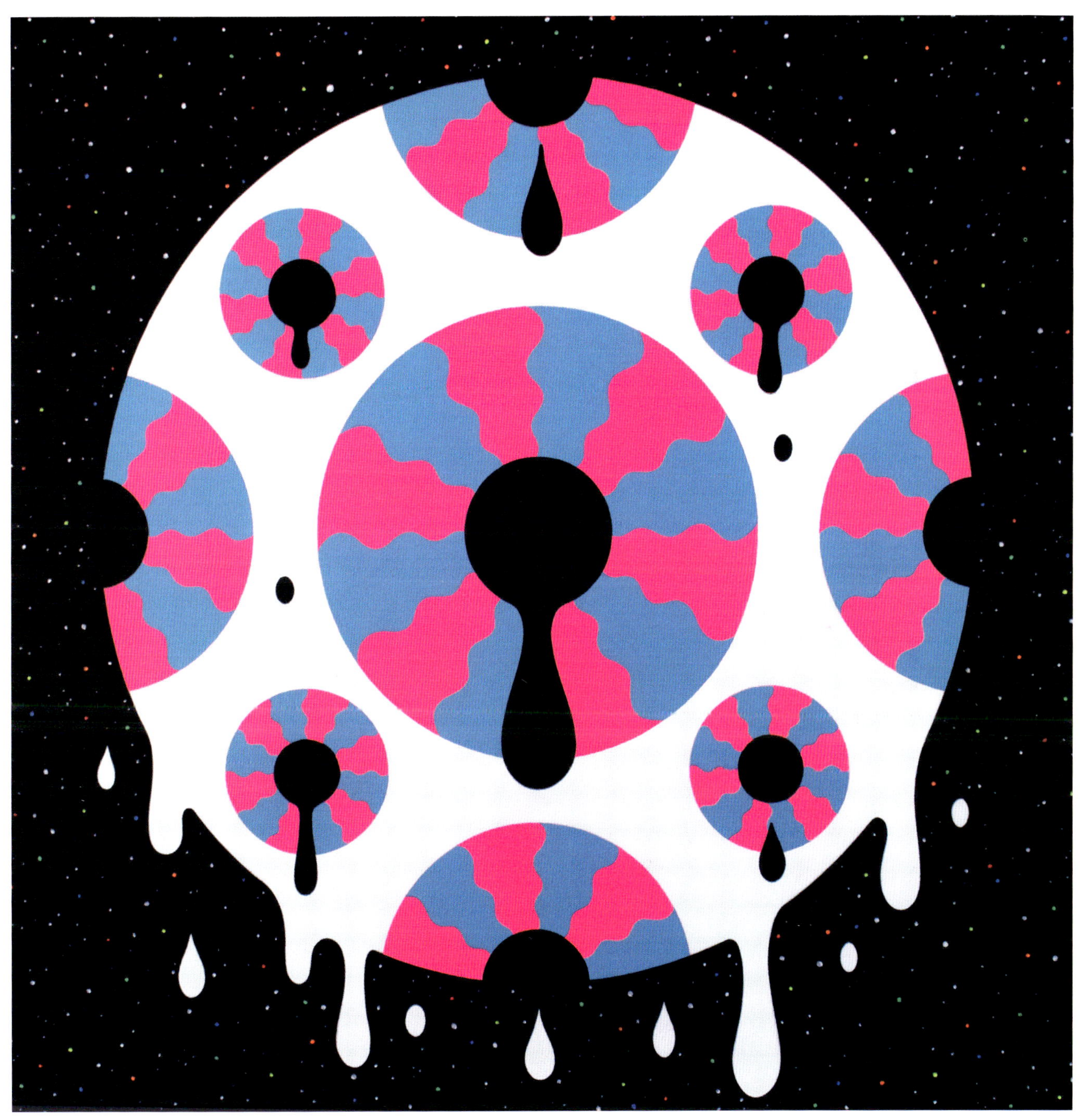

Chapter Two:

Illustrations & Works on Paper

Possibly even more prevalent than in his paintings, Oliver's illustrations and preliminary sketches display his predilection for symmetry and balance. Many works are bisected, expertly counterweighted halves, each detail plotted out against its mirrored twin. While many of the most beloved psychedelic artists—Martin Sharp and Keiichi Tanaami to name two—employed collage in their busy allover works (showing their reverence for Dada and the surrealists), Oliver maintains a comparatively stripped-down simplicity to his compositions. In the absence of color (shown in several sketches here in this chapter), the value of the line becomes paramount, like the foundation of a building. Deftness of draftsmanship provides the crucial outline skeleton on which Oliver's bold, confrontational colors can be hung.

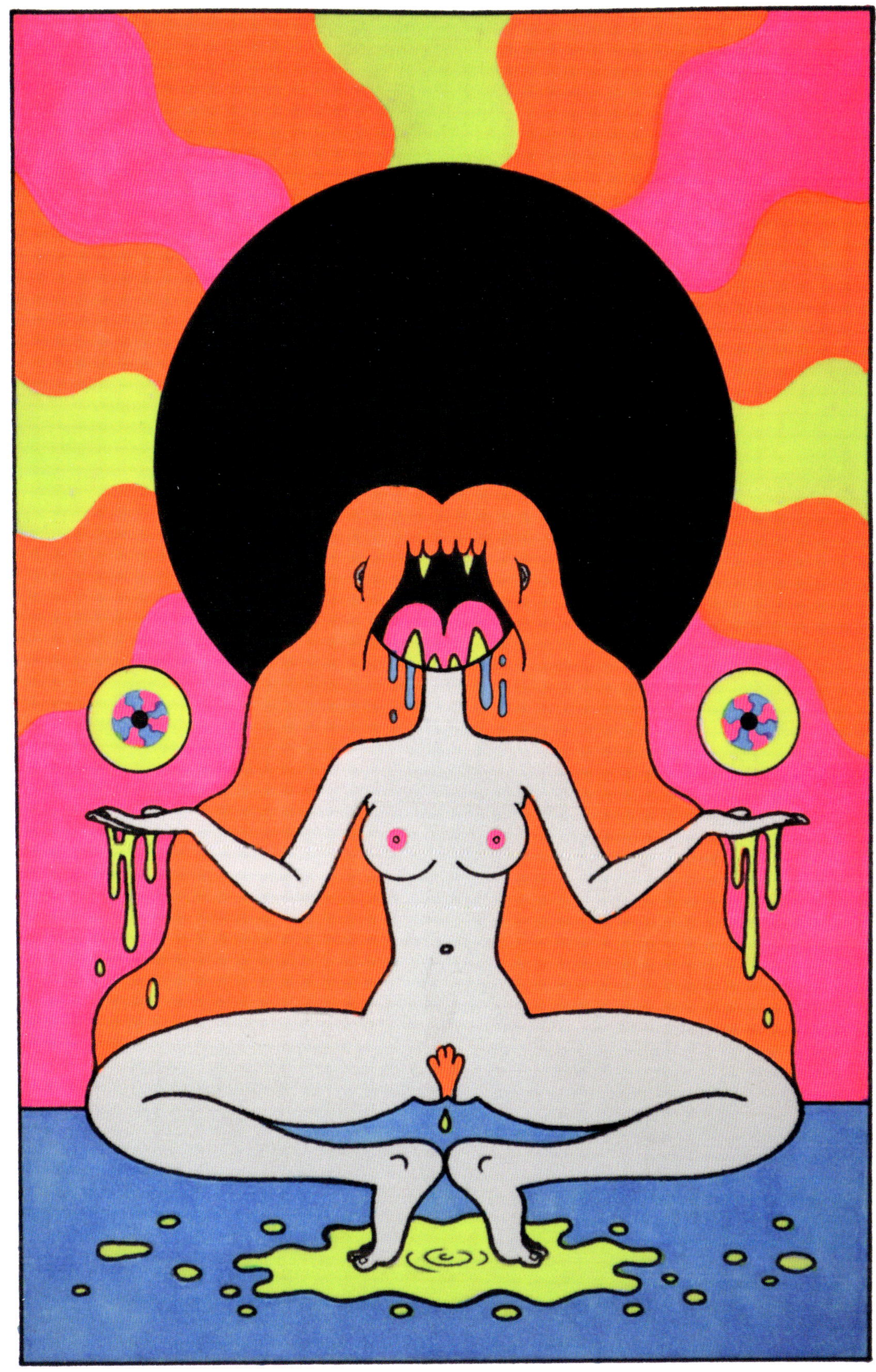

Eat The Sun

"The night time is the right time. I truly do hate the sun."

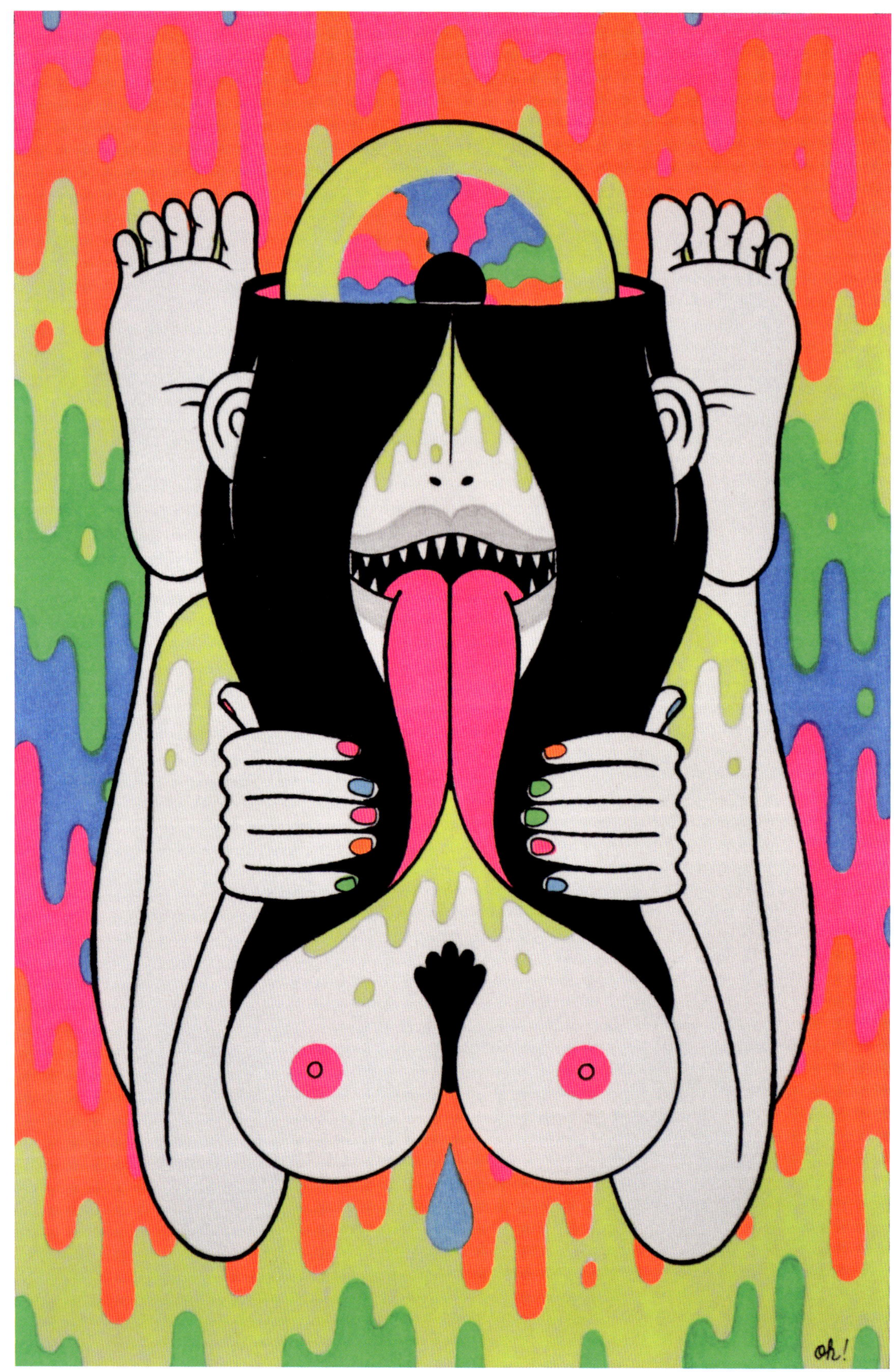

The Creeper

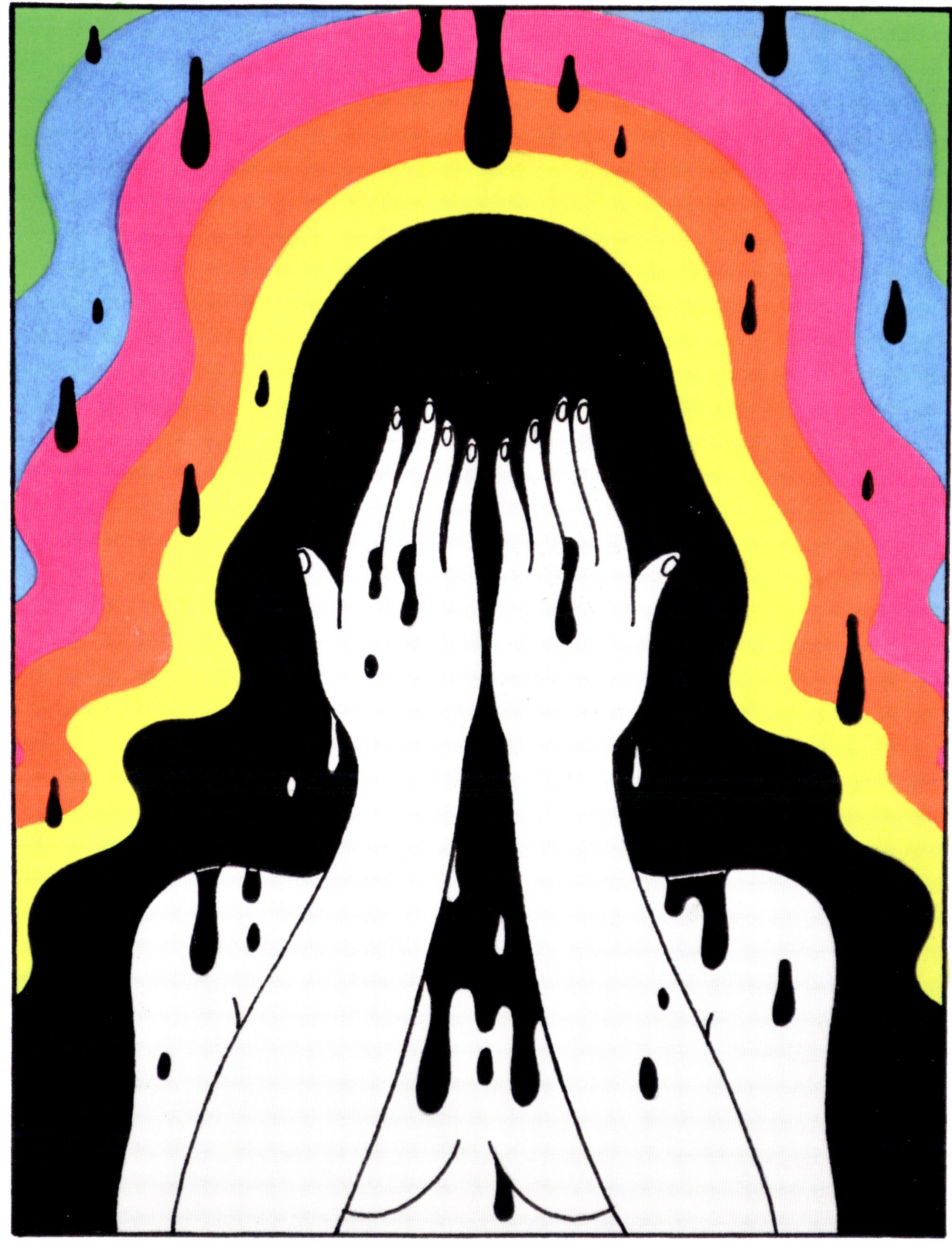

Goodnight

"We all feel like this at times, but we must not forget the rainbow around us."

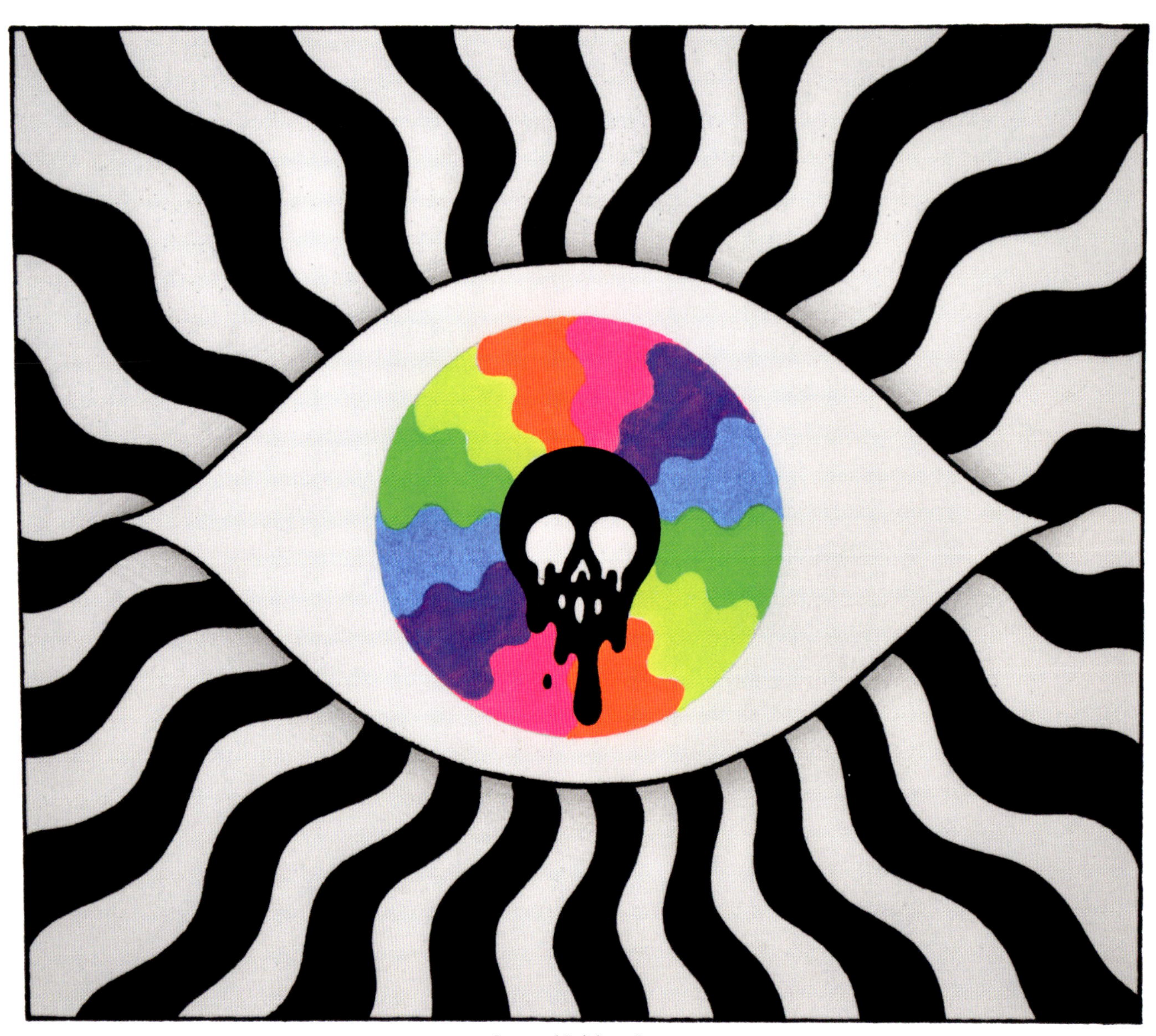

Doomed Rainbow Eye
(color test study)

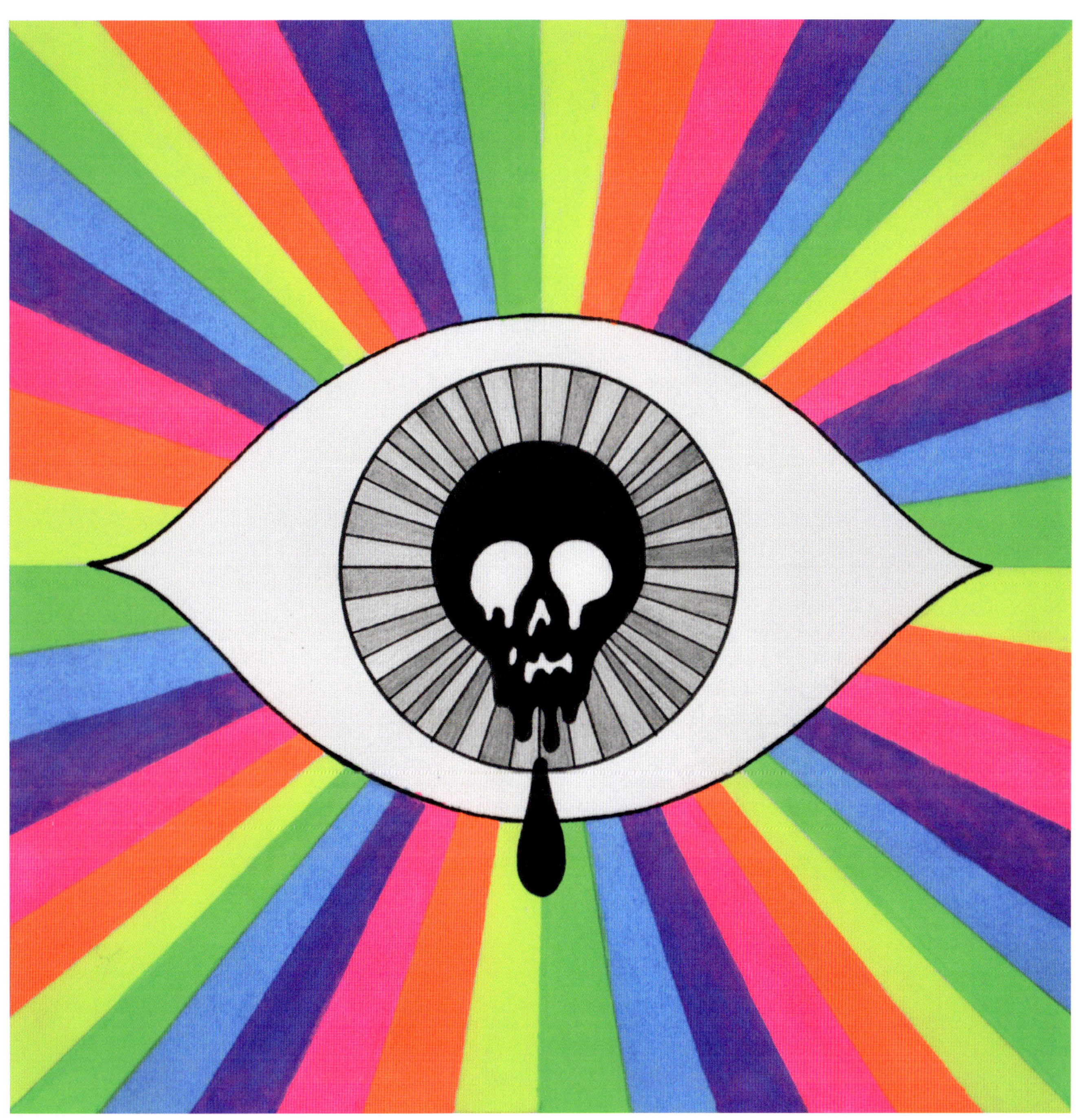

Doomed Rainbow Eye
(color test study)

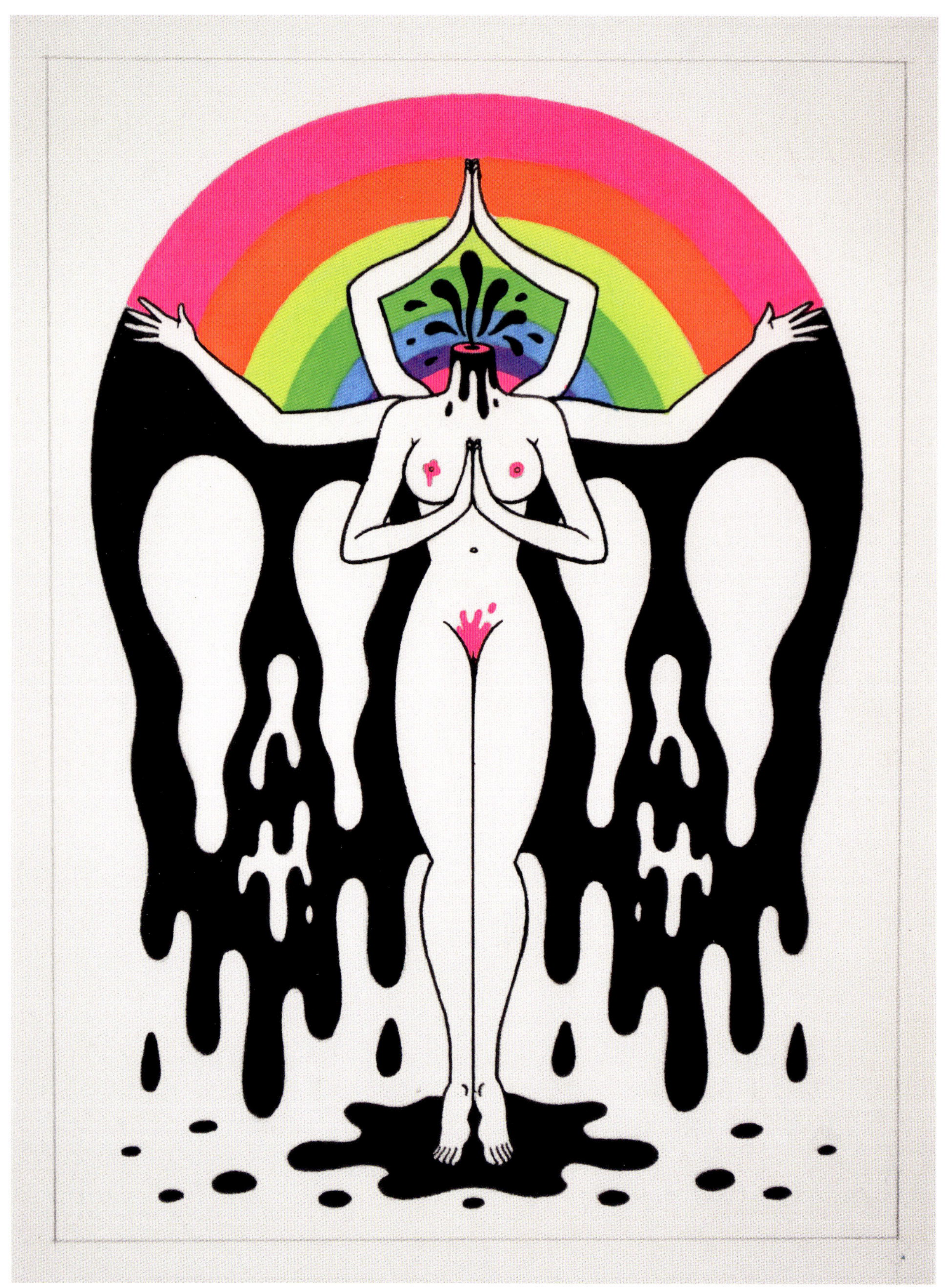

Untitled

"One of my favorites from the *Rainbow Death* series"

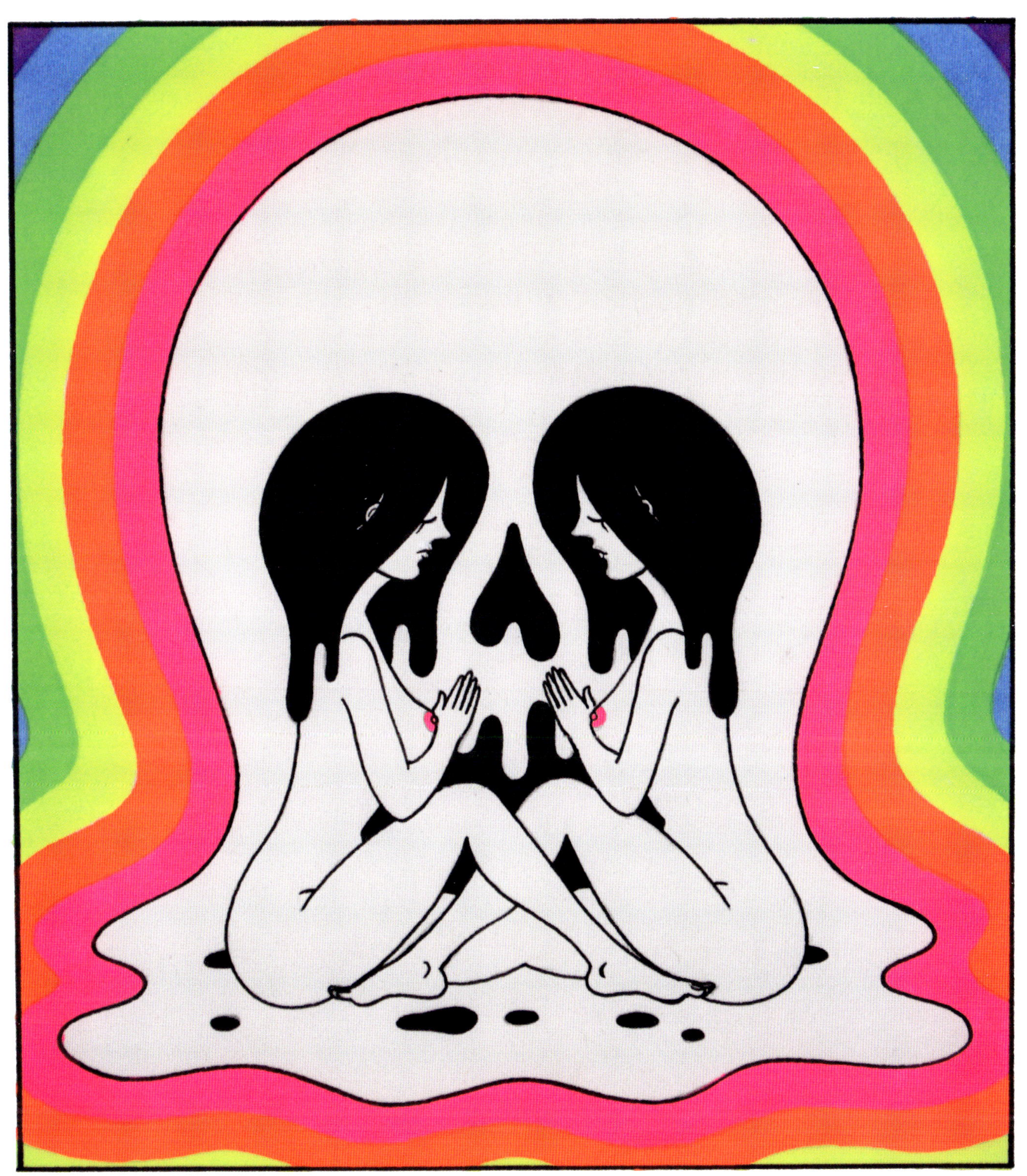

Secret Rainbow Séance

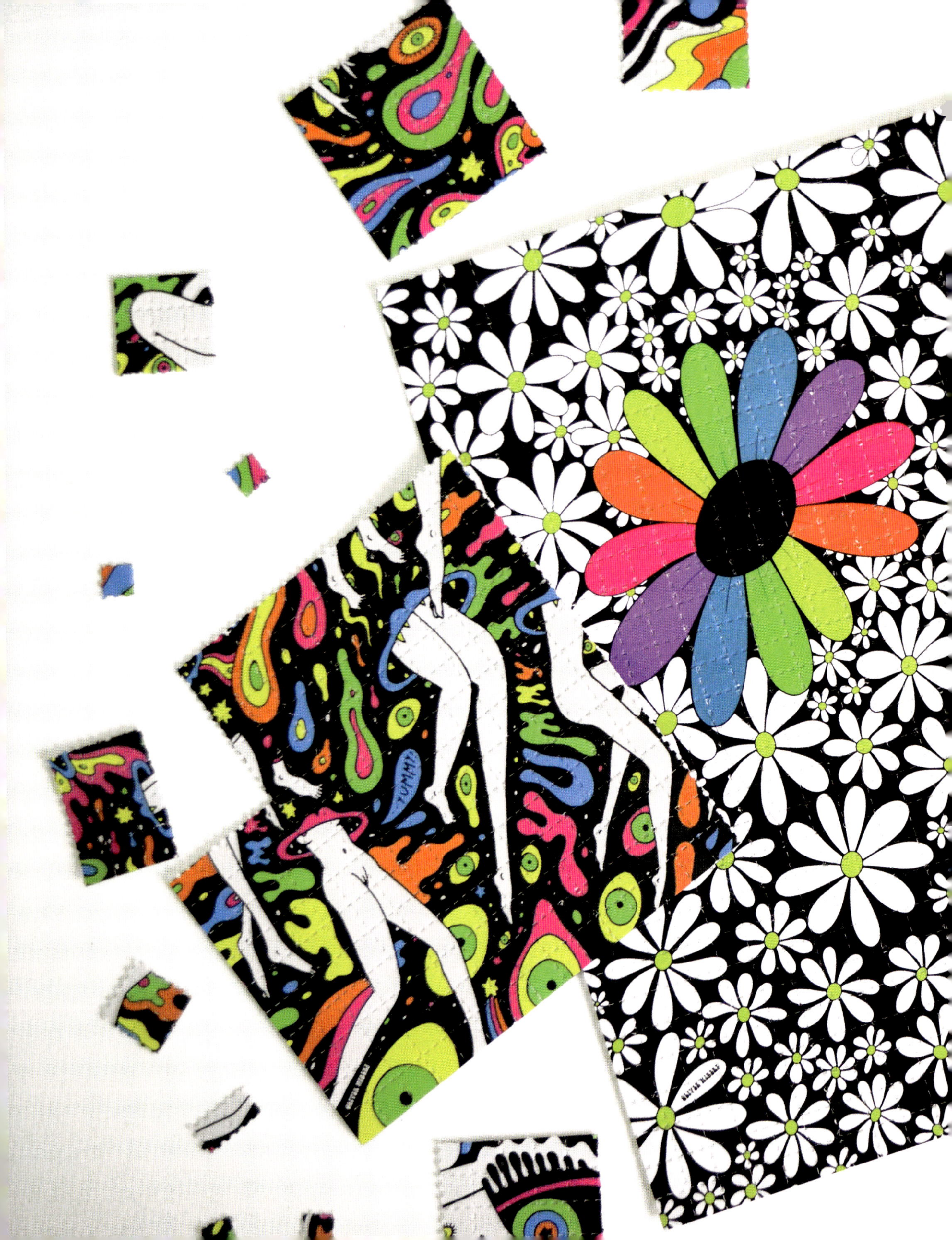
YUMMY!!

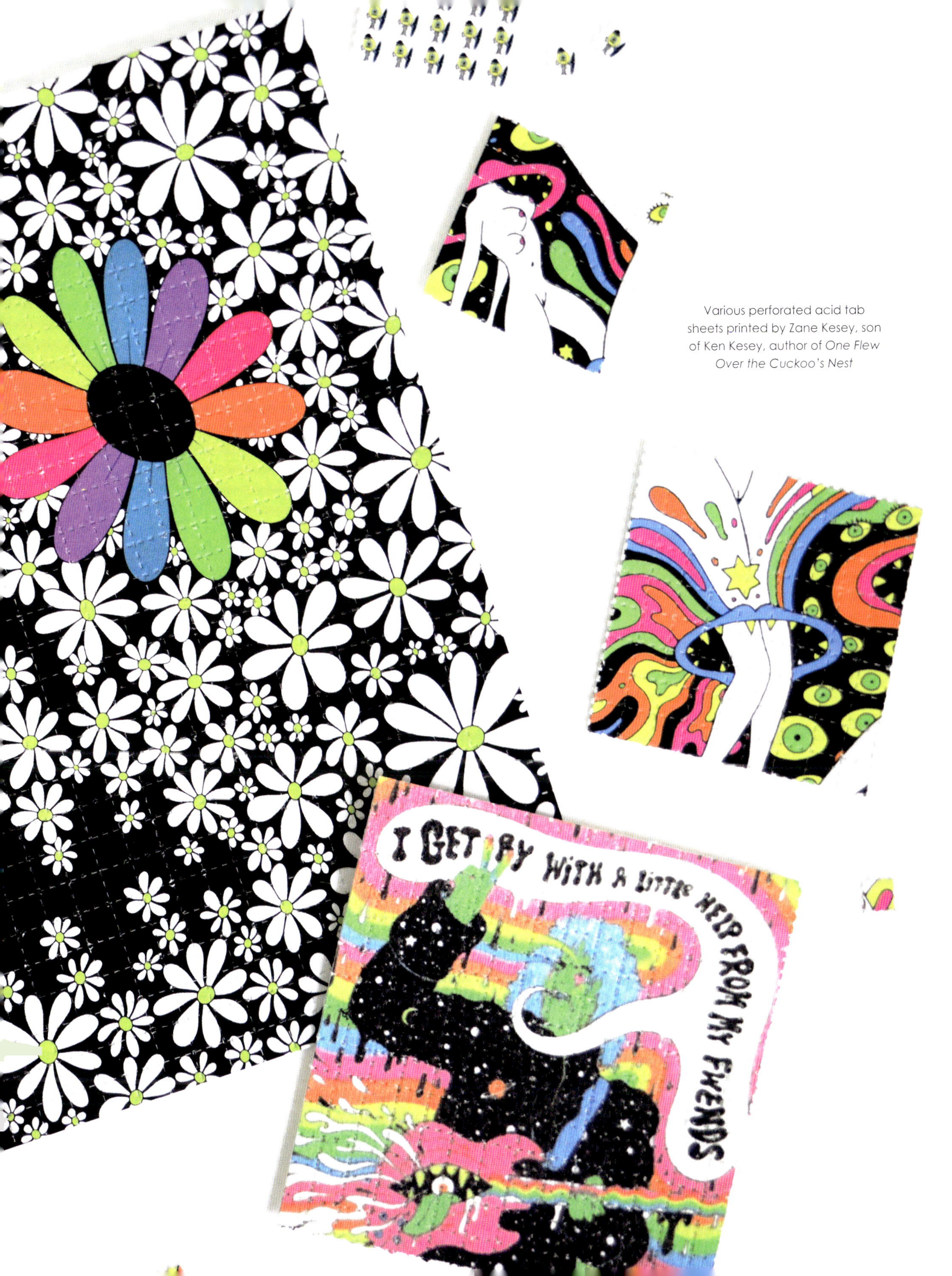

Various perforated acid tab sheets printed by Zane Kesey, son of Ken Kesey, author of *One Flew Over the Cuckoo's Nest*

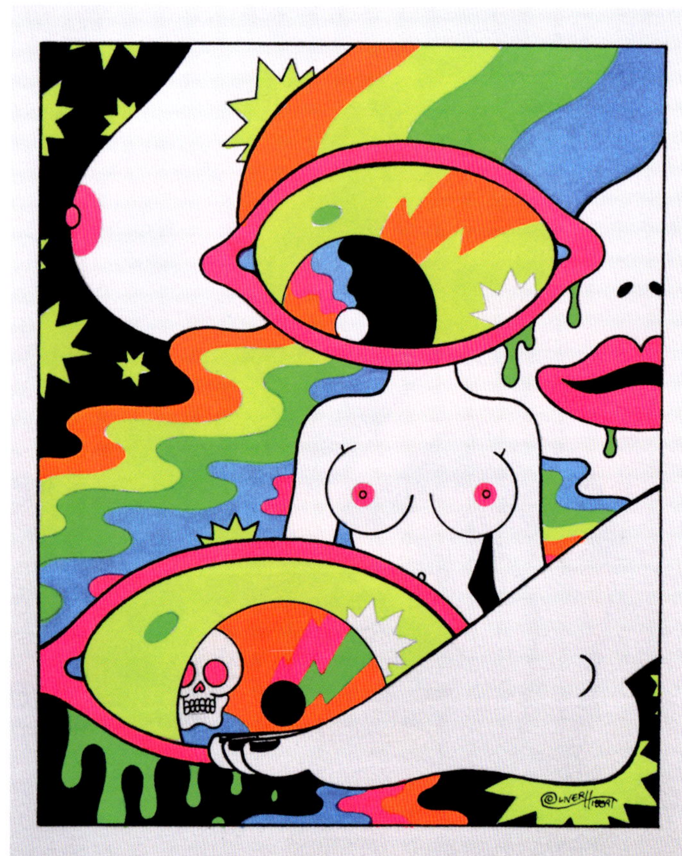

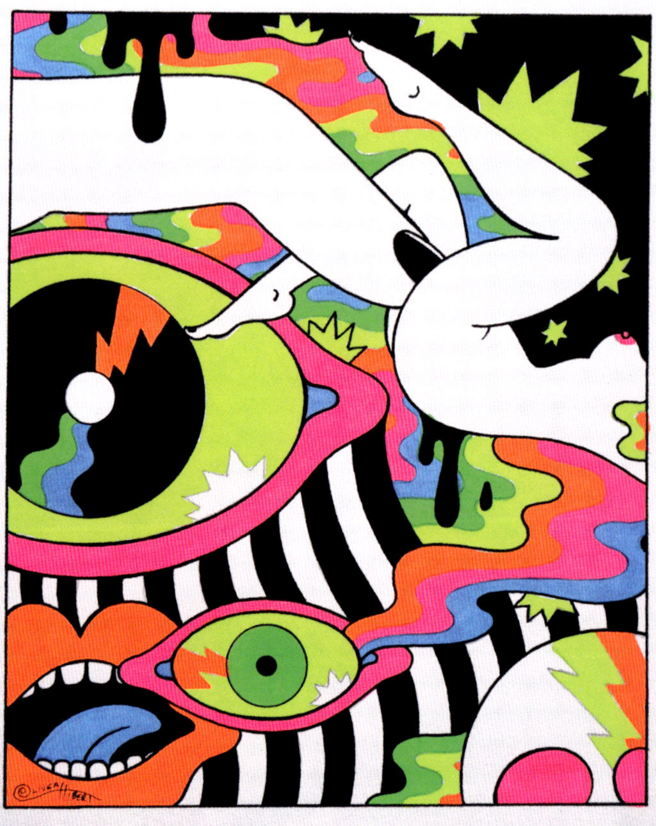

***Love Pop Suicide*, Numbers 1–4**

"From my Technicolor Nightmare art show"

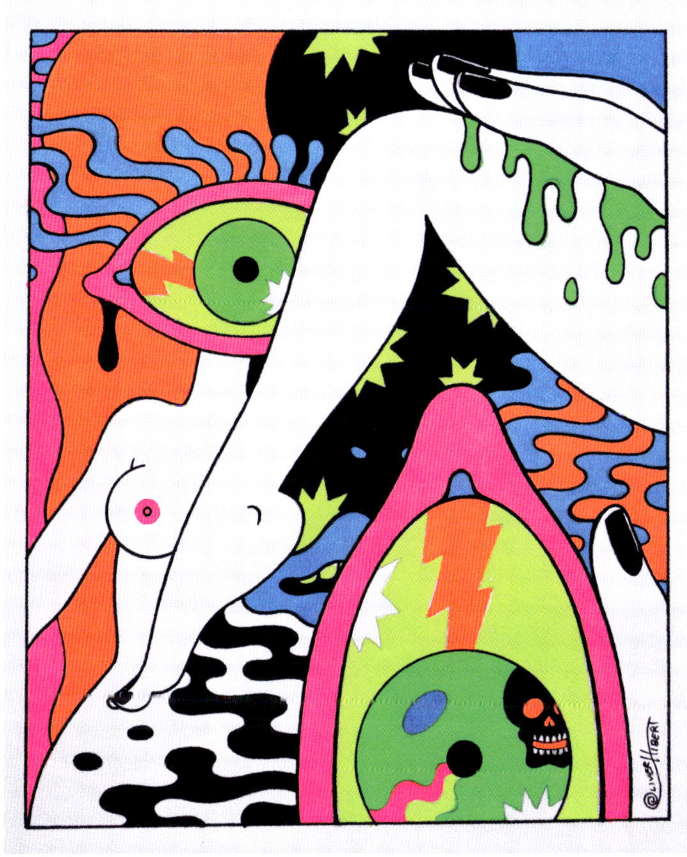

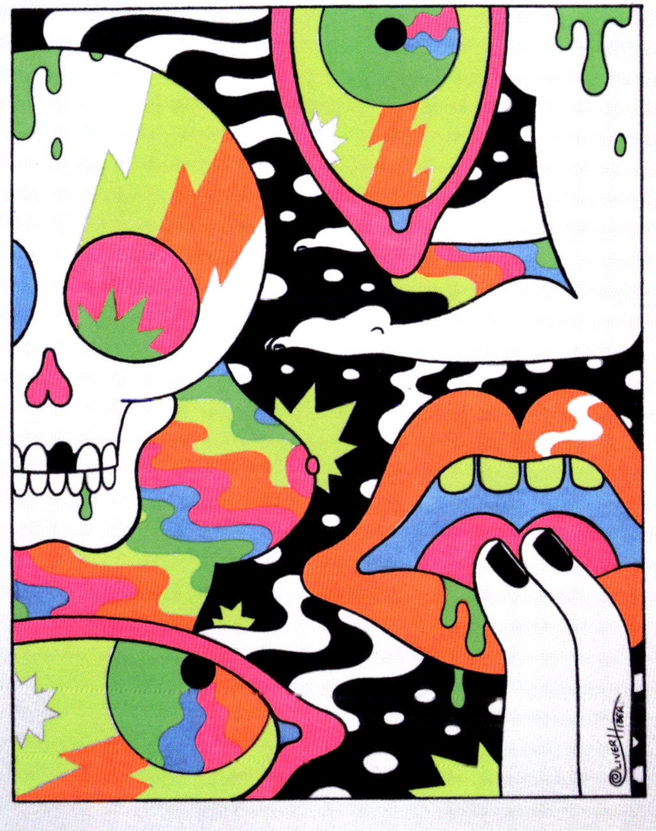

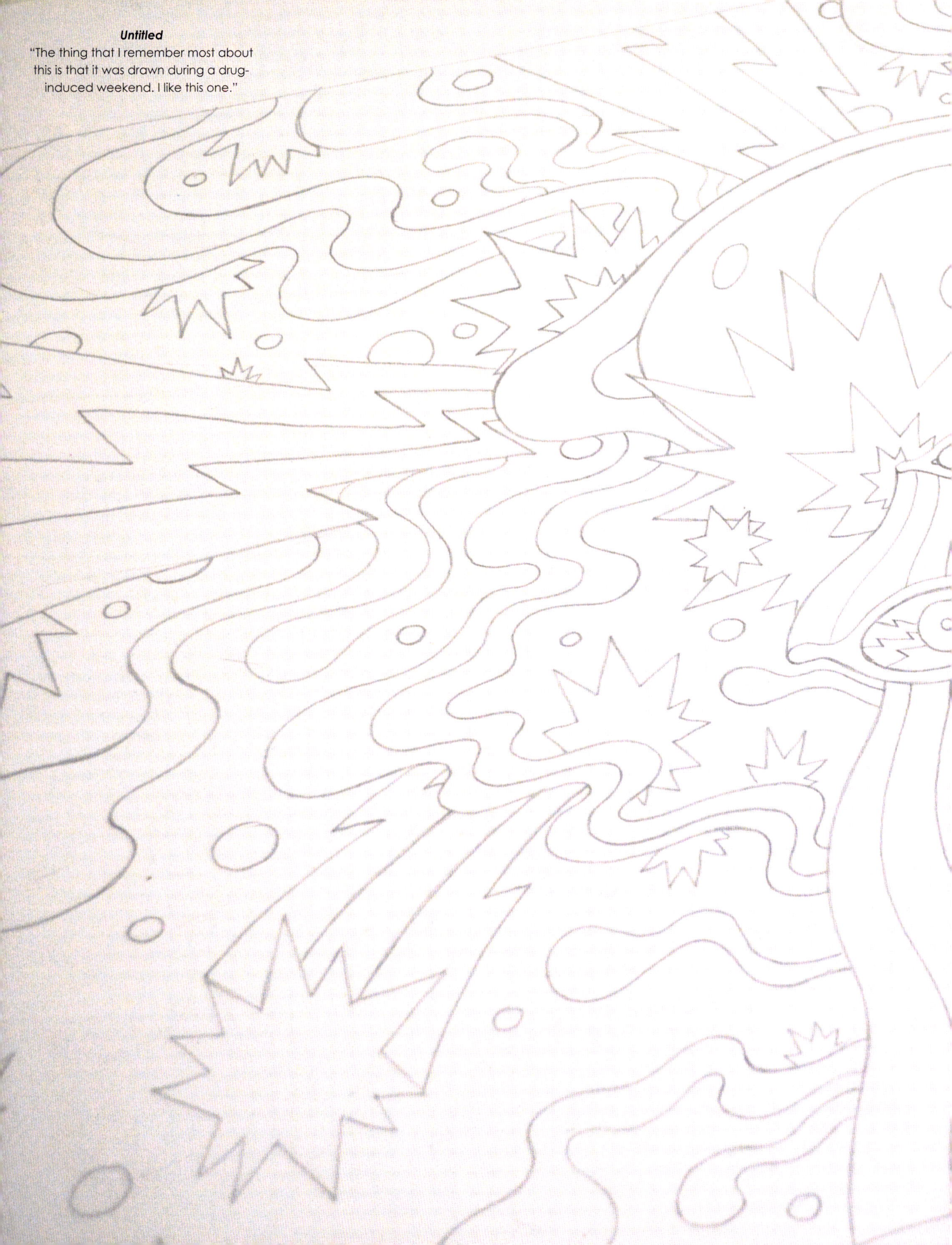

Untitled

"The thing that I remember most about this is that it was drawn during a drug-induced weekend. I like this one."

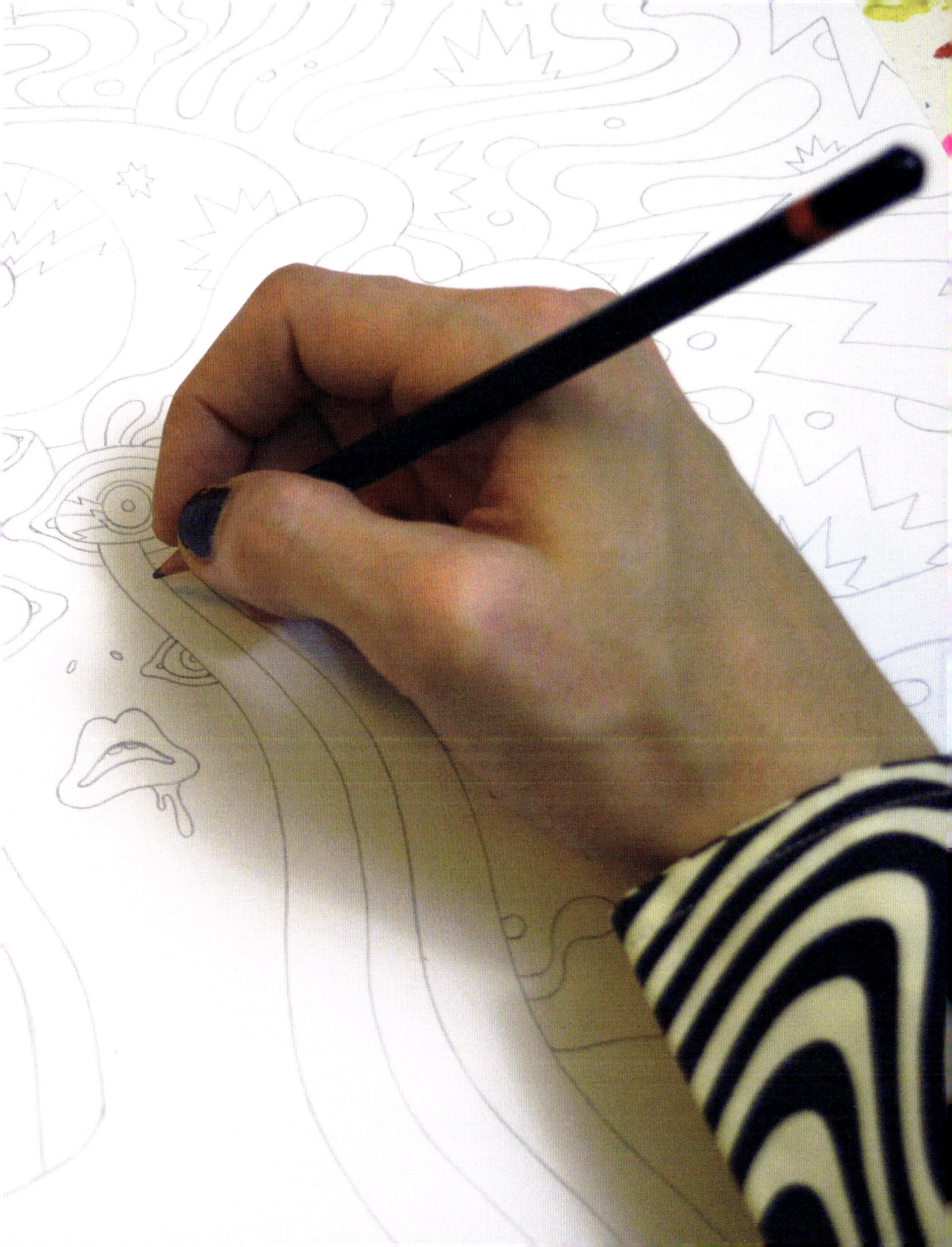

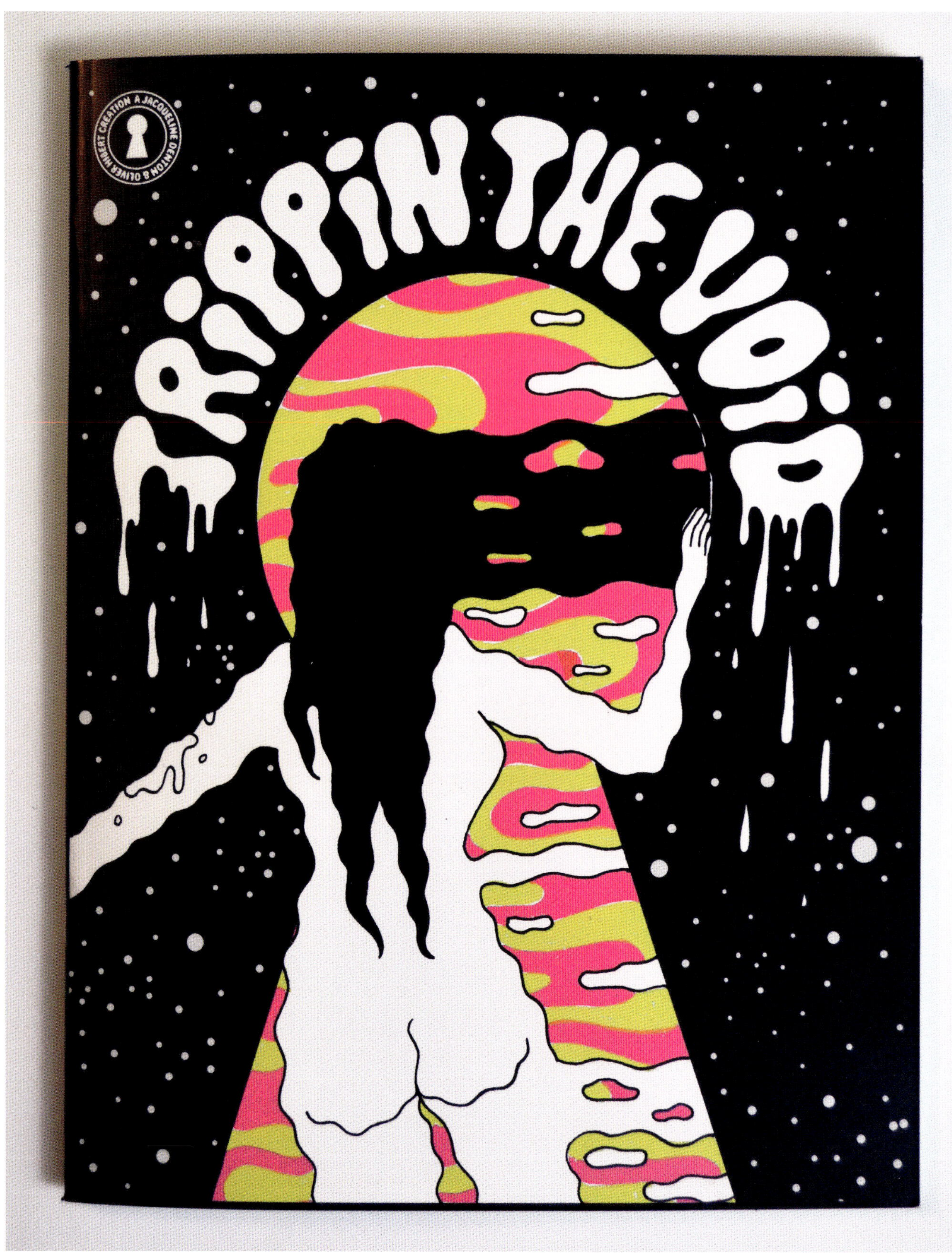

"This was from a collaboration with Jacqueline Denton for a magical 50-page comic book we made."

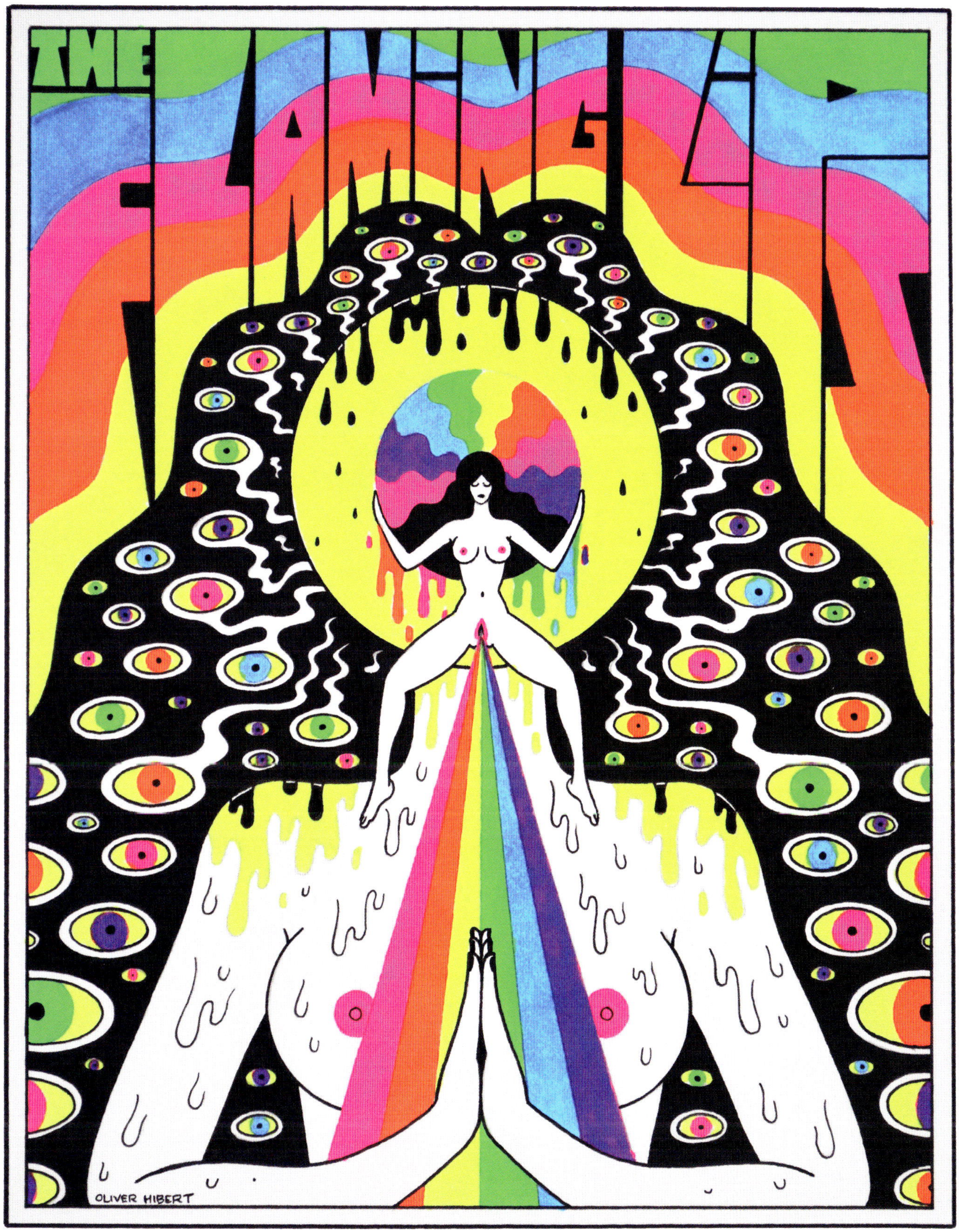

Original drawing for The Flaming Lips Levitation/Psychfest 2015 rock poster

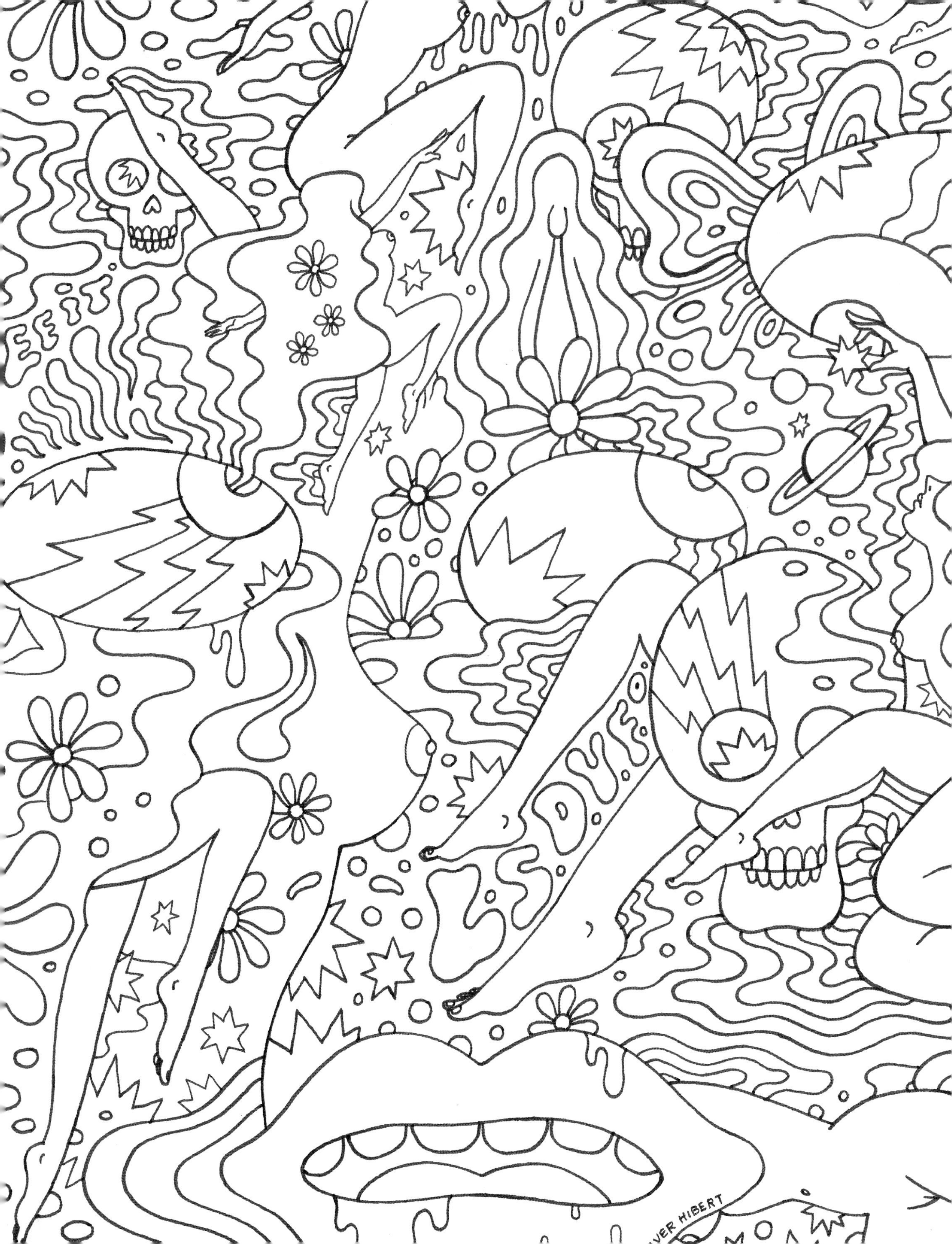
VER HIBERT

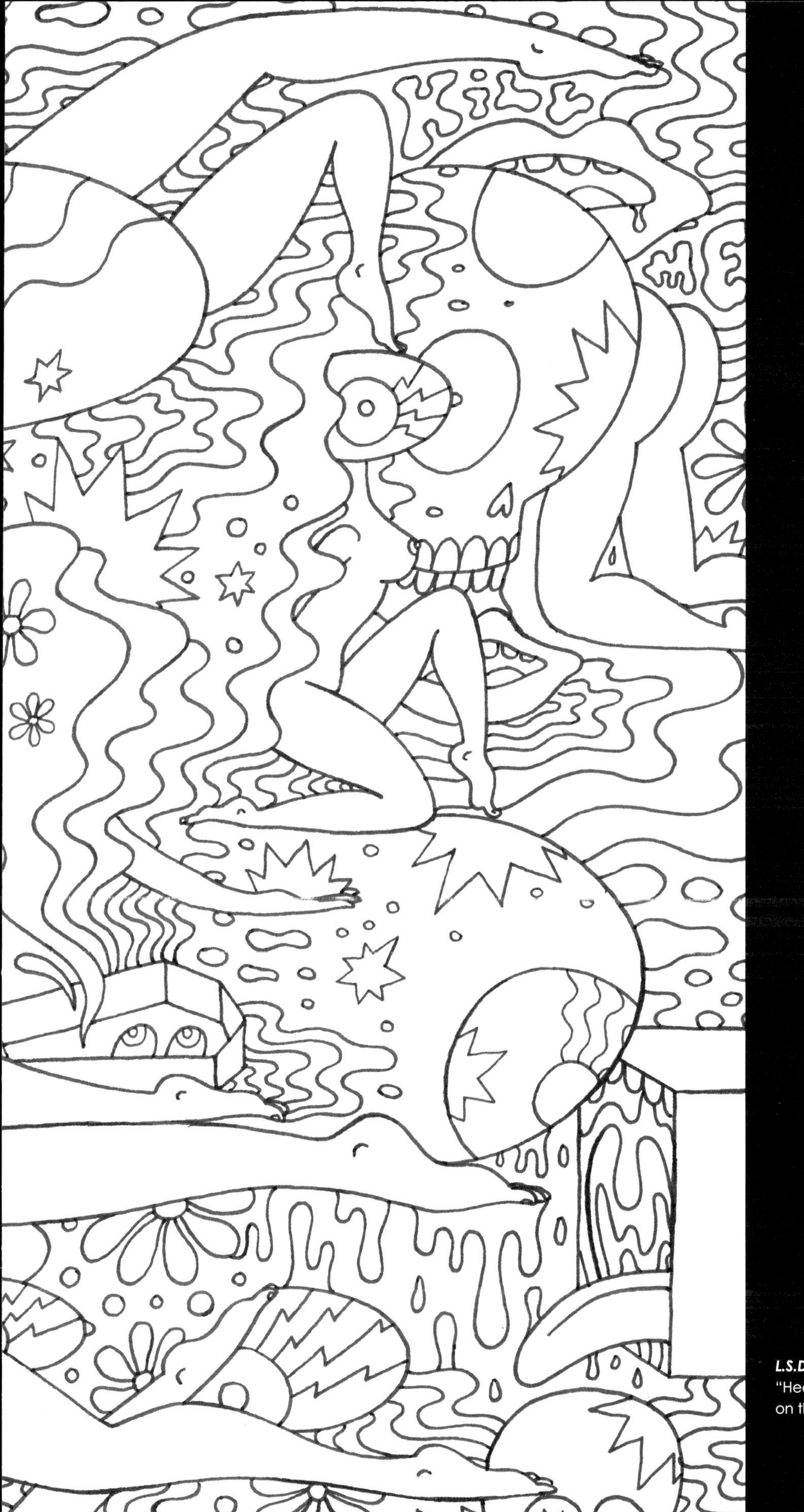

L.S.D.U.F.O
"Heavily influenced from psychedelics on this drawing . . . 'nuff said."

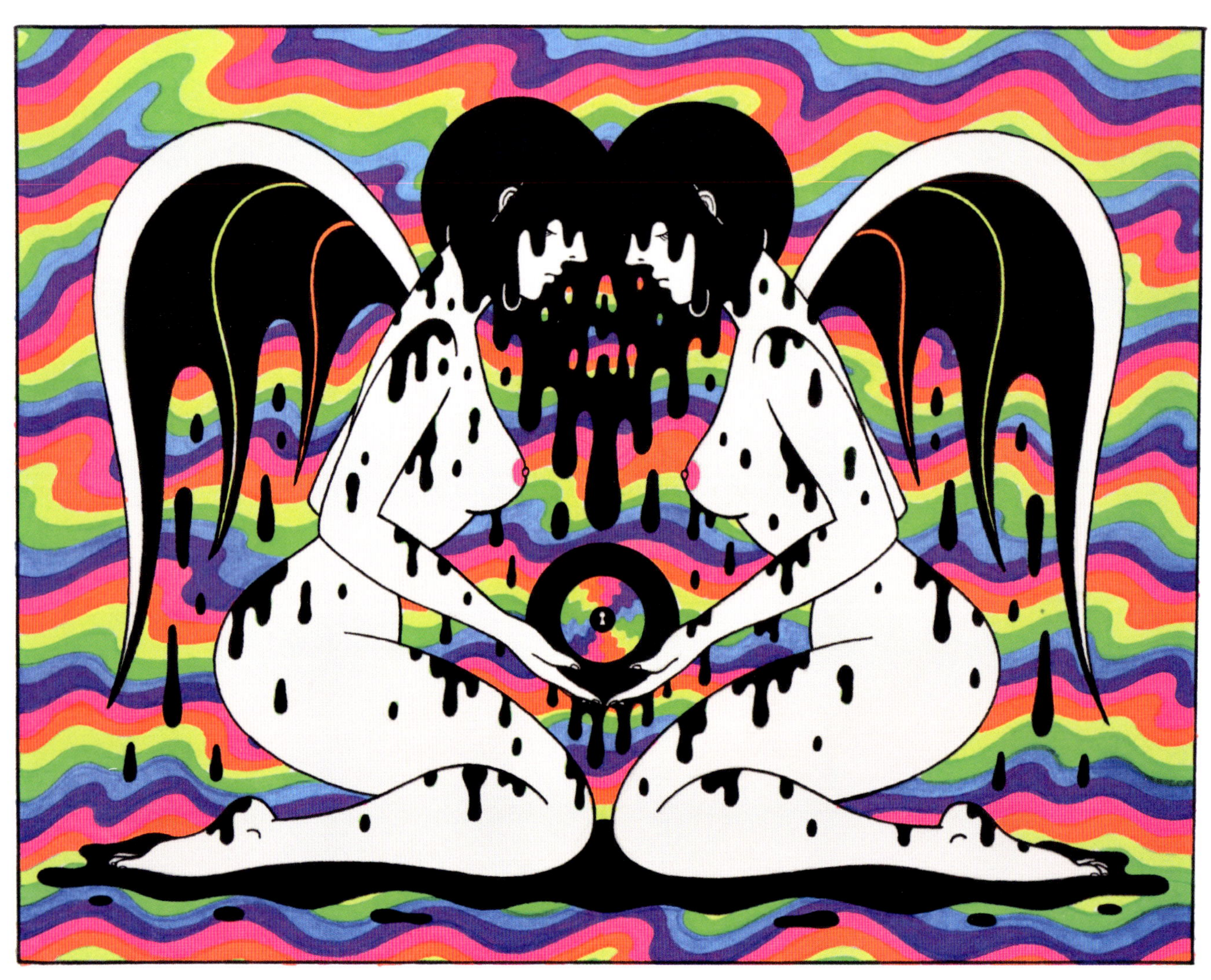

A Psychedelic Séance in the Castle of Your Heart
"Love is the fuel for this one."

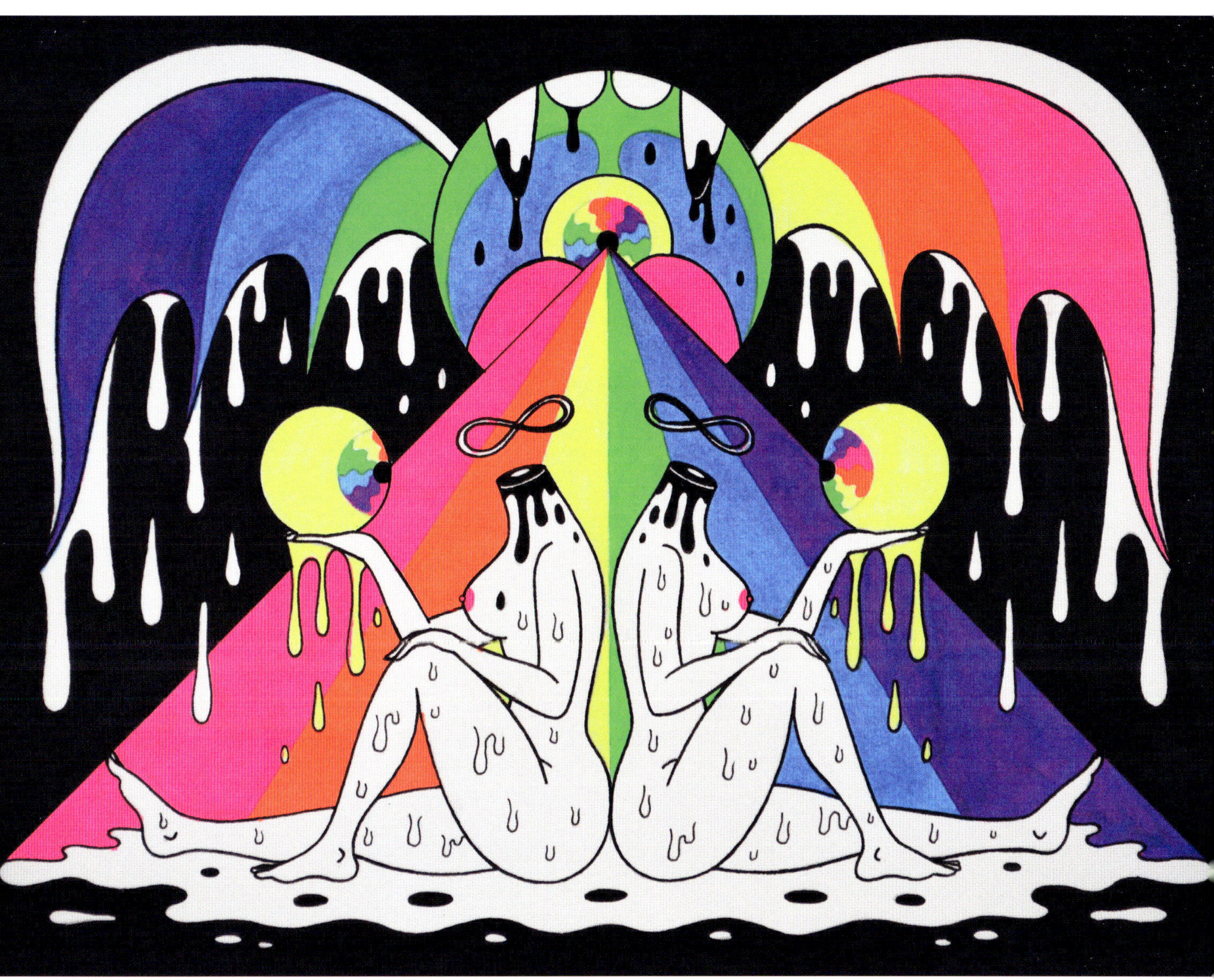

You and Me and Me and You

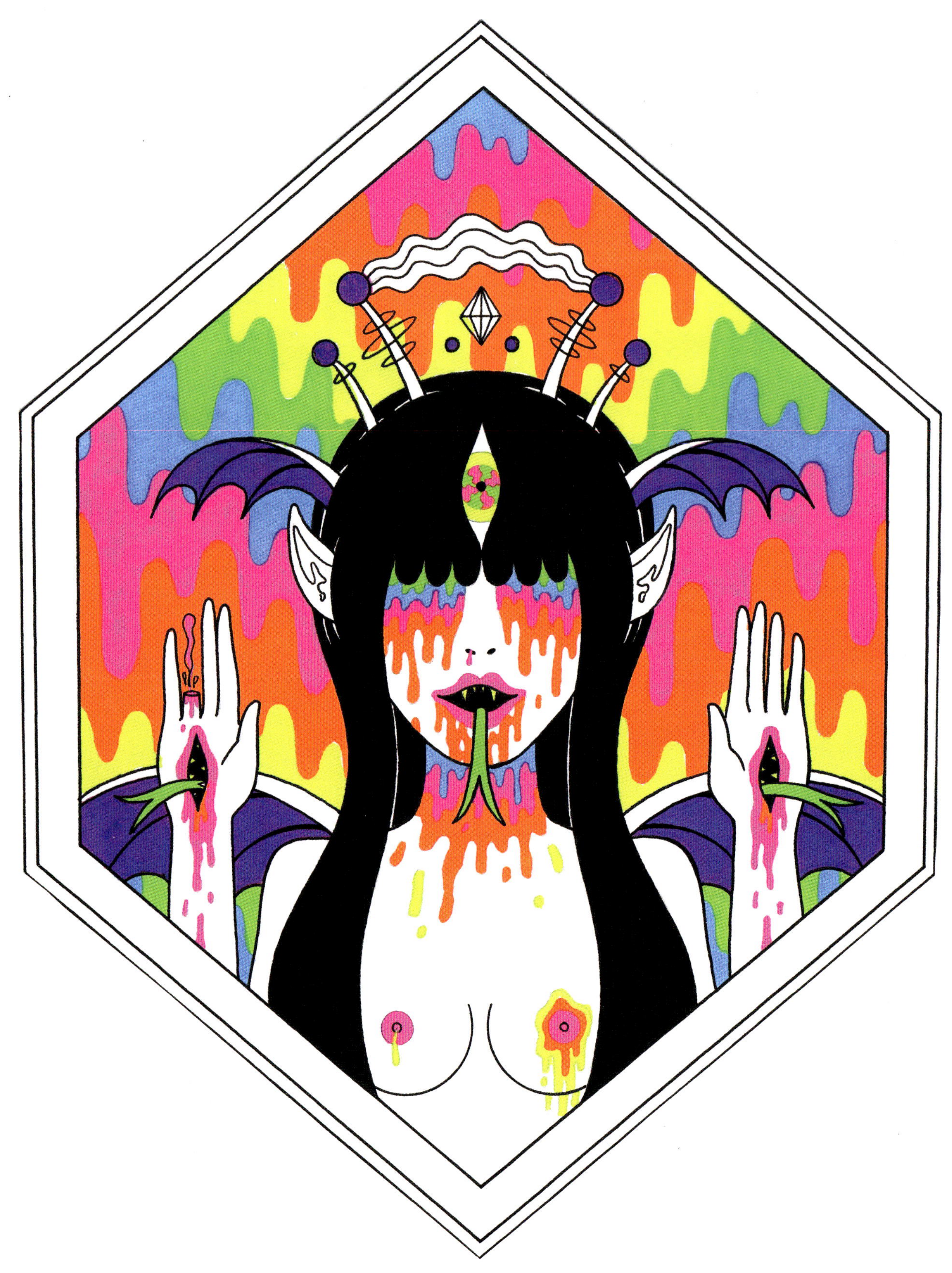

Hexed Out Vortex Vamp
"Vampire girls and colored swirls dry dripping flowers make cats cry."

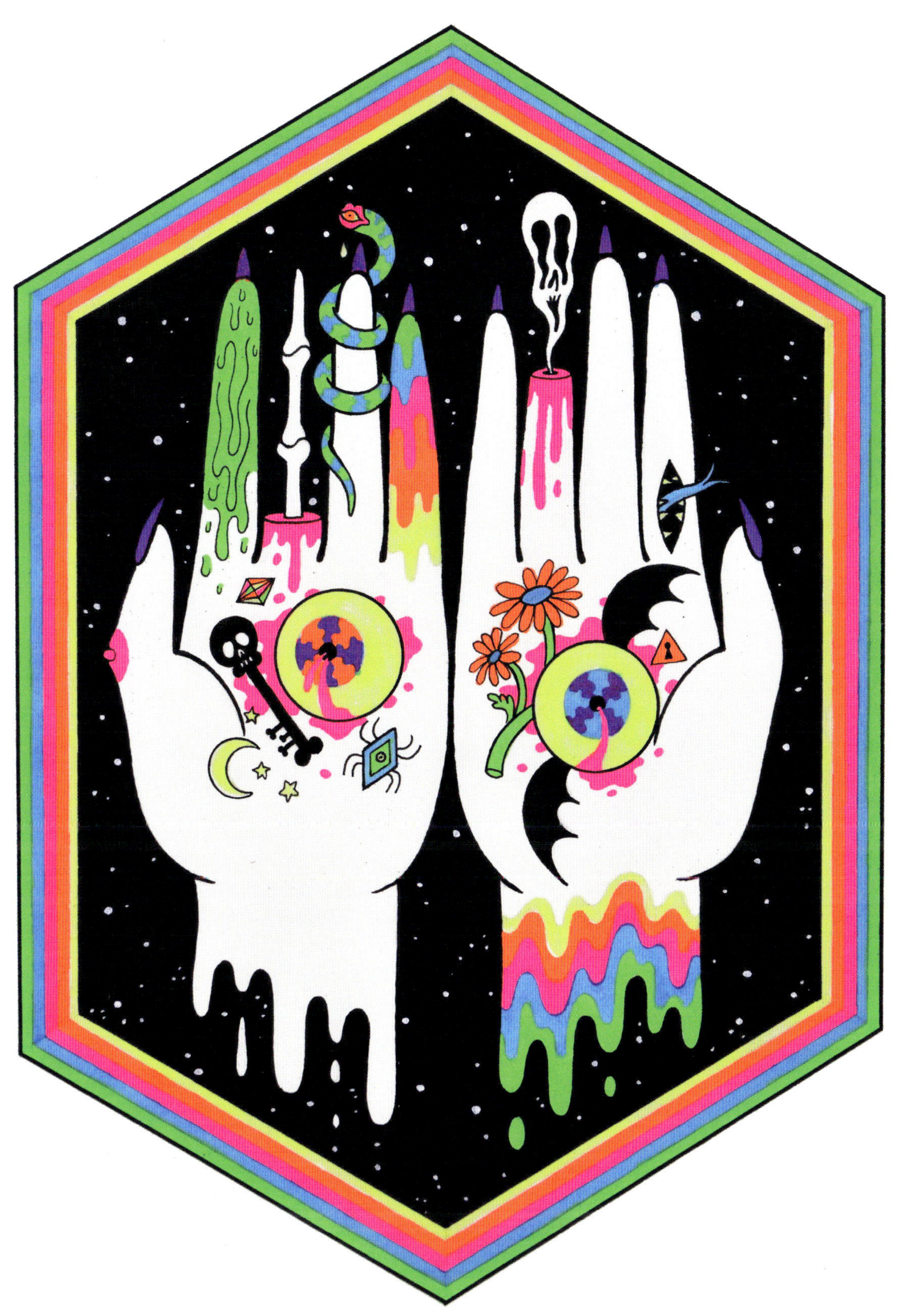

Poisonous Possessions

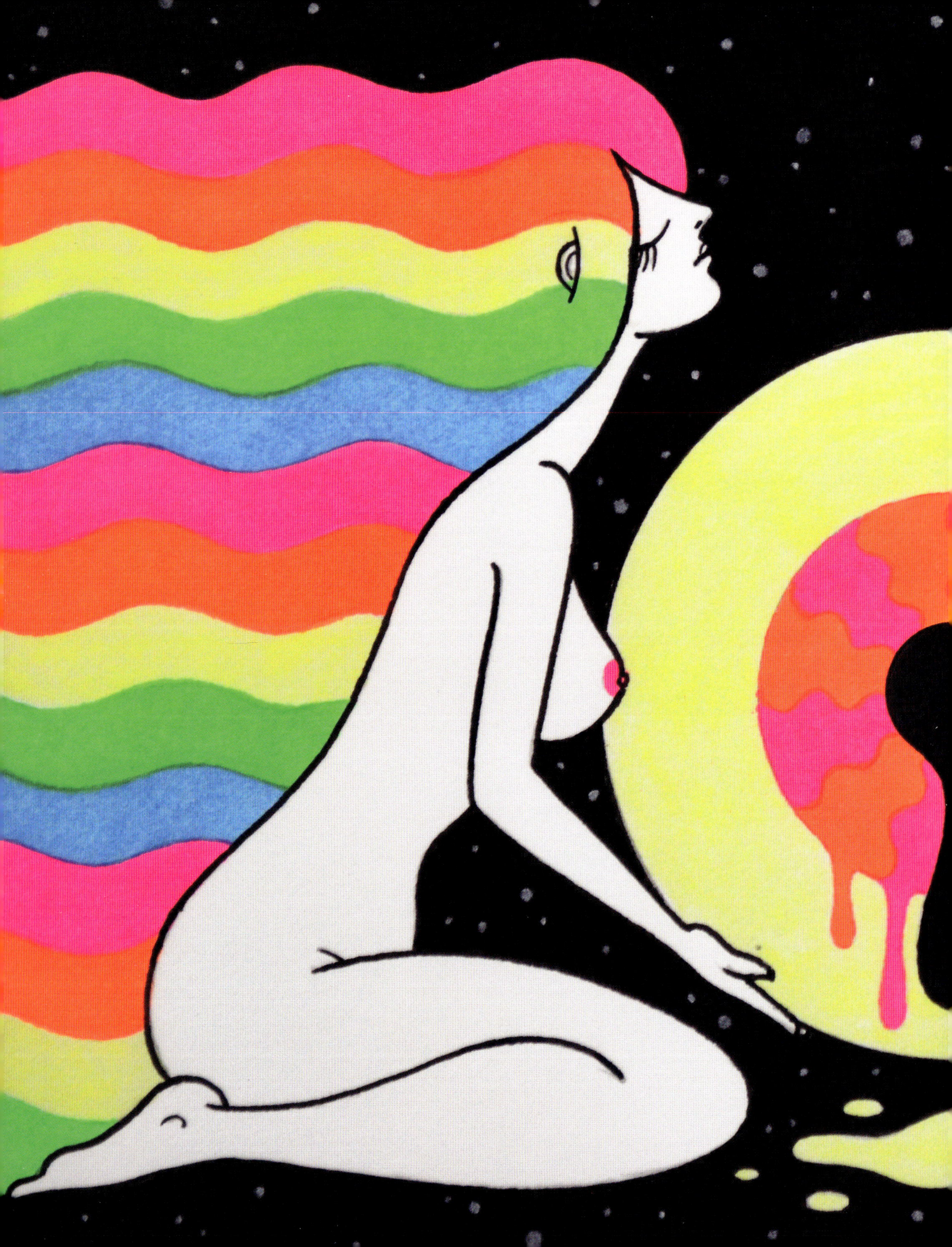

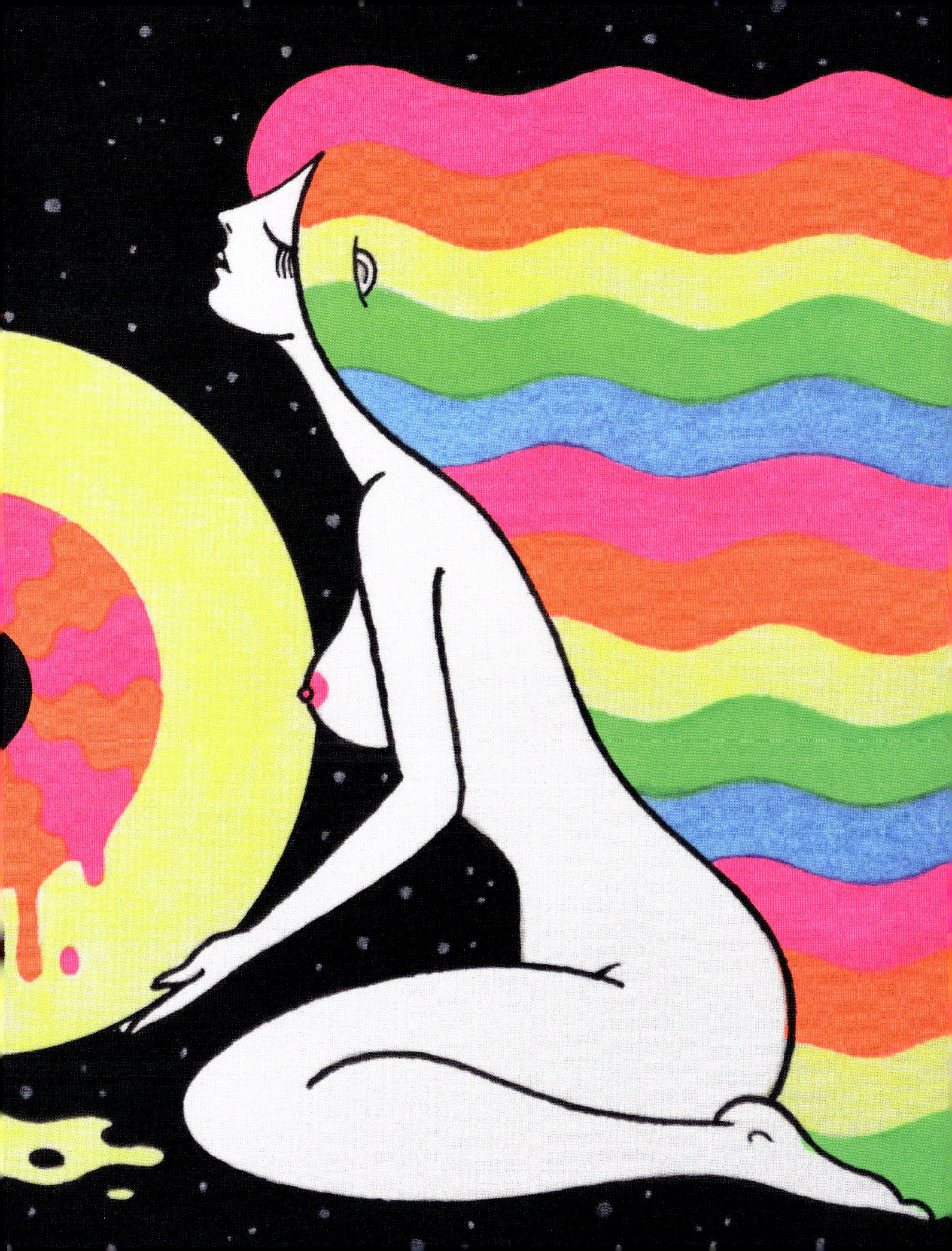

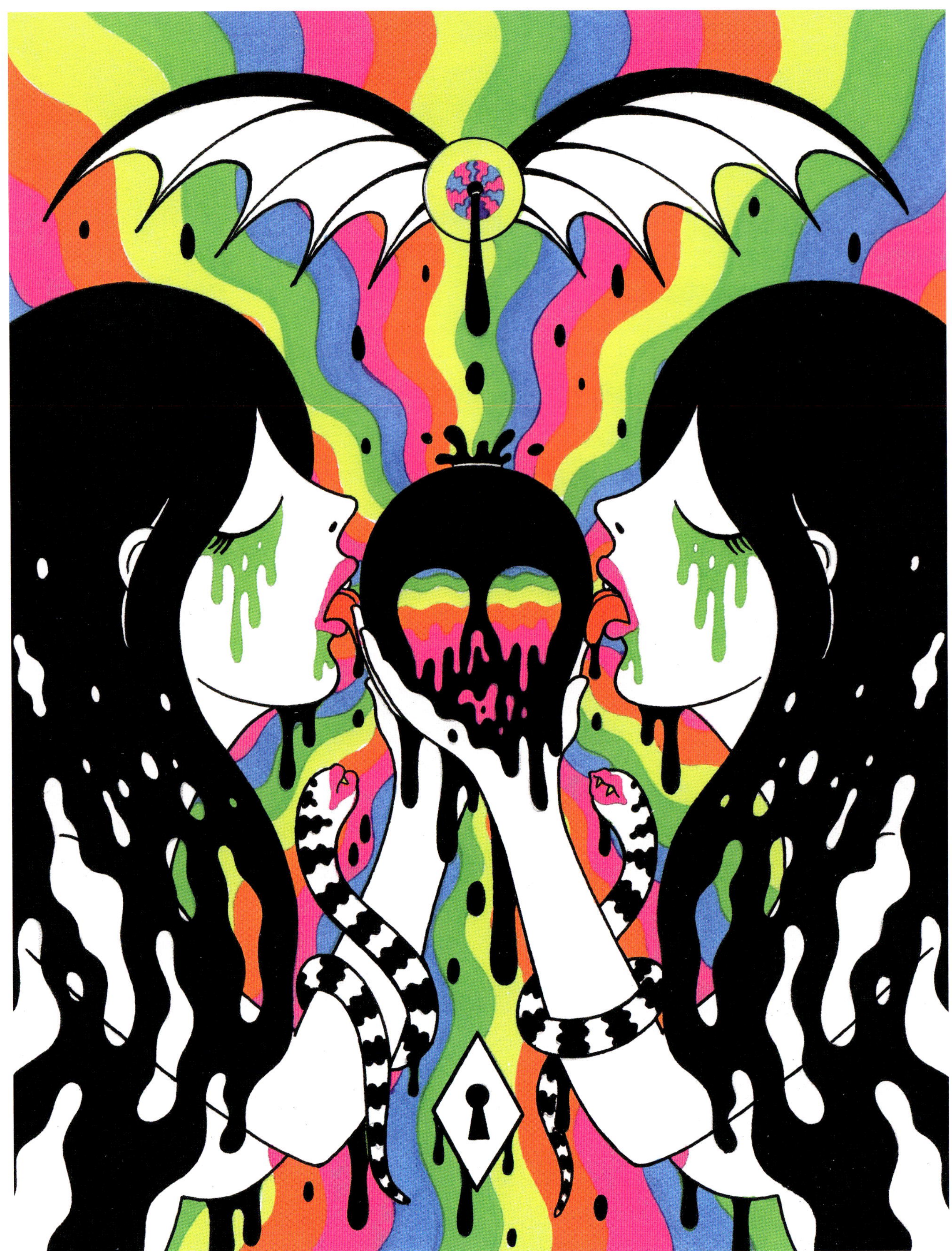

Taste the Fuck

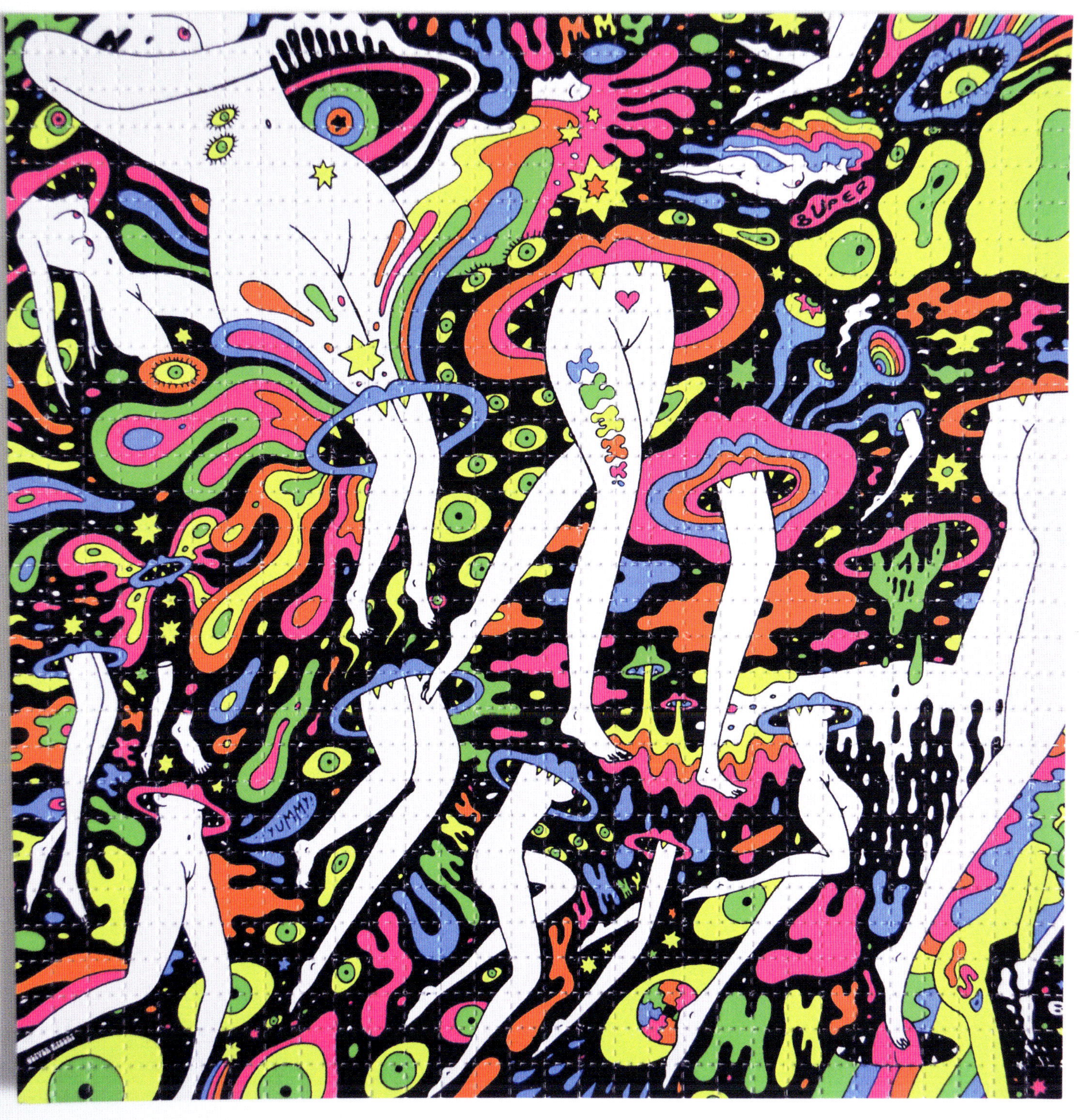

Yummy

"A definite psychedelic breakthrough for me. The night I drew this ended up being really important. I opened up a new door within myself and my mind to break some of my own rules as far as proportion and symmetry are concerned."

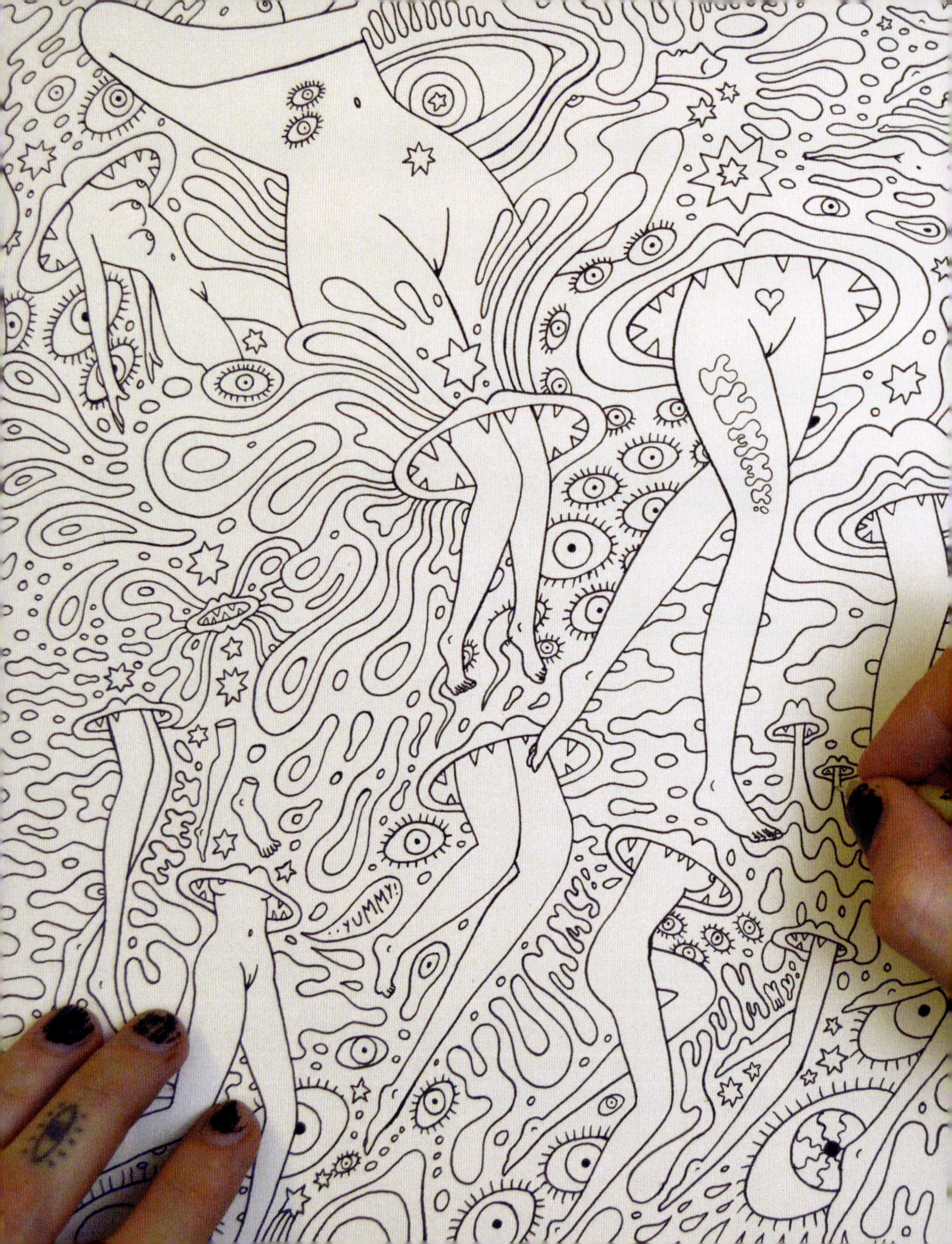
YUMMY!

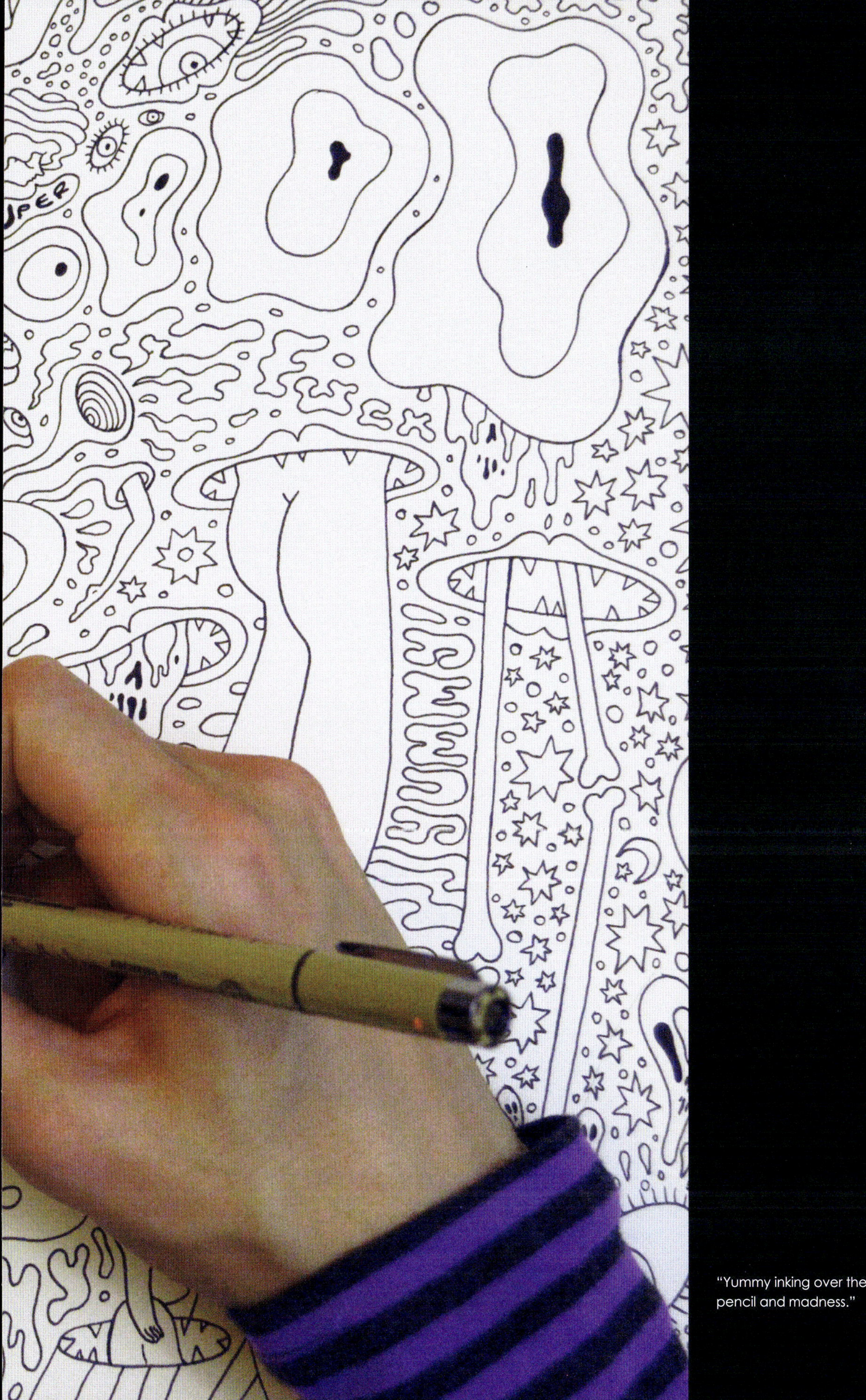

"Yummy inking over the pencil and madness."

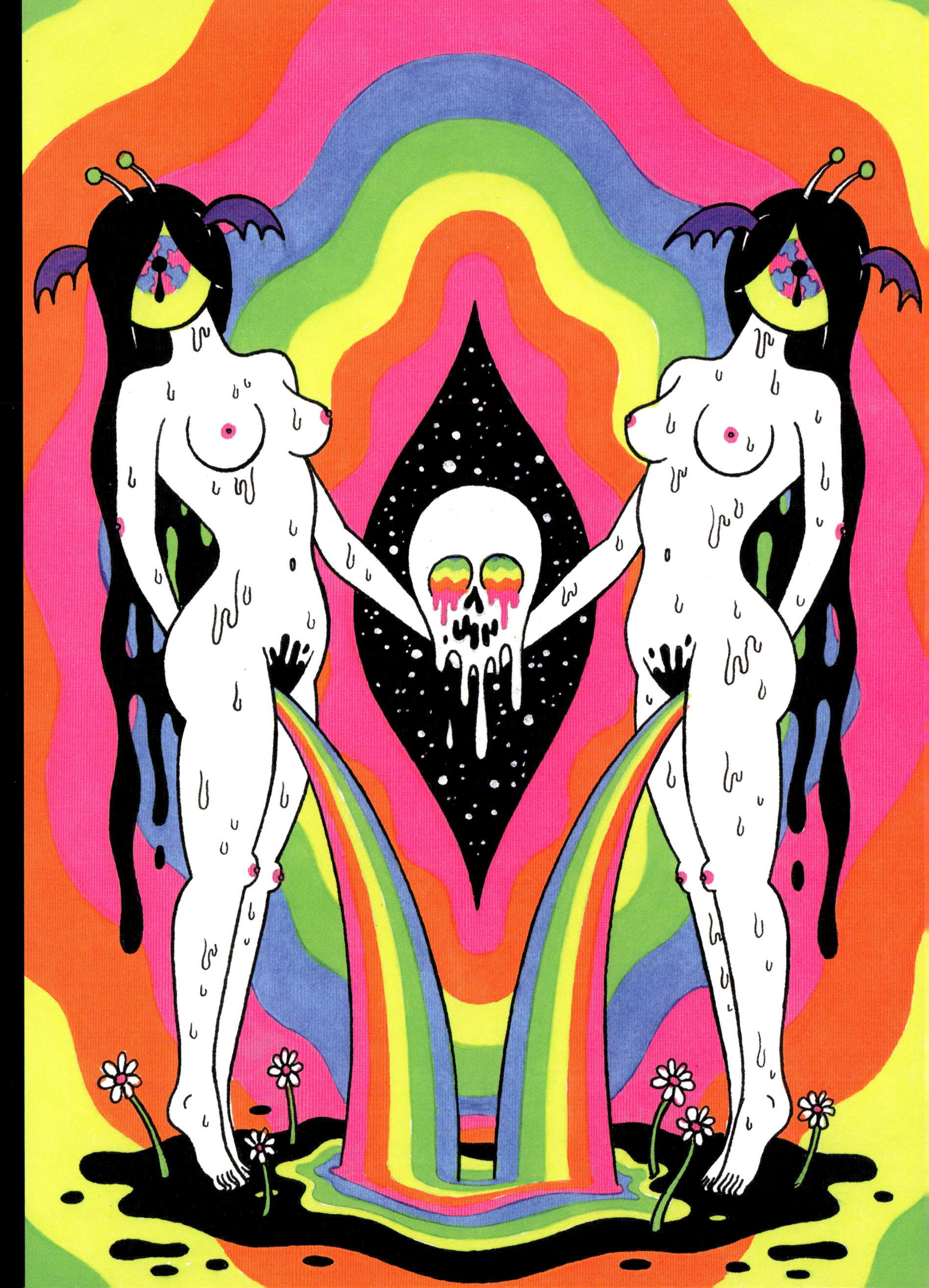

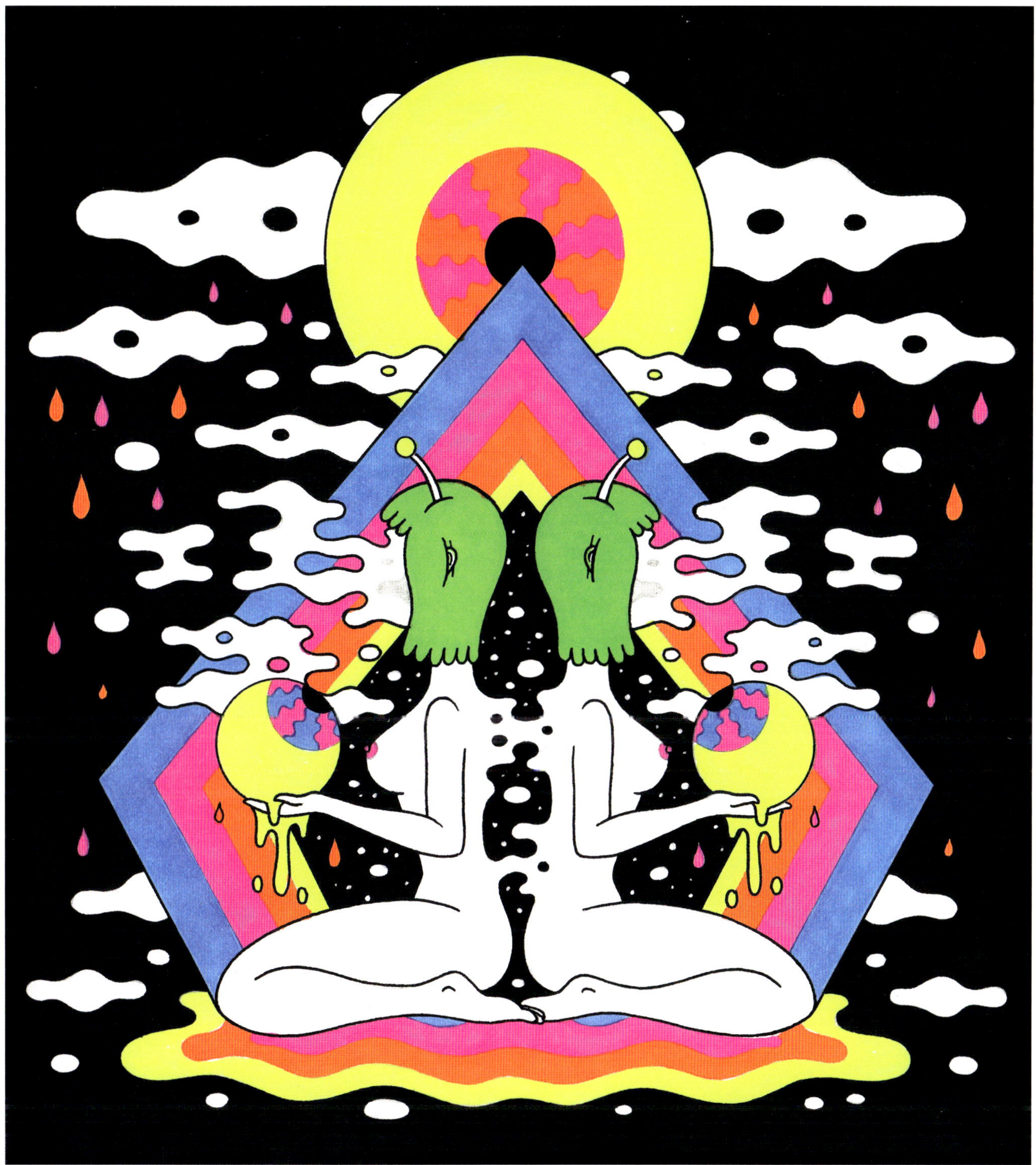

Double Hex

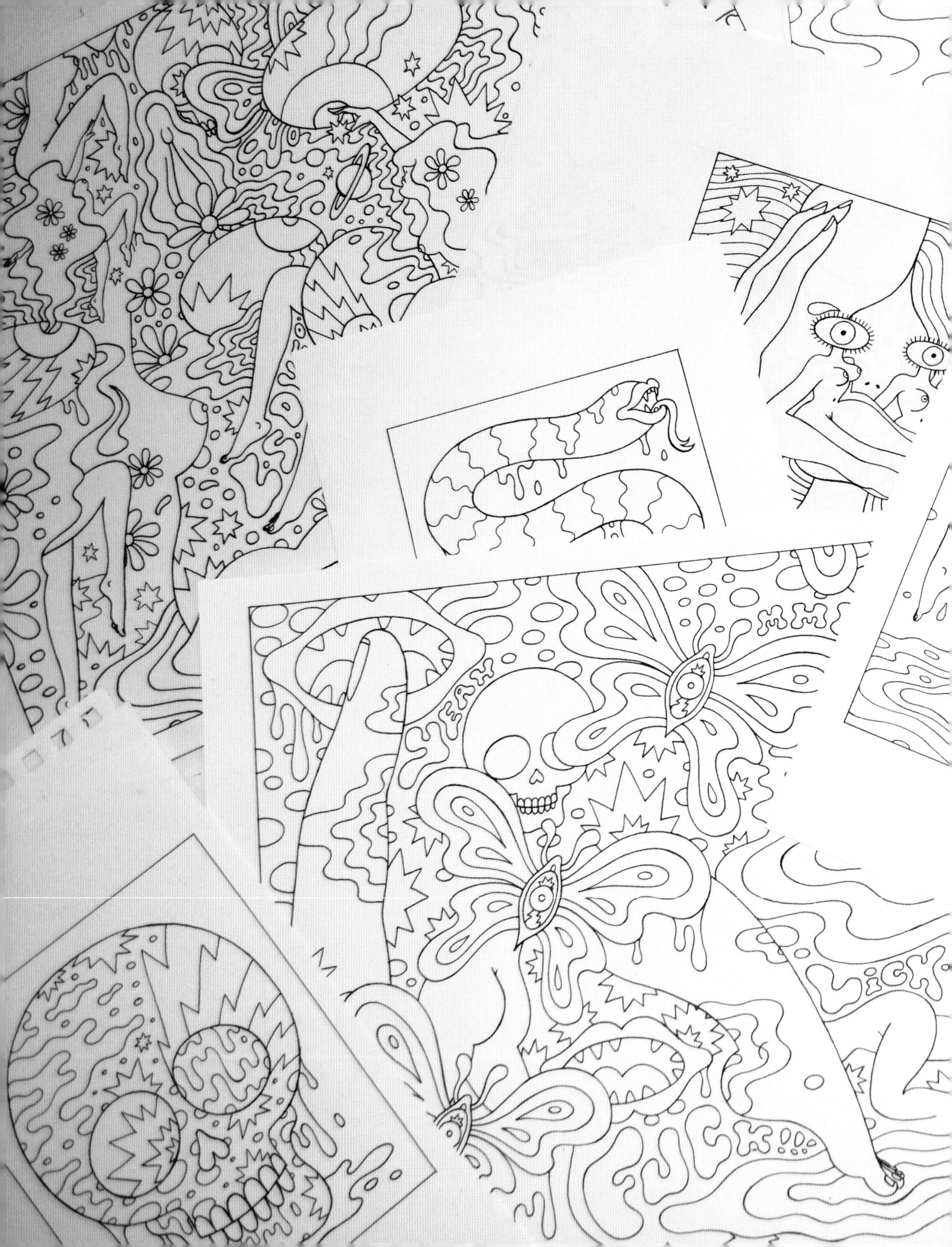

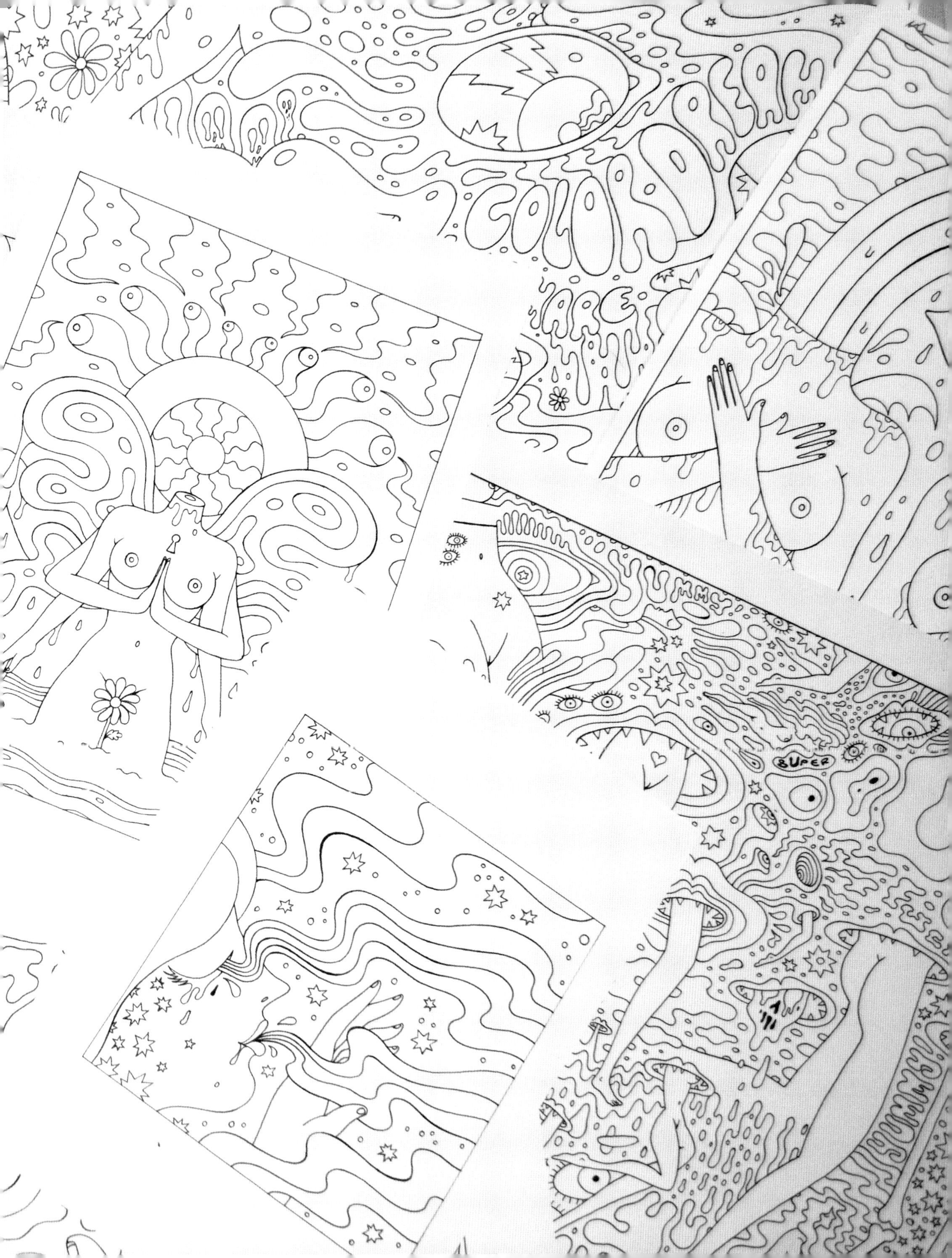

ARE
YUMMY
SUPER

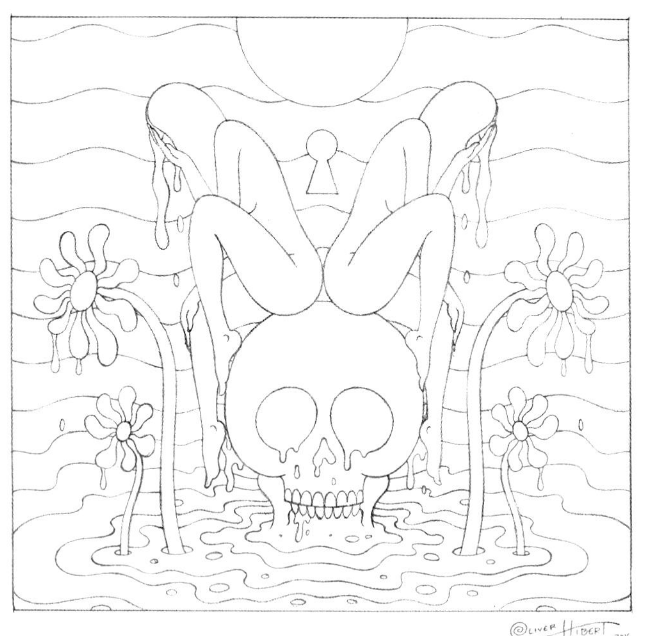

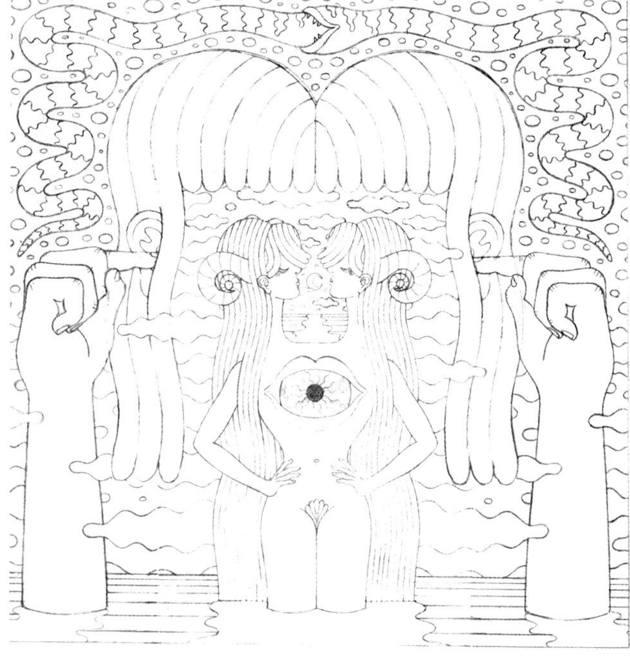

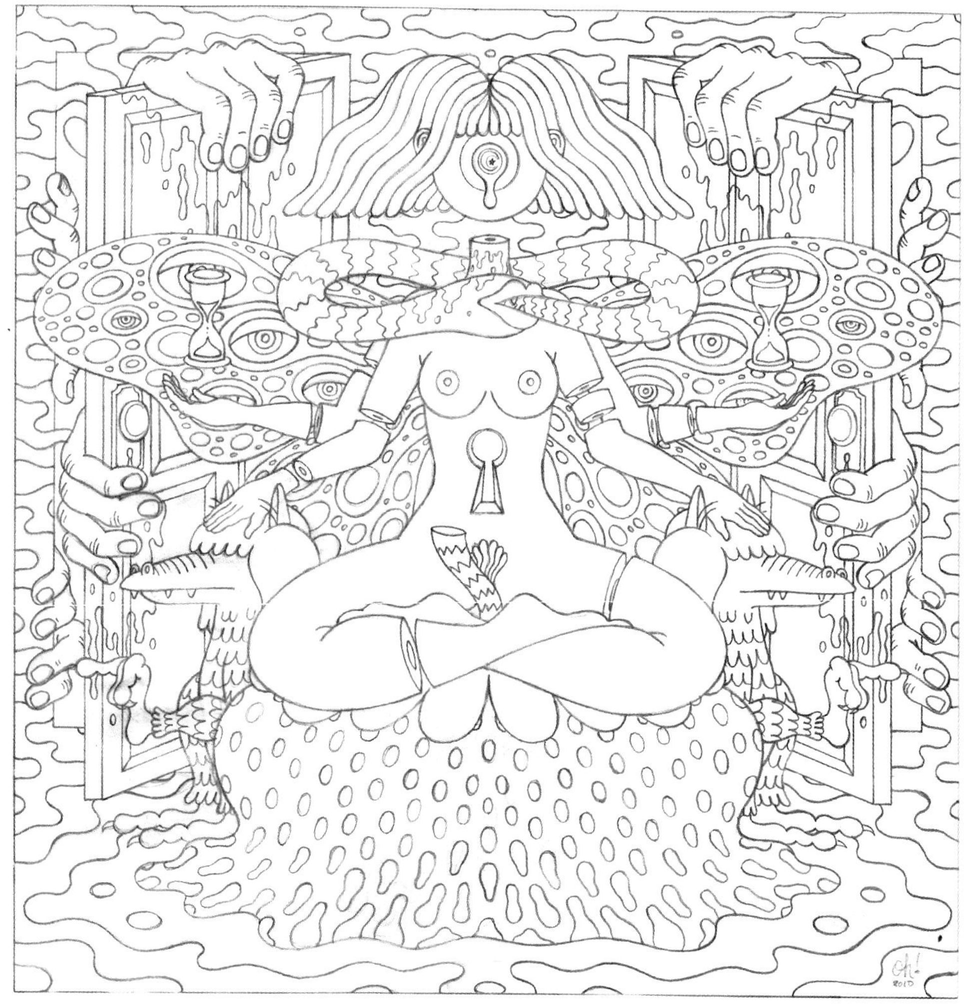

"Various drawings, sketches, studies for paintings, etcetera . . ."

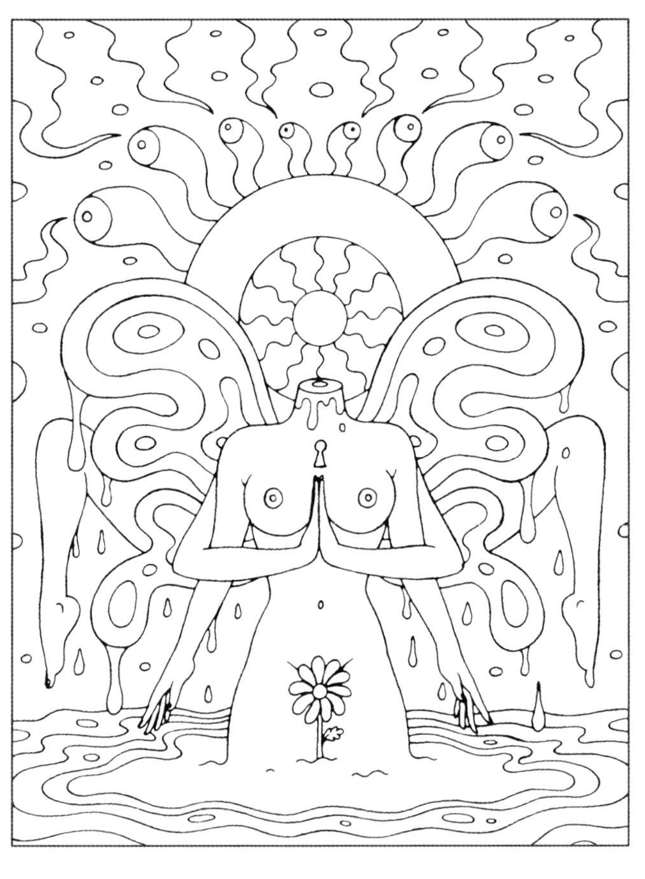

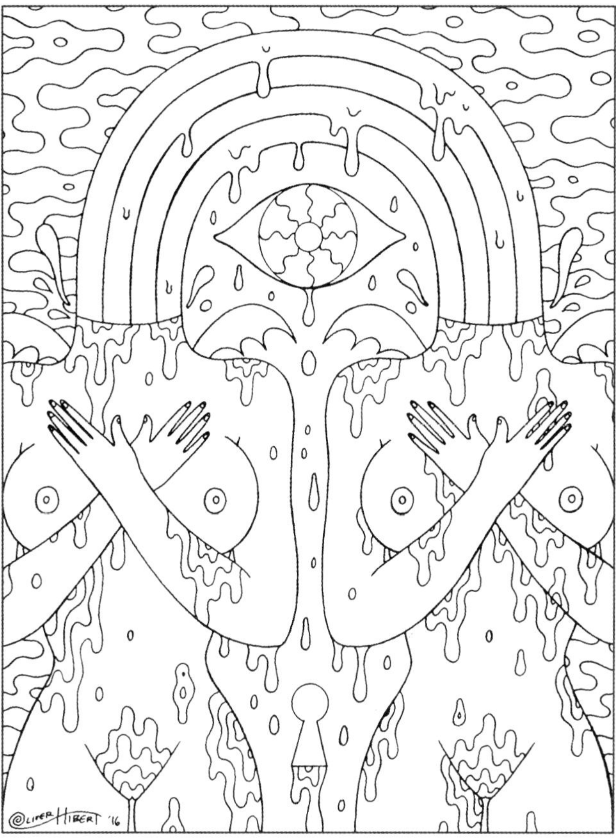
Oliver Hibert '16

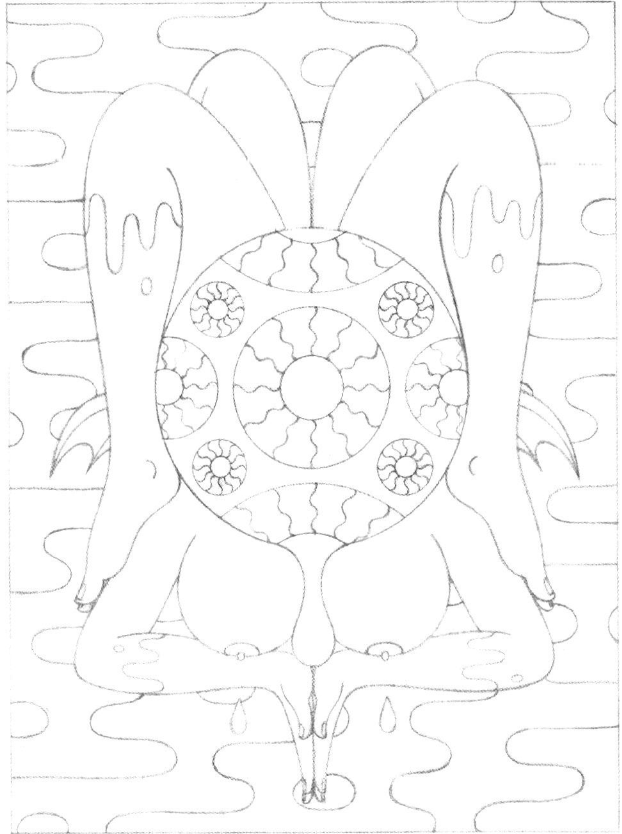

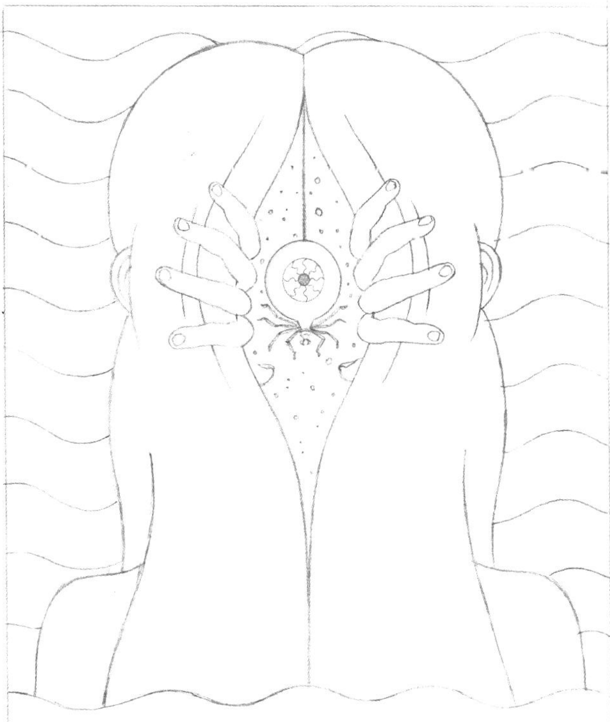

Chapter Three:

Prints & Editions

The flat, bold colors and heavy, exacting outlines of Oliver's work lend well to the processes of screenprinting and lithography. As Oliver's original paintings are executed with a flatness that belies the human hand, making mechanical prints of his works seems only logical.

The rock poster was, if not created by, perfected by The Family Dog artists Wes Wilson, Chet Helms, Victor Moscoso, Stanley Mouse, Alton Kelley, and others for the seminal concerts at the Avalon Ballroom and the Fillmore. While The Family Dog's artists had a penchant for reappropriating imagery often culled from art deco and art nouveau, Oliver eschews employing found imagery in his posters, just as in his fine art. That being said, there remains clear and deliberate nods to classic psychedelic poster art throughout Oliver's work. Considering, for example, Oliver's Halloween Blood Bath poster, one need look no further than Bob Schnepf's famed 1968 Iron Butterfly handbill to trace a direct path back to classic rock poster art. Typeface also takes center stage in Oliver's designs, as weight and shape of text plays heavily into his patented symmetrical compositions, often defining the layout, as seen in his My Bloody Valentine poster. While the original rock poster artists often used psychedelic lettering as a secret code of sorts—only those who were "tuned in" were intended to be able to decipher the copy—Oliver's posters never sacrifice legibility for style. The text is as clear and punchy as the graphics with which they share the page. As with his paintings and drawings, Oliver achieves a gooey, weirdo beauty while maintaining a cleanly engineered image, always crisp and exacting.

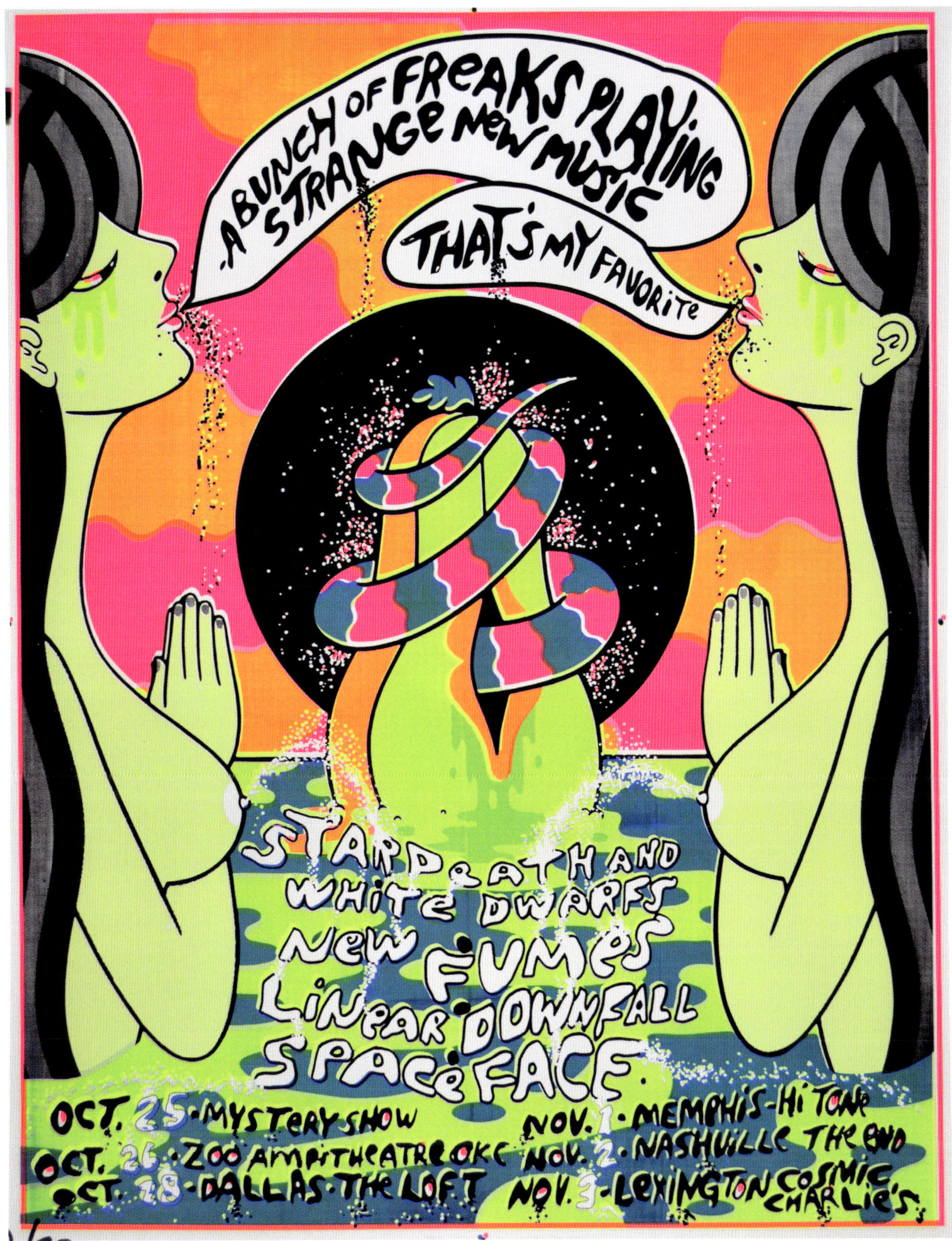

A Bunch of Strange Freaks rock poster collaboration, with text and bits by Wayne Coyne

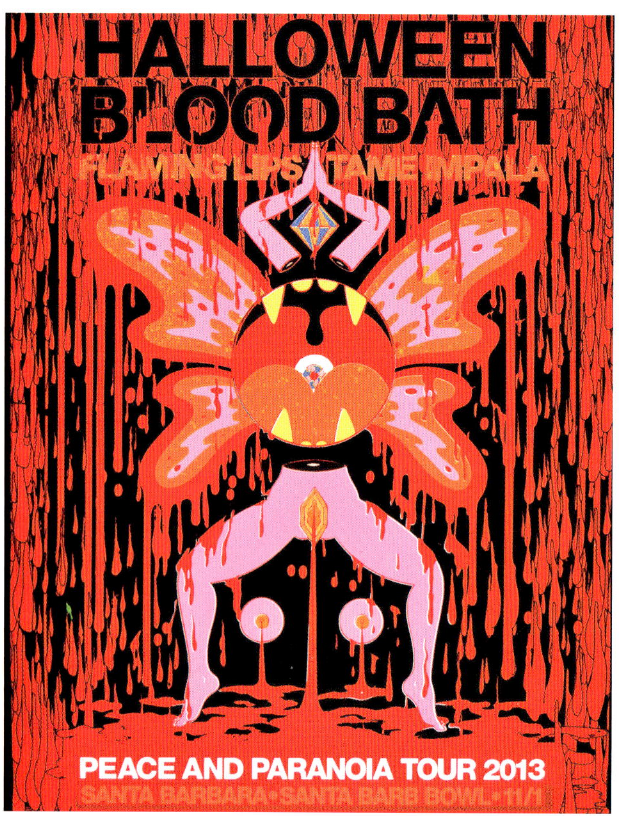

Halloween Blood Bath rock poster for
The Flaming Lips and Tame Impala

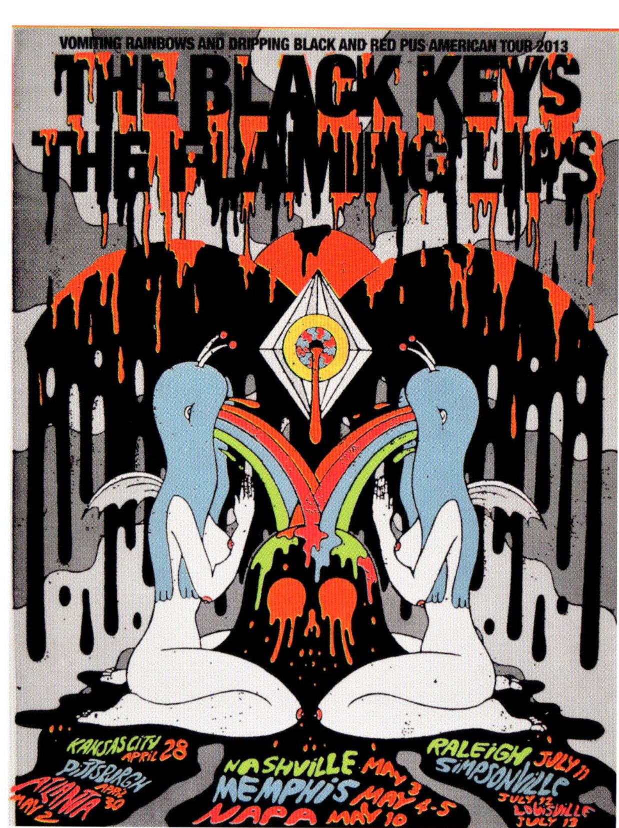

Rock poster for The Black Keys and The Flaming Lips,
with text and bits by Wayne Coyne

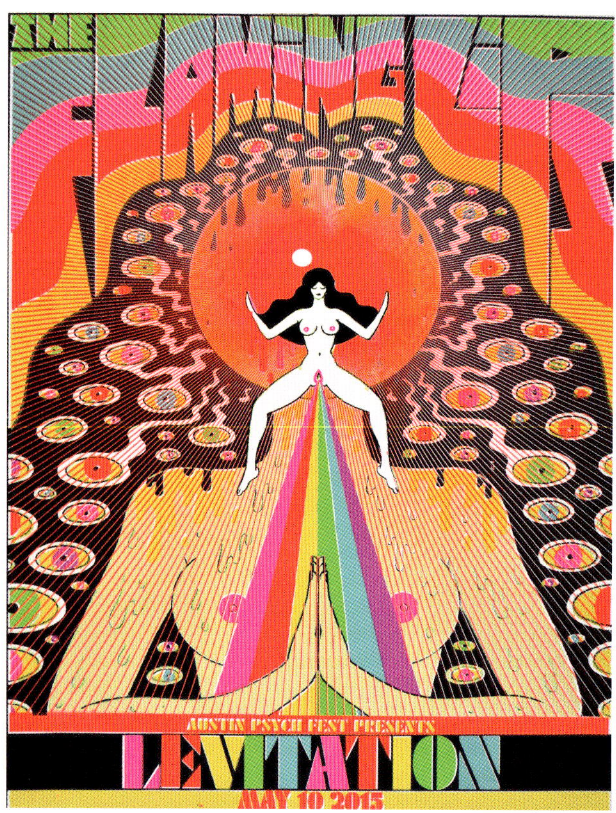

Rock poster for The Flaming Lips
and Def Rain at Levitation Psychfest

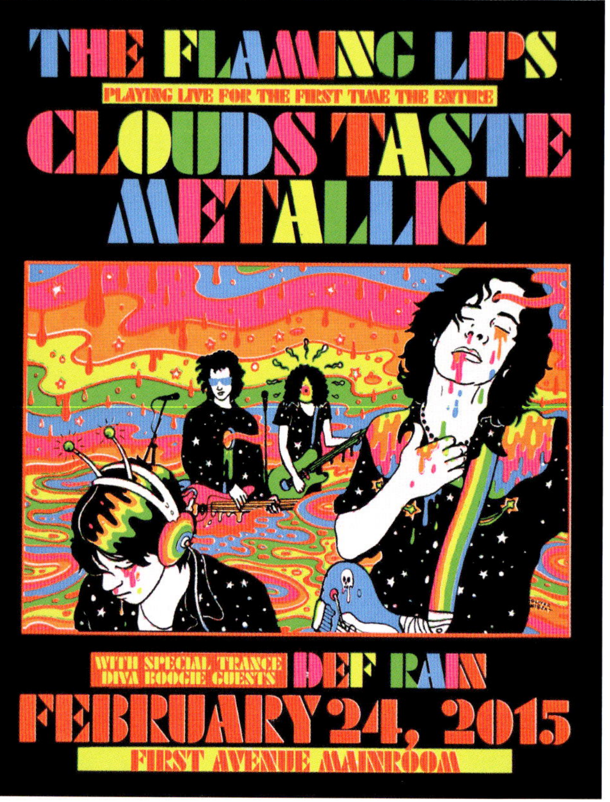

Rock poster for The Flaming Lips'
Clouds Taste Metallic tour

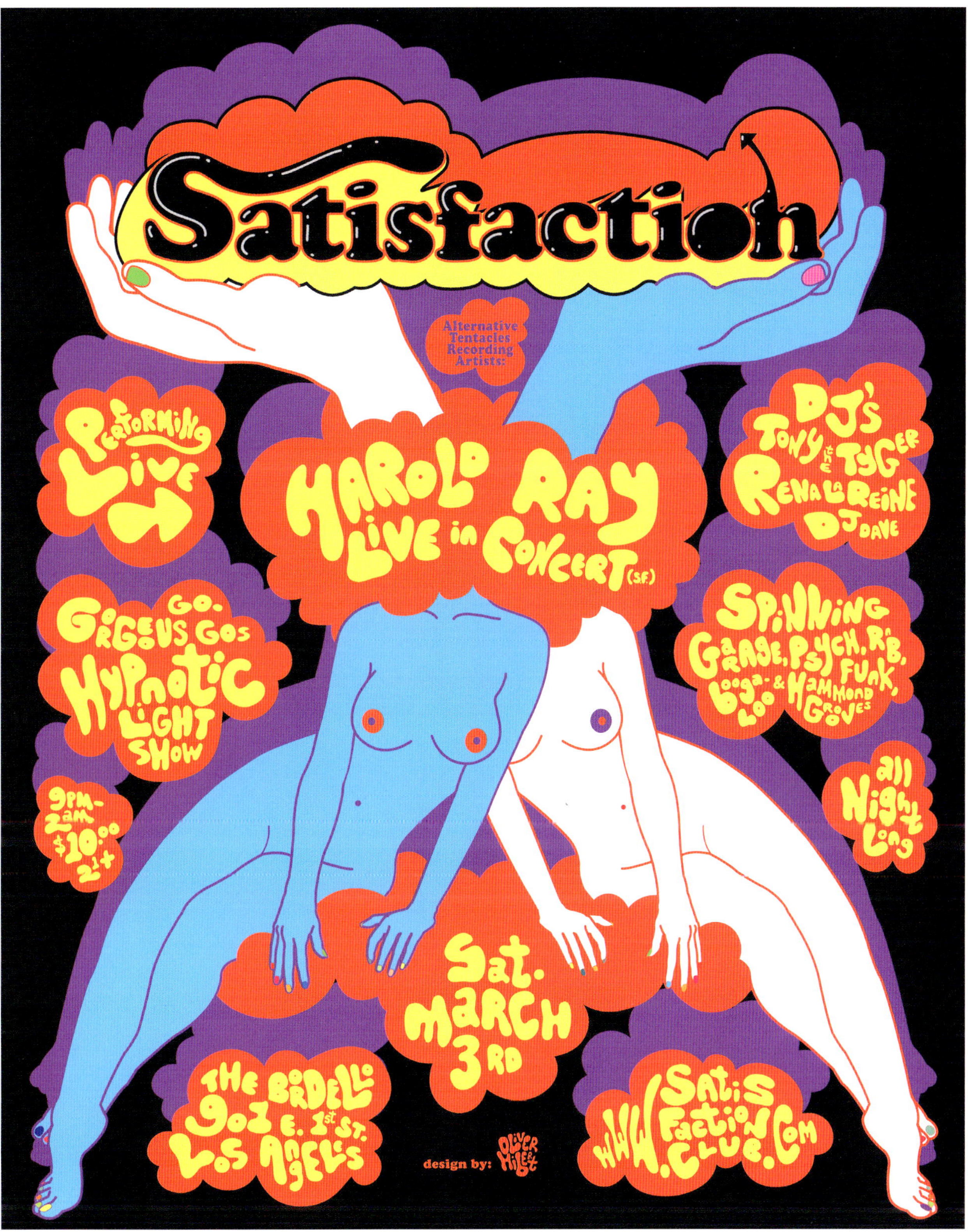

"Satisfaction poster for a random show in LA. This was the first rock poster I ever did, from some time in the mid 2000s. What a blur."

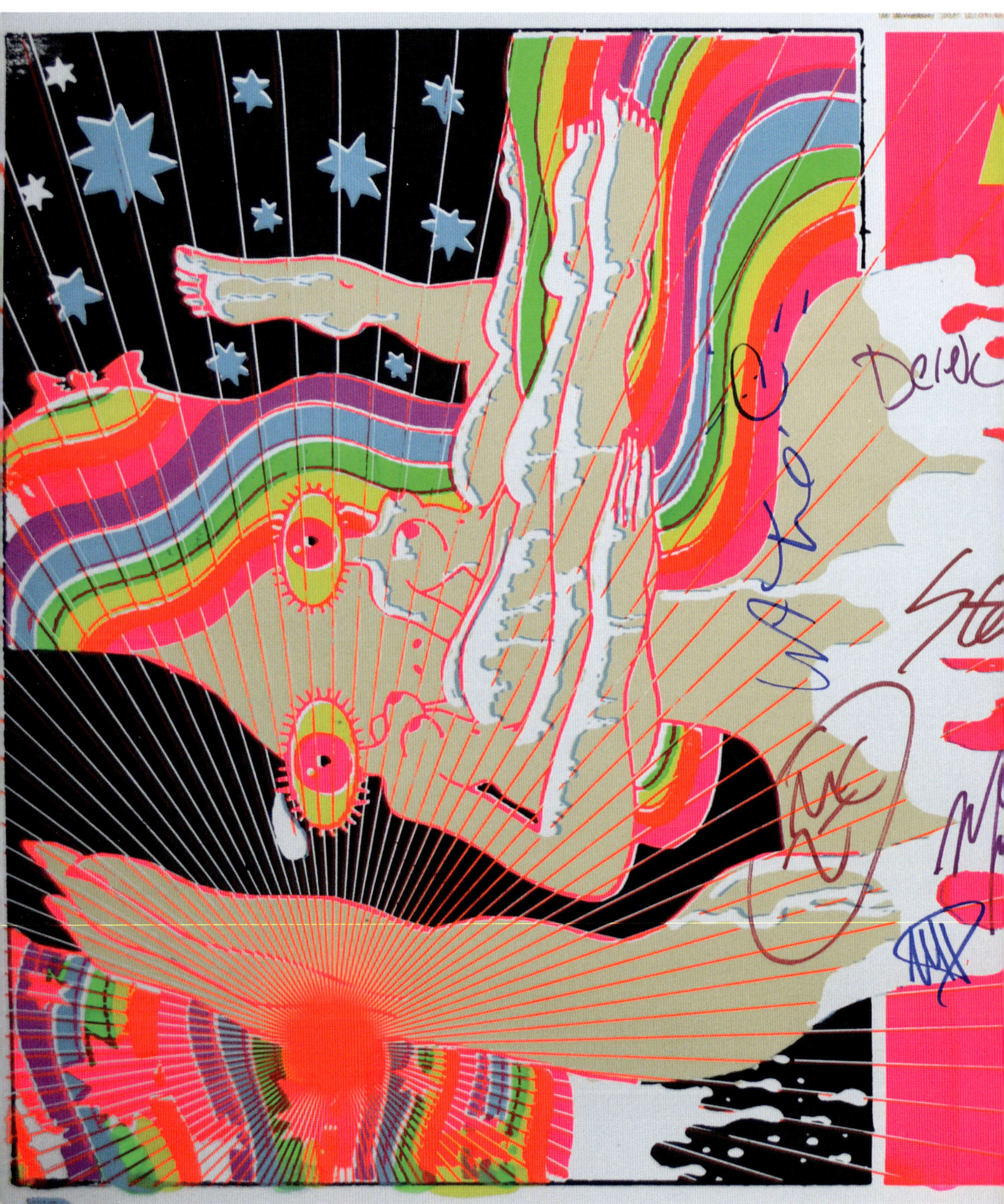

Rock poster for The Flaming Lips and Miley Cyrus & Her Dead Petz tour, with bits of Wayne Coyne drips

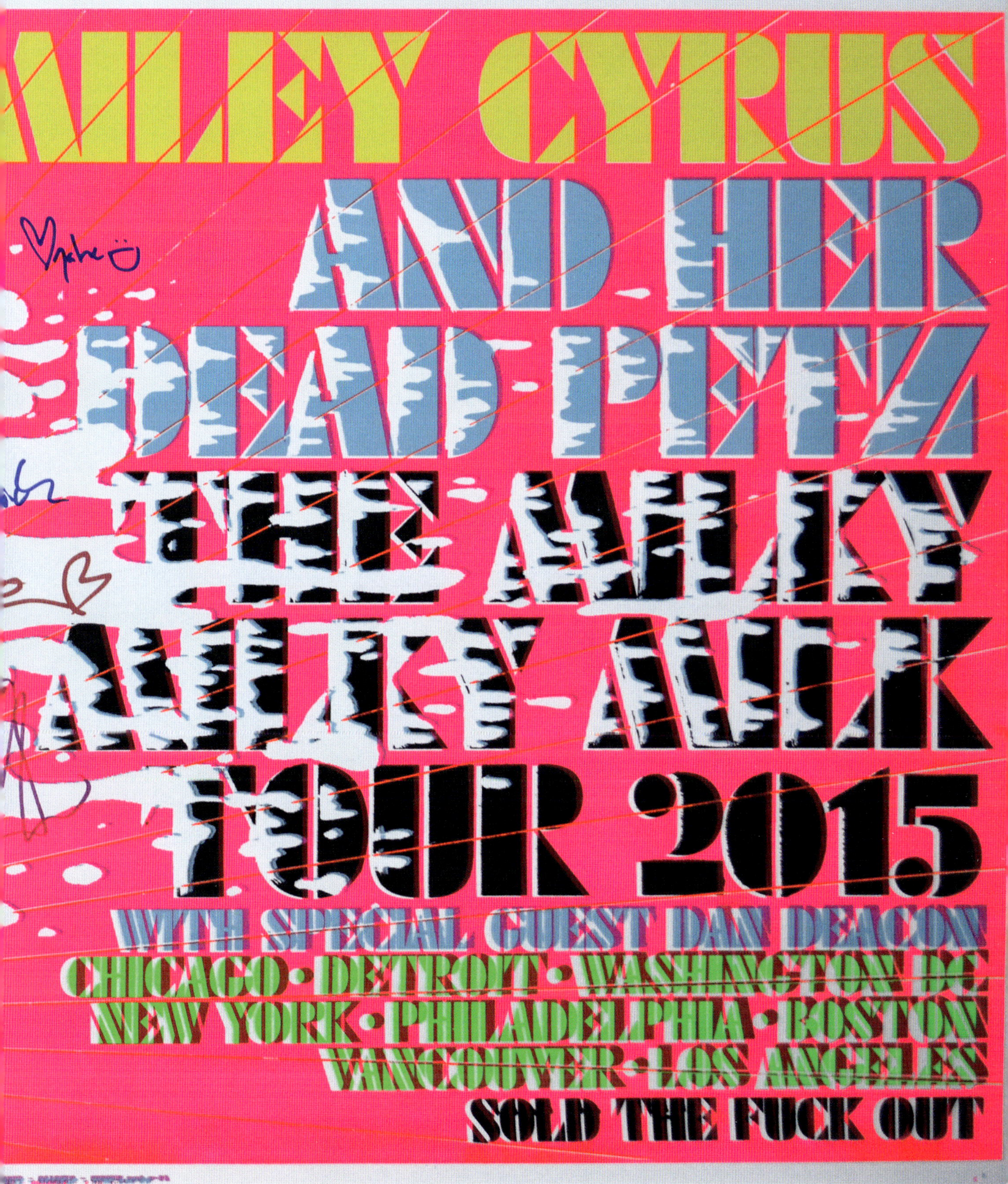
ILEY CYRUS
AND HER
DEAD PETZ
THE MILKY
MILKY MILK
TOUR 2015
WITH SPECIAL GUEST DAN DEACON
CHICAGO • DETROIT • WASHINGTON DC
NEW YORK • PHILADELPHIA • BOSTON
VANCOUVER • LOS ANGELES
SOLD THE FUCK OUT

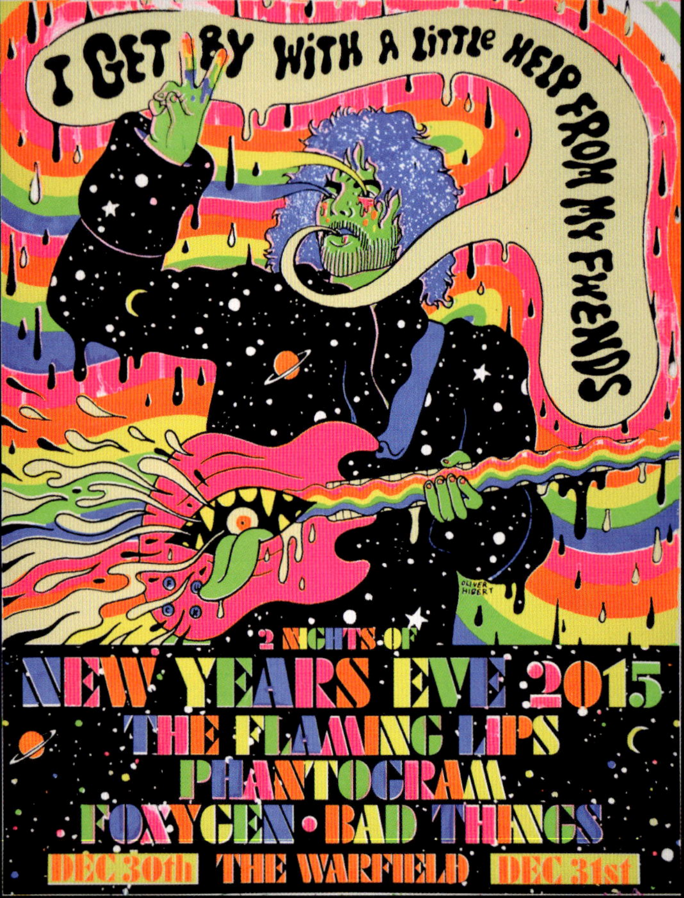

Rock poster for The Flaming Lips' Fwends tour

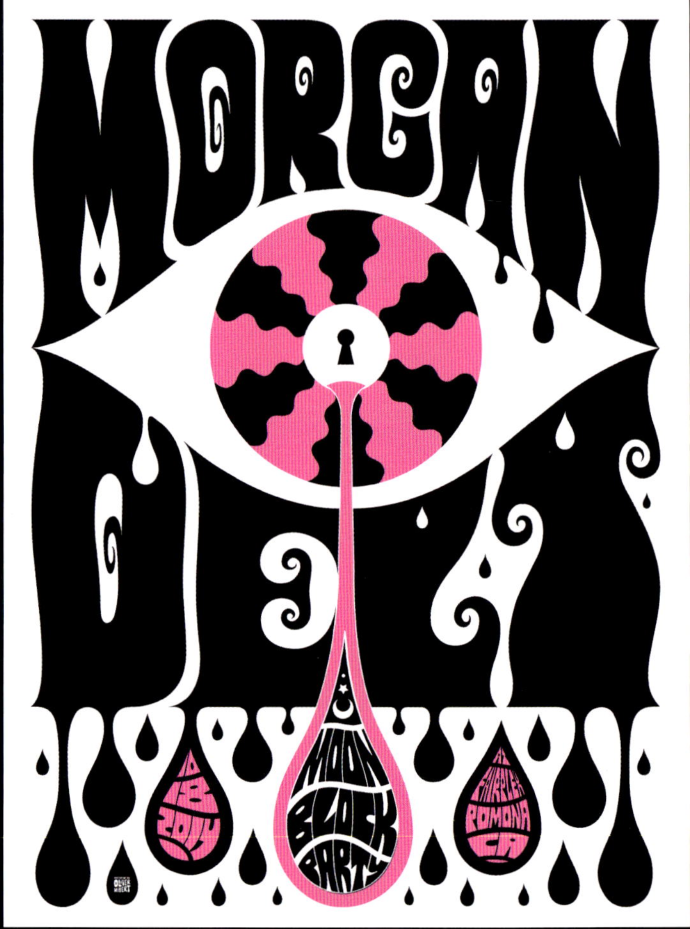

Rock poster for Psychedelic master of sound, Morgan Delt

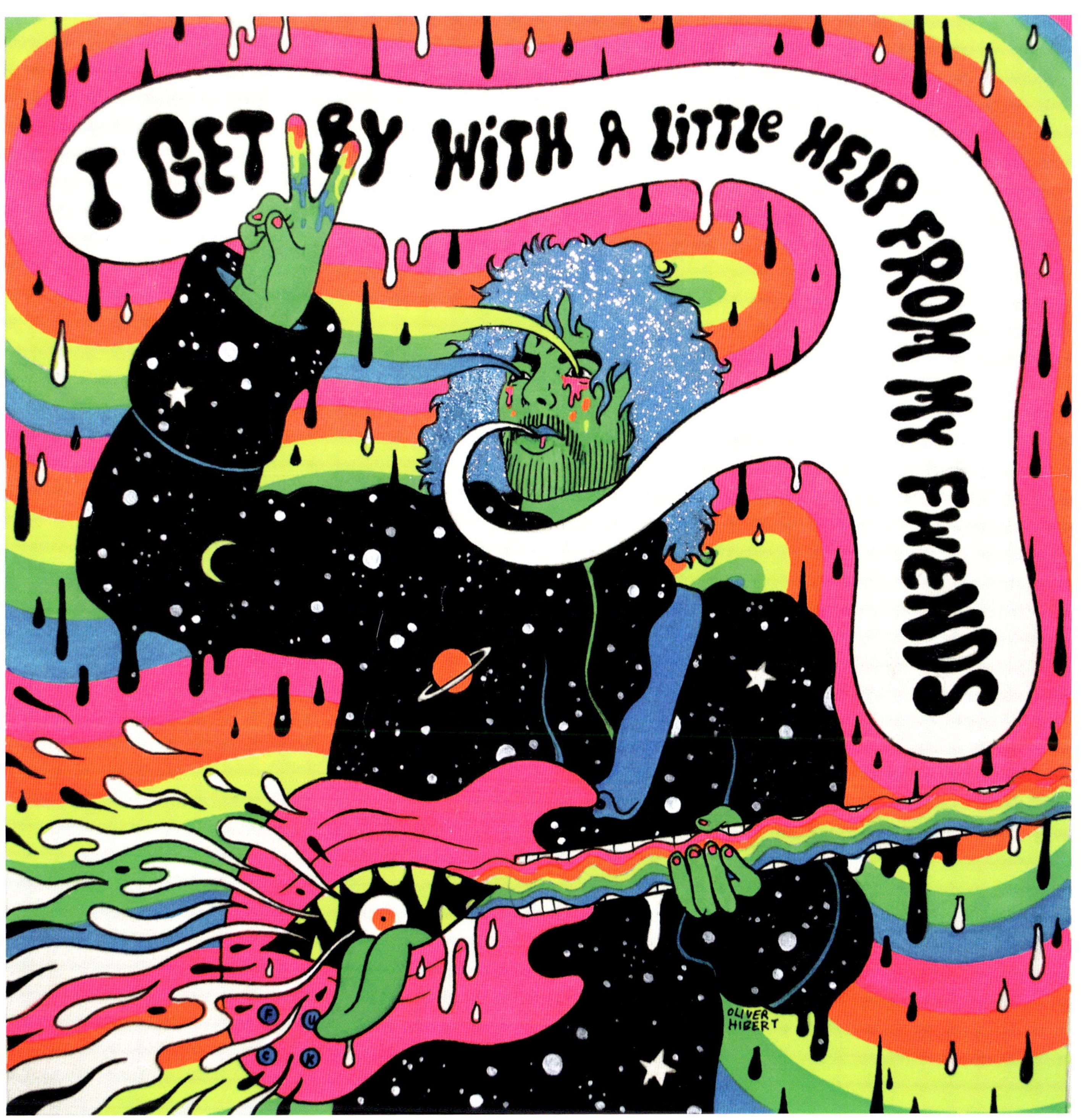

Detail of Fwends rock poster art

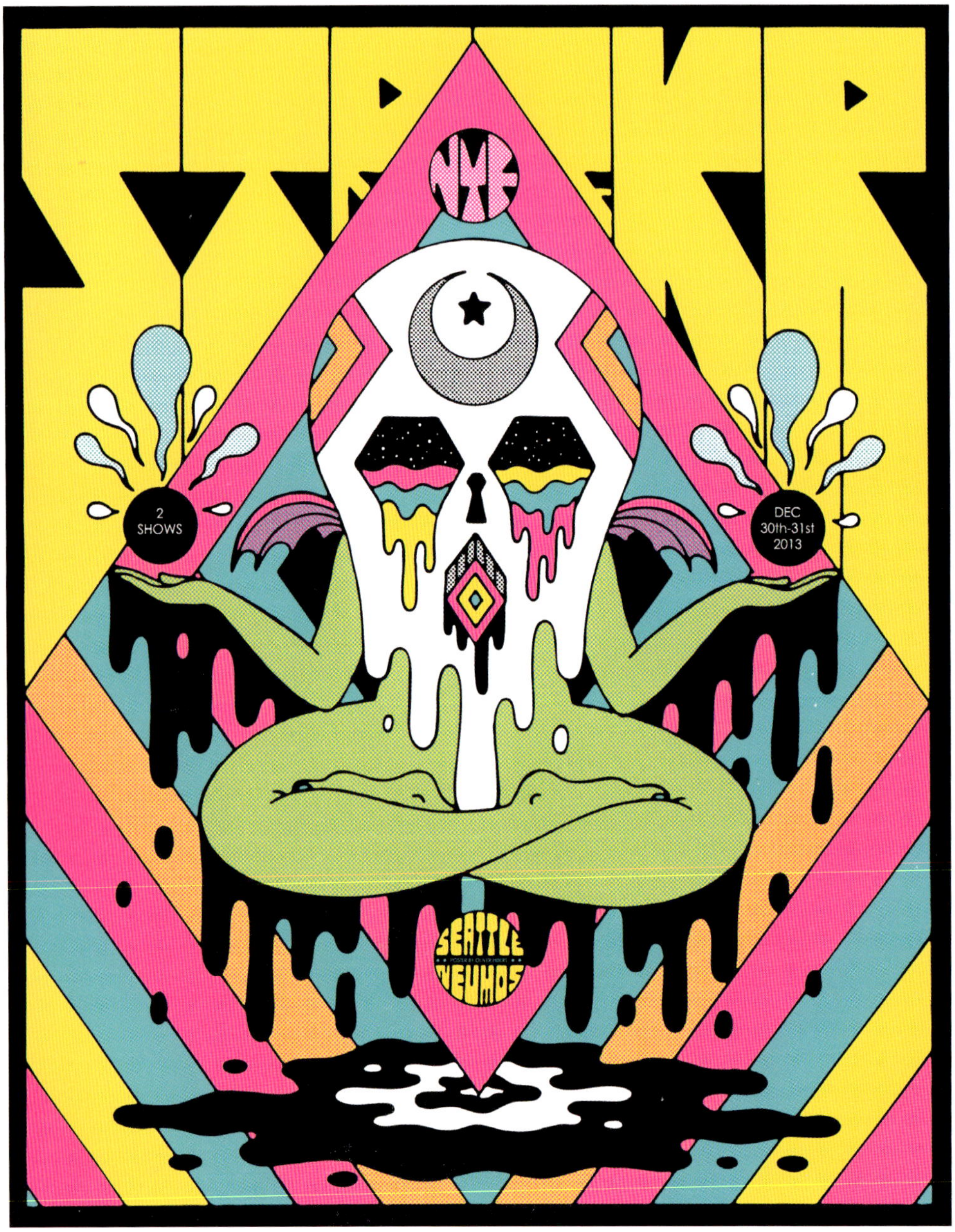

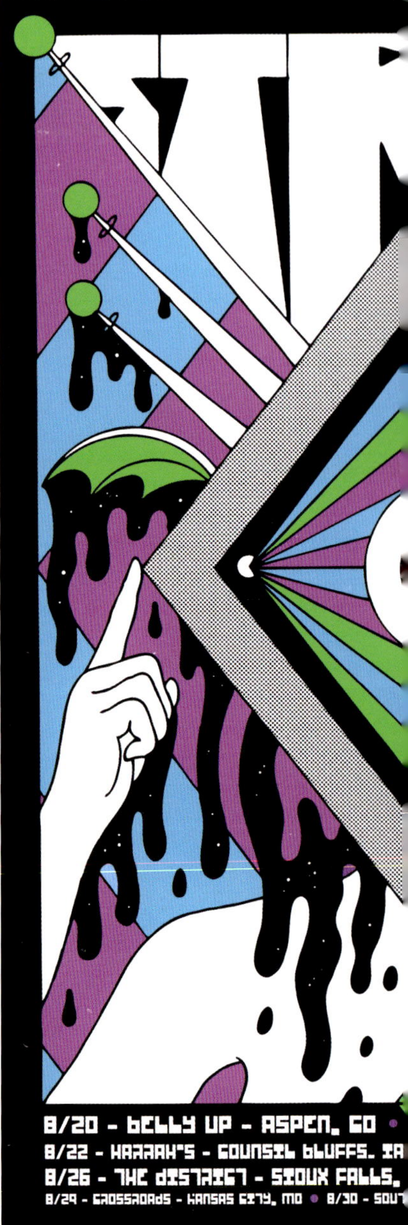

"Three consecutive New Year's Eve rock posters for my friends STRFKR. These guys are always fun to hang out with!"

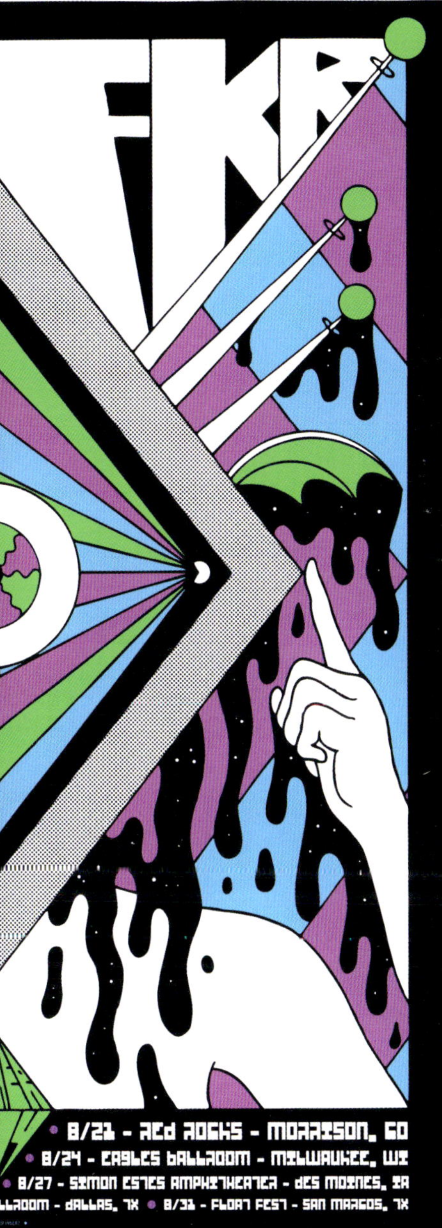
8/21 - Red Rocks - Morrison, CO
8/24 - Eagles Ballroom - Milwaukee, WI
8/27 - Simon Estes Amphitheater - Des Moines, IA
llroom - Dallas, TX • 8/31 - Float Fest - San Marcos, TX

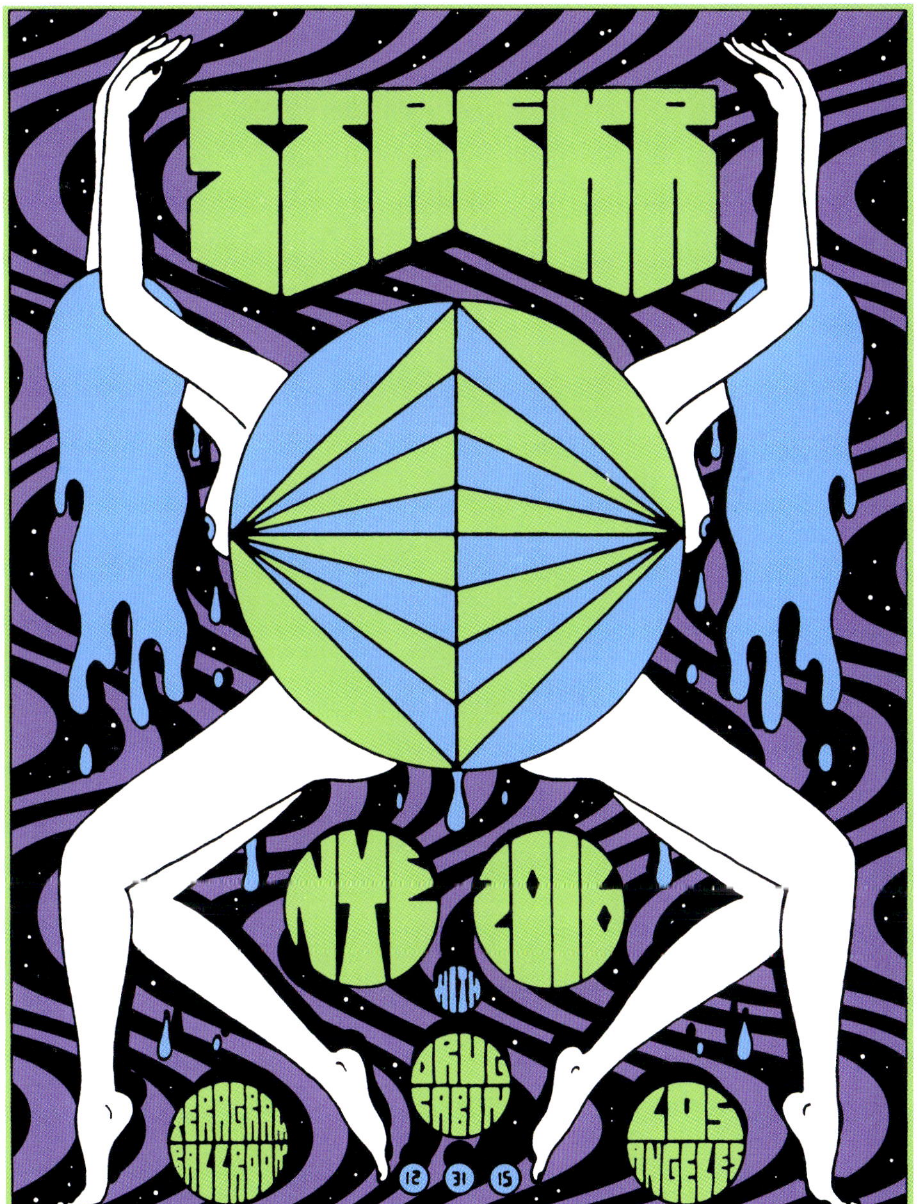

STRFKR
NYE 2016
with
Drug Cabin
Teragram Ballroom
12 31 15
Los Angeles

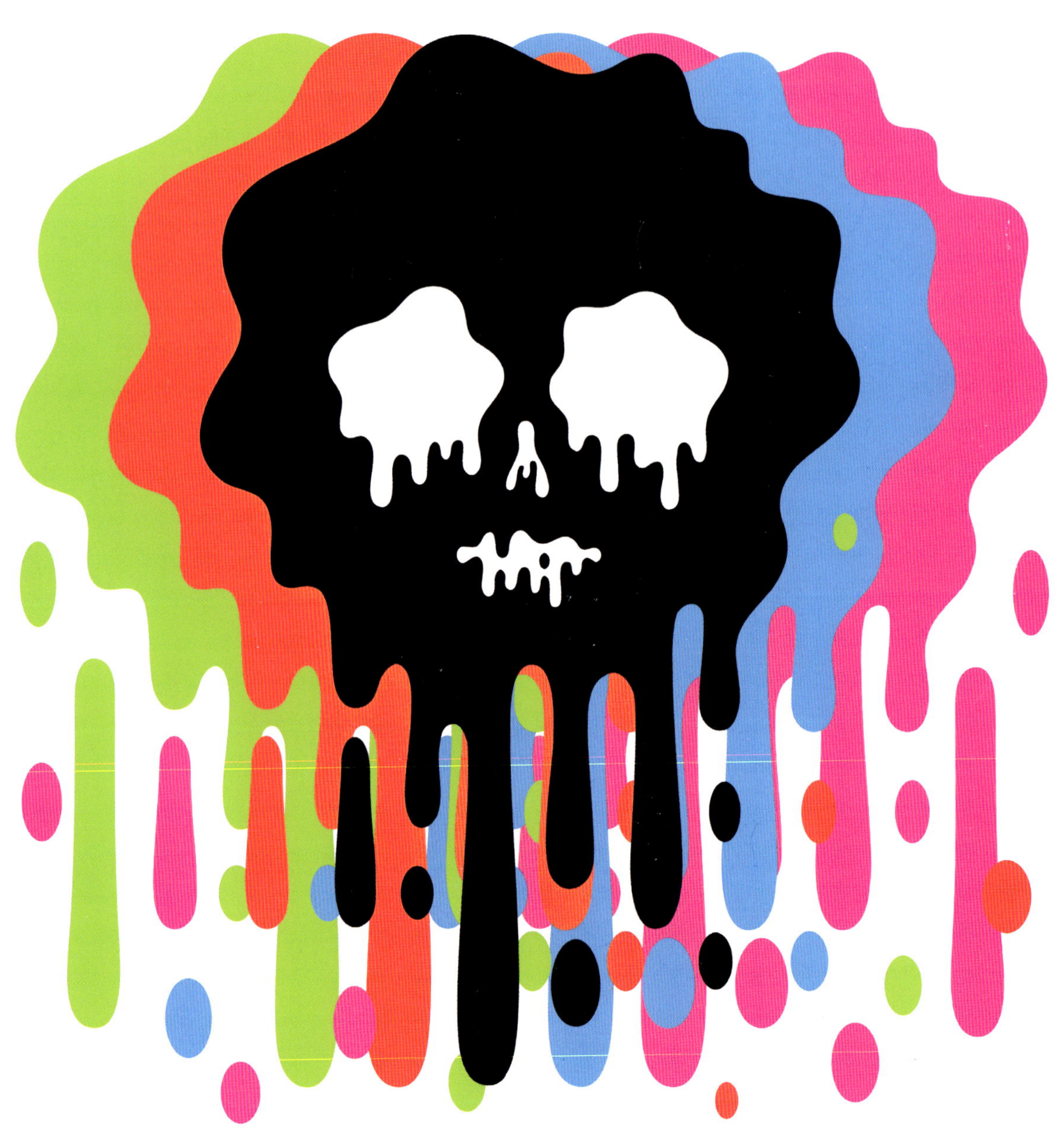

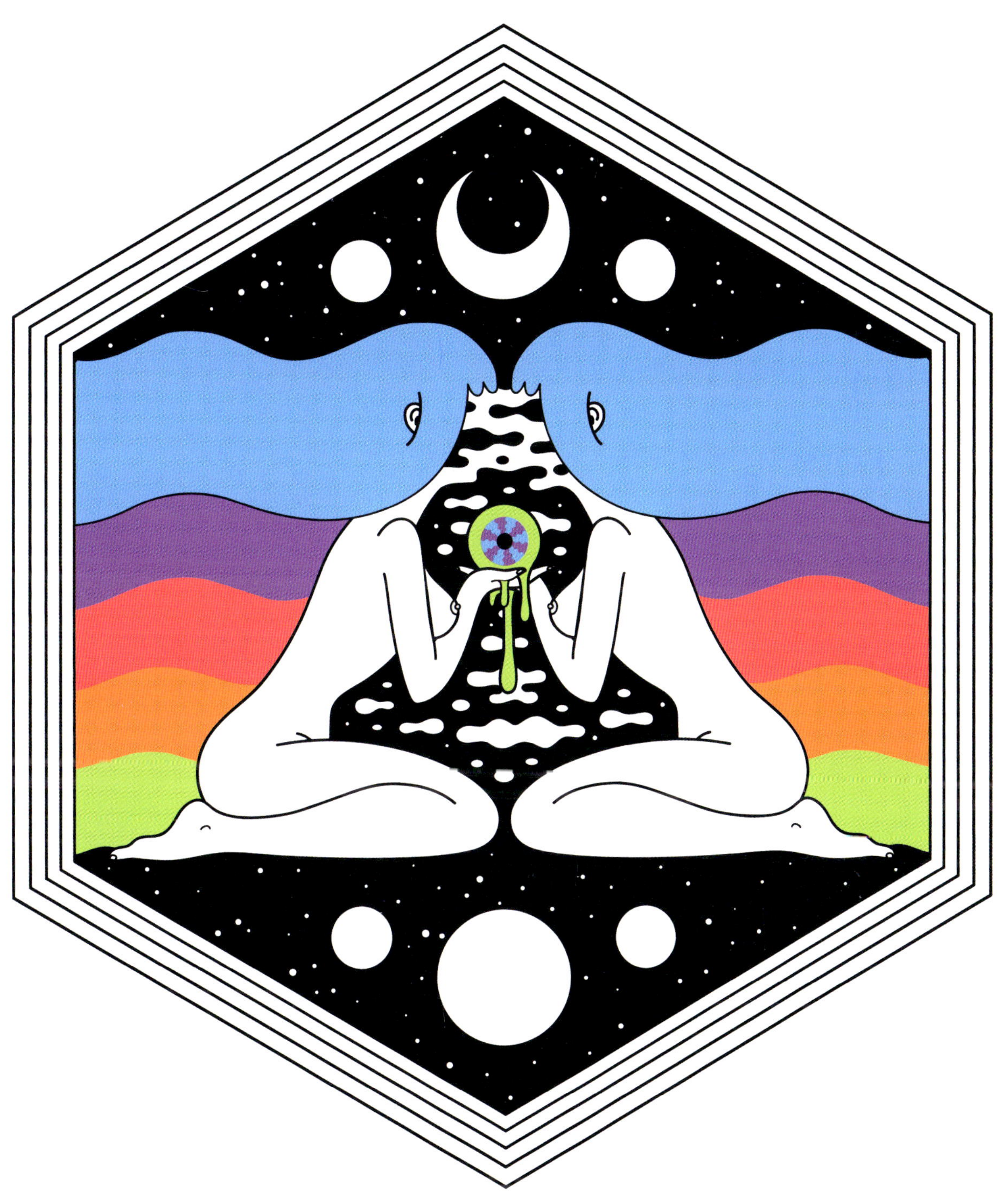

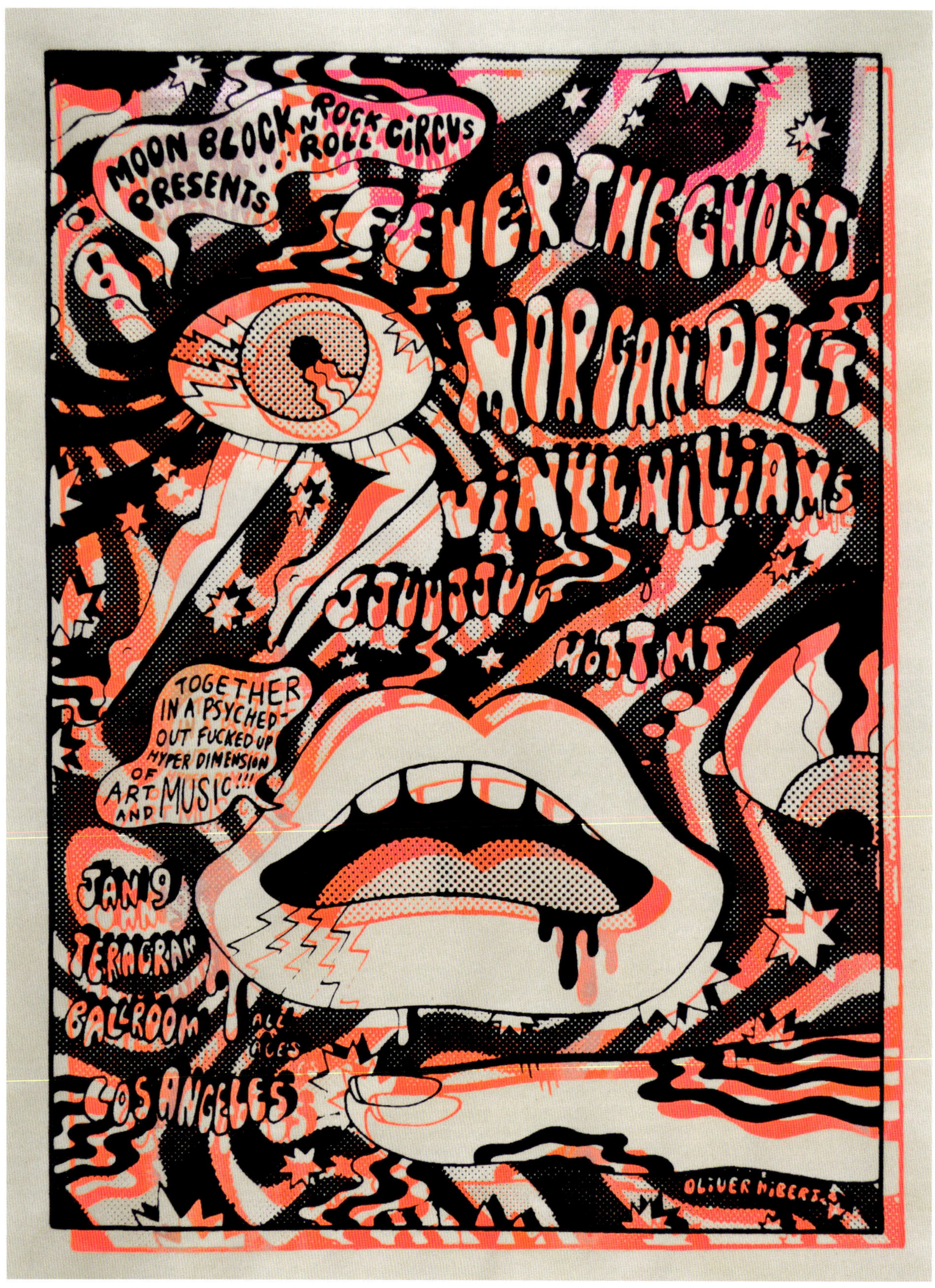

"Last minute punk rock, self-screenprinted poster for Fever The Ghost show in LA. I think I had maybe eight hours or so to make these and then drive six hours to make it in time for the show. Always good times with my friends Fever The Ghost."

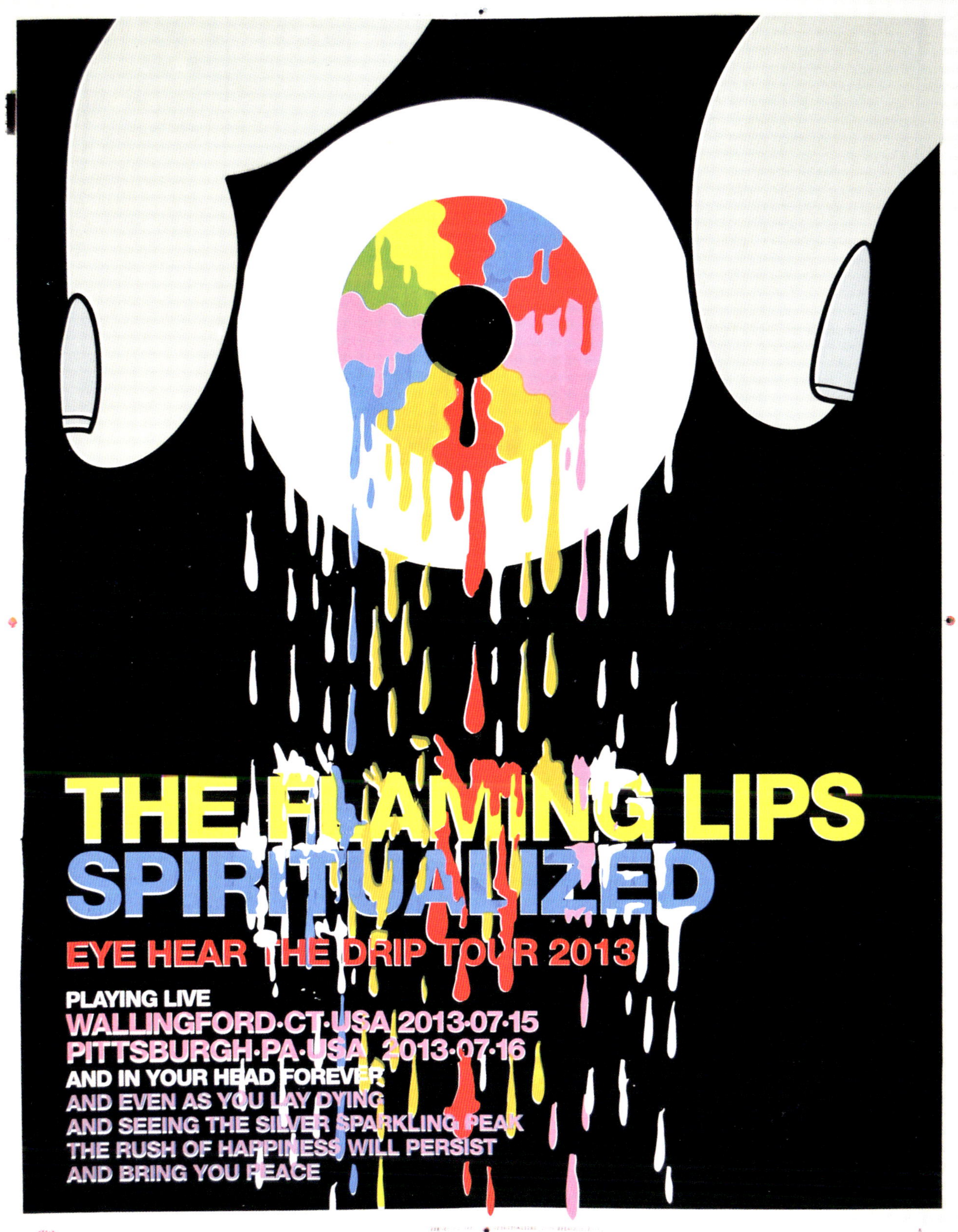

"Rock poster for The Flaming Lips and Spiritualized tour. All the drips were drawn by Wayne. He loves fucking with my art."

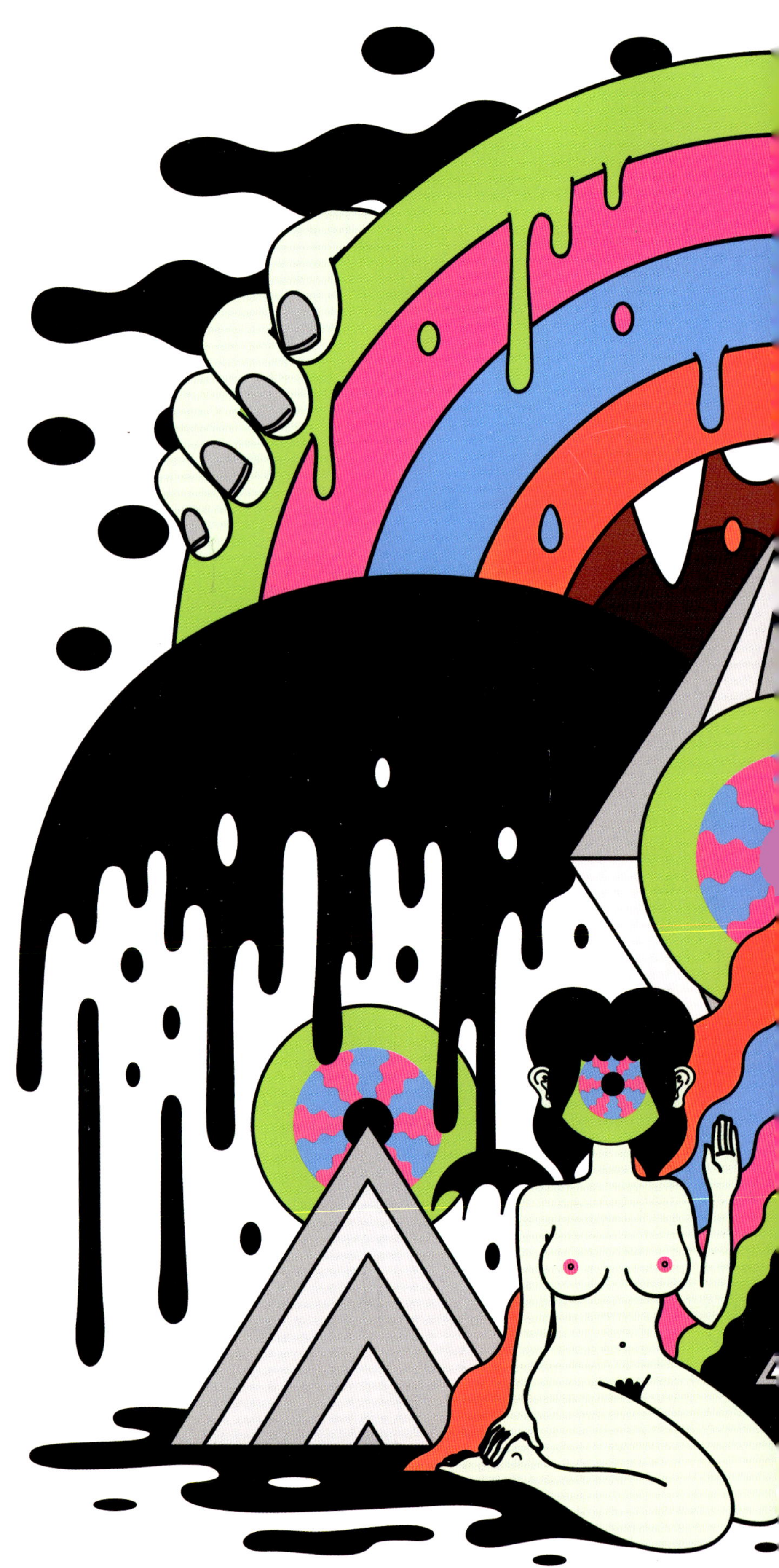

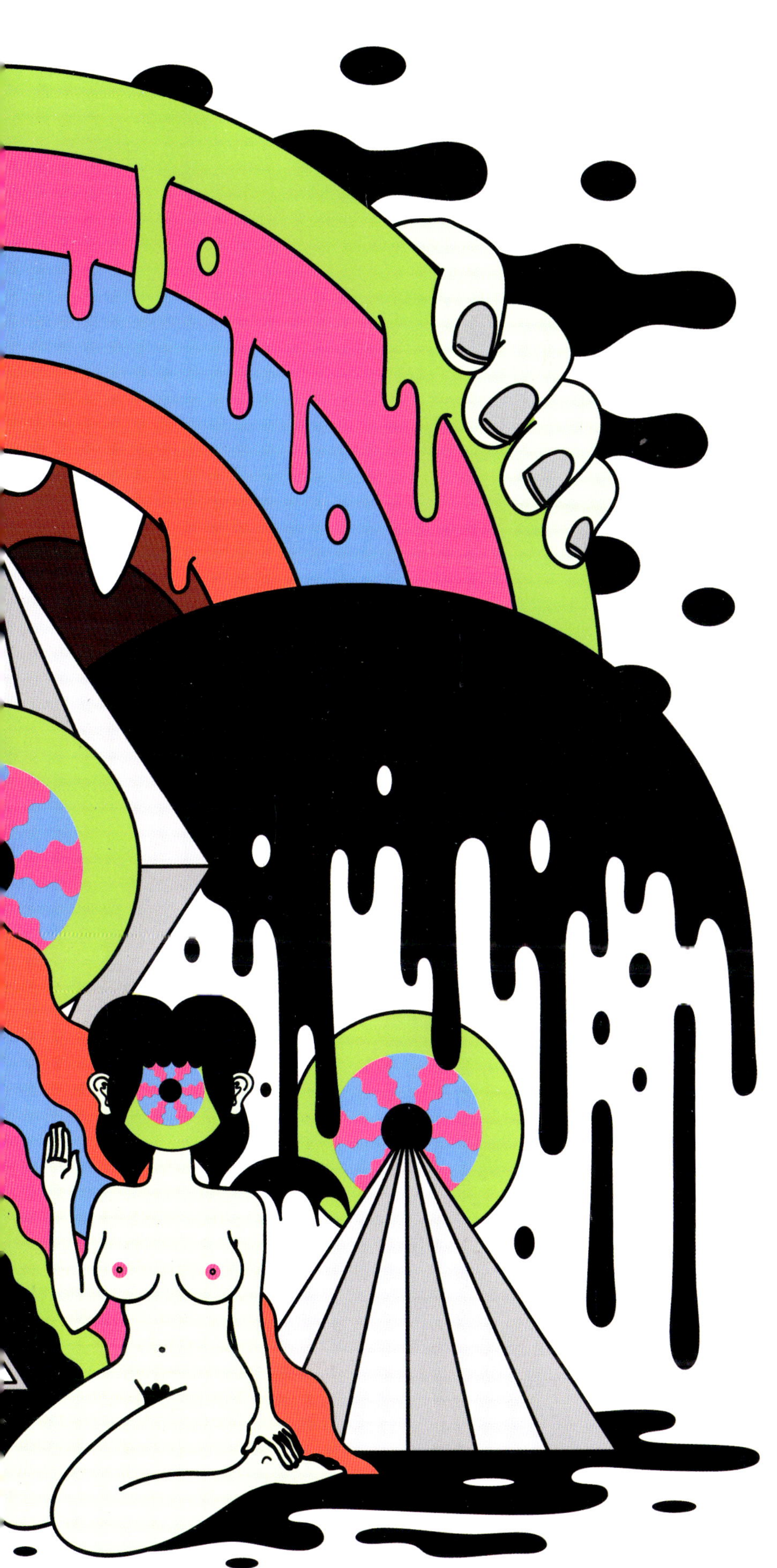

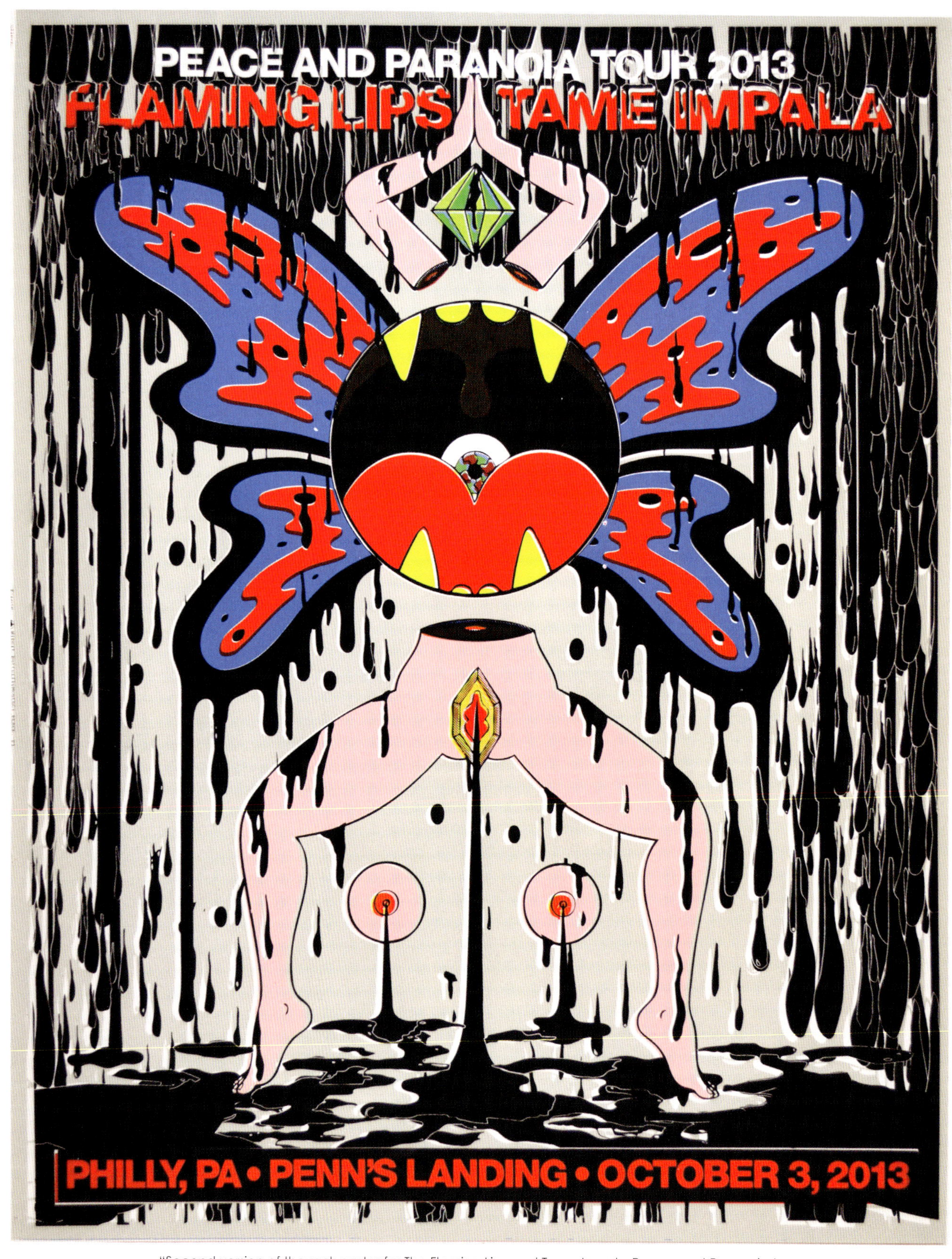

"Second version of the rock poster for The Flaming Lips and Tame Impala *Peace and Paranoia* tour. I had drips on this, and by the time Wayne got his hands on it, he went completely drip-nuts. Haha!"

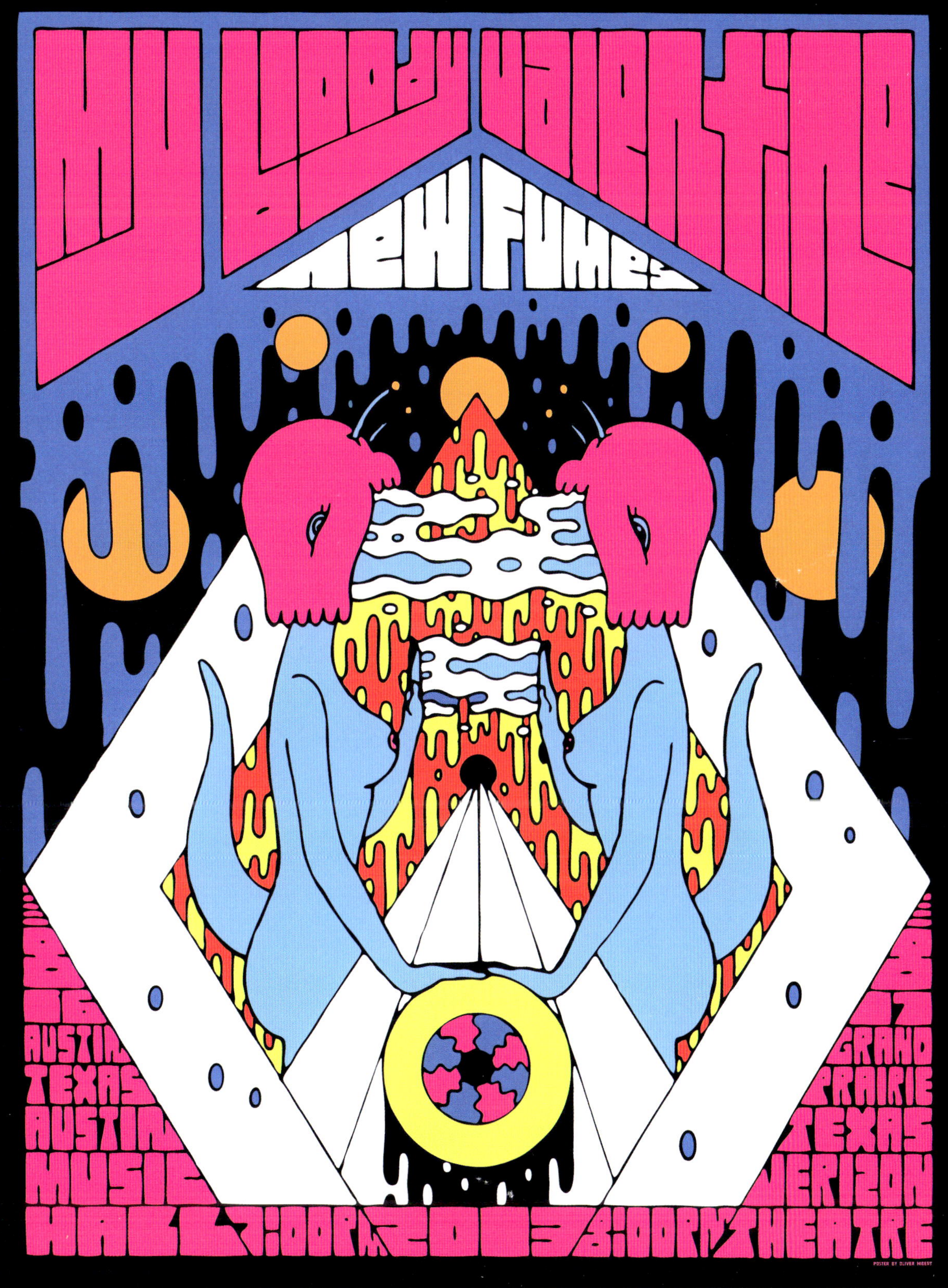

Rock poster for My Bloody Valentine and New Fumes
"One of my favorites"

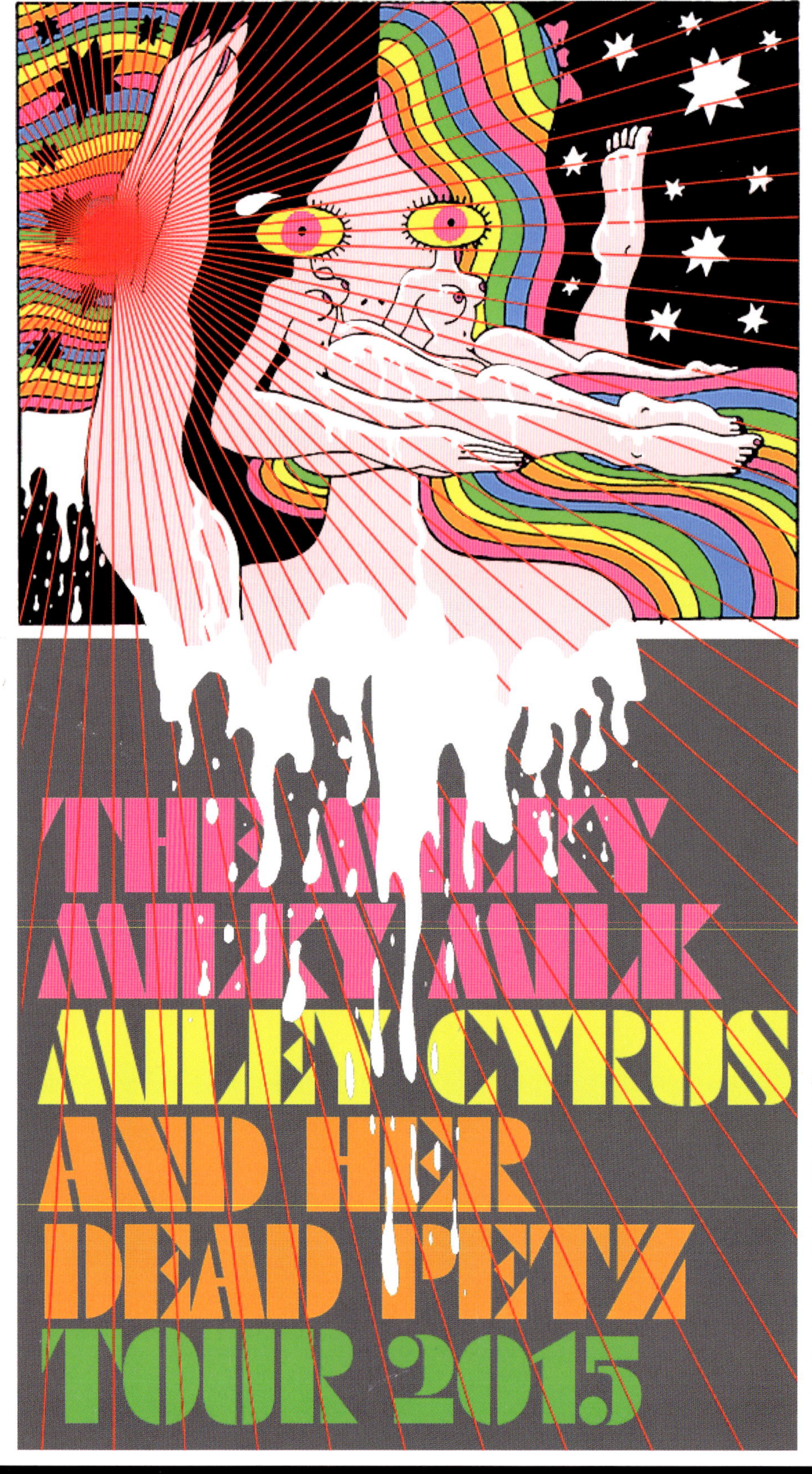

Rock poster for The Flaming Lips and Miley Cyrus & Her Dead Petz tour, with drips by Wayne Coyne

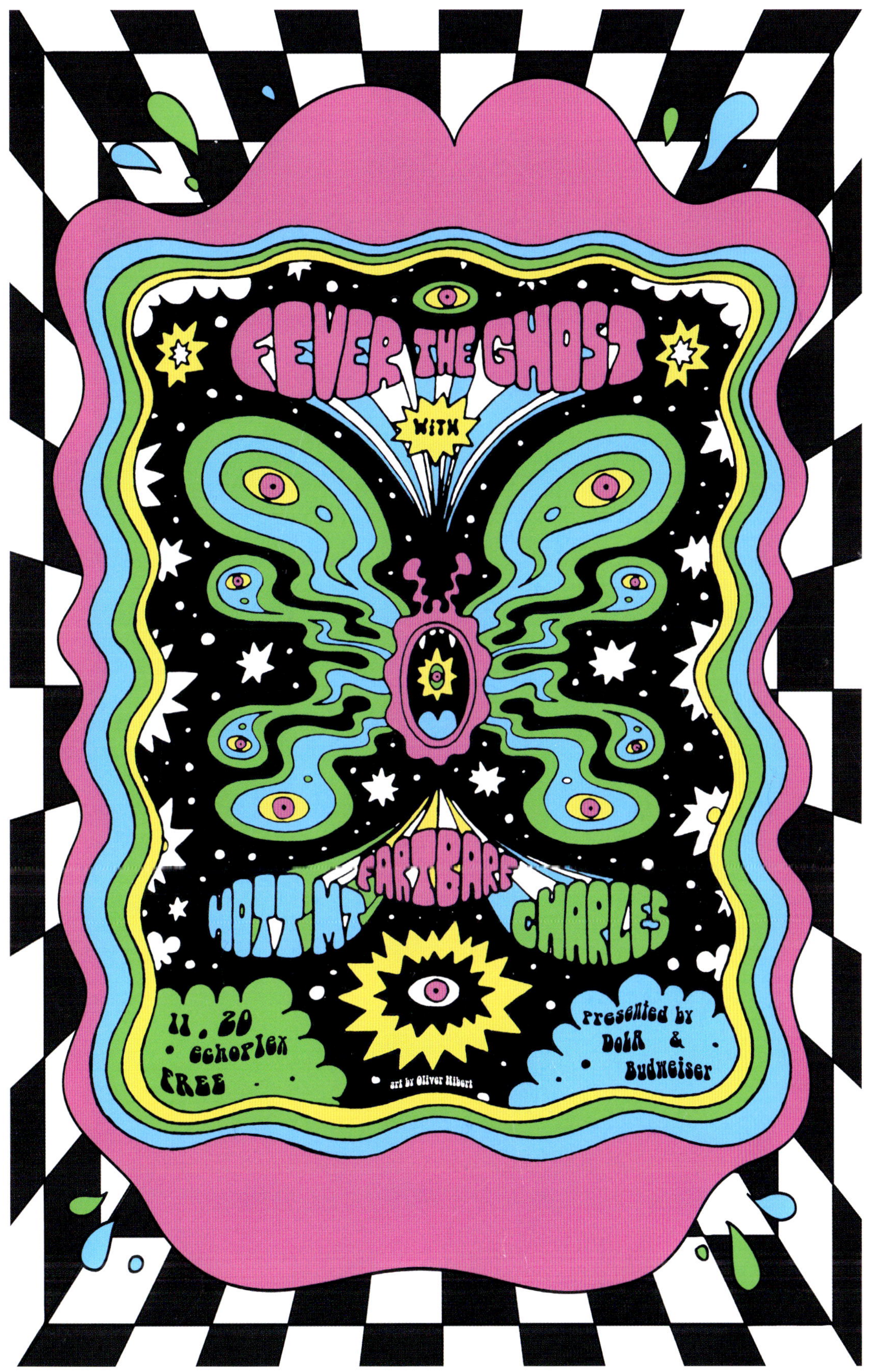

"Another rock poster for my friends, Fever The Ghost."

Chapter Four:

The Tarot

Illustrated by Pamela Colman Smith in 1909, the Rider-Waite tarot deck (also known as the Rider-Waite-Smith deck, or the Waite-Smith deck), is the best-known and most recognizable version of the tarot. As it was the first modern edition to be mass produced and marketed, the Rider-Waite tarot has become the standard bearer, even though tarot cards in some form have existed since at least the fourteenth century.

Pamela Colman Smith was a part of the English occult society The Hermetic Order of the Golden Dawn, in which she found herself meeting and collaborating with fellow members Aleister Crowley and William Butler Yeats. Yeats himself had indoctrinated Smith into the organization, after meeting her in a theater group managed by *Dracula* author Bram Stoker. It was with The Hermetic Order of the Golden Dawn that Smith met A.E. Waite, who commissioned the young artist to create the tarot deck. Smith's name was not credited (hence, the deck was known as the Rider-Waite tarot), nor was she compensated for her incredible work. Sadly, Smith, a gifted artist and performer, died penniless and unknown in 1951. The original artwork used to produce her tarot cards were assumed to have been destroyed completely in the many bombing raids that struck England during World War II, with not a single card known to have survived.

Oliver Hibert's redux of Pamela Colman Smith's tarot deck is far from simple homage. Having broken away from the Jehovah's Witnesses in his pre-teens, the tarot (like rock music and modern art) represents that which was once considered taboo and evil in his formative years. Being brought up in a sheltered environment, only knowing of the tarot as some undefined sinful thing to be avoided, this notorious occult touchstone became for Oliver something he was now free to explore.

While the composition of each card holds remarkably close to the original illustrations by Pamela Colman Smith, the artwork is undeniably Oliver's. The hallmarks of Oliver's work (floating eyeballs, melting skulls, etc.)—not to mention his vivid color palette—grace every card. Yet, in revisiting the controversial tarot deck, Oliver reminds us that Smith's illustrations were graceful, clever works of art, each card fascinating and beautiful. While Oliver's version can and does function as a normal tarot deck in that it can be read, every card is a fully realized painting in and of itself. By researching and recreating the tarot deck, Oliver has attempted to embrace and understand what was once forbidden to him.

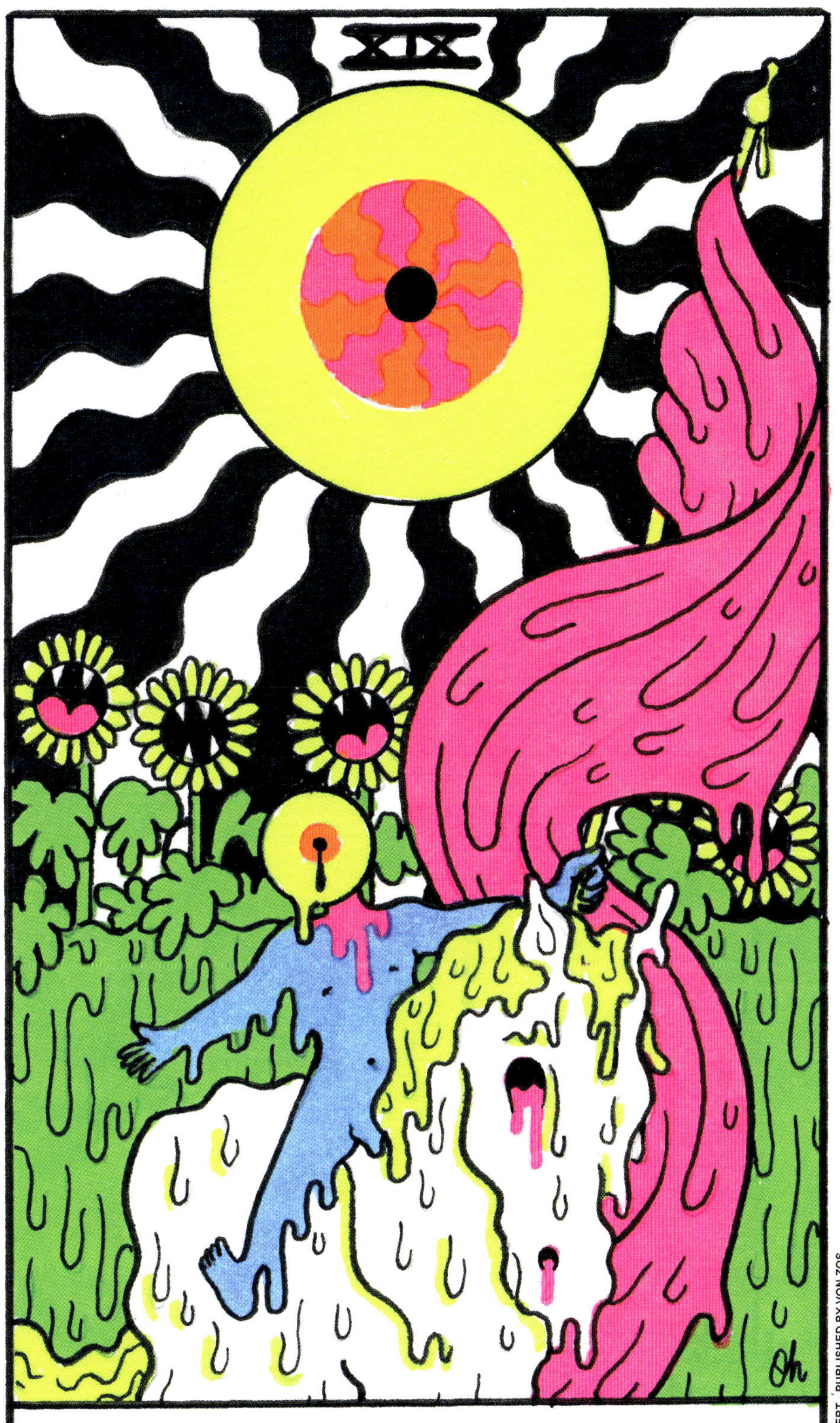

THE SUN.

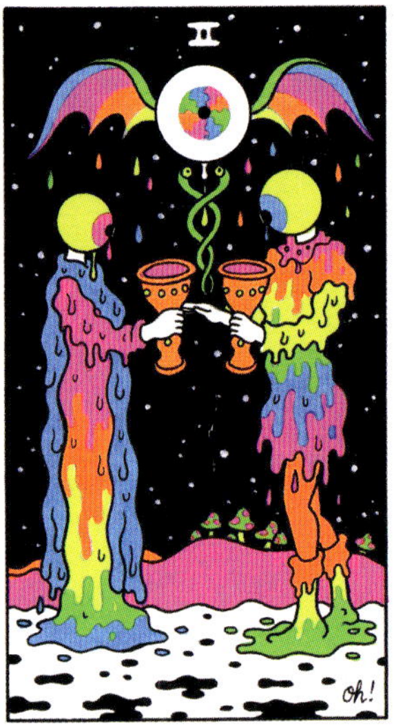

II

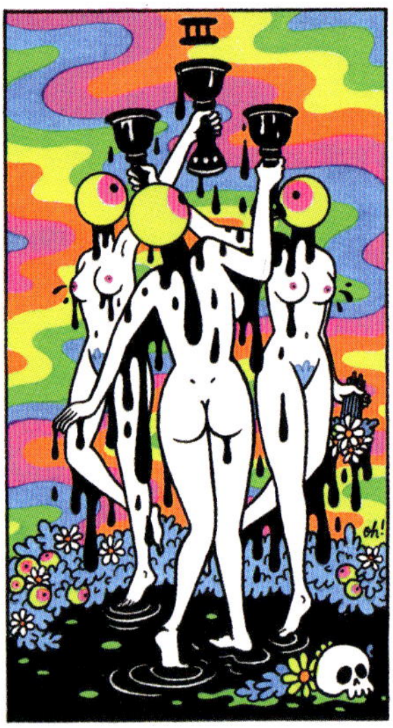

III

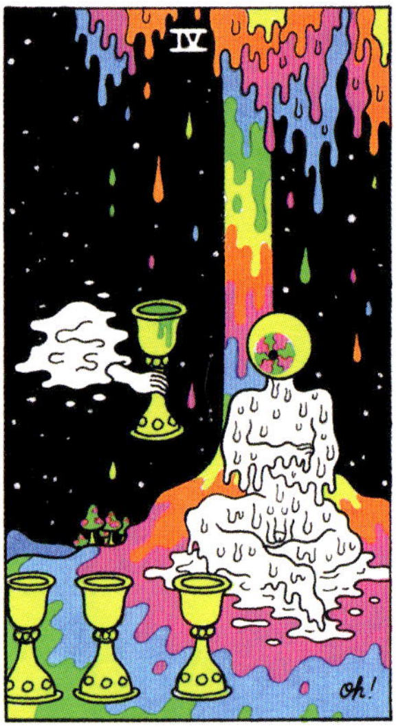

IV

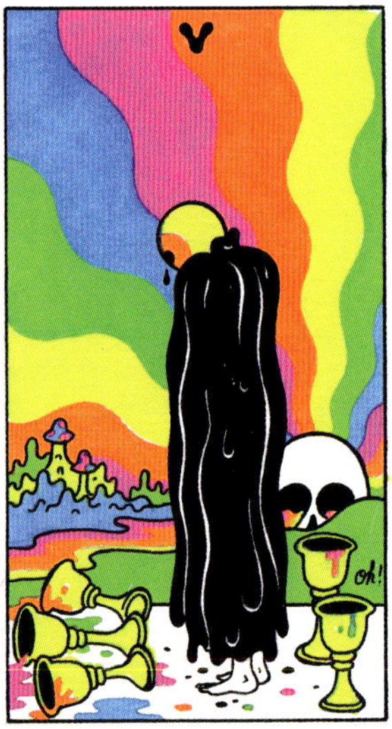

V

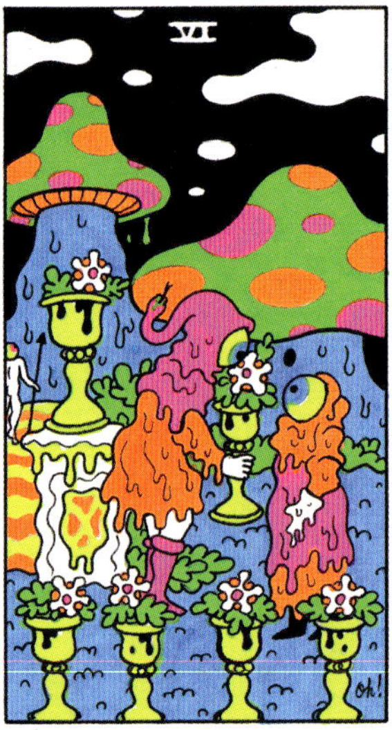

VI

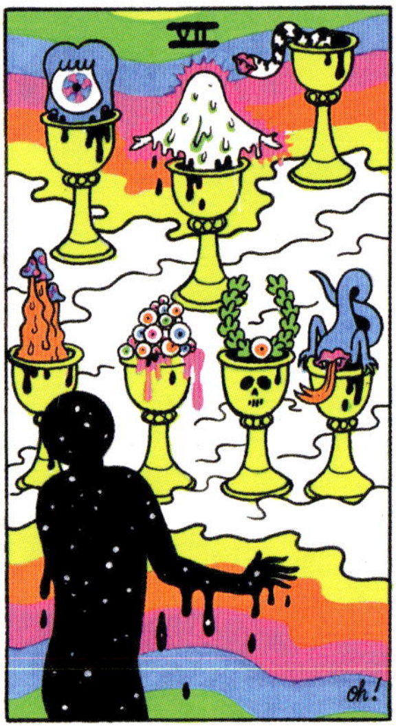

VII

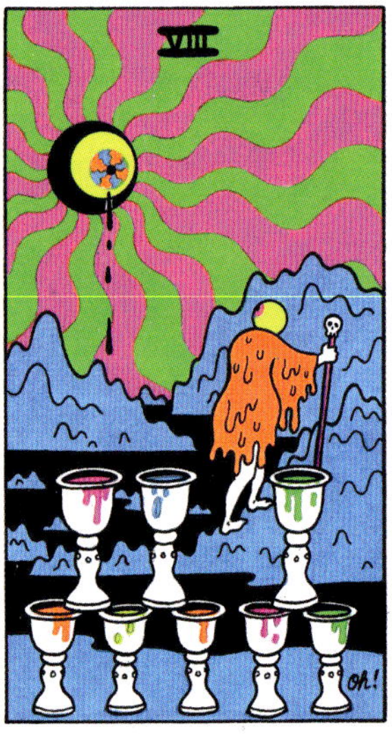

VIII

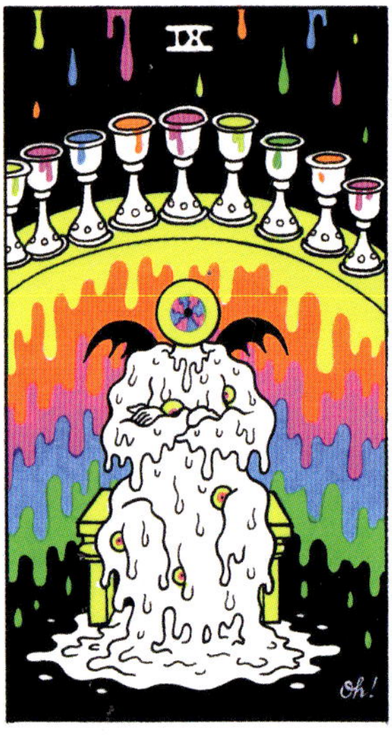

IX

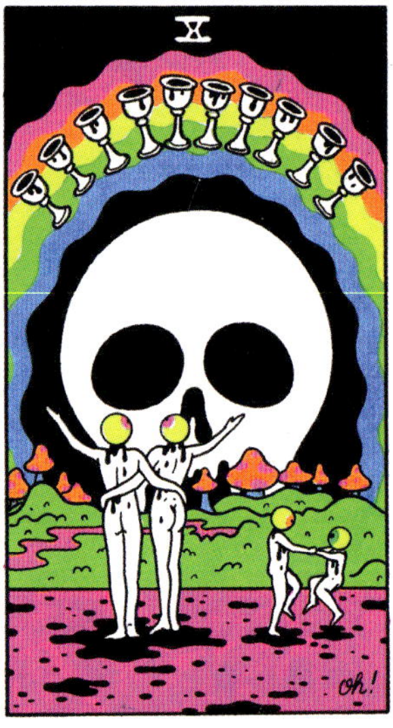

X

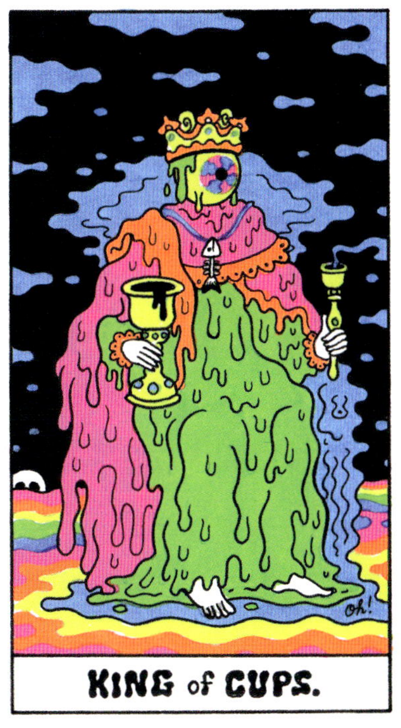
oh!
KING of CUPS.

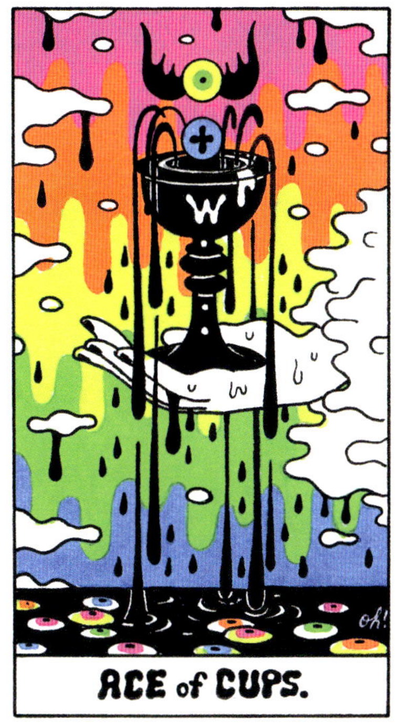
oh!
ACE of CUPS.

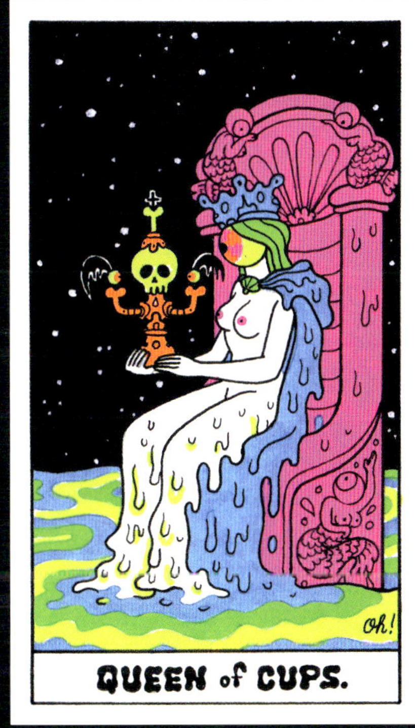
Oh!
QUEEN of CUPS.

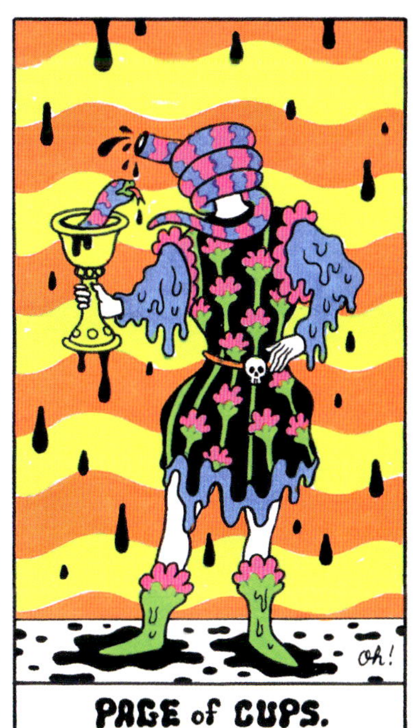
Oh!
PAGE of CUPS.

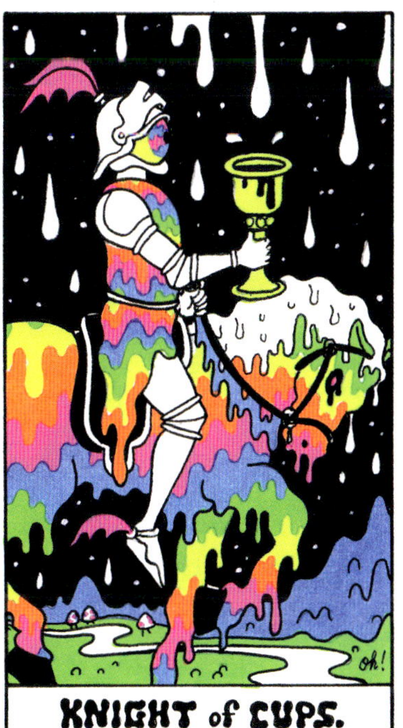
oh!
KNIGHT of CUPS.

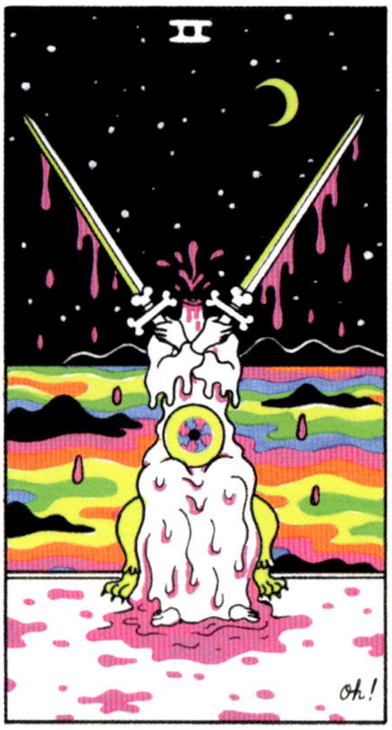

II

Oh!

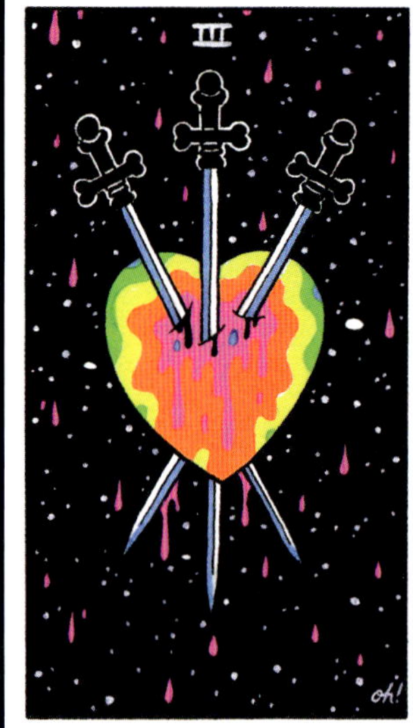

III

Oh!

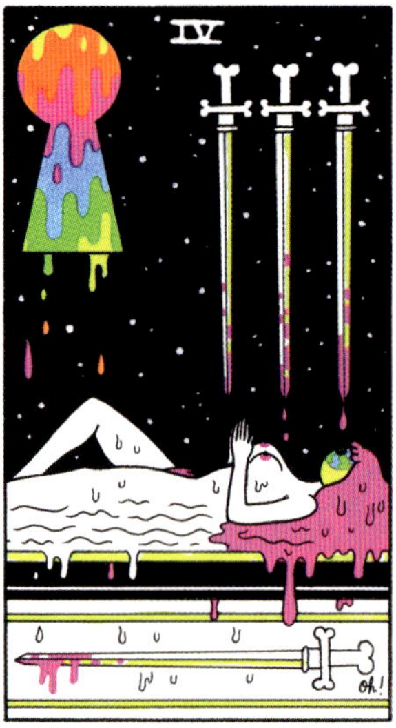

IV

Oh!

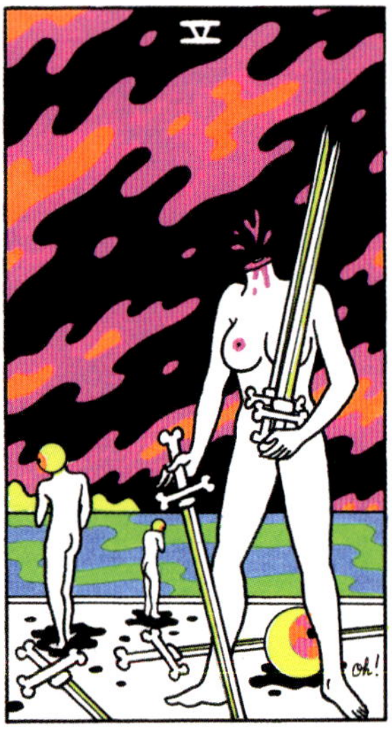

V

Oh!

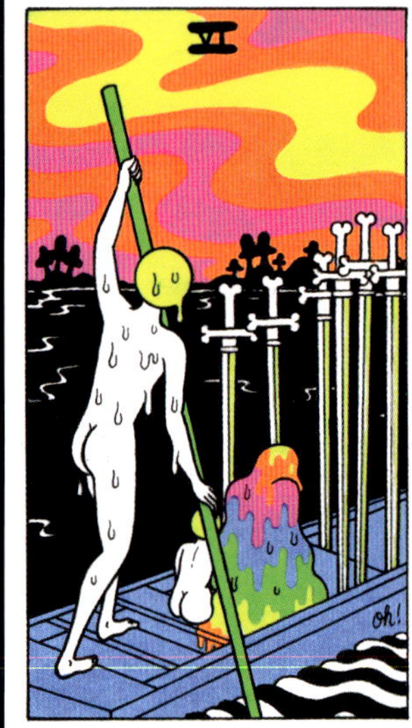

VI

Oh!

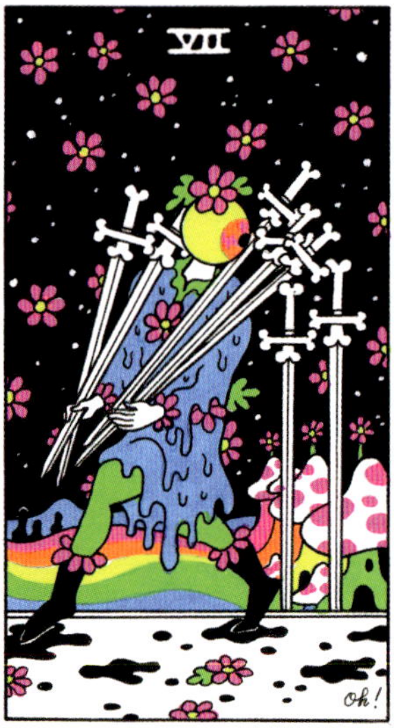

VII

Oh!

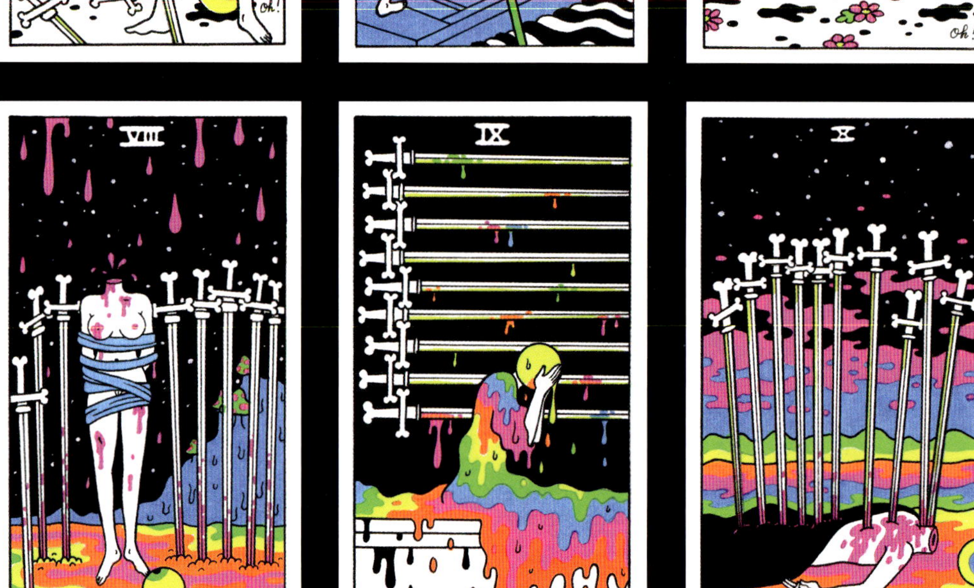

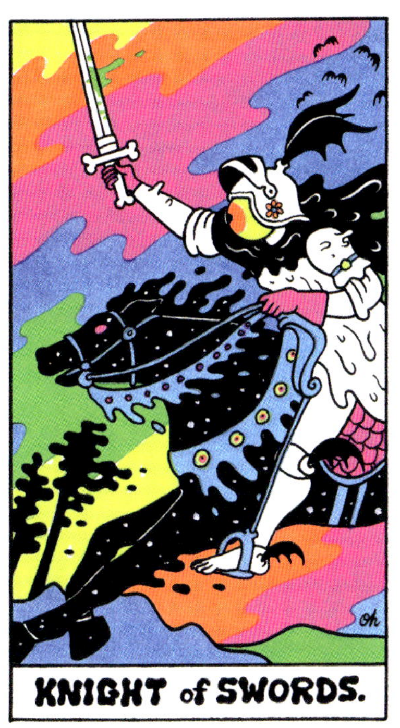
oh
KNIGHT of SWORDS.

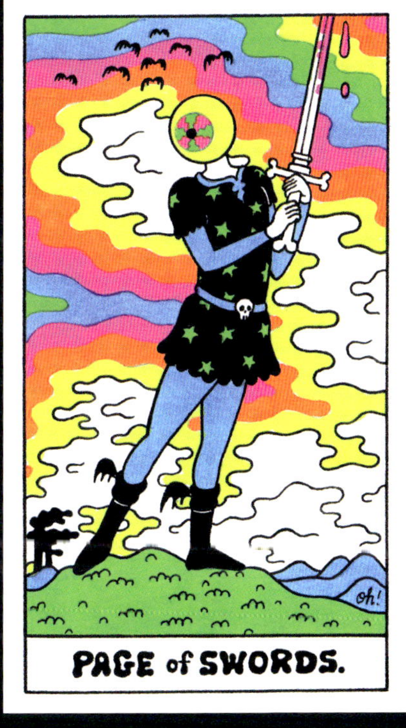
oh!
PAGE of SWORDS.

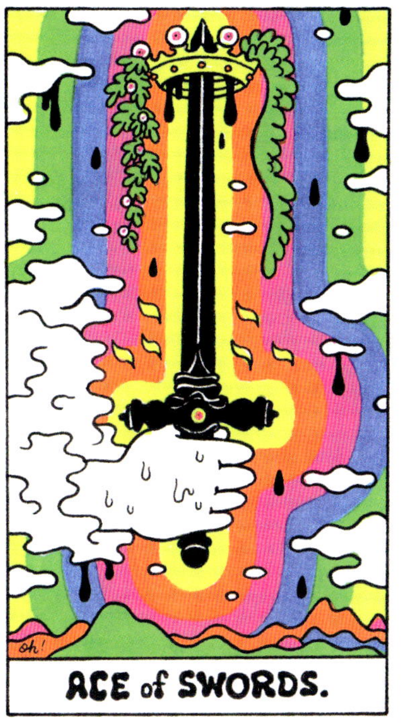
oh!
ACE of SWORDS.

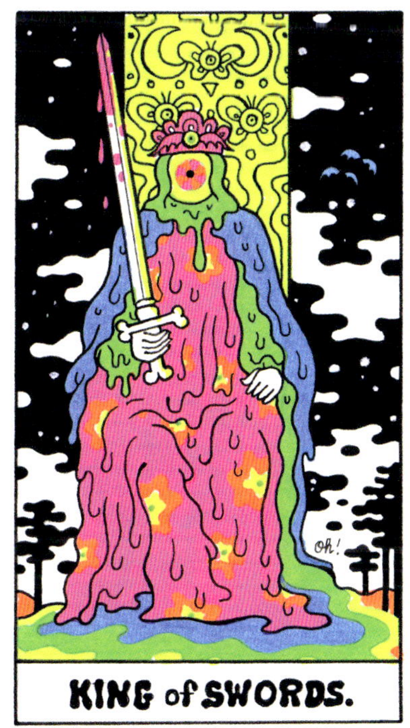
oh!
KING of SWORDS.

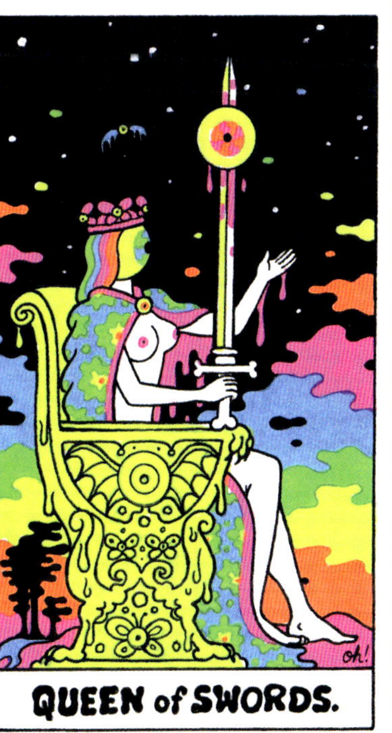
oh!
QUEEN of SWORDS.

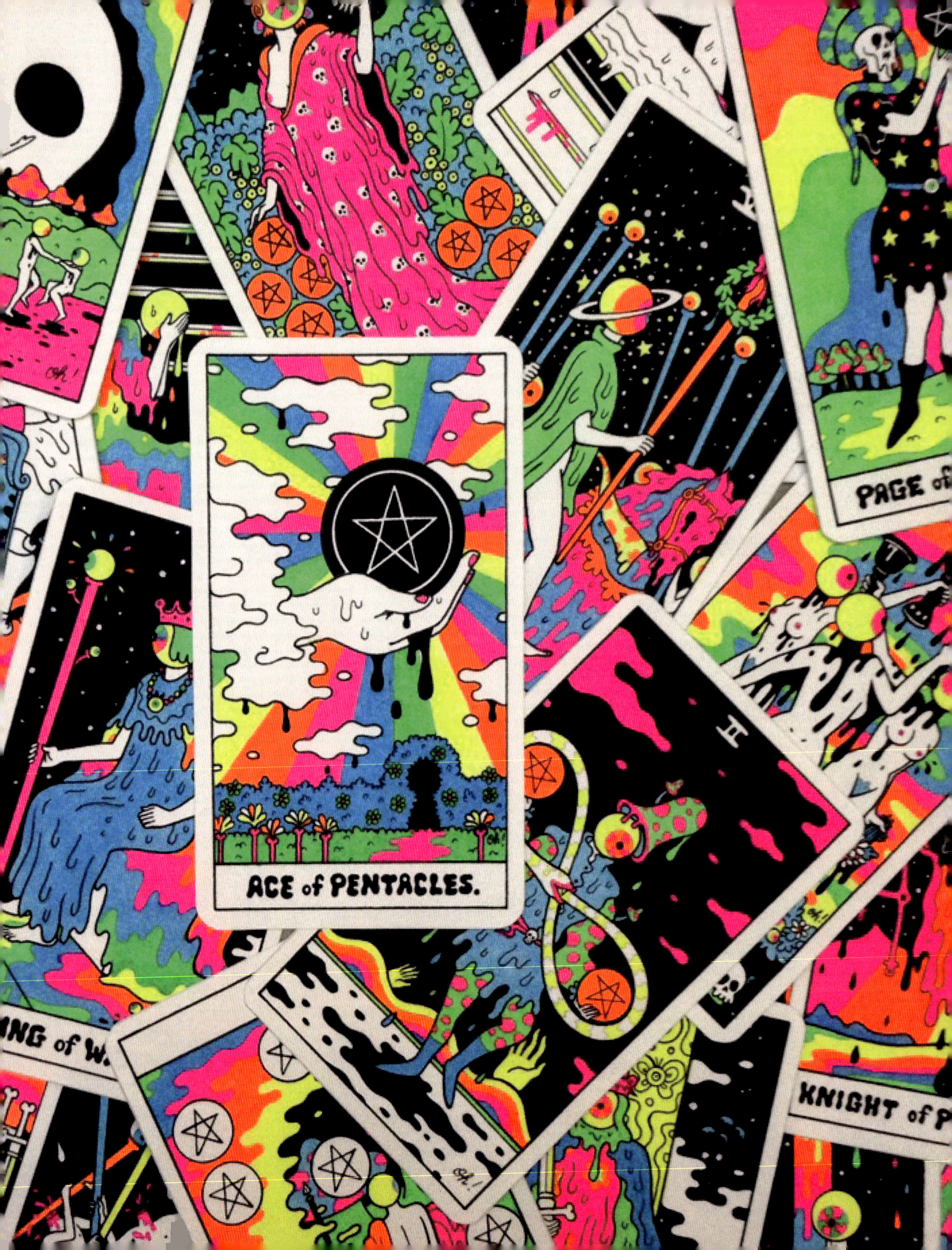
ACE of PENTACLES.
PAGE of
KNIGHT of

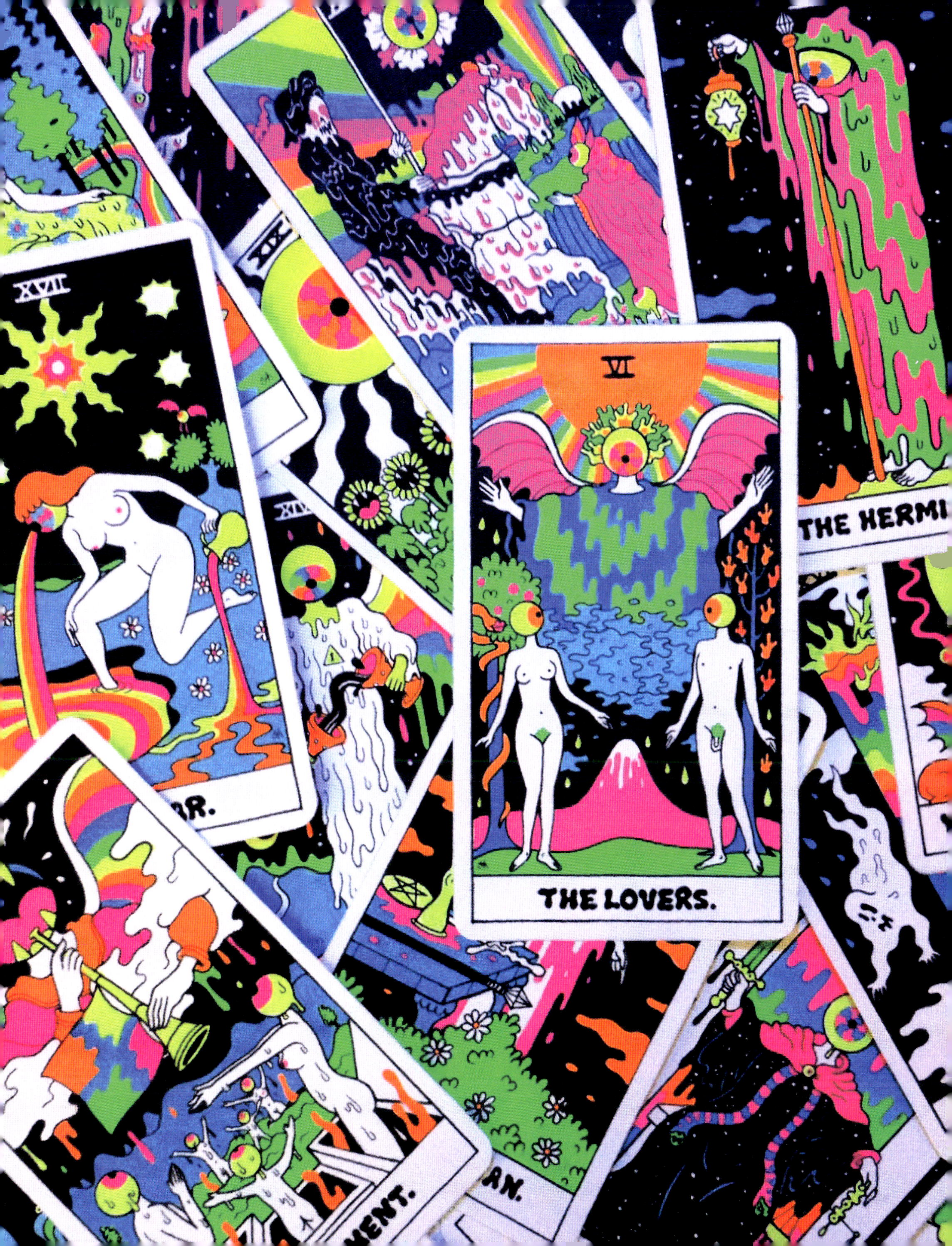
XVII
XIX
VI
THE LOVERS.
THE HERMI

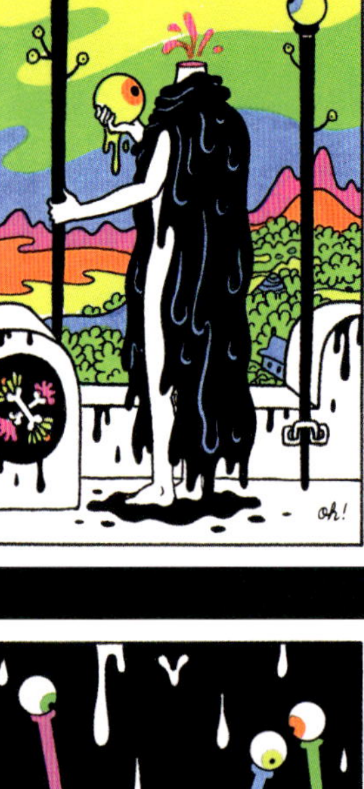
II
oh!

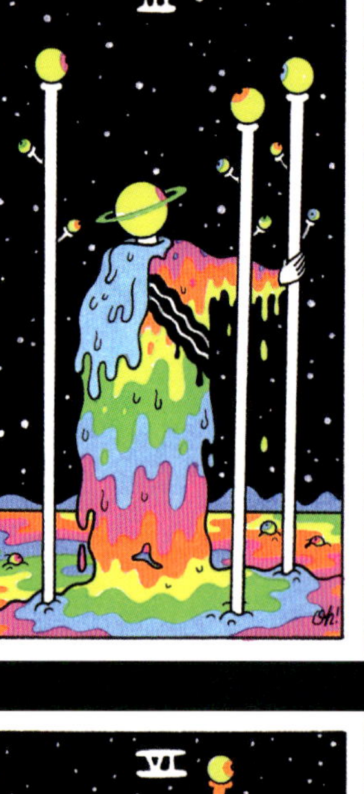
III
oh!

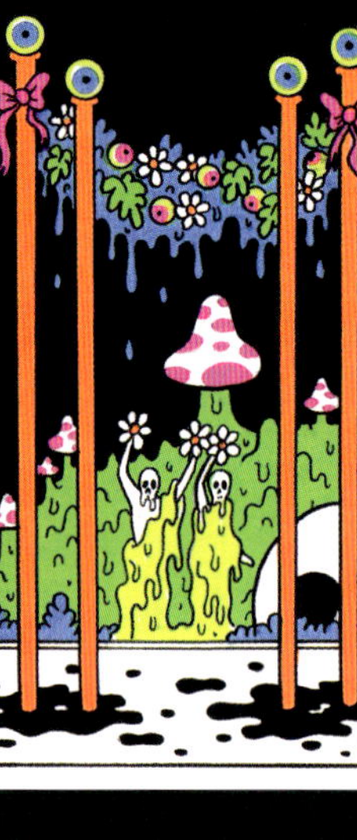
IV
oh!

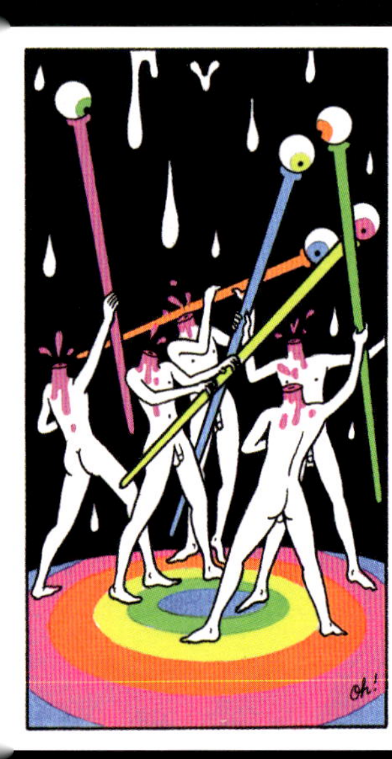
V
oh!

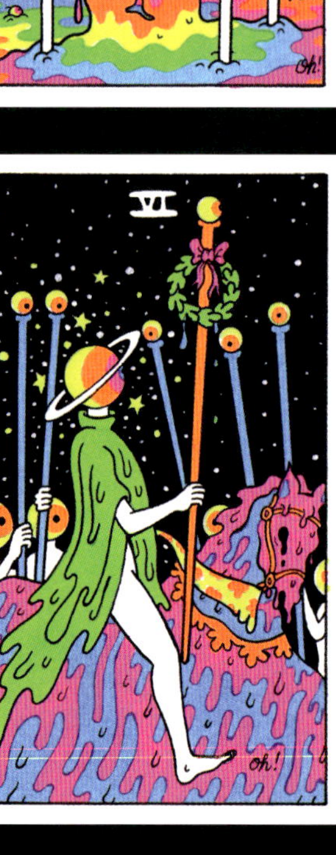
VI
oh!

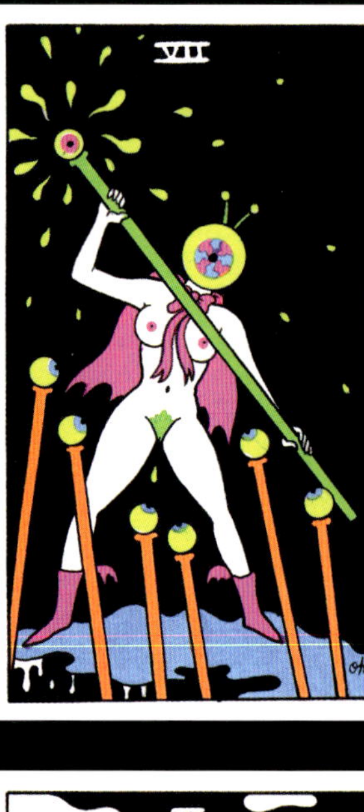
VII
oh!

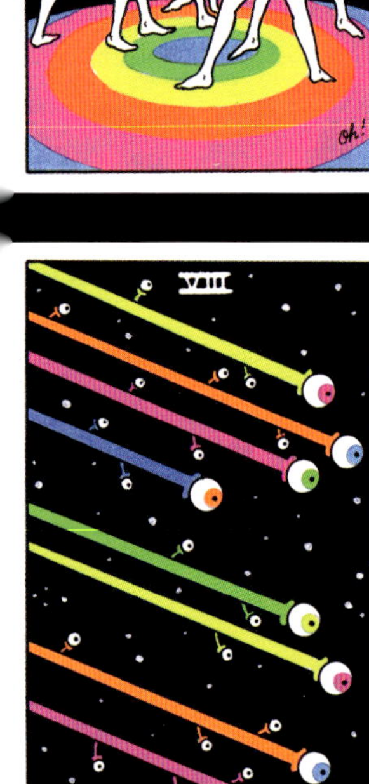
VIII
oh!

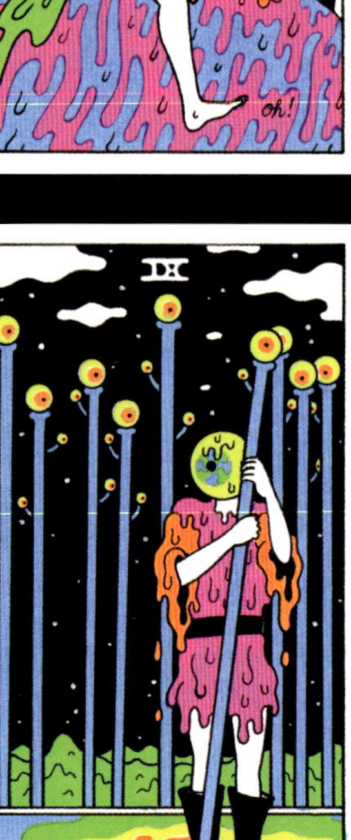
IX
oh!

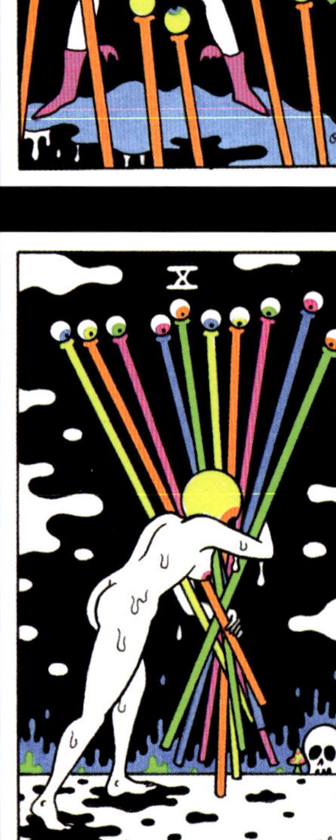
X
oh!

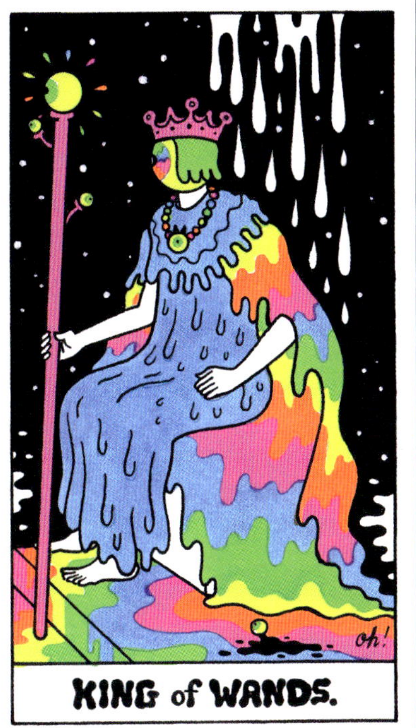
oh!
KING of WANDS.

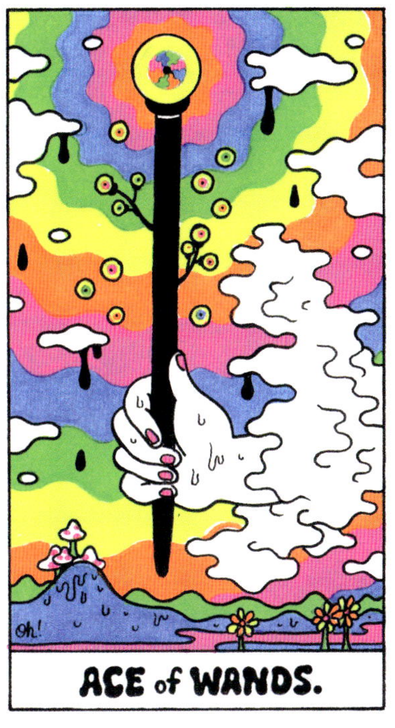
oh!
ACE of WANDS.

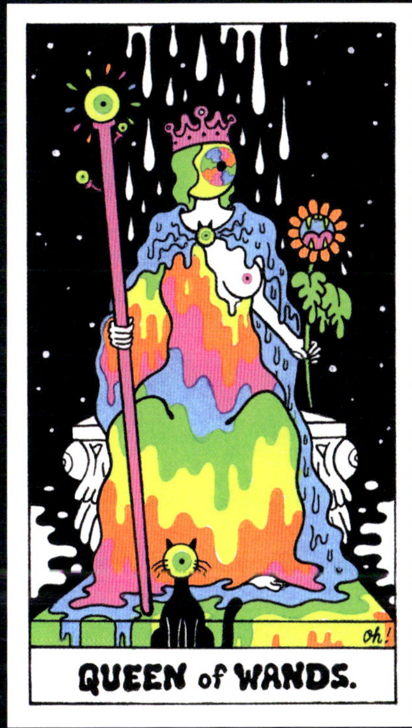
oh!
QUEEN of WANDS.

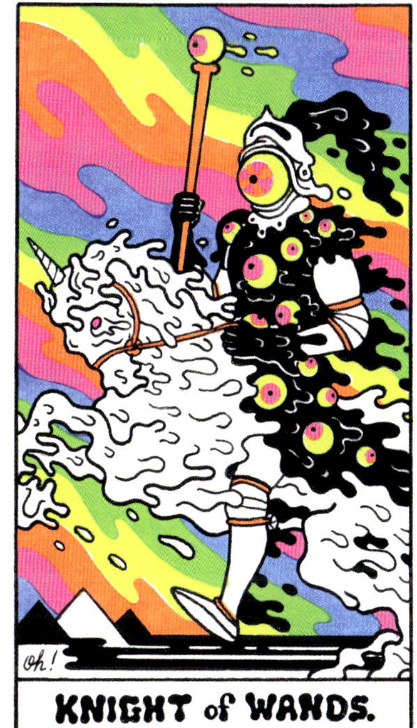
oh!
KNIGHT of WANDS.

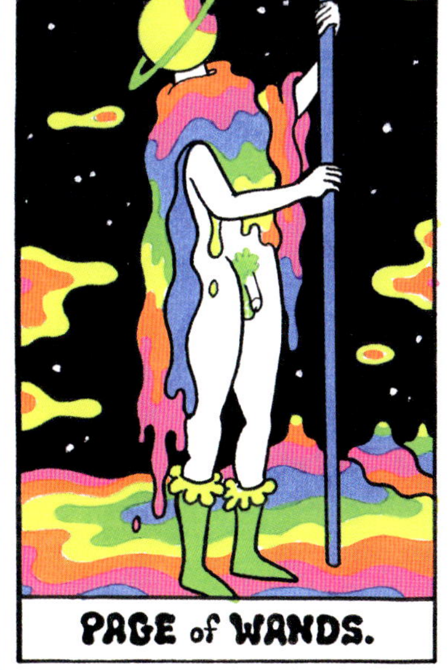
PAGE of WANDS.

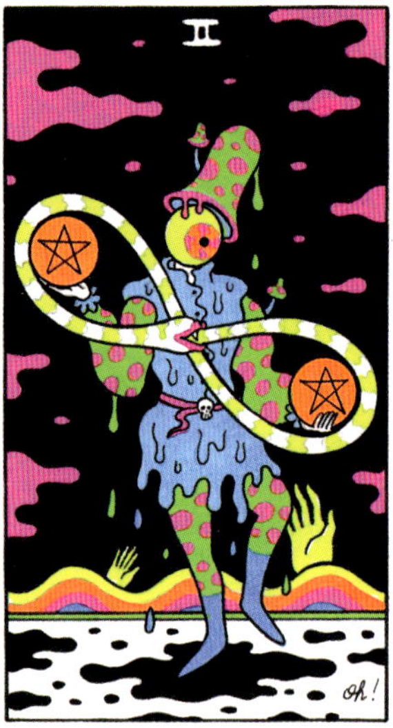

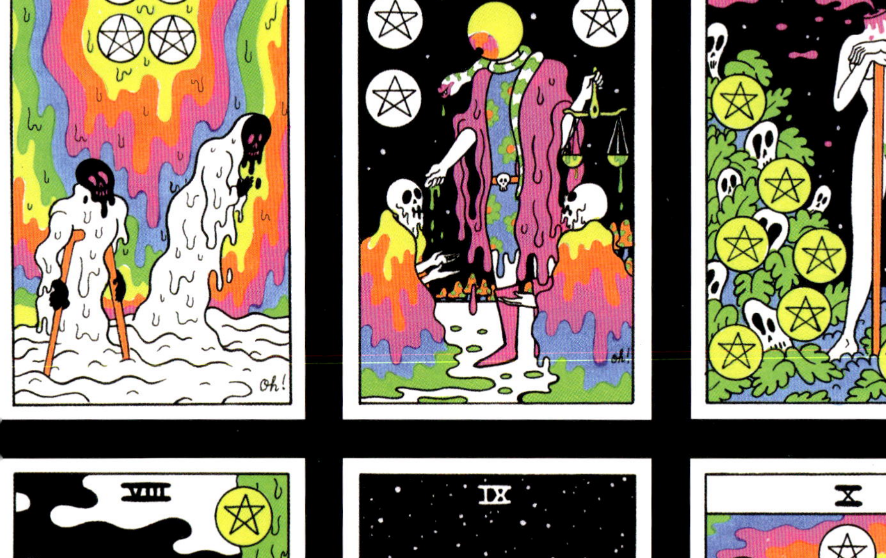
VI
VII
Oh!
Oh!
Oh!

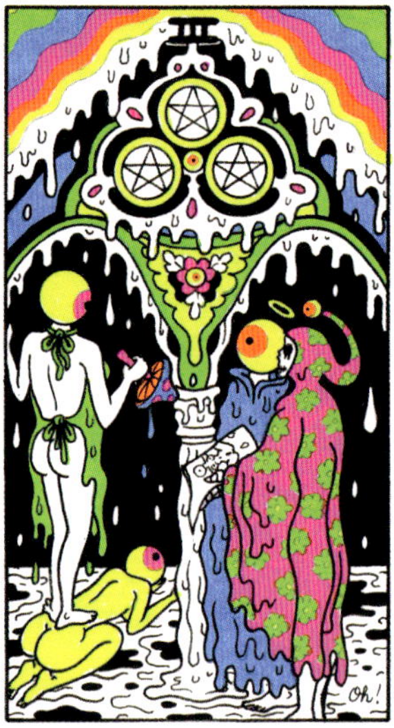

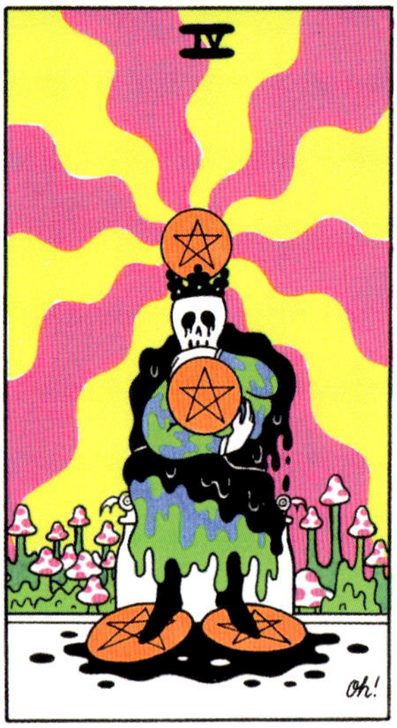

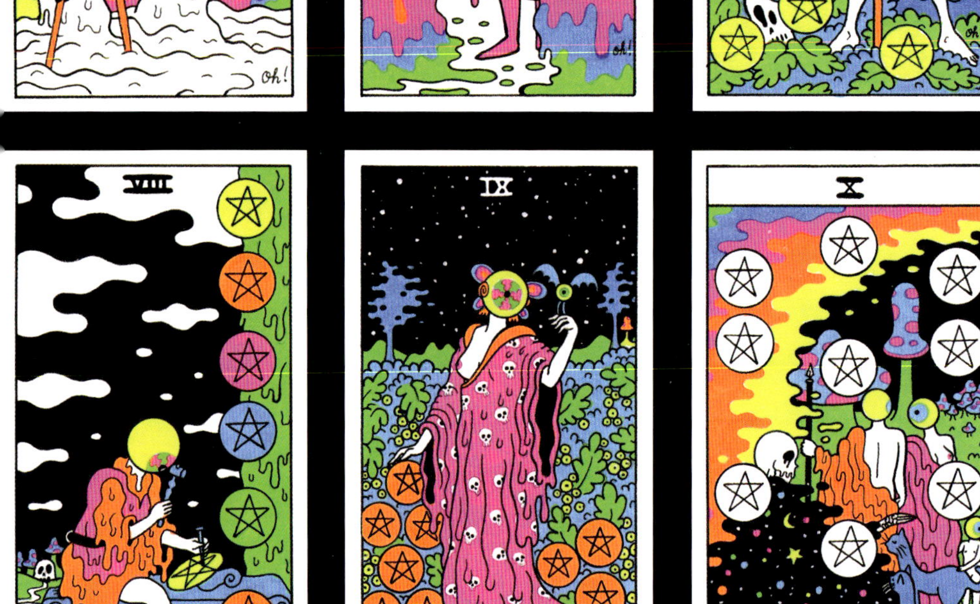
VIII
IX
X
Oh!
Oh!
Oh!

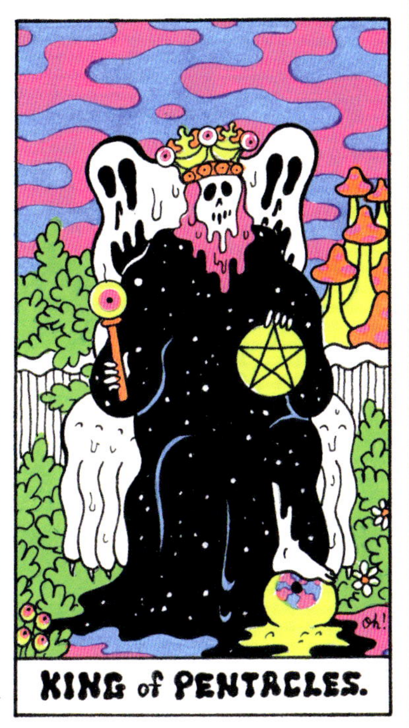
oh!
KING of PENTACLES.

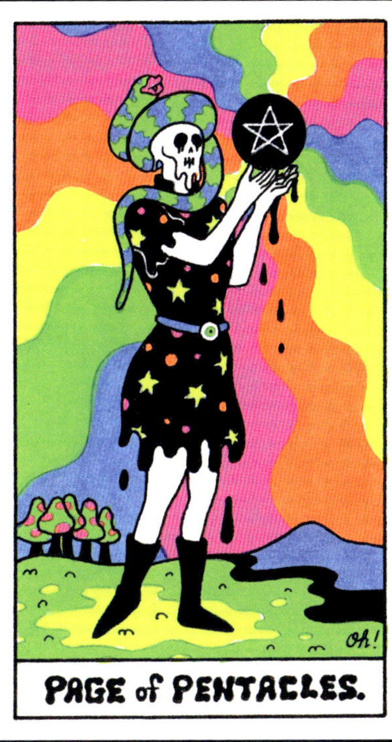
oh!
PAGE of PENTACLES.

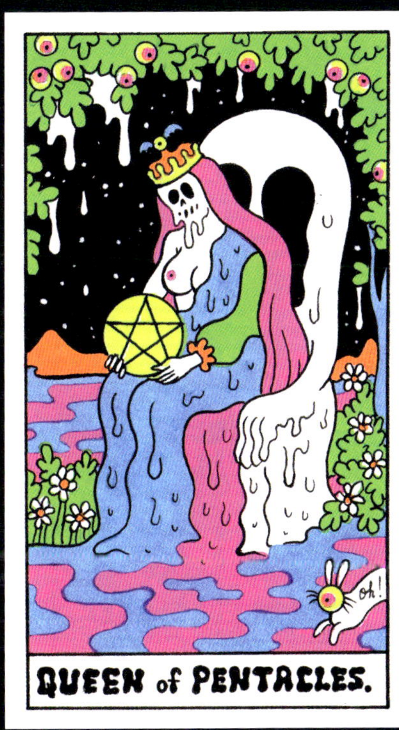
oh!
QUEEN of PENTACLES.

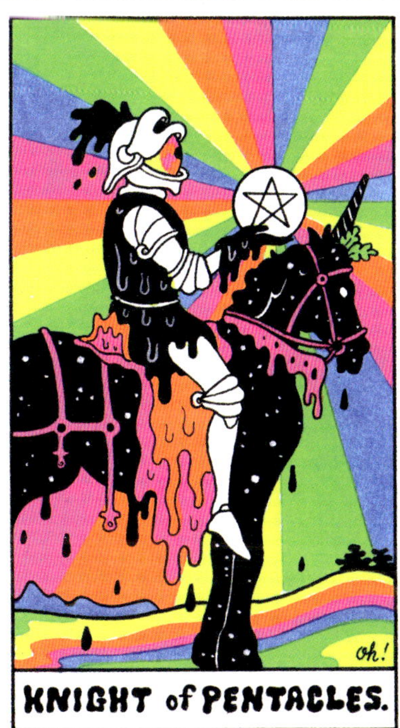
oh!
KNIGHT of PENTACLES.

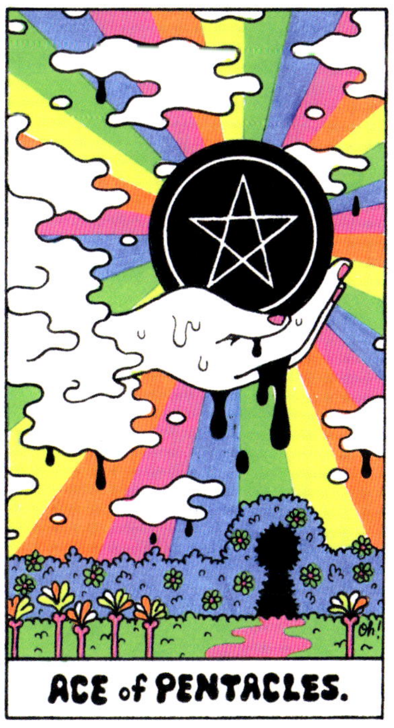
oh!
ACE of PENTACLES.

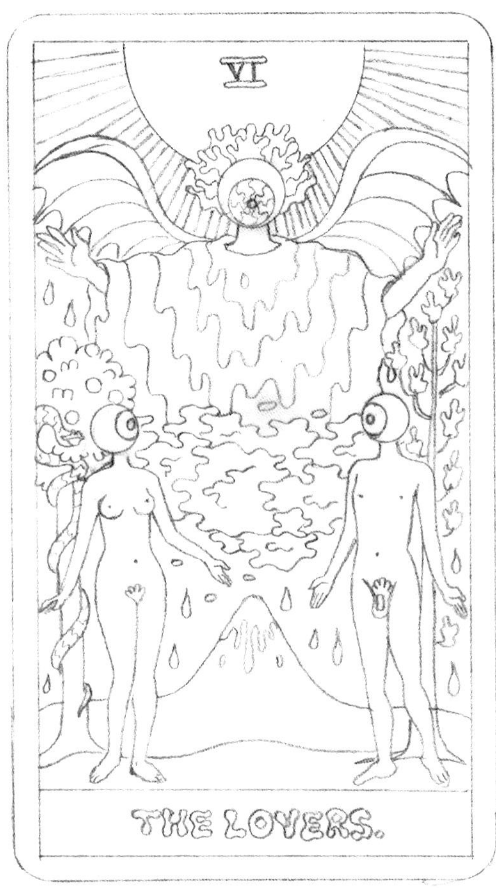

Preliminary sketch for "The Lovers"

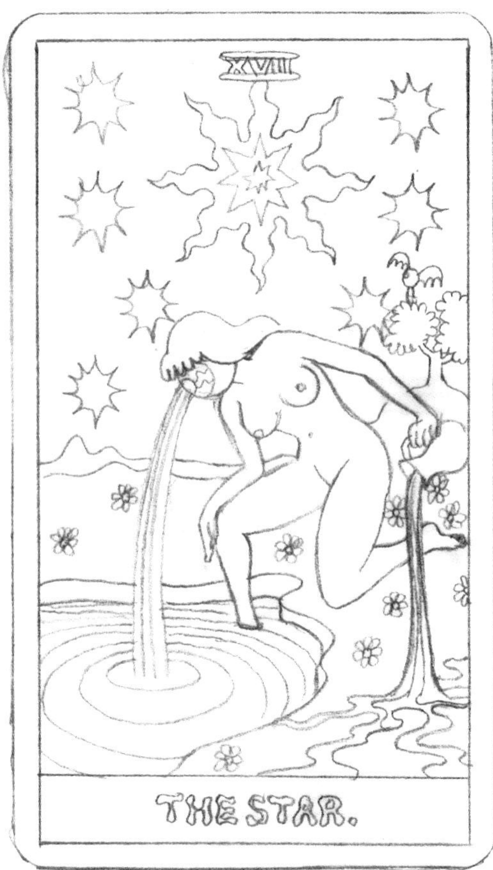

Preliminary sketch for "The Star"

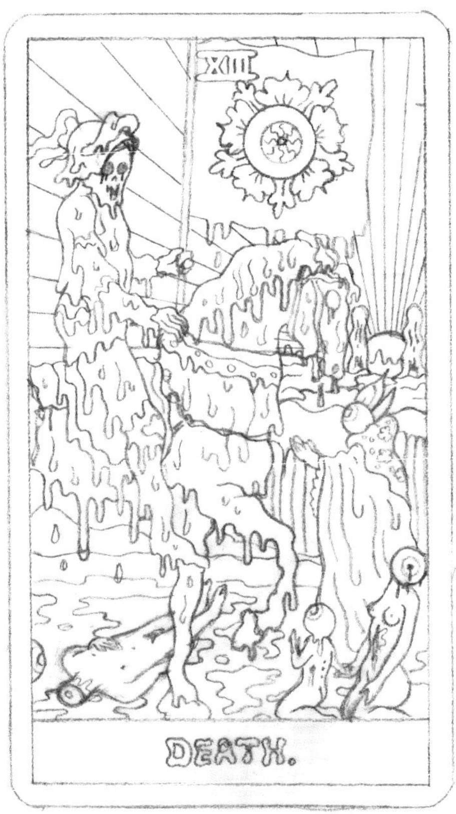

Preliminary sketch for "Death"

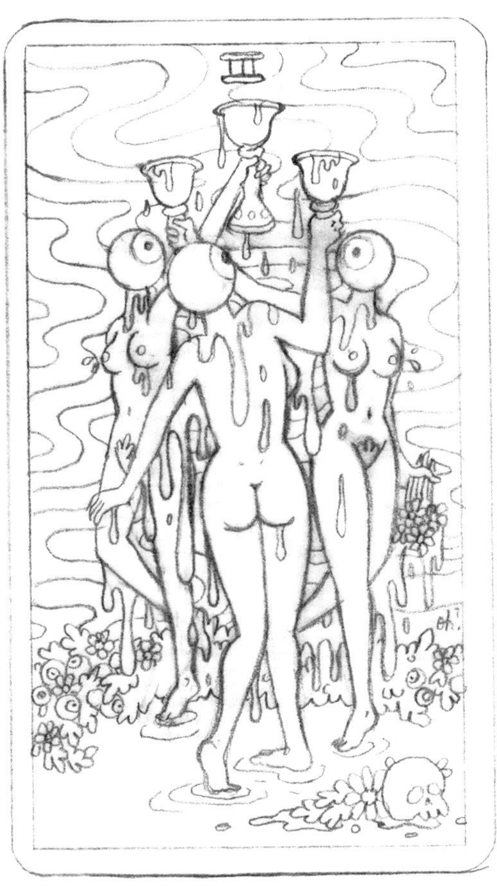

Preliminary sketch for "Three of Cups"

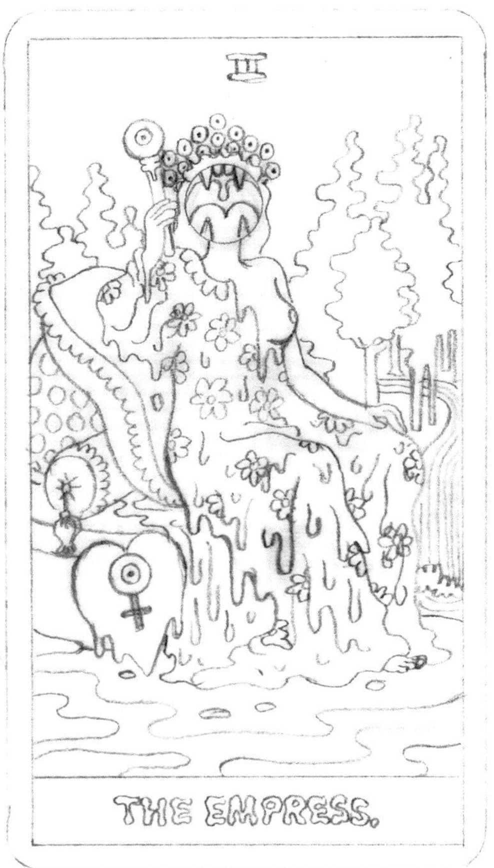

Preliminary sketch for "The Empress"

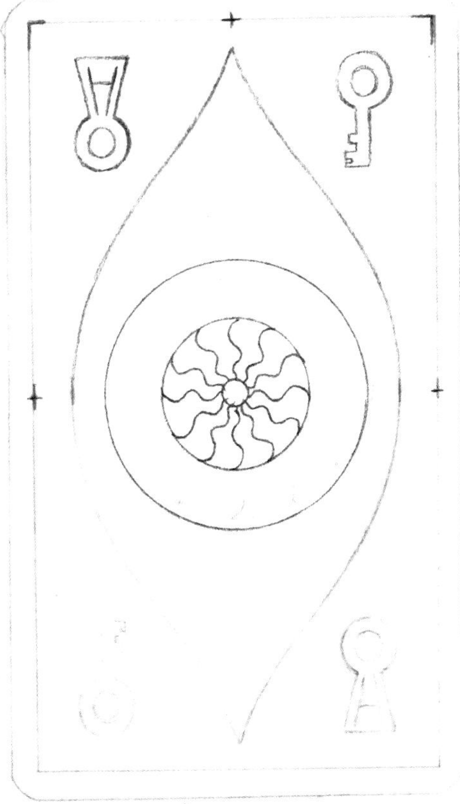
Preliminary sketch for card back

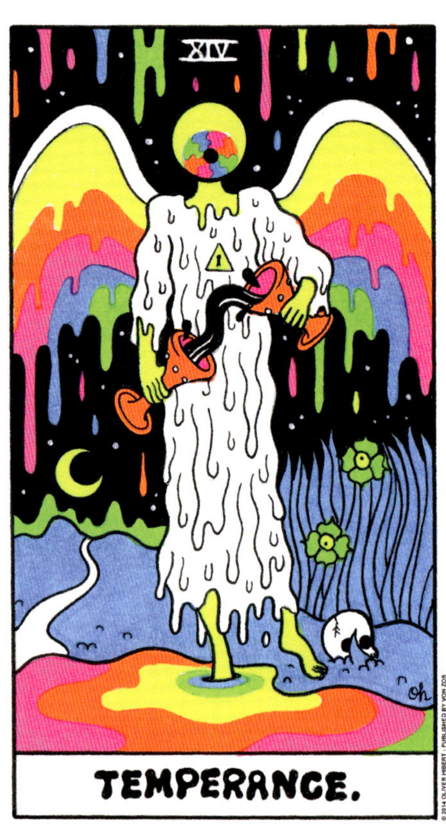
XIV
TEMPERANCE.
© 2014 OLIVER HIBERT · PUBLISHED BY VON ZOS

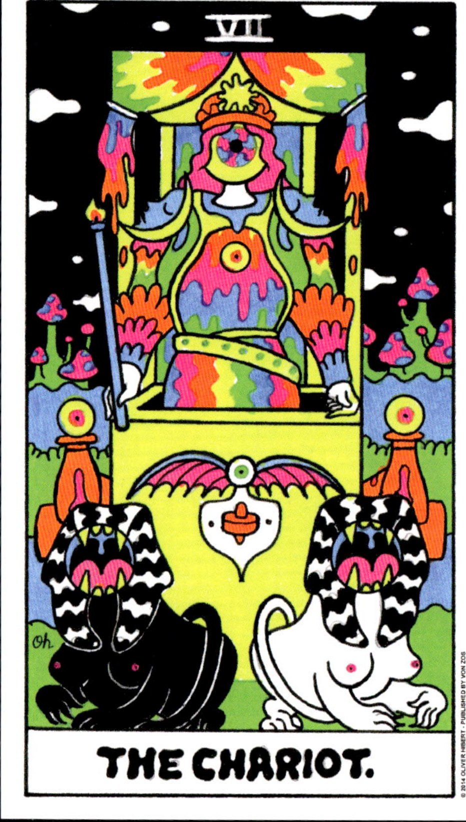
VII
THE CHARIOT.
© 2014 OLIVER HIBERT · PUBLISHED BY VON ZOS

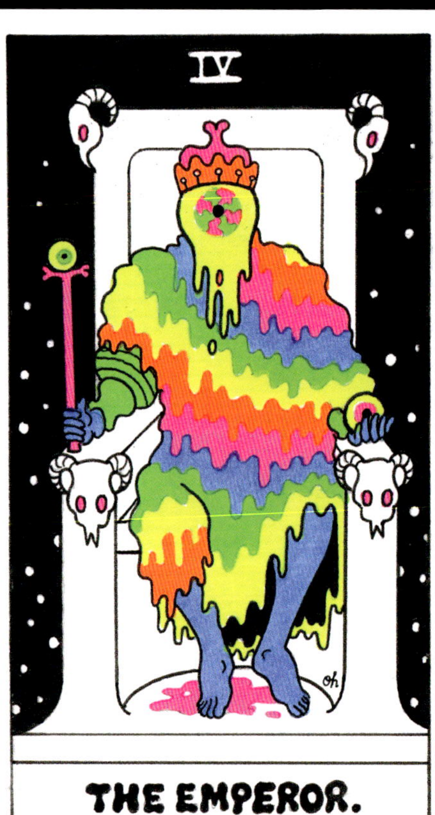
IV
THE EMPEROR.
© 2014 OLIVER HIBERT · PUBLISHED BY VON ZOS

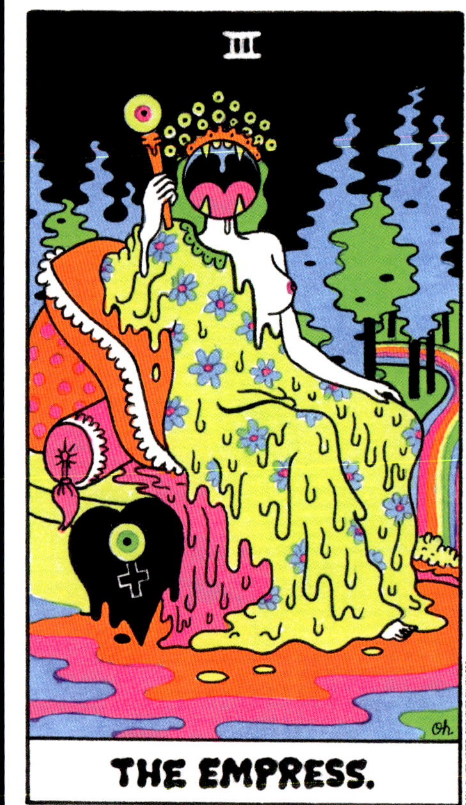
III
THE EMPRESS.
© 2014 OLIVER HIBERT · PUBLISHED BY VON ZOS

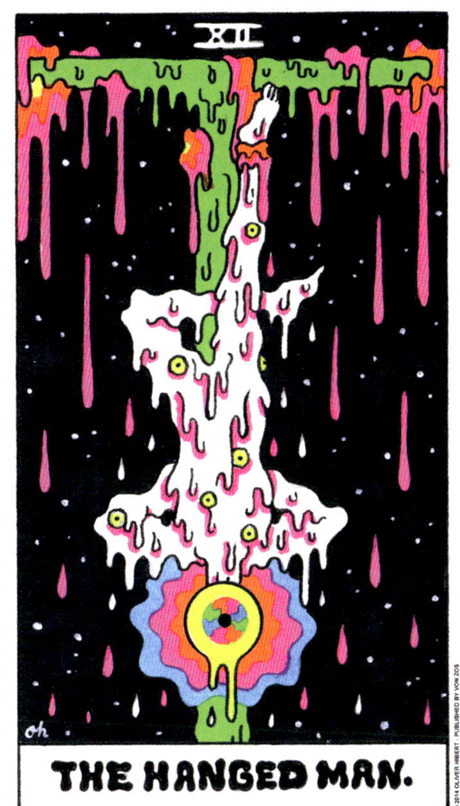
XII
THE HANGED MAN.
© 2014 OLIVER HIBERT · PUBLISHED BY VON ZOS

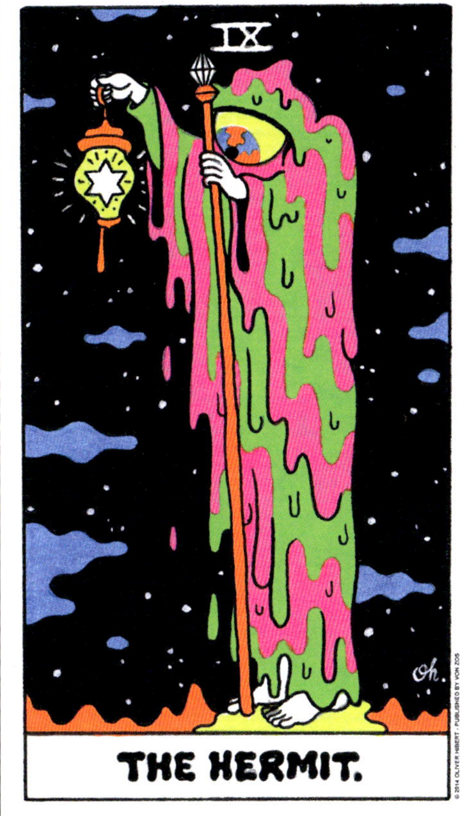
IX
THE HERMIT.
© 2014 OLIVER HIBERT · PUBLISHED BY VON ZOS

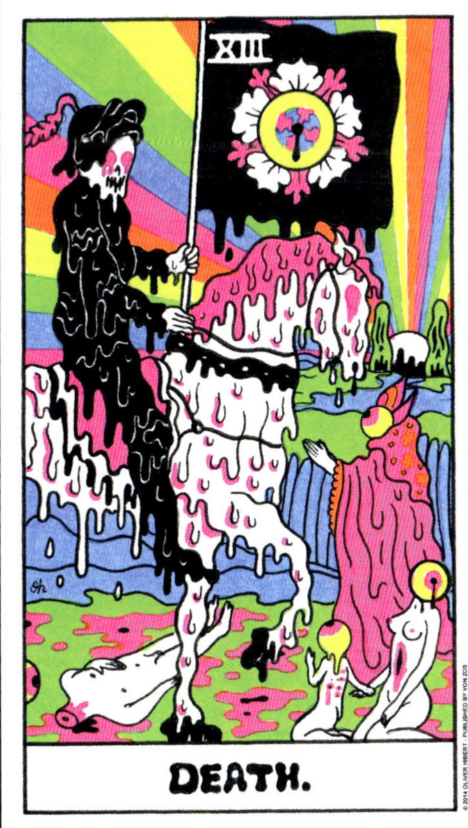
XIII
DEATH.
© 2014 OLIVER HIBERT · PUBLISHED BY VON ZOS

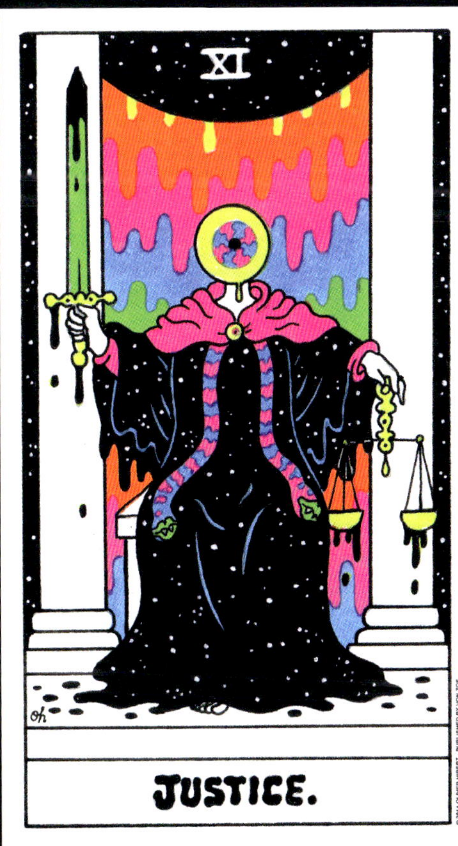
XI
JUSTICE.
© 2014 OLIVER HIBERT · PUBLISHED BY VON ZOS

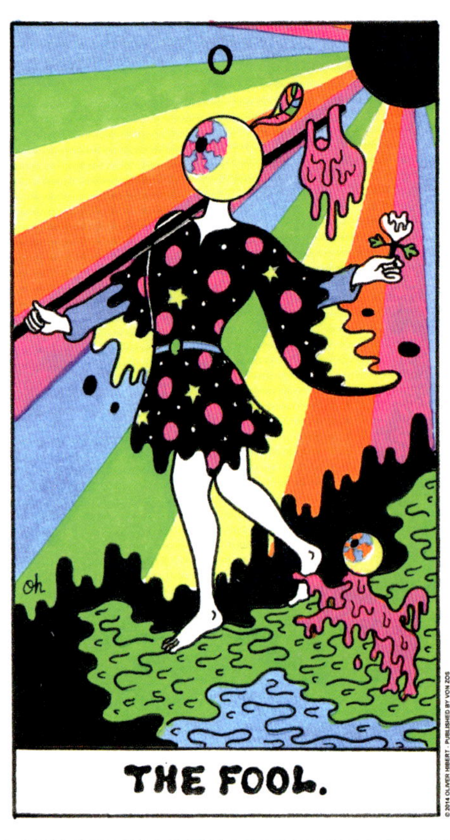
0
oh
THE FOOL.
© 2014 OLIVER HIBERT · PUBLISHED BY VON ZOS

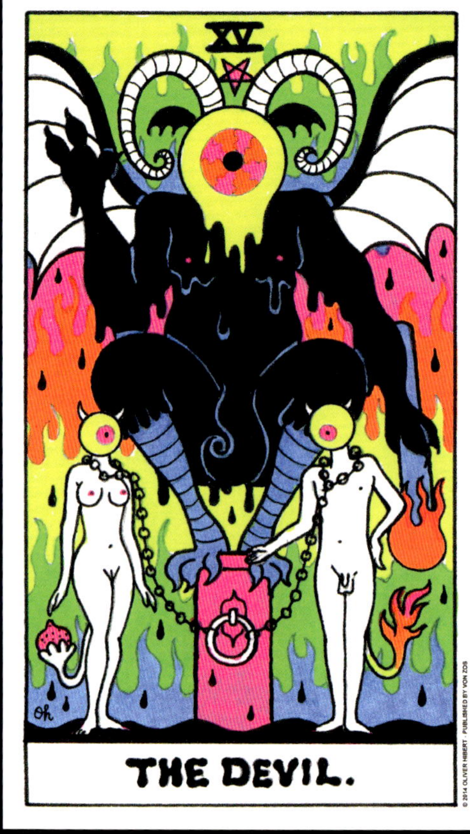
XV
oh
THE DEVIL.
© 2014 OLIVER HIBERT · PUBLISHED BY VON ZOS

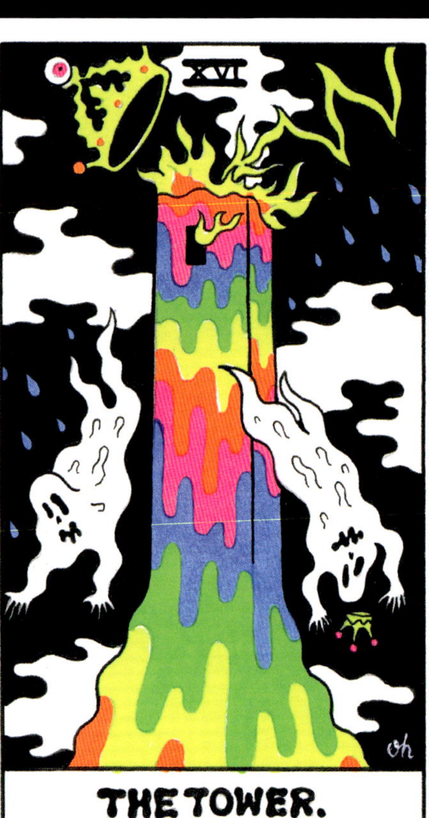
XVI
oh
THE TOWER.
© 2014 OLIVER HIBERT · PUBLISHED BY VON ZOS

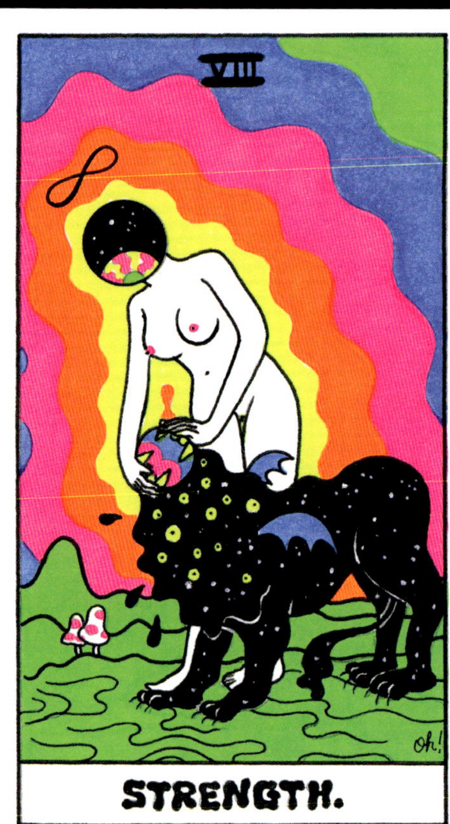
VIII
oh!
STRENGTH.
© 2014 OLIVER HIBERT · PUBLISHED BY VON ZOS

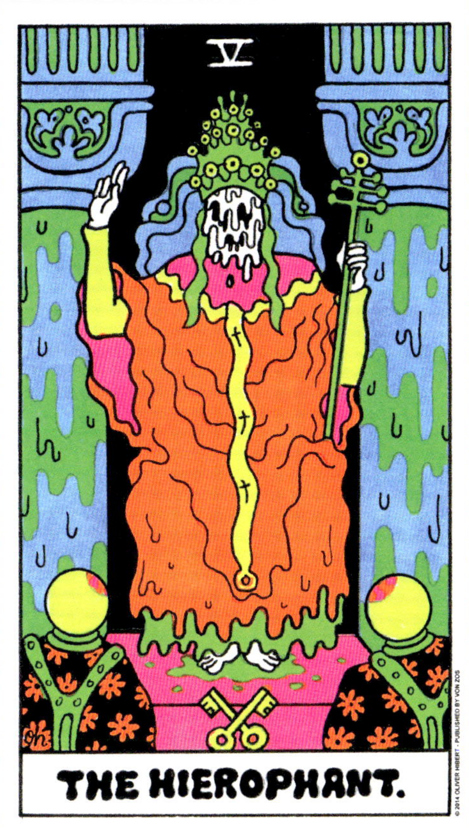
V
THE HIEROPHANT.
© 2014 OLIVER HIBERT · PUBLISHED BY VON ZOS

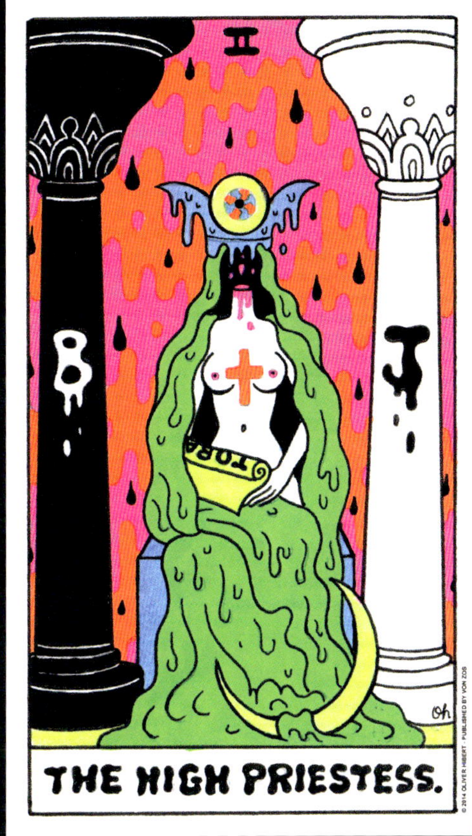
II
B
J
TORA
THE HIGH PRIESTESS.
© 2014 OLIVER HIBERT · PUBLISHED BY VON ZOS

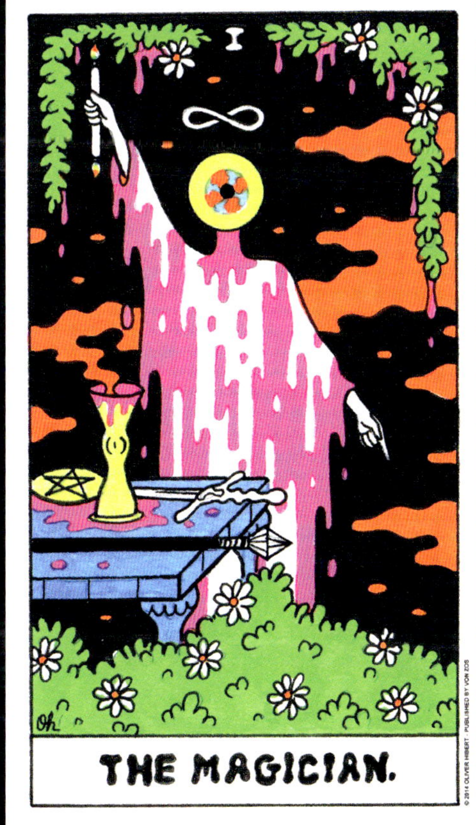
I
THE MAGICIAN.
© 2014 OLIVER HIBERT · PUBLISHED BY VON ZOS

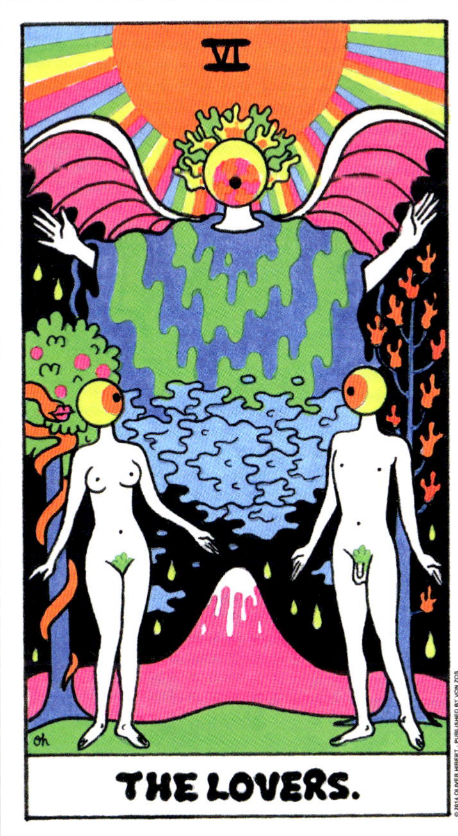
VI
THE LOVERS.
© 2014 OLIVER HIBERT · PUBLISHED BY VON ZOS

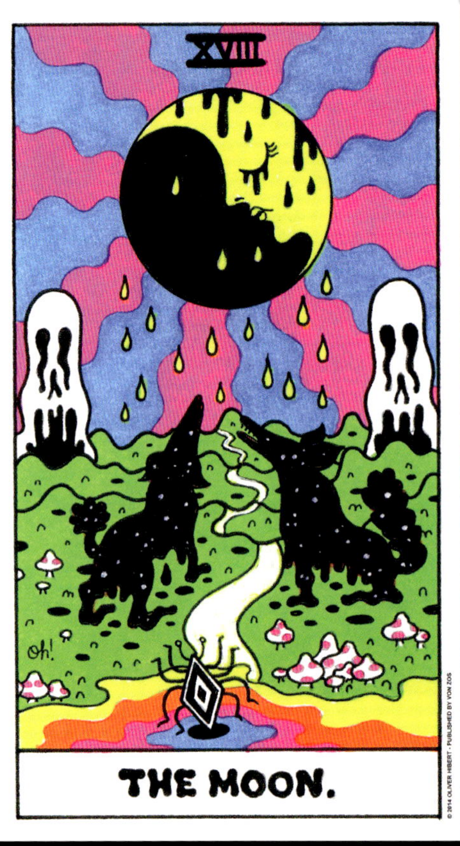
XVIII
oh!
THE MOON.
© 2014 OLIVER HIBERT · PUBLISHED BY VON ZOS

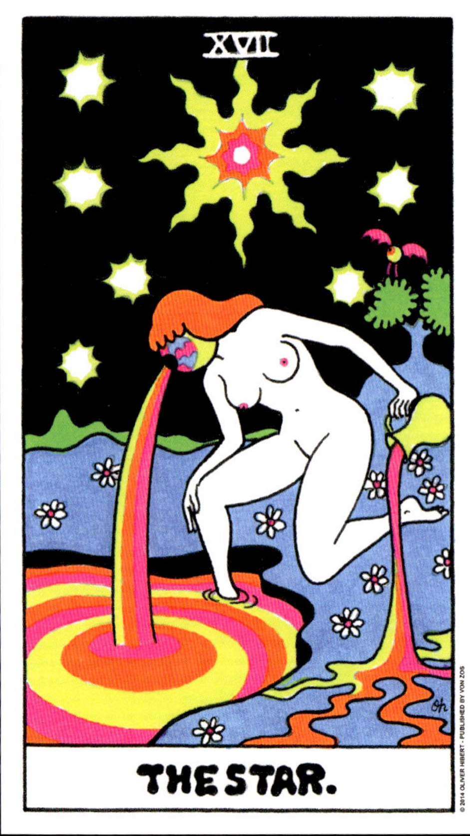
XVII
oh
THE STAR.
© 2014 OLIVER HIBERT · PUBLISHED BY VON ZOS

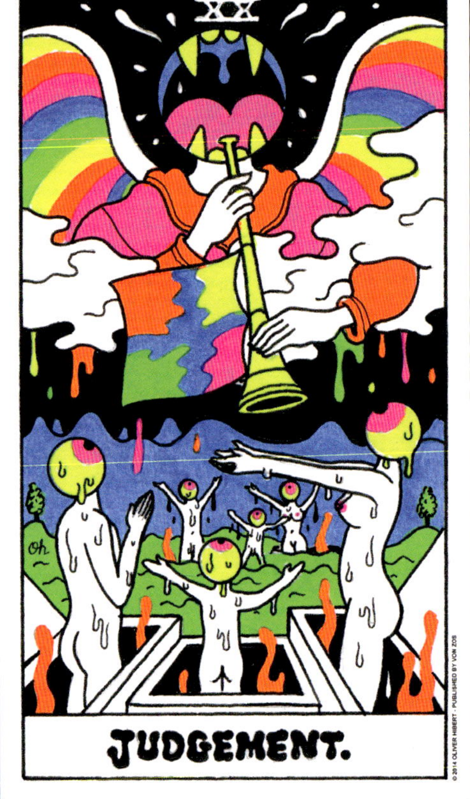
XX
oh.
JUDGEMENT.
© 2014 OLIVER HIBERT · PUBLISHED BY VON ZOS

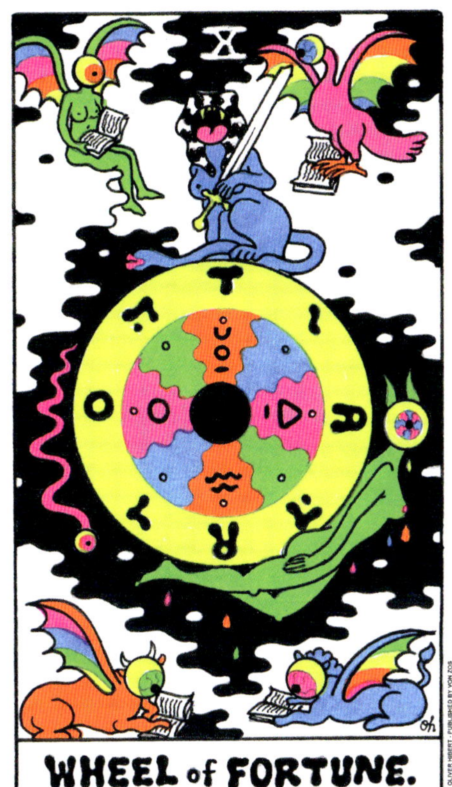
X
WHEEL of FORTUNE.
© 2014 OLIVER HIBERT · PUBLISHED BY VON ZOS

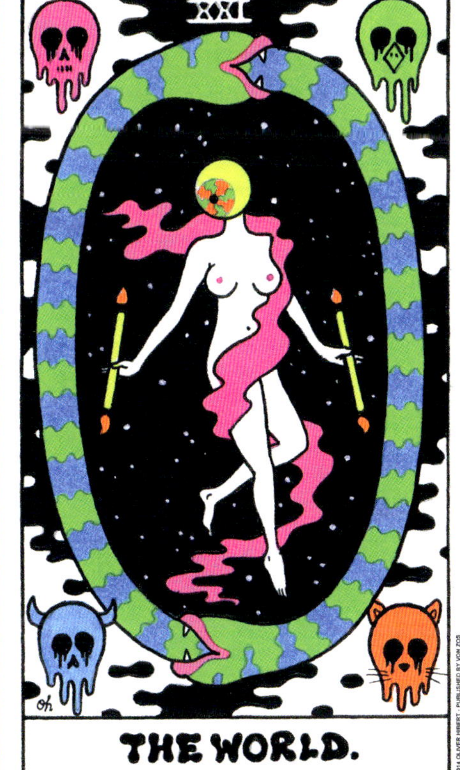
XXI
THE WORLD.
© 2014 OLIVER HIBERT · PUBLISHED BY VON ZOS

Chapter Five:

Graphic Design

For many artists, graphic design can be seen as, at best, a means to an end and, at worst, an unacceptable sacrifice. Yet, for other artists, even when creating for an employer, the challenge is invigorating, and the outcome often still feels like their studio work. Consider Robert Rauschenberg's album cover for The Talking Heads' *Speaking In Tongues*, Richard Prince's "Lemon Fizz" drink for Arizona Beverage Company, or Barry McGee and Margaret Kilgallen's skate deck creations for HUF and Toy Machine. Each product was a success in that it contained the look of the artist's work (as was intended) and not simply a faceless task for a generic product.

Post-Warhol, the concept of artist-as-brand has essentially negated the cries of "sellout," even though one may take favor or umbrage with any of the more notable artist/brands going, be they Jeff Koons, Damien Hirst, Shepard Fairey, Murakami, or KAWS. Whatever side of the fence you may personally fall on, what is undeniable is the ability they all have to consistently recreate the look of their studio art, be it on t-shirts, designer toys, or home décor, while also meeting the approval of their clients.

This same attitude exists in Oliver's commercial work —there's the overwhelmingly obvious symbiotic nature of his album and apparel design for The Flaming Lips, of course—but even when attacking something seemingly unconventional like a pair of sneakers or a snowboard, the result is overwhelmingly Oliver every time. Oftentimes the parameters of a commercial assignment can prove to be a stimulating challenge, leading to new ideas or practices that can in turn inform one's own studio work. Oliver's textile designs for scarves provide lessons about symmetry as well as working with fabric. Creating skate decks offers the challenge of making a legible design and having it fit aesthetically alongside the hardware of skateboard trucks and wheels. And lastly, anytime you can land the opportunity to create anything for a band as legendary as The Zombies, well, that's just about as good as it gets.

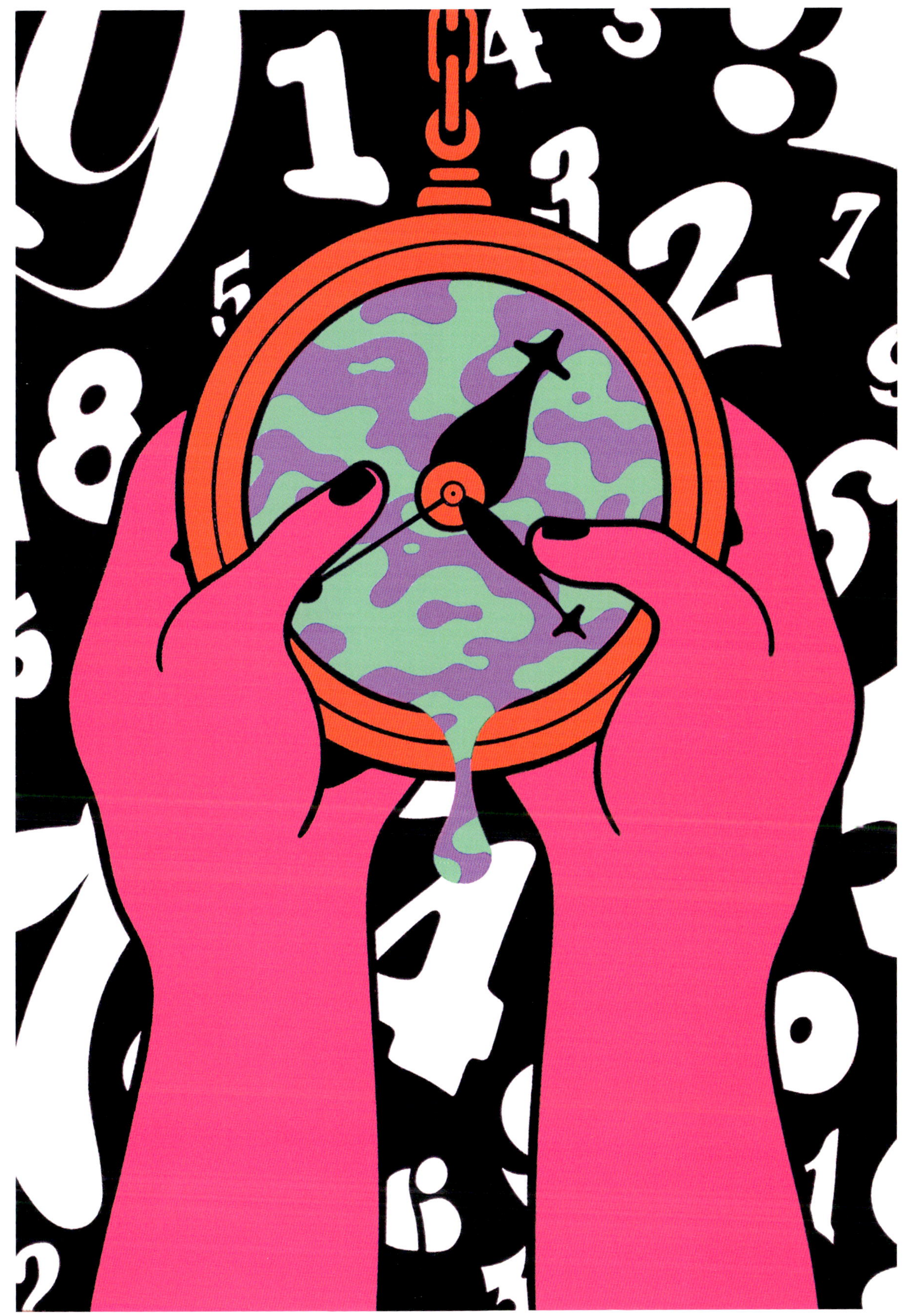

Tic Tic Tic

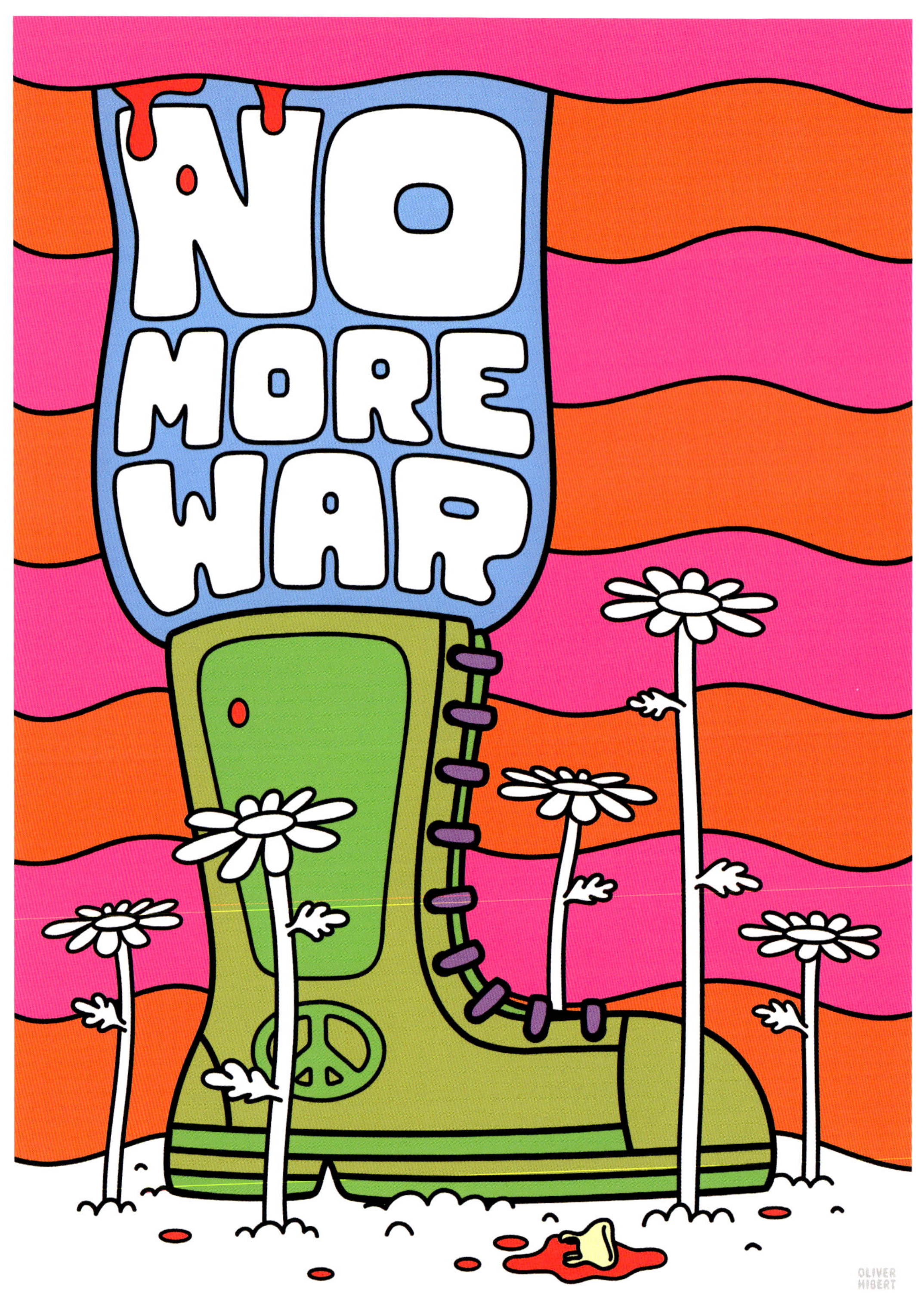

"These are from a series of self-made posters during the whole going to war with Iraq/Afghanistan bullshit. I don't often try to acknowledge the horrible things that go on in this world sometimes, even through my art. Sometimes you can't really control it or avoid it, and you just have to speak up. I might as well keep this series going now that I think about it, because I don't think the wars will ever end."

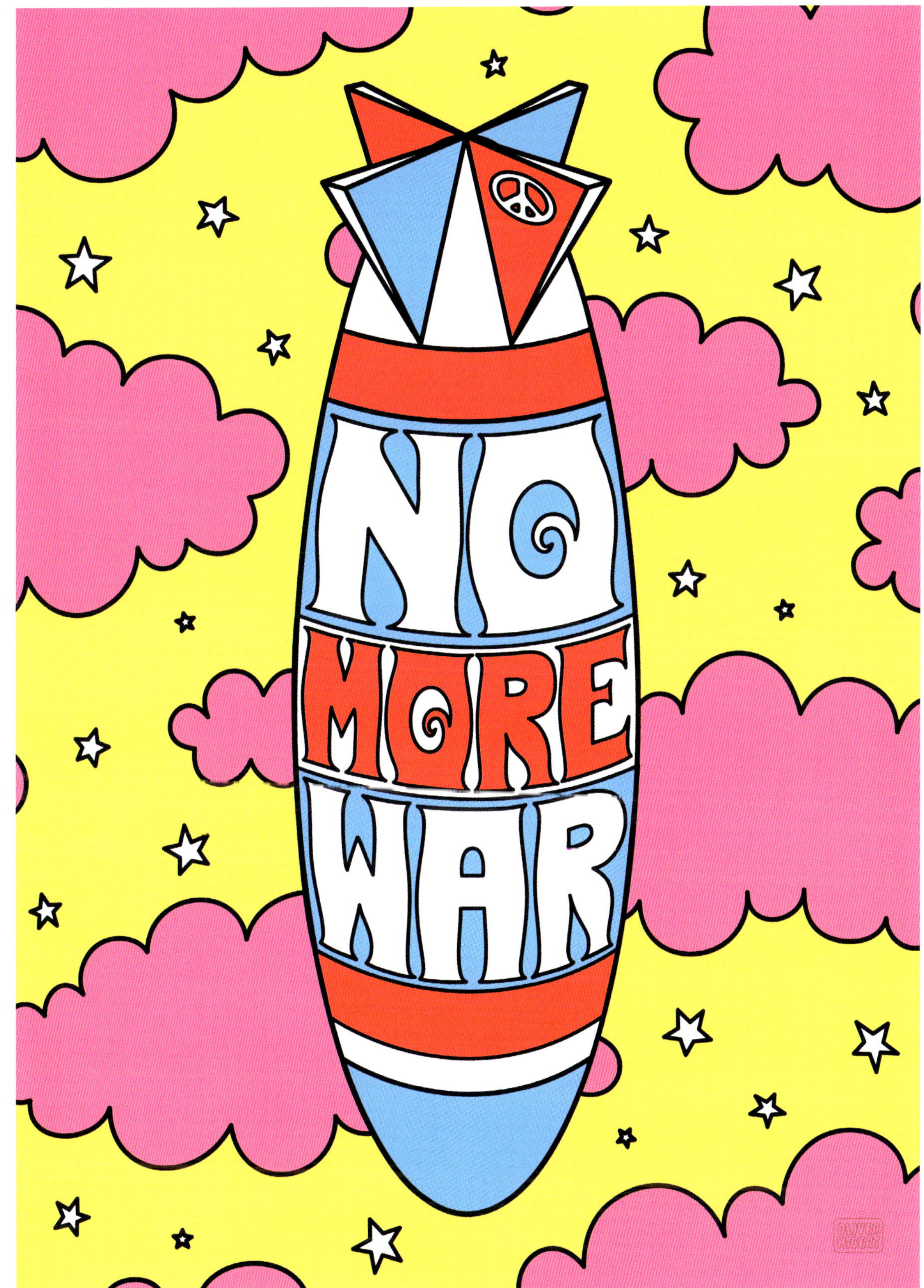
NO
MORE
WAR

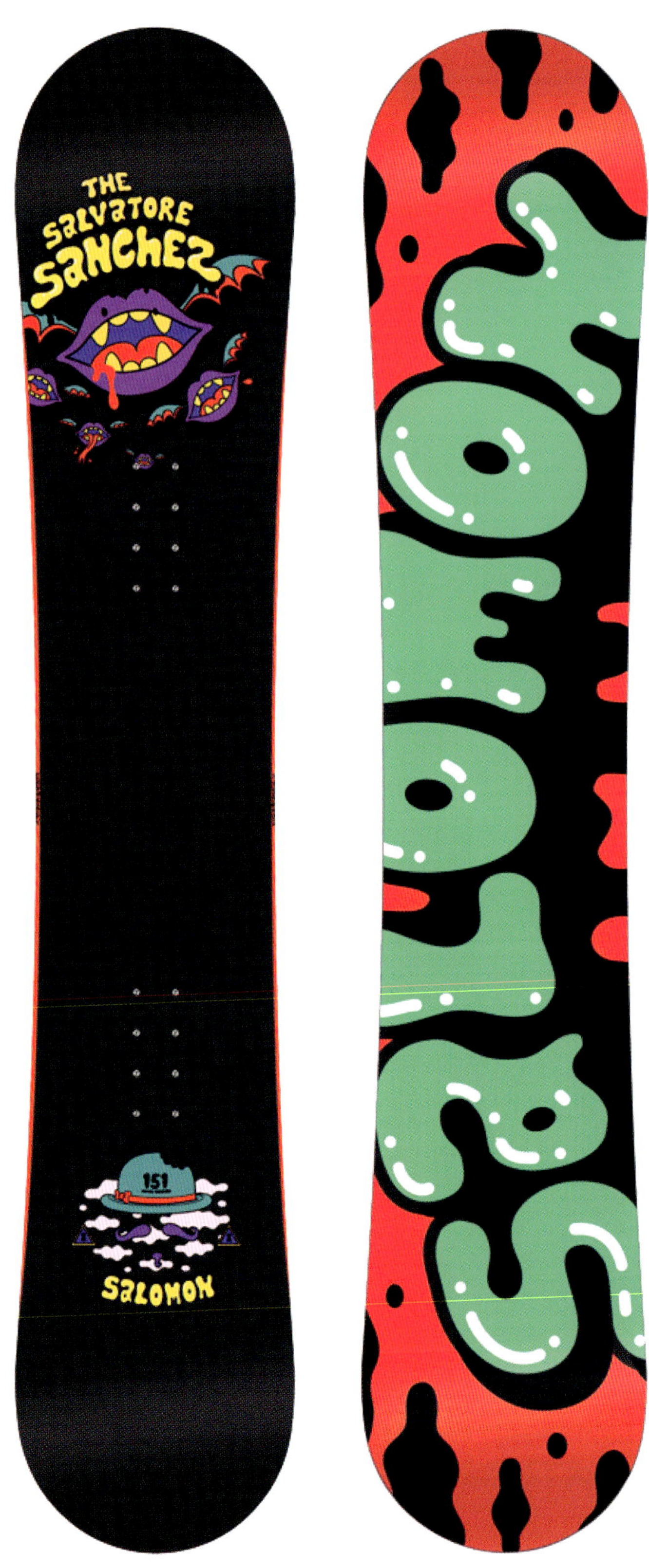

"A fun little fancy series of board graphics I did for Salomon Snowboards."

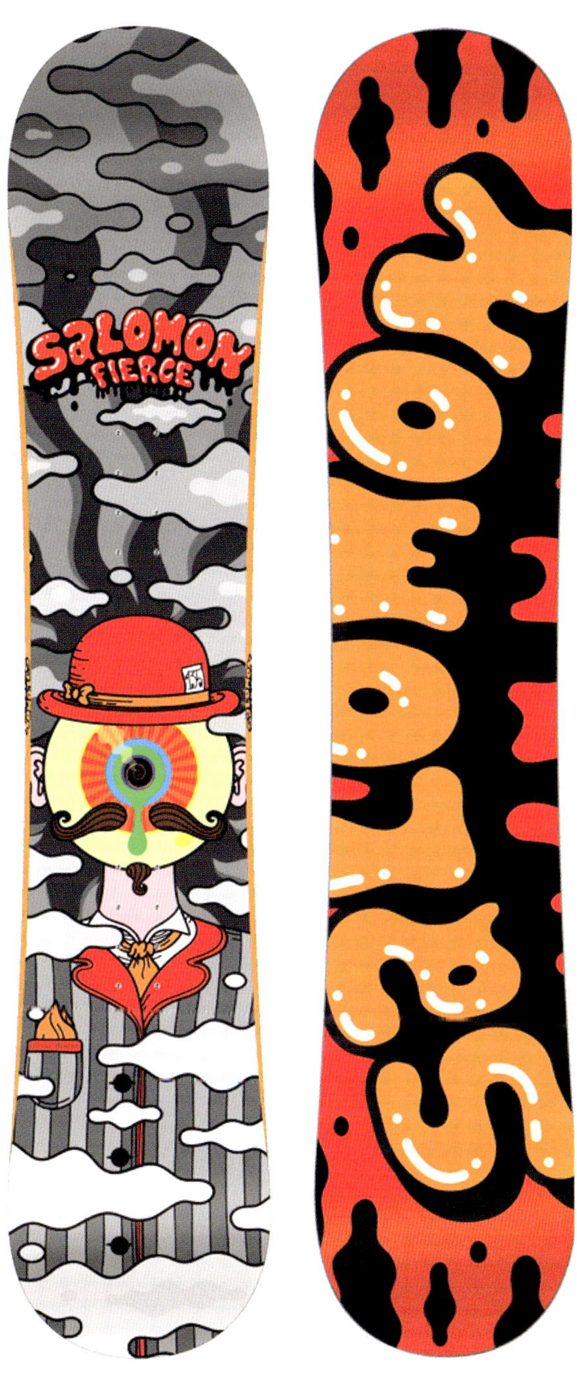
SALOMON
FIERCE
SALOMON

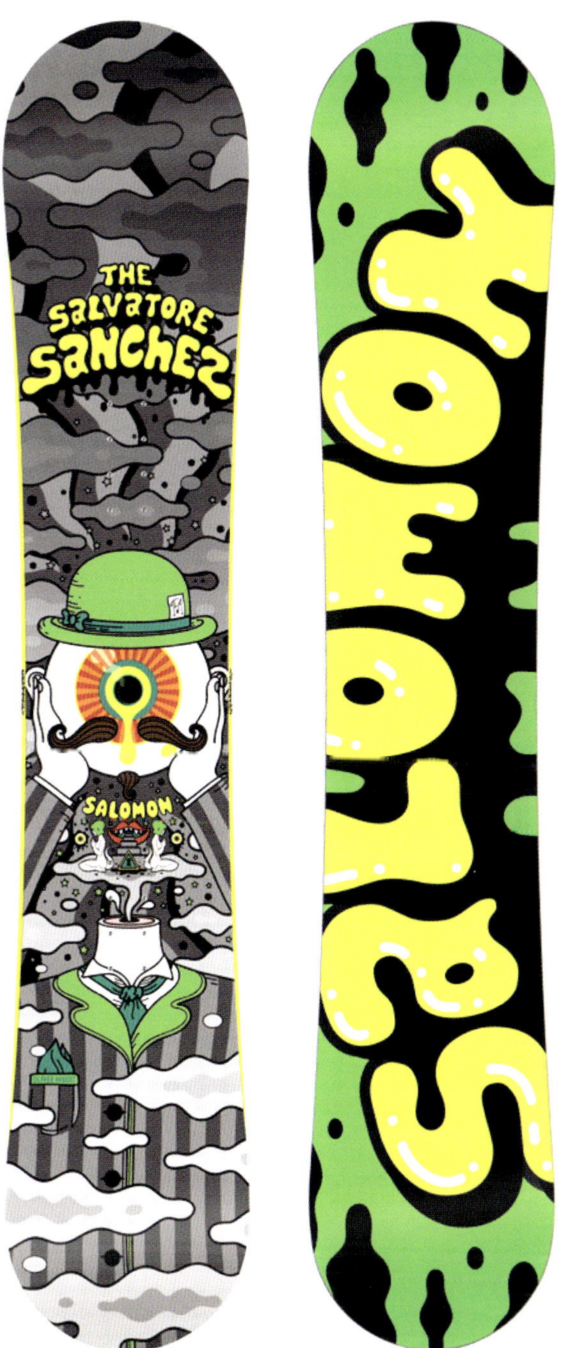
THE
SALVATORE
SANCHEZ
SALOMON
SALOMON

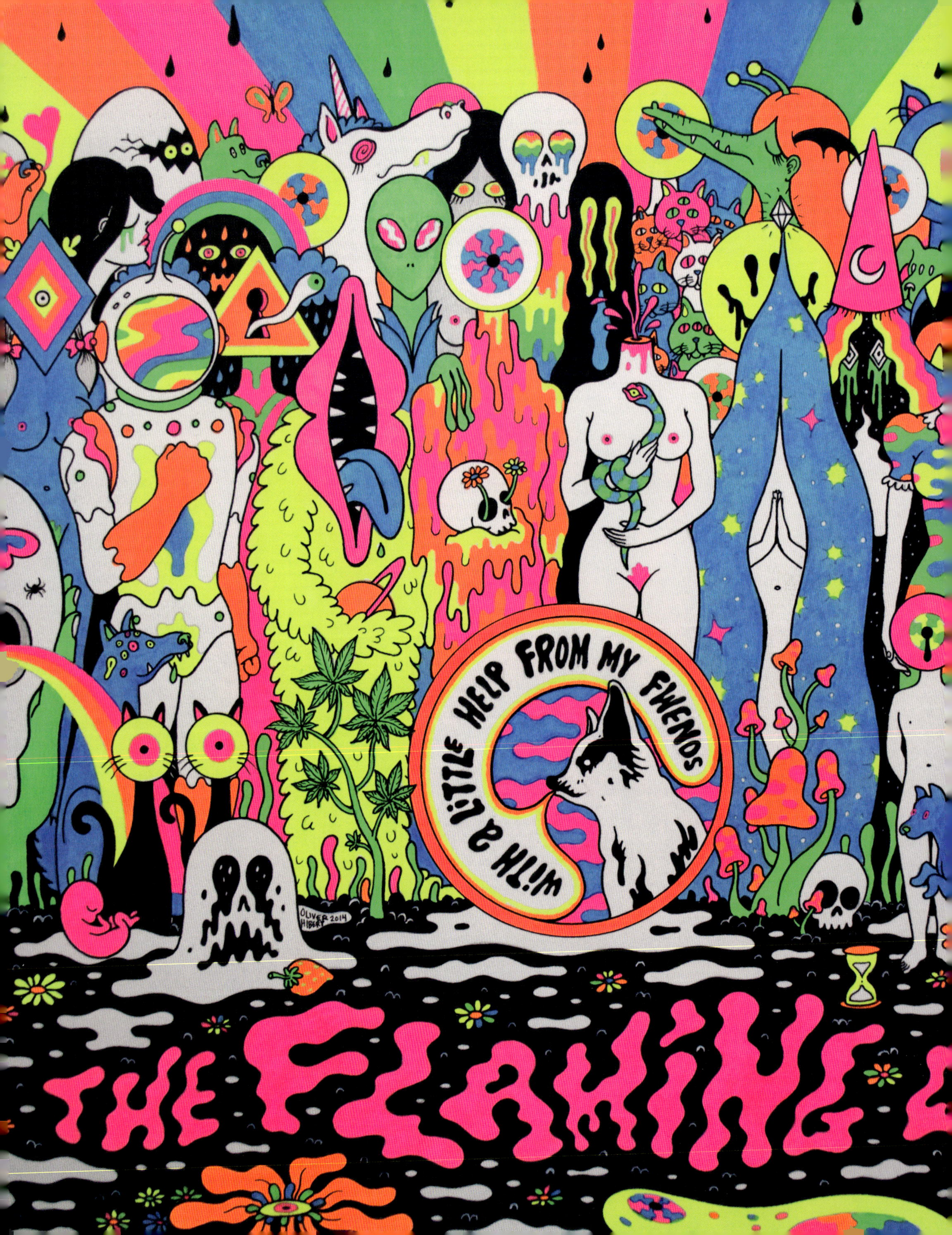

WITH A LITTLE HELP FROM MY FWENDS
OLIVER HIBERT 2014
THE FLAMING

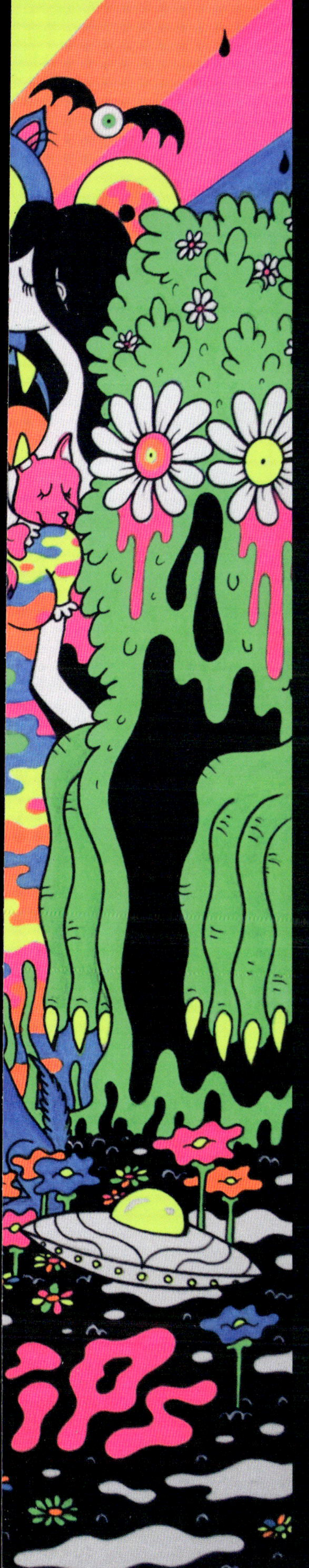

"Inside cover art for The Flaming Lips record *With a Little Help from My Fwends*. This was a Sgt. Pepper tribute album, with many other bands involved. All the work and art I did for this album was pretty intense, as the deadline was extremely short and last-minute. The funny thing about this image was that it had been intended for the front cover of the album. From what I heard, The Beatles' people weren't too into letting that happen, so we used it for the inside cover instead. I had to design an entirely different image for the front cover with an insanely small amount of time to do so. Totally not complaining though, as I like the challenge of time and spontaneity."

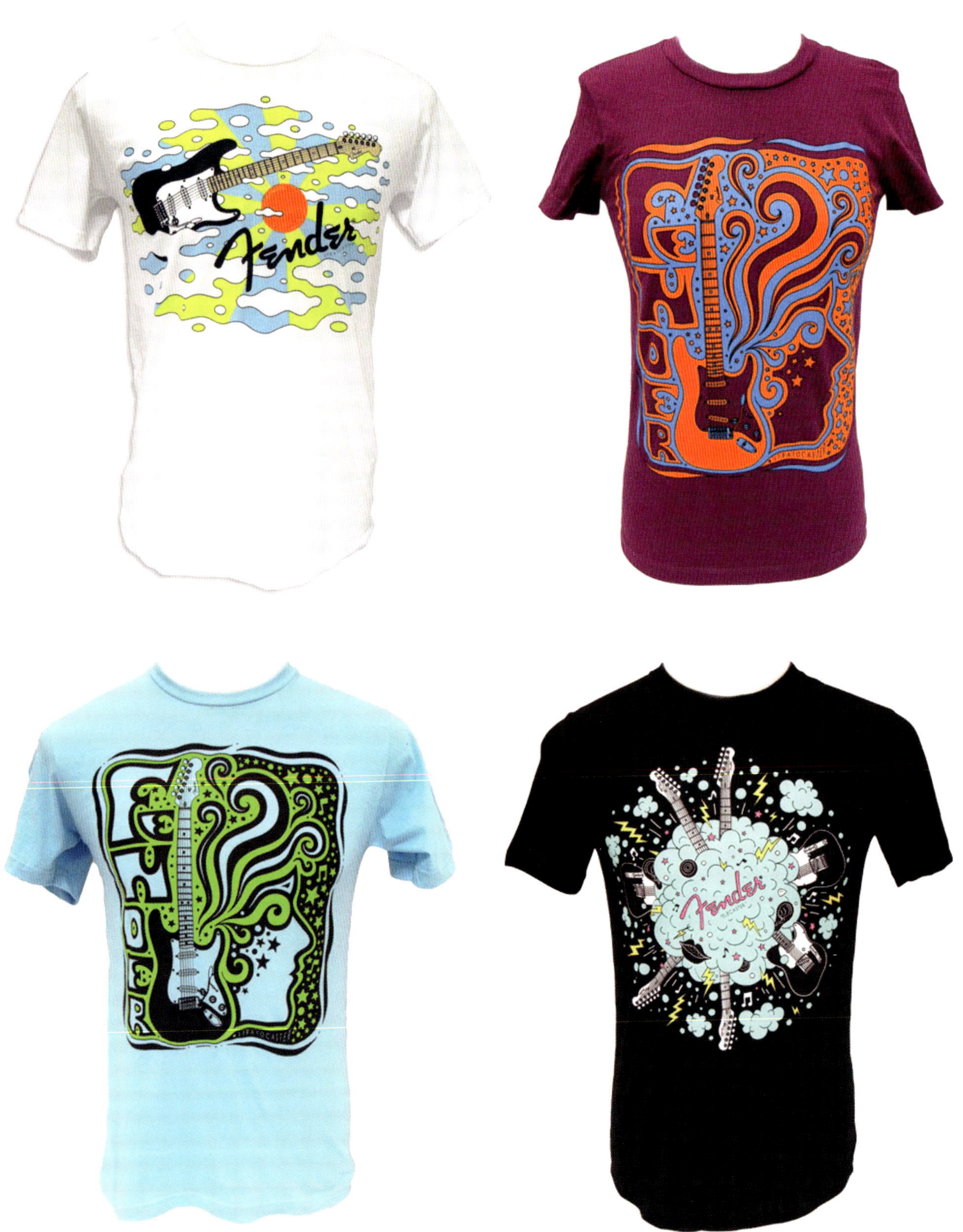

"Various shirts I did for my friends at Fender. Always fun and cool to work with them."

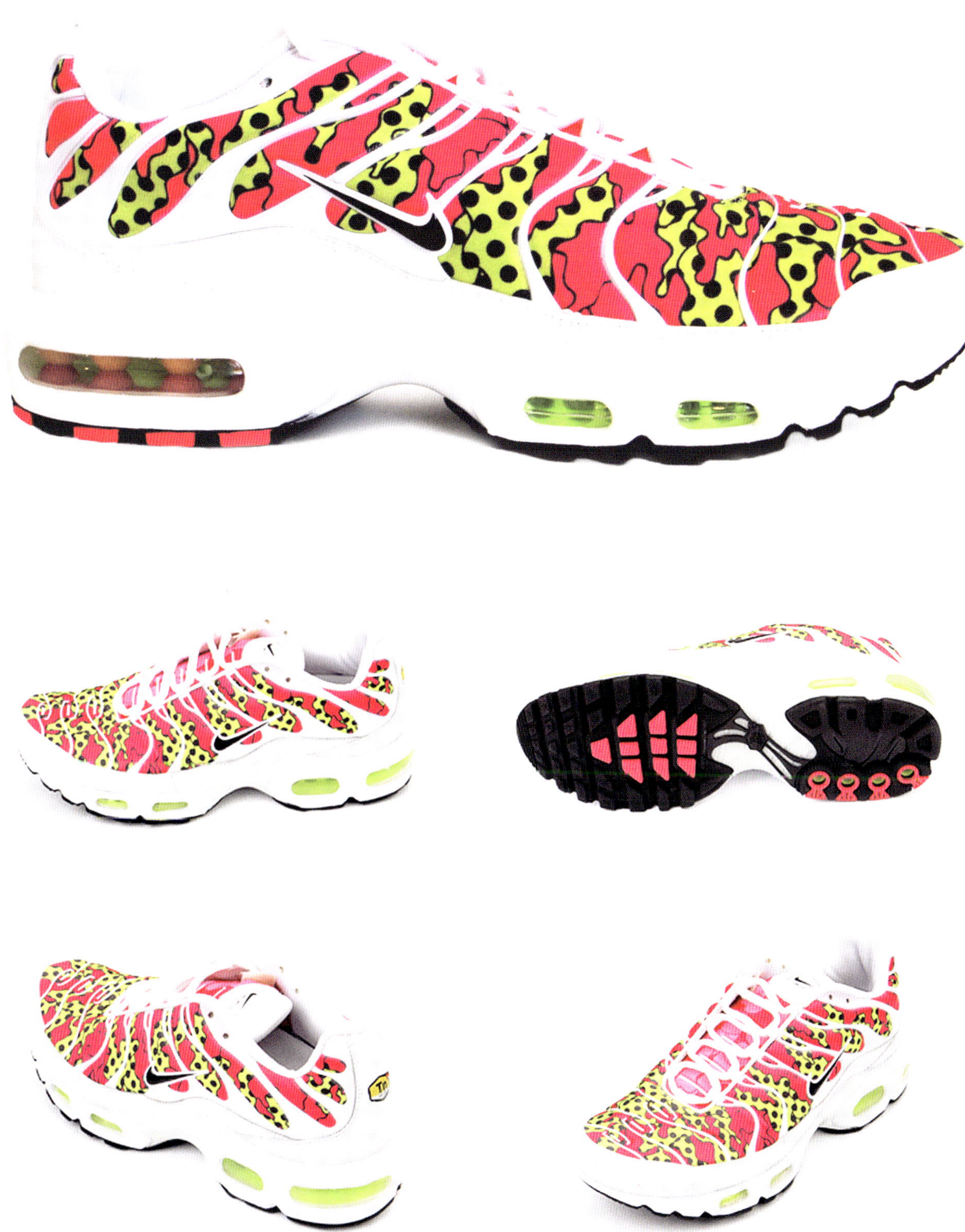

"Textile graphics I designed for Nike in the mid-2000s. This was a limited production for Paris Fashion Week. There were four color ways released for these shoes, but these were my favorite."

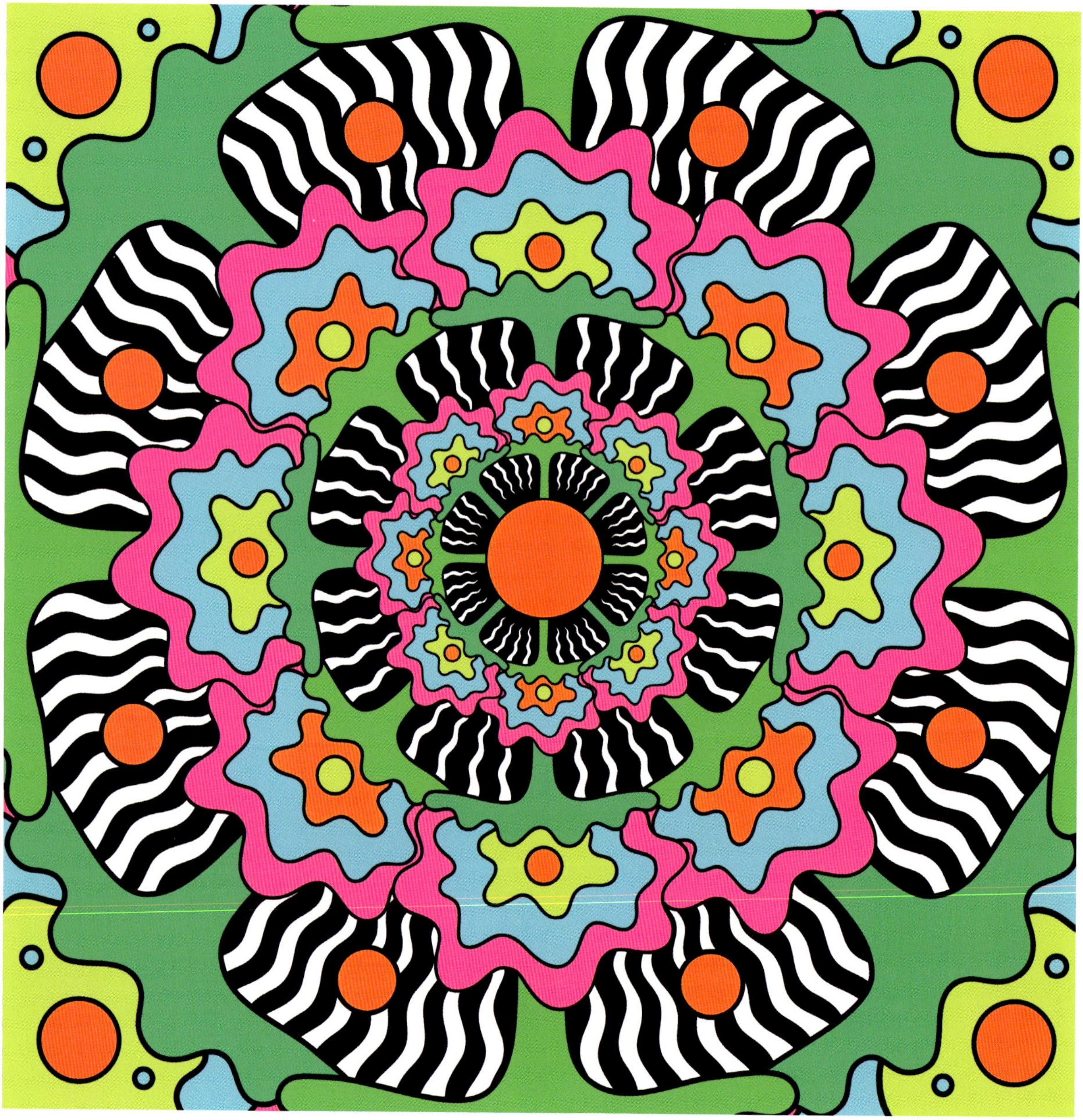

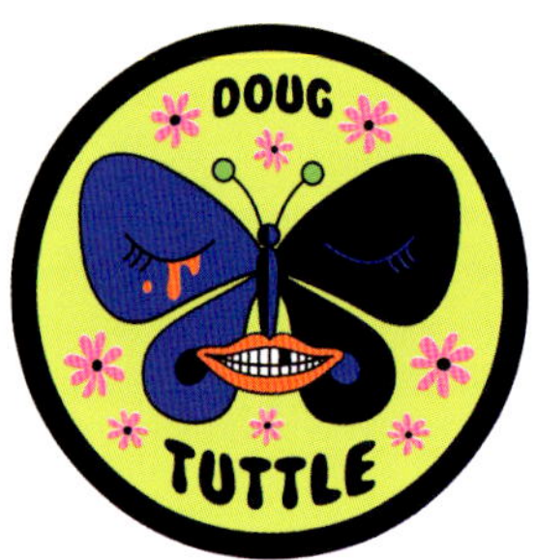

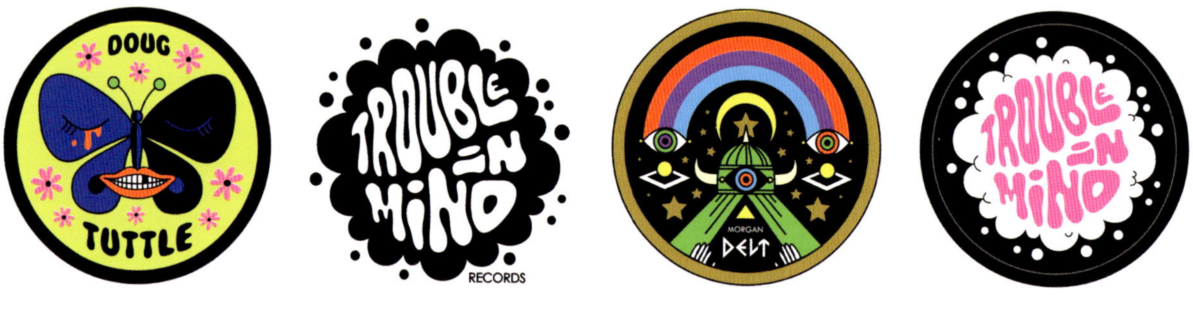

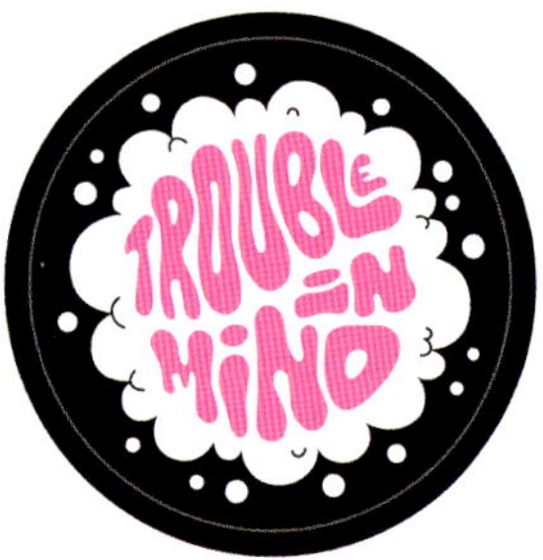

"Various designs of patches for Trouble In Mind Records.
Two of them include my friends Morgan Delt and Doug Tuttle. Cool record company and amazing musicians."

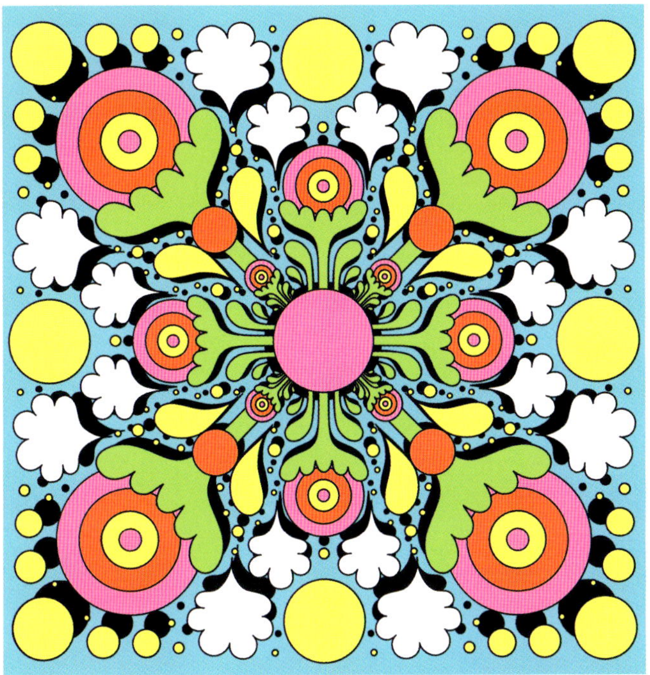

"A textile design I created for LUSH Ltd."

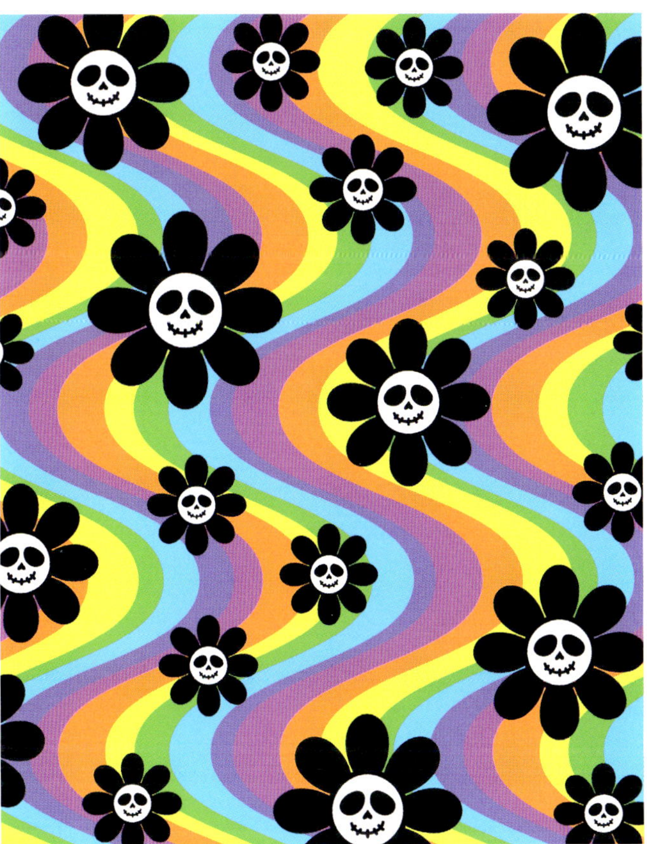

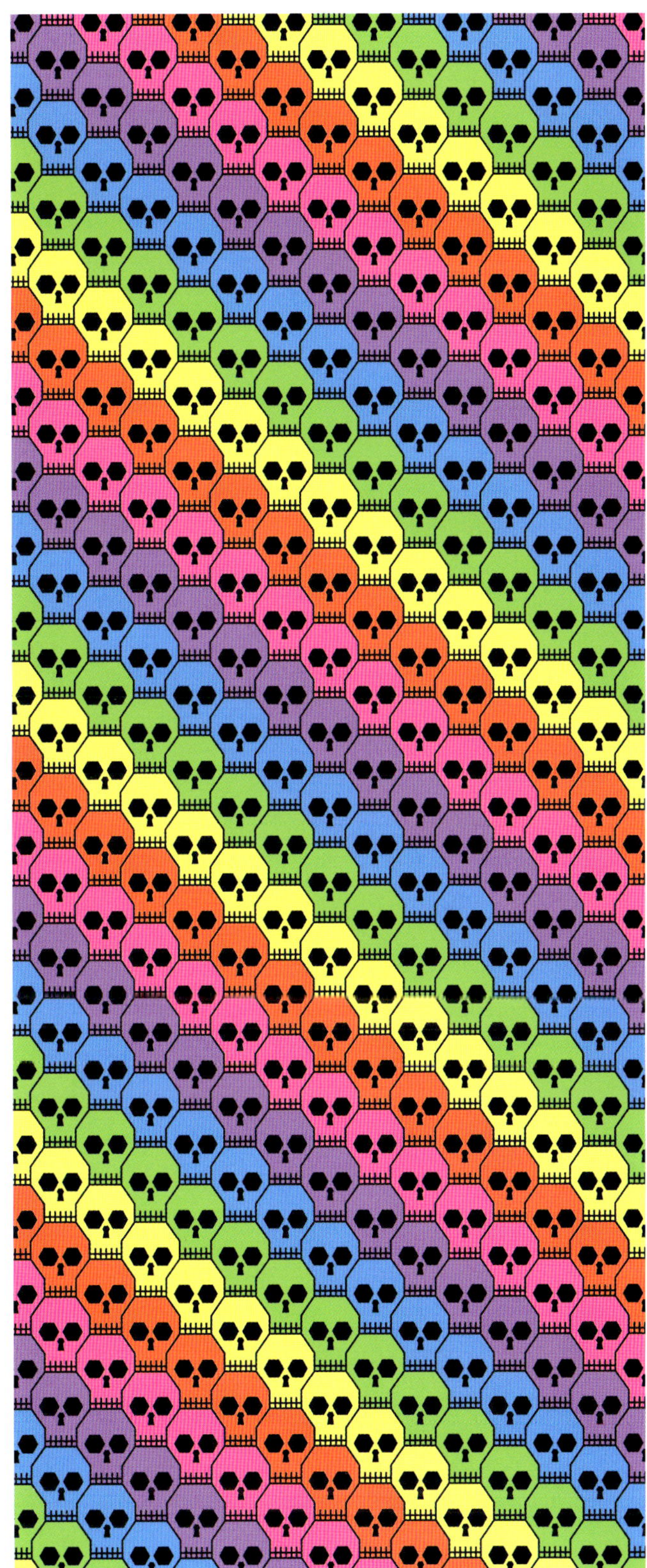

Various textile patterns/designs

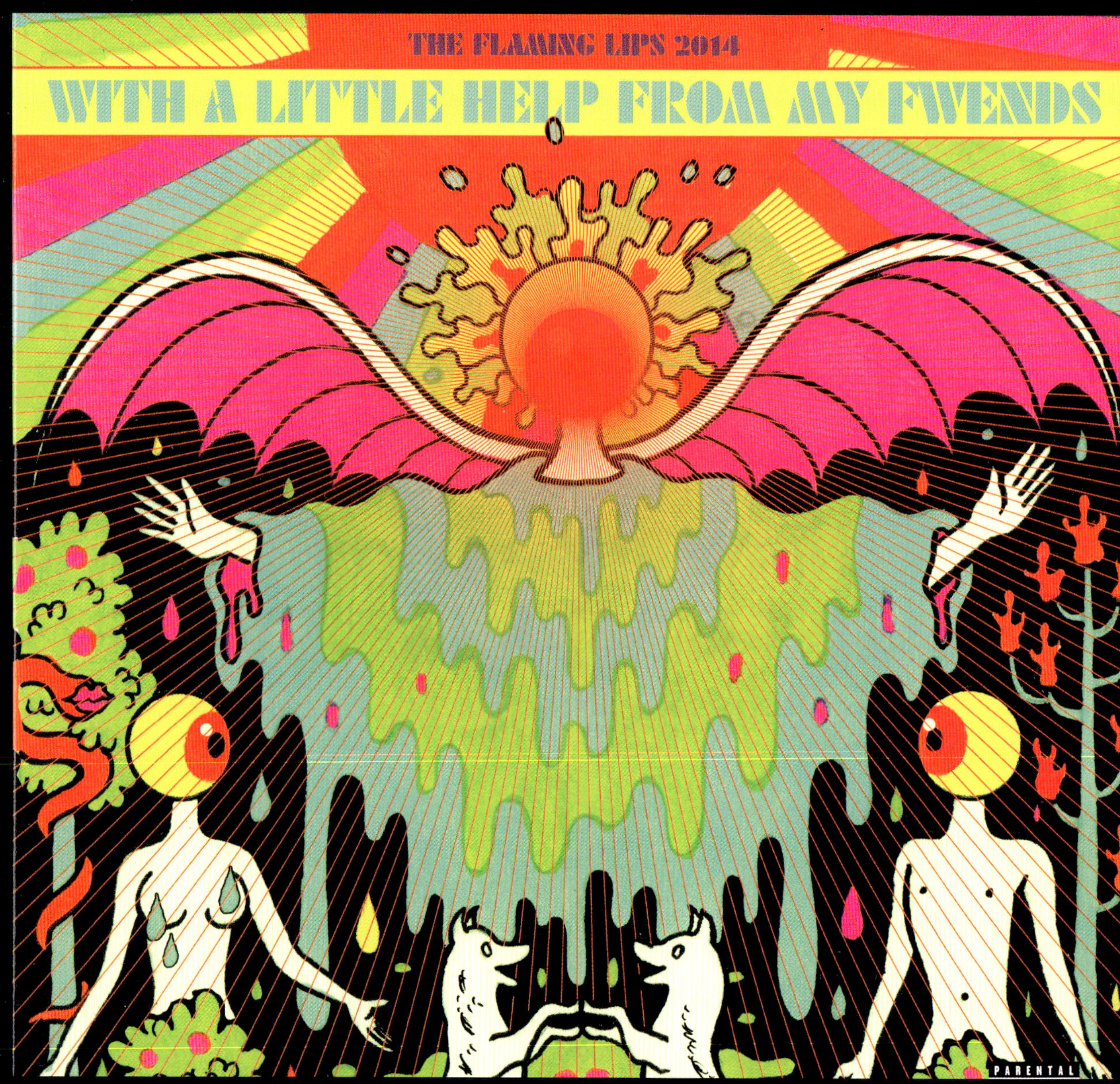

"Original and final artwork that was used for The Flaming Lips' 2014 album *With a Little Help from My Fwends*. I was so honored to do this one."

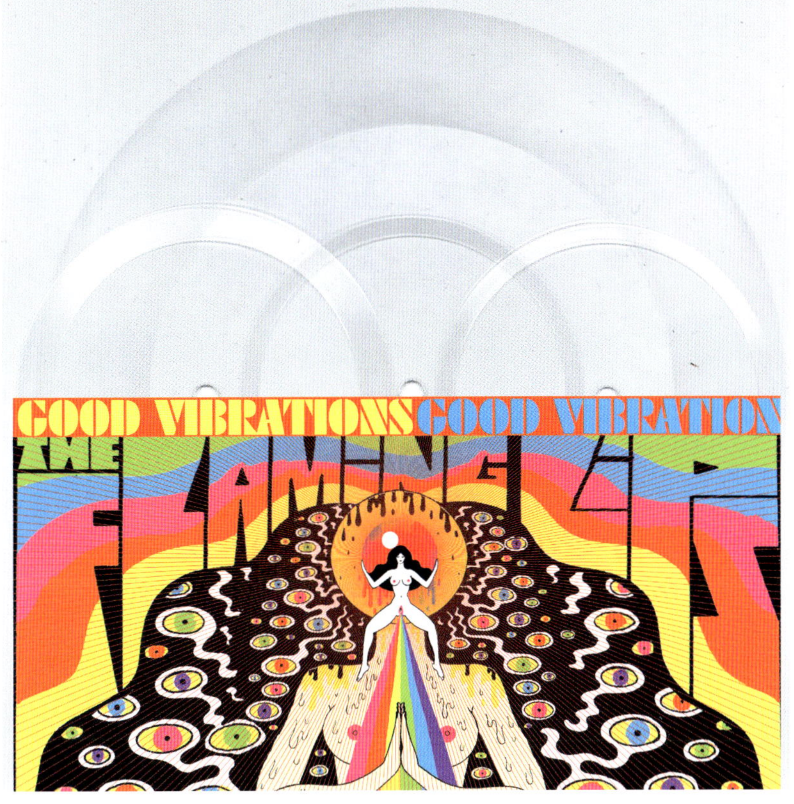

"The Flaming Lips album cover/sleeve design for a super-rare and cool little record that was released and sold only at the Levitation/Psychfest music festival in 2015."

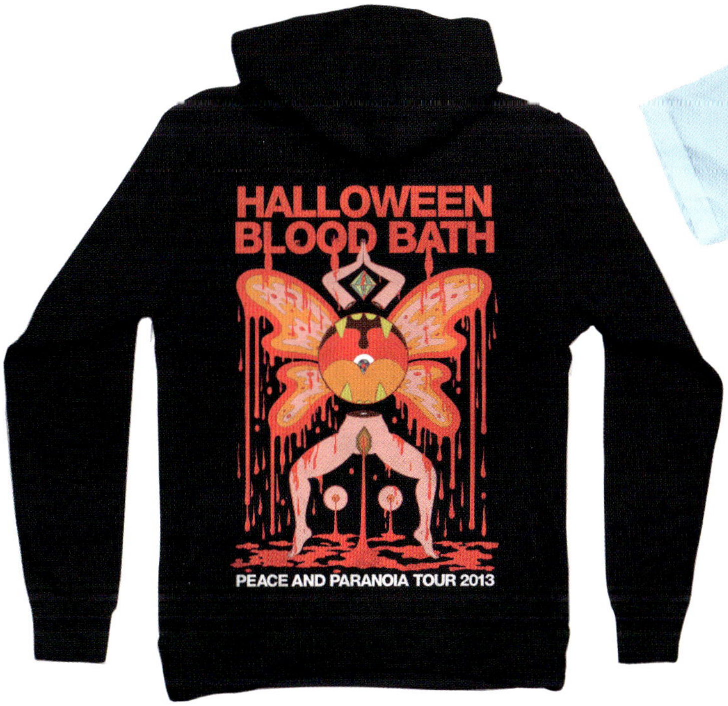

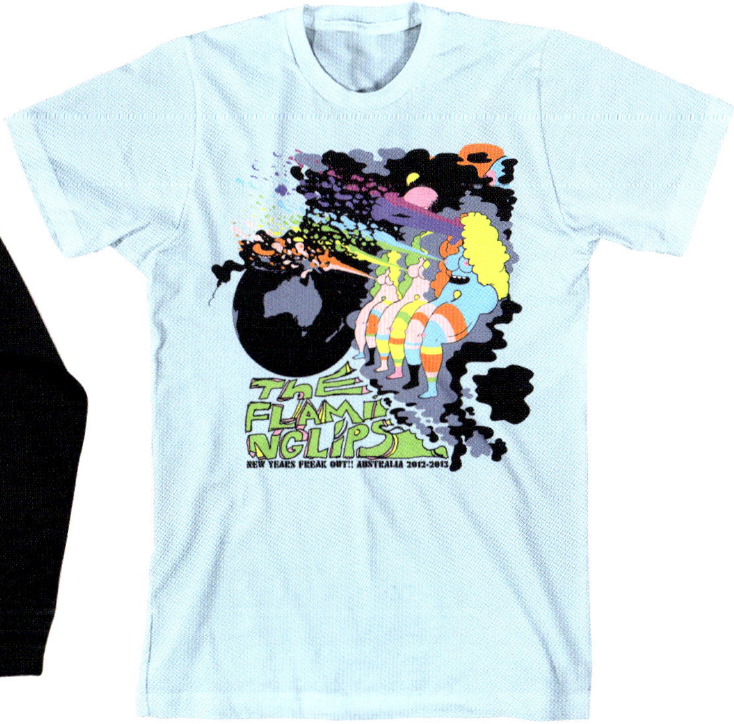

"A few of the various clothing merchandise items I've made for The Flaming Lips. I can't even remember how many shirts we have created to date, but there has been a ton!"

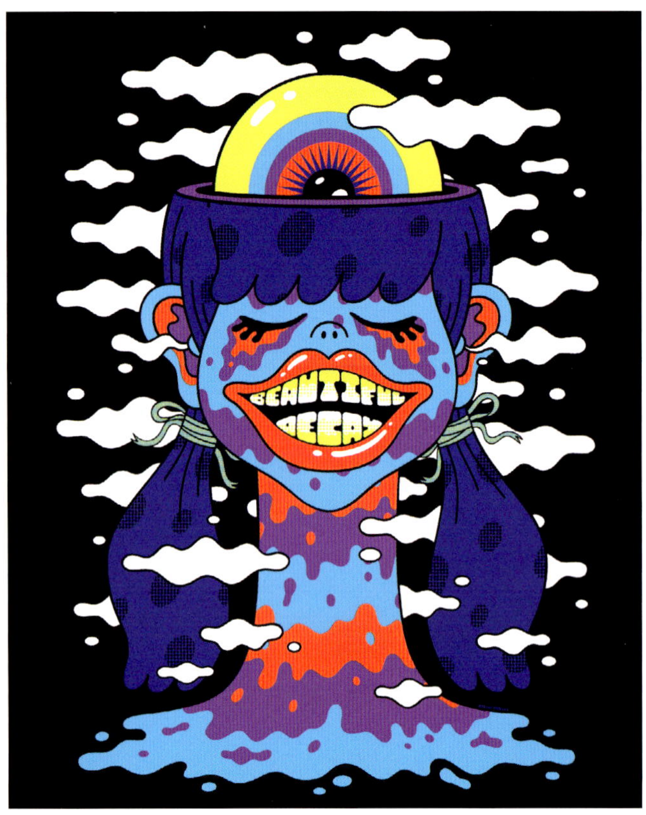

T-shirt illustration for *Beautiful Decay* Magazine

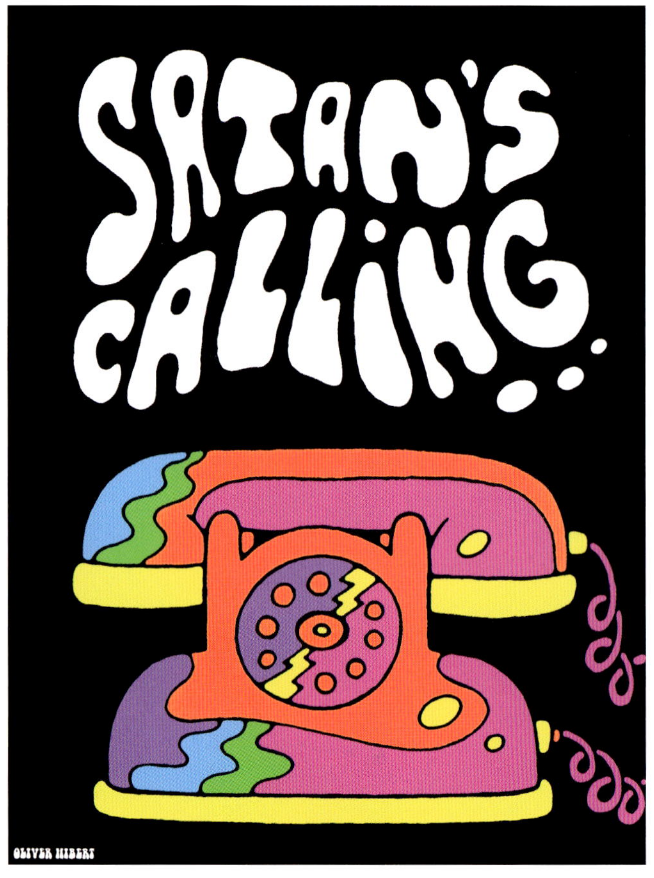

Satan's Calling

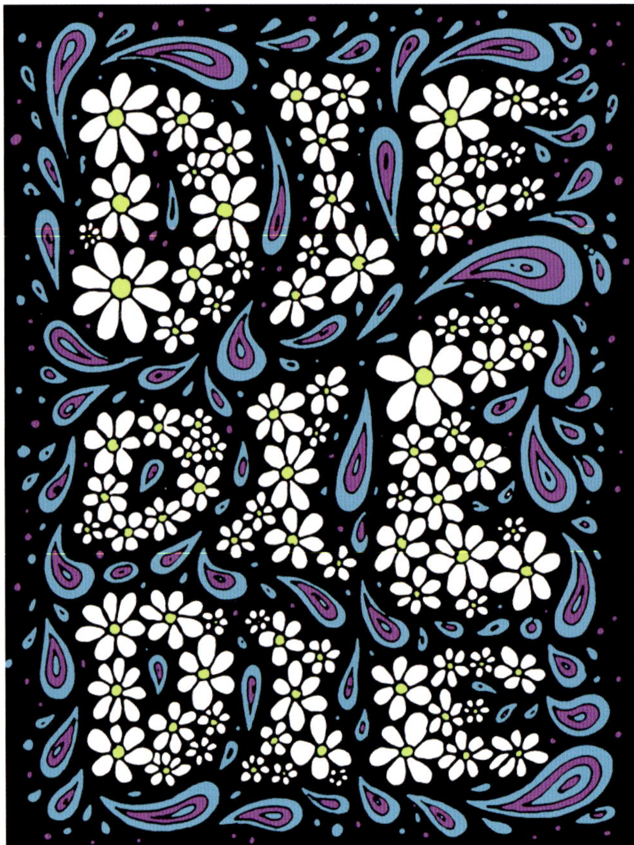

Die Die Die
"Fun illustration for *Spoopadelic* #1,
a zine by Jacqueline Denton and me."

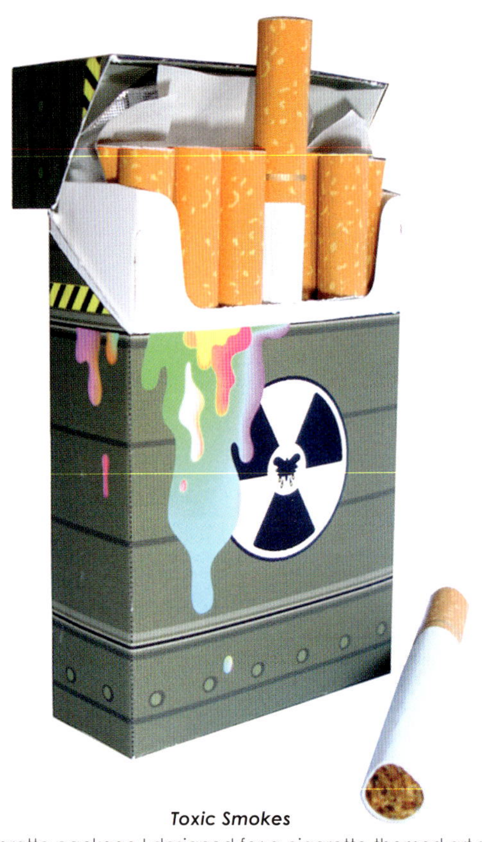
Toxic Smokes
"3-D cigarette package I designed for a cigarette-themed art show."

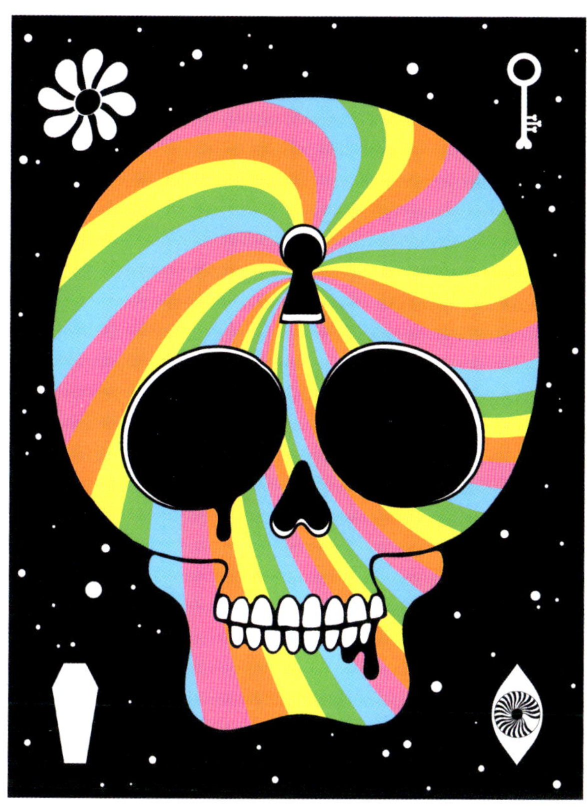

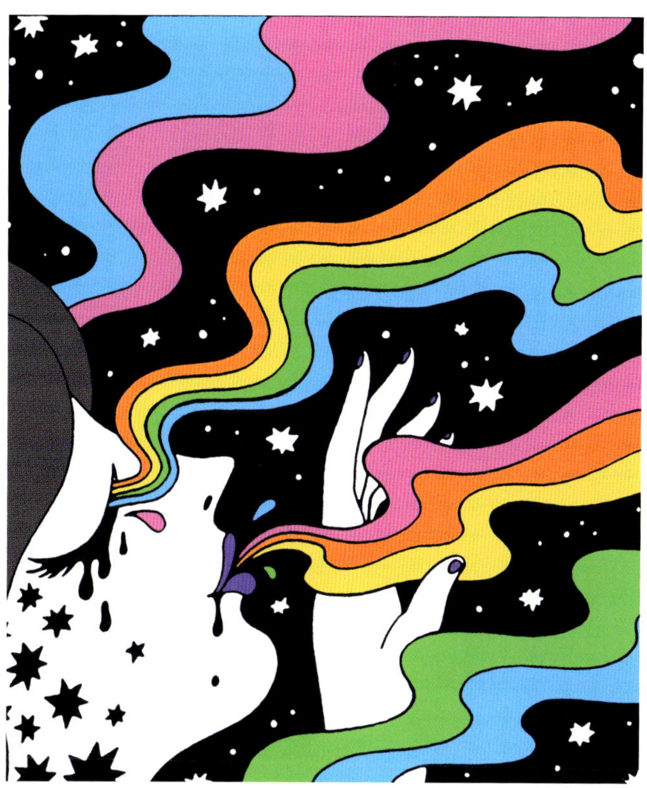

Secret Rainbow of Doom

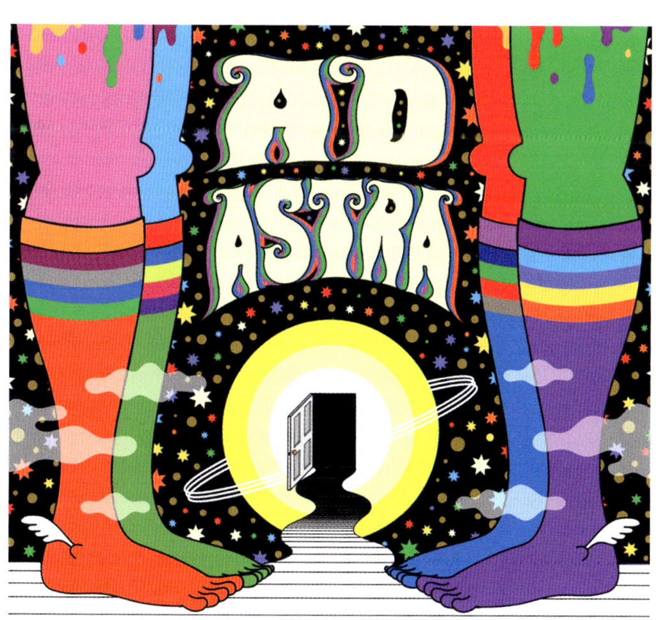

Ad Astra

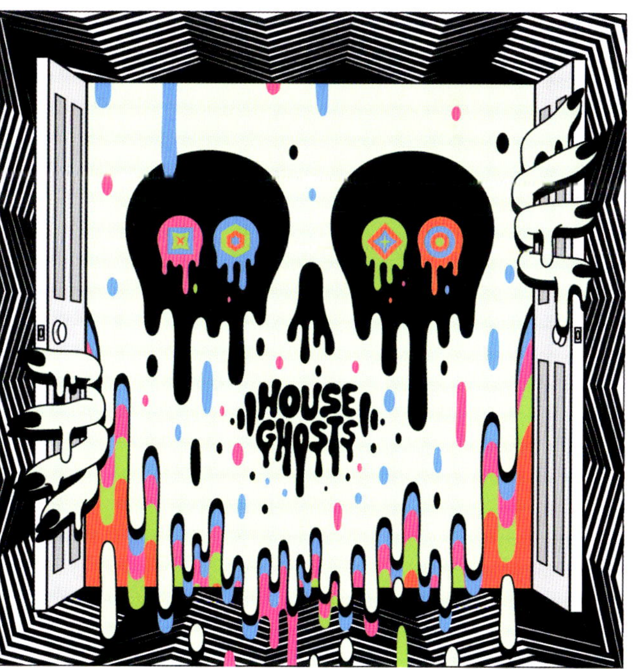

Album cover illustration for House Ghosts

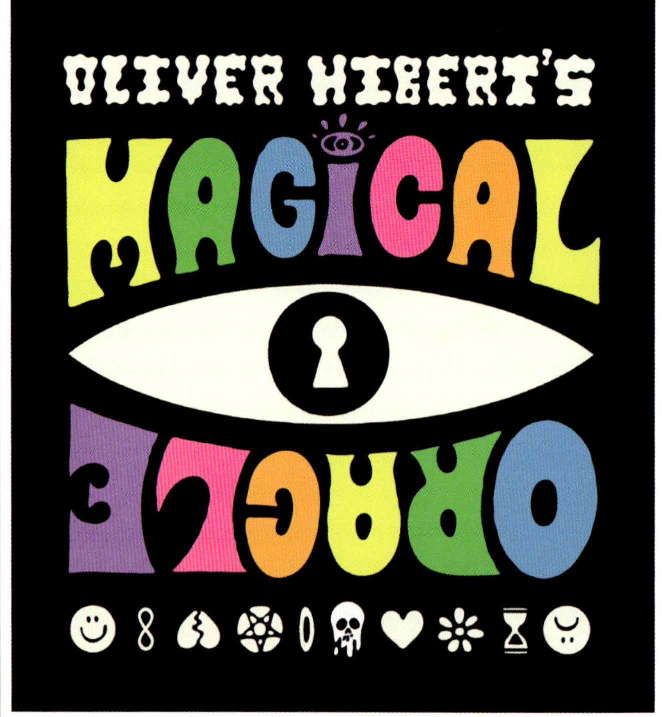

The Magical Oracle

"This was a spiritual communicative board game I designed and released with Von Zos. I was really excited about this project. And to those of you who have purchased one, keep the creepy stories coming!"

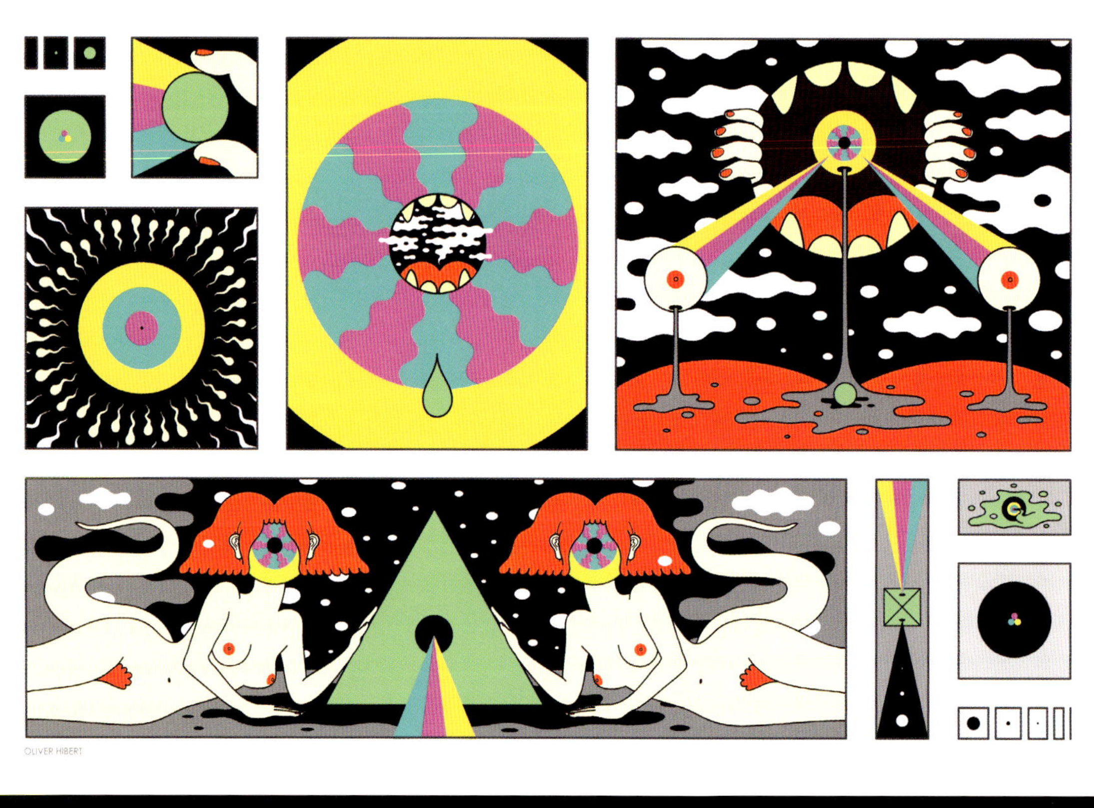

"A strange and very short comic I made that has something to do with atoms and protons and weird stuff. I don't know what was going on at the time I made this."

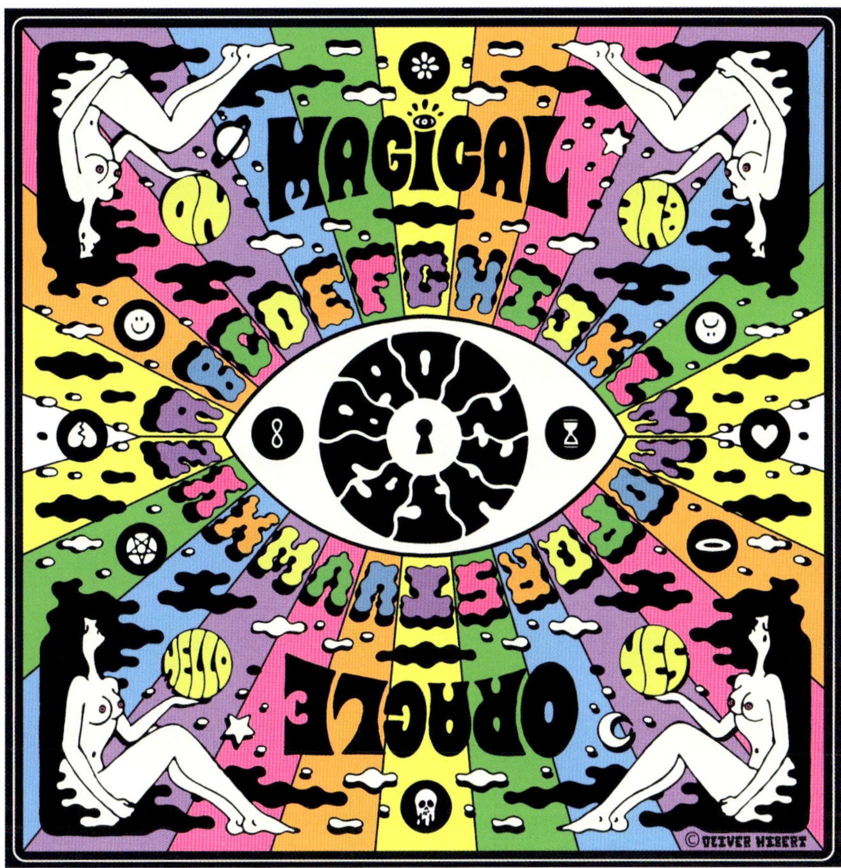

The Magical Oracle game board

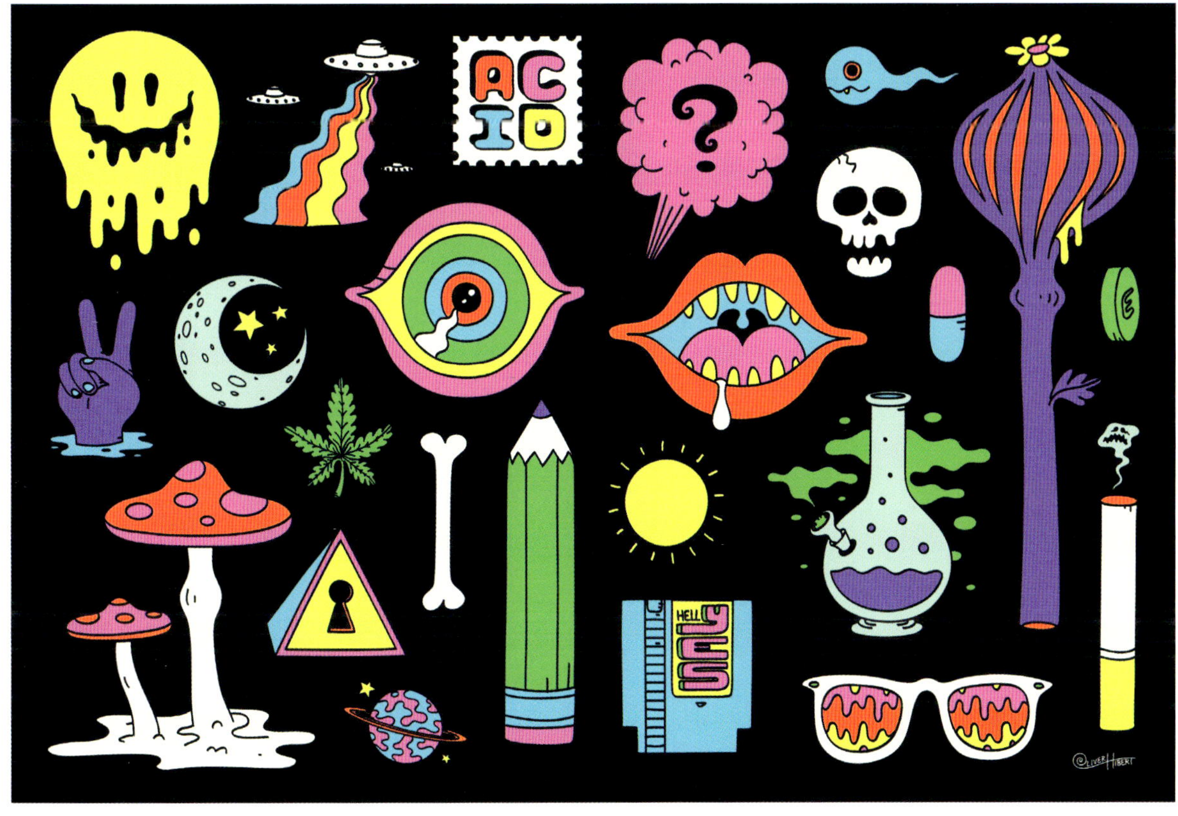

Drugs and Stuff

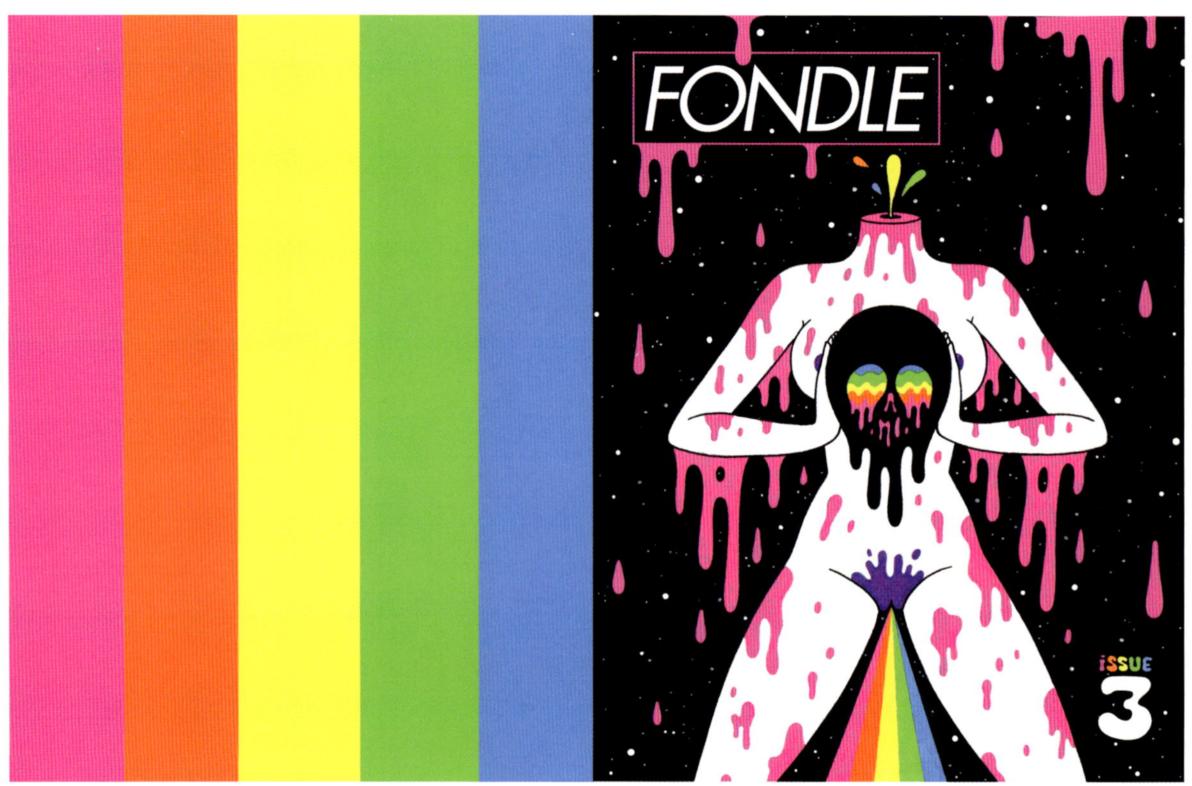

"Front and back covers for *Fondle* Magazine out of LA. You've got to appreciate those commercial projects that will actually let you draw rainbows shooting out of vaginas. Thanks guys!"

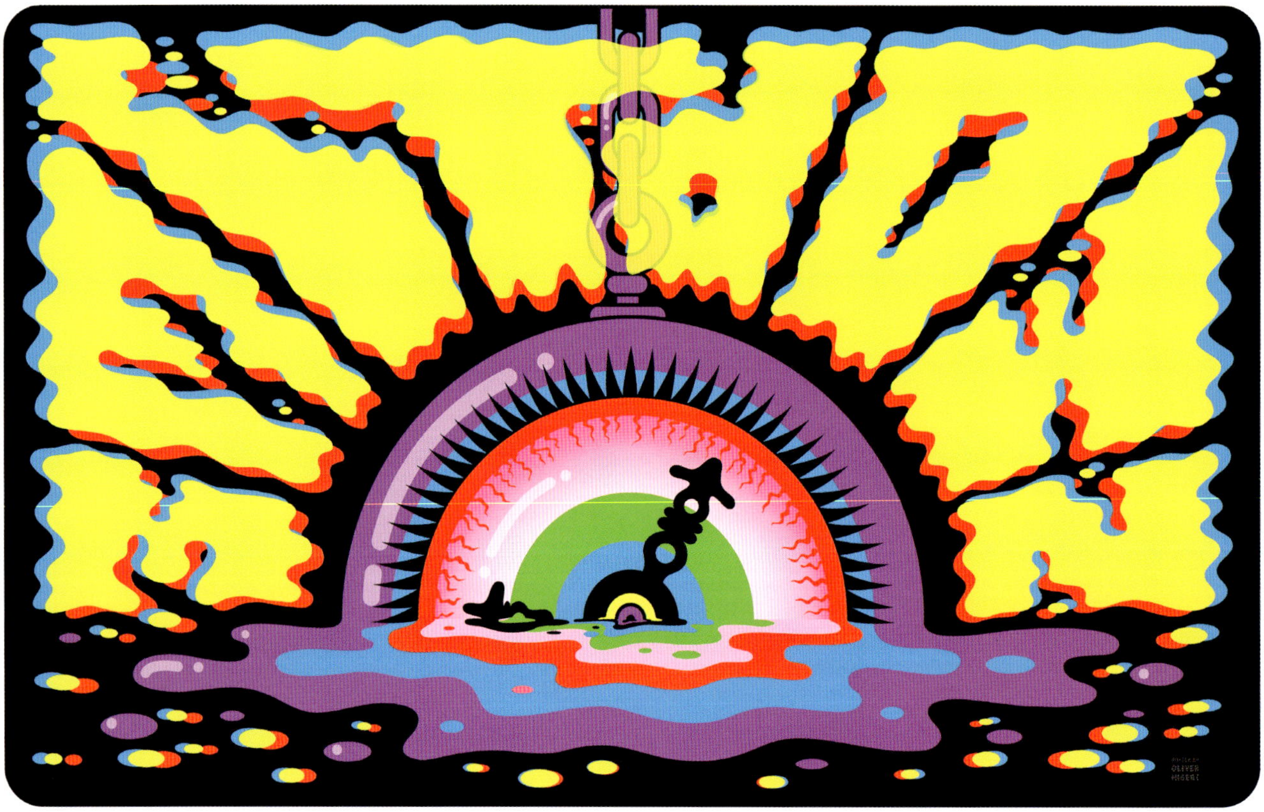

Meltdown art show poster

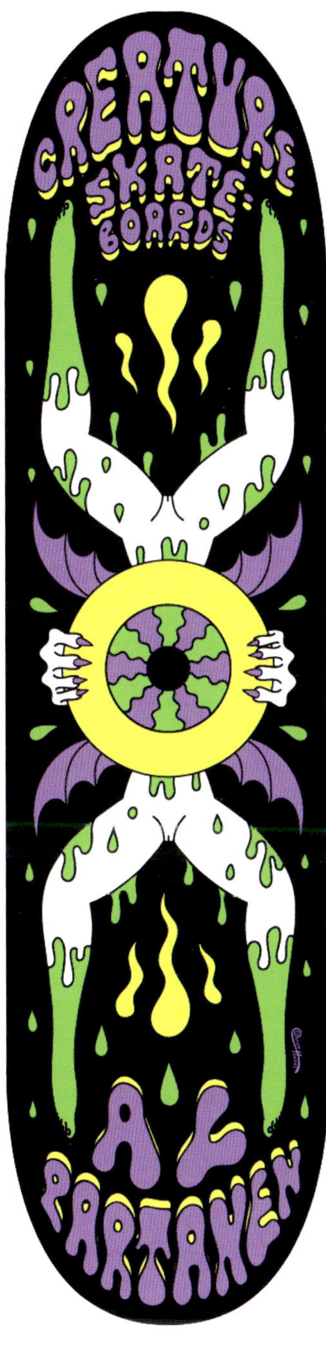

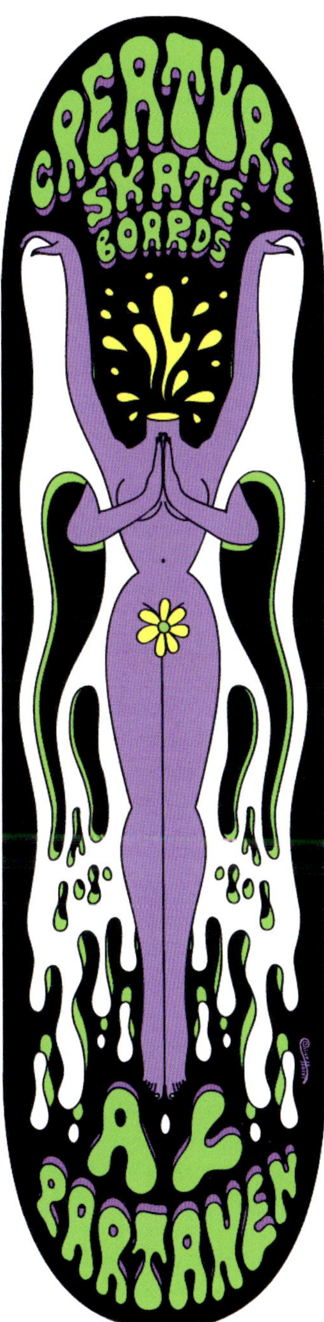

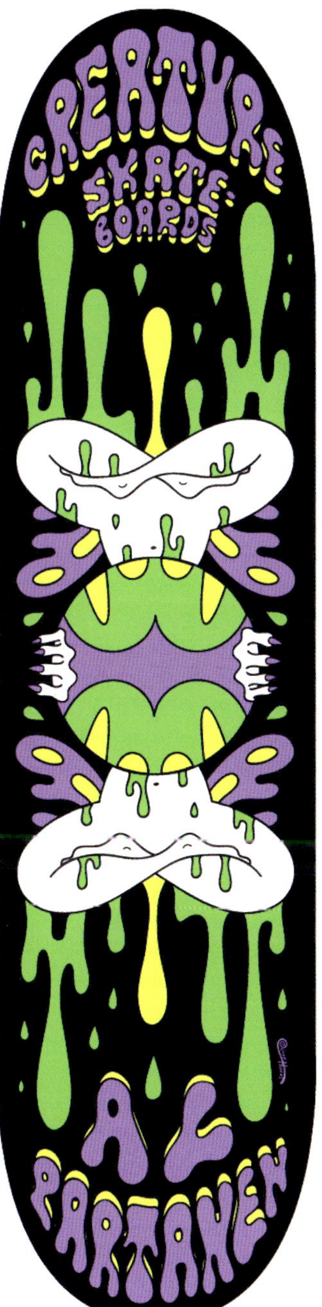

Artwork for Creature Skateboards

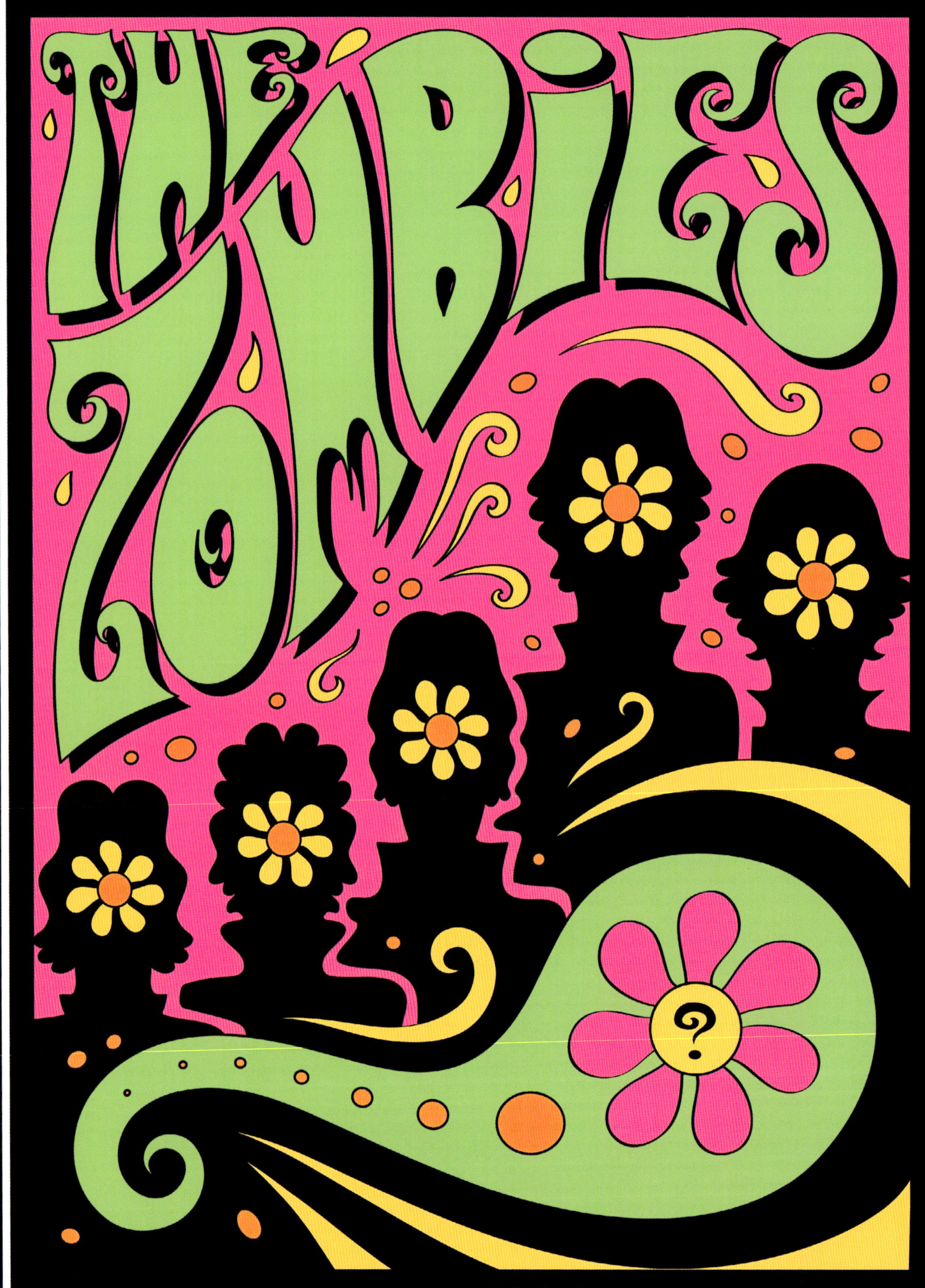

Editorial illustration for The Zombies

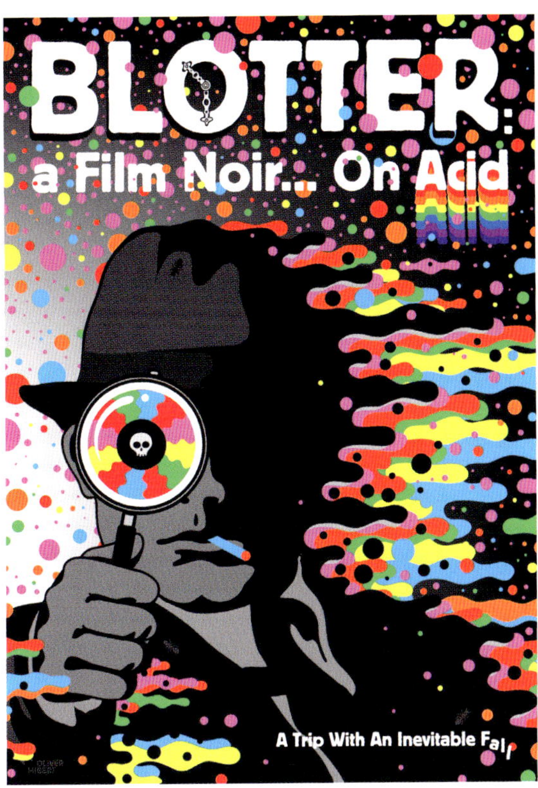

Blotter, a Film Noir on Acid DVD cover art

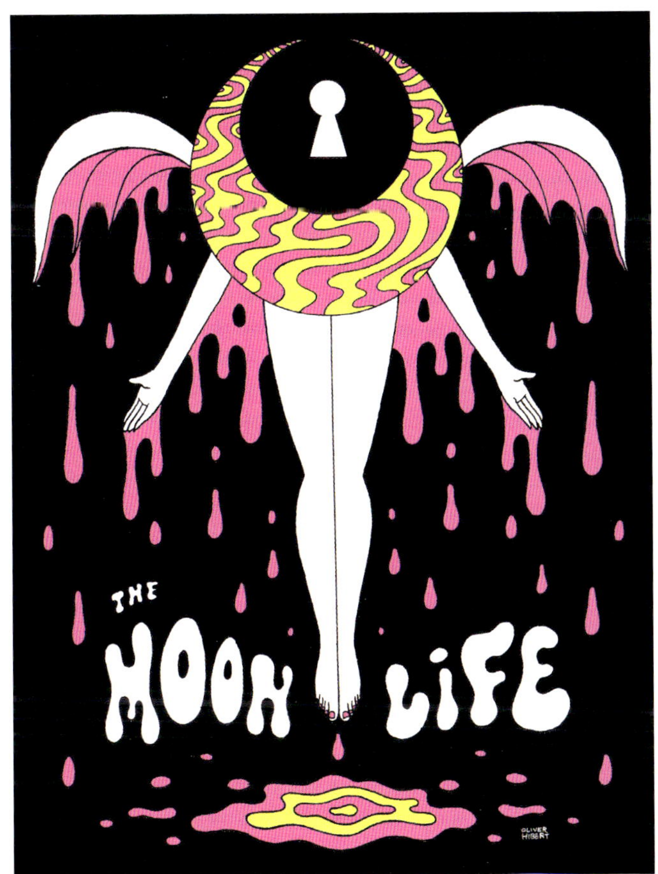

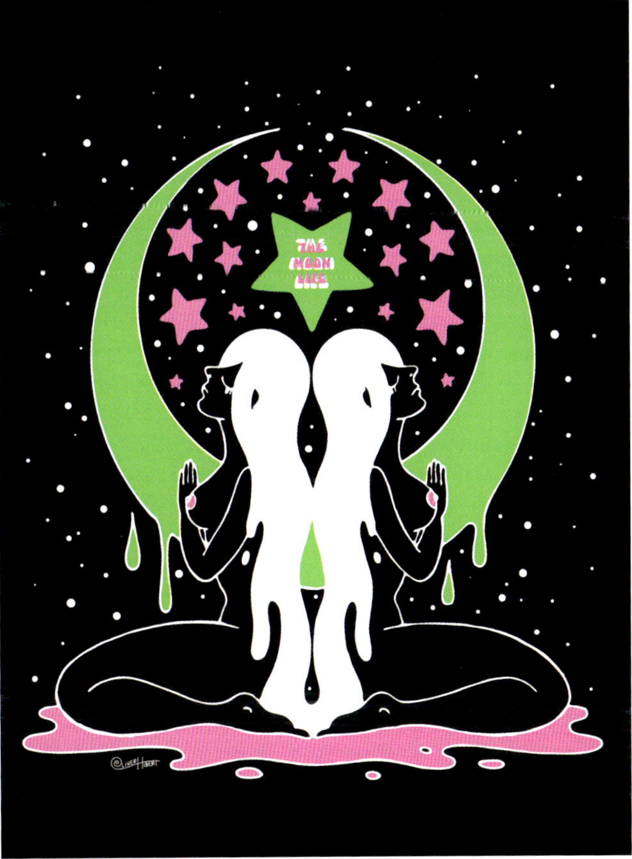

T-shirt graphics for The Moonlife clothing company

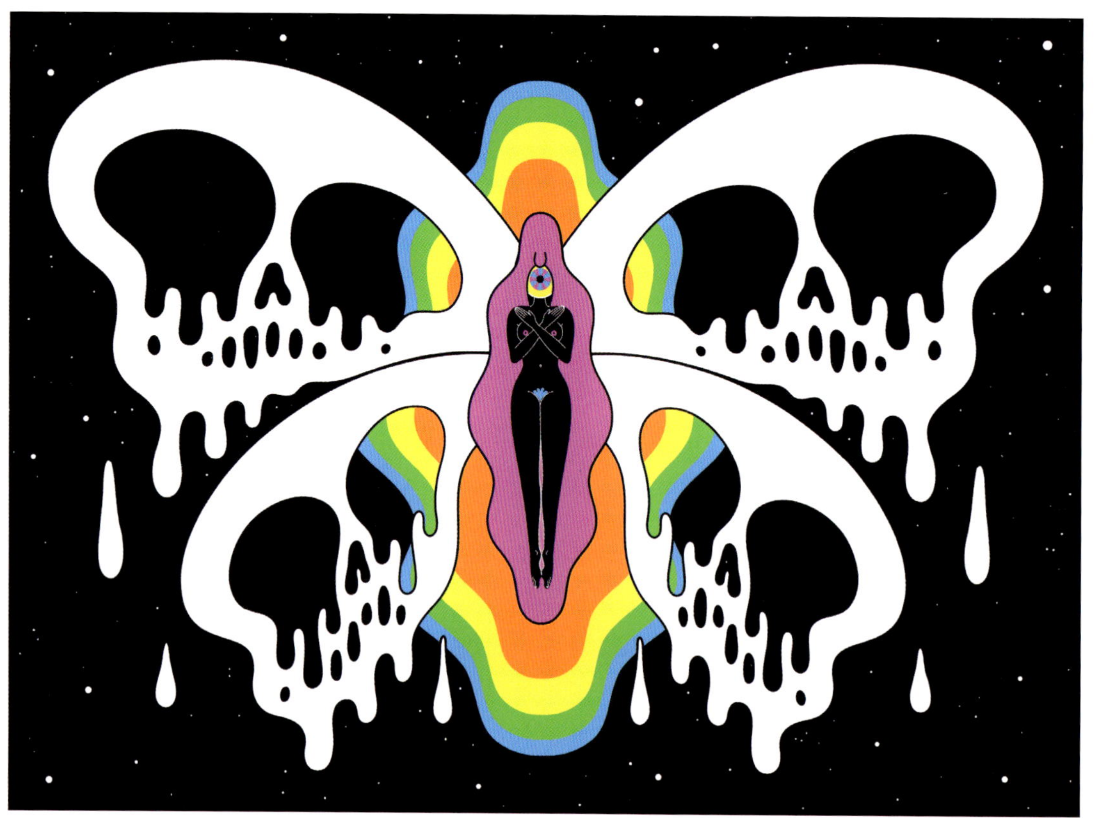

Decorus Mortem

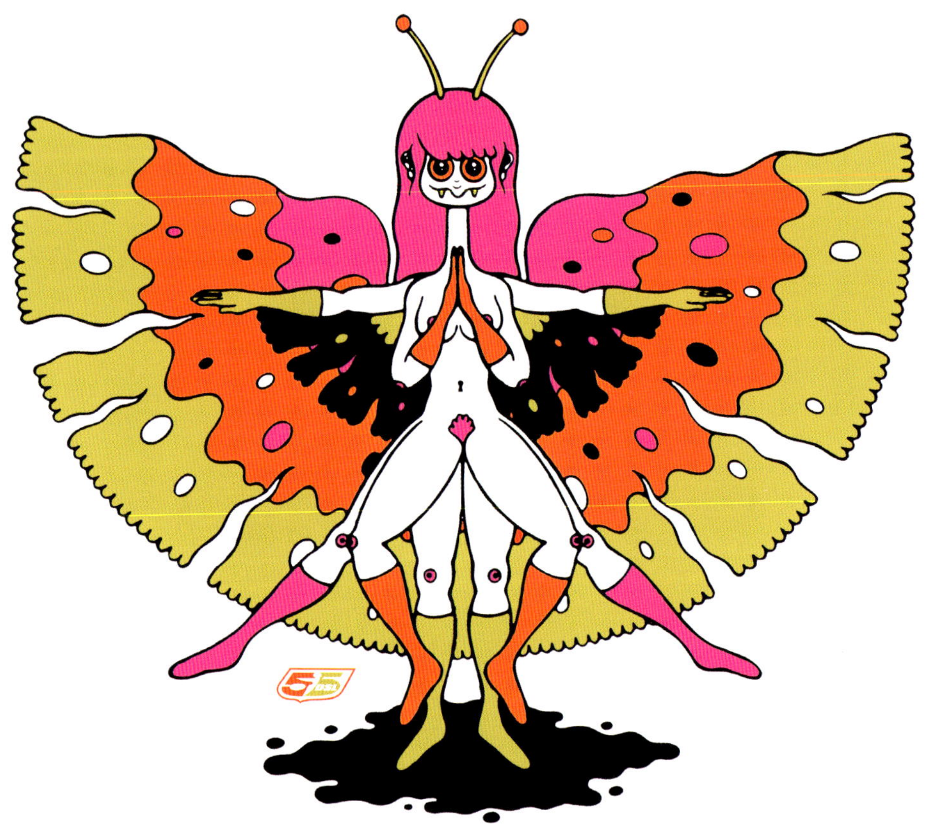

T-shirt graphics for DSL55 clothing company

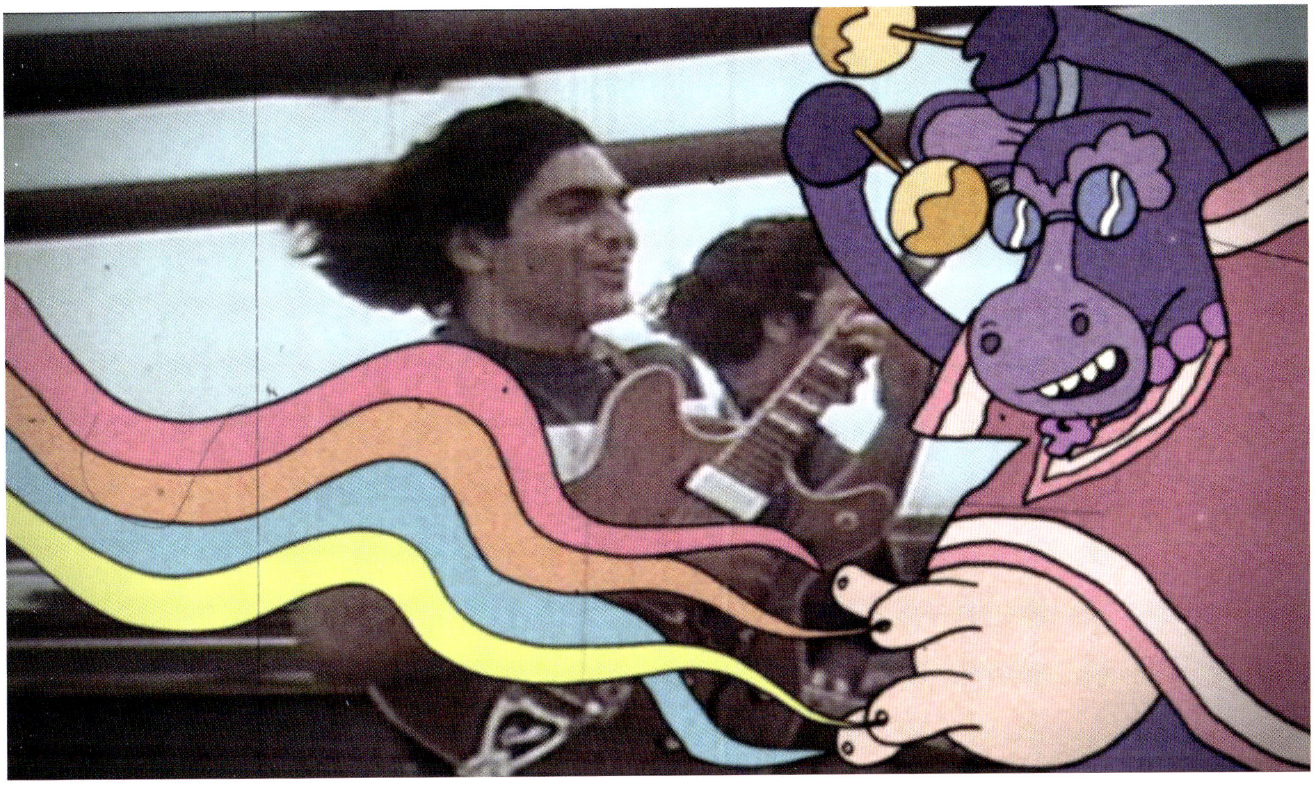

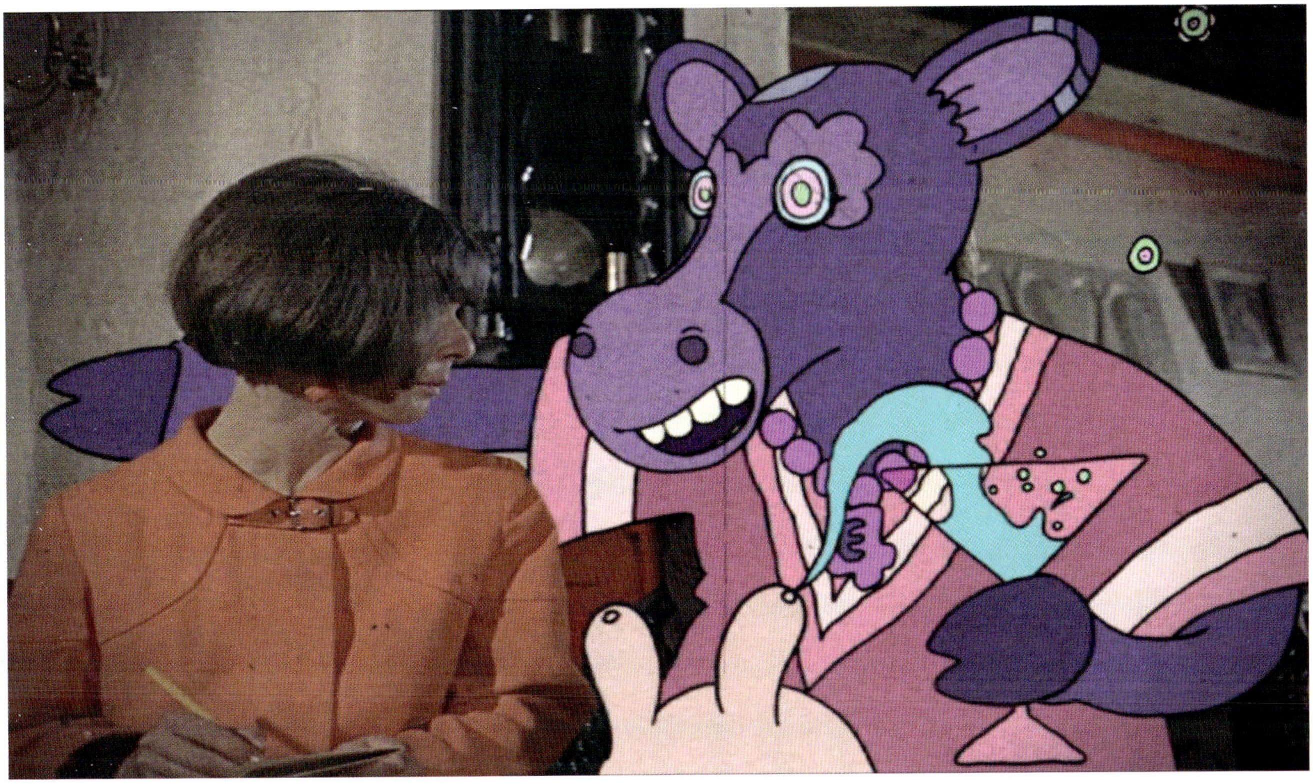

Animated commercial character design for the UK's E4 Udderbelly music festival

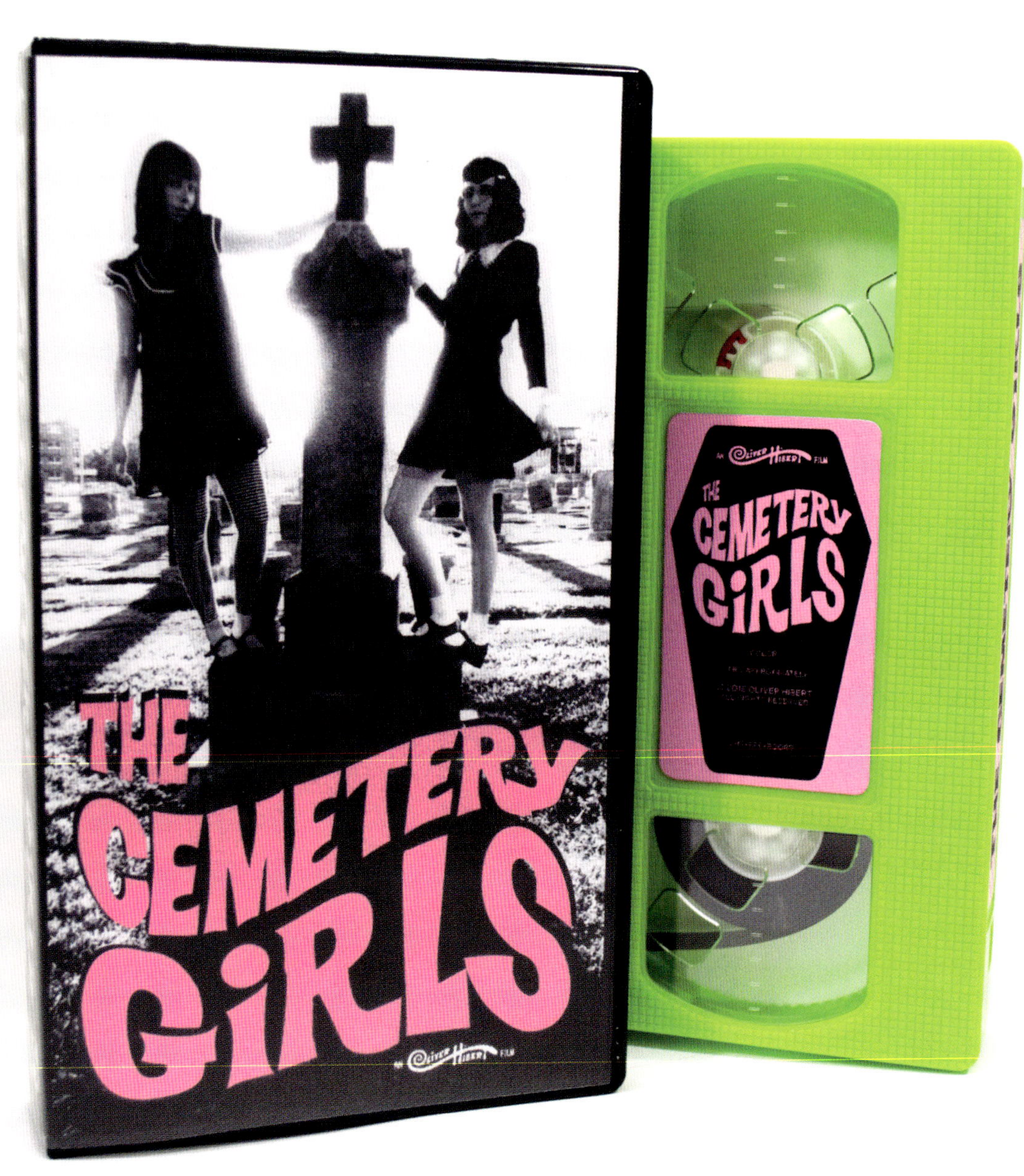

The Cemetery Girls VHS

"My first psychedelic silent short film. Catch it if you can."

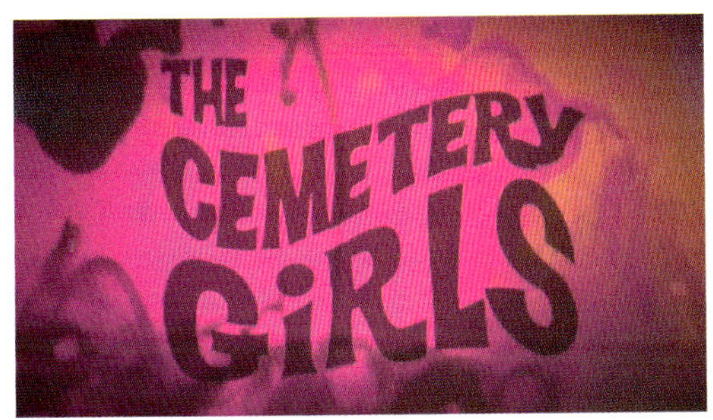

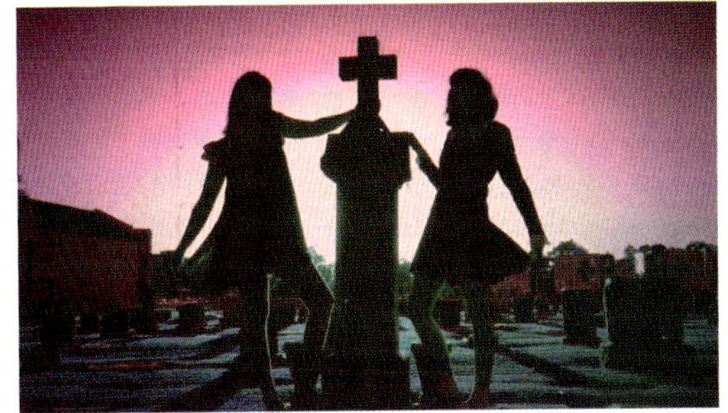
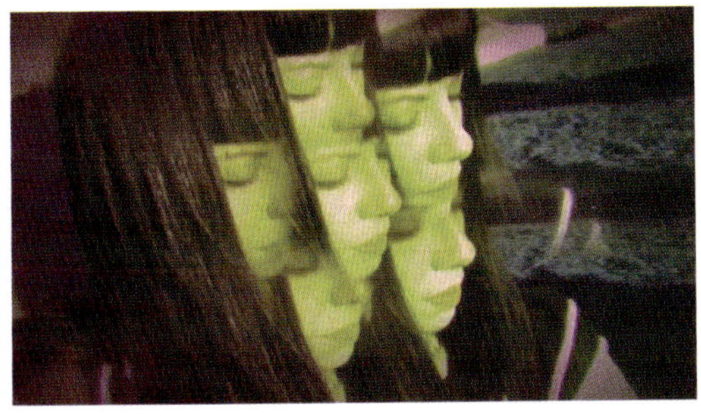
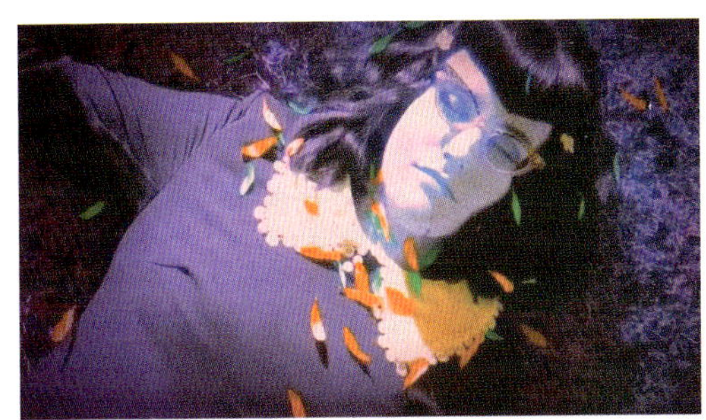
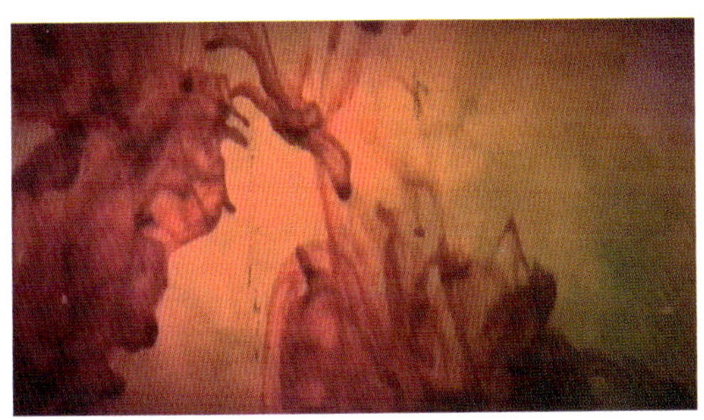
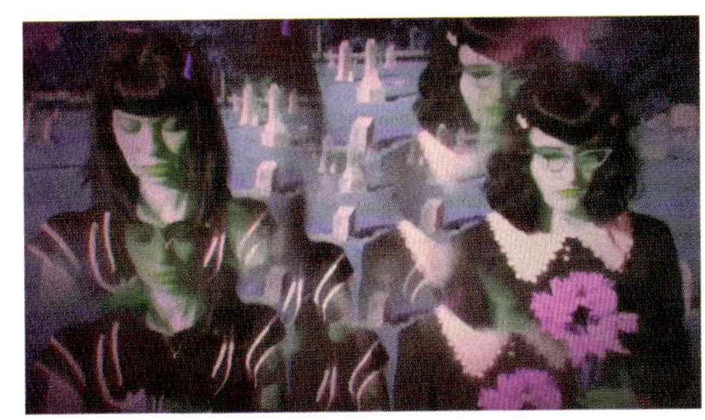
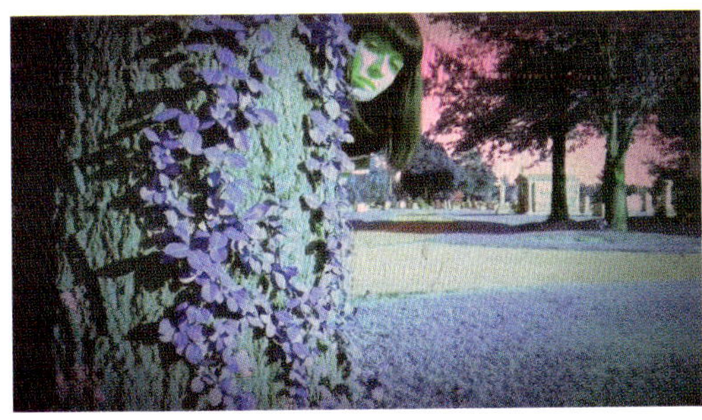
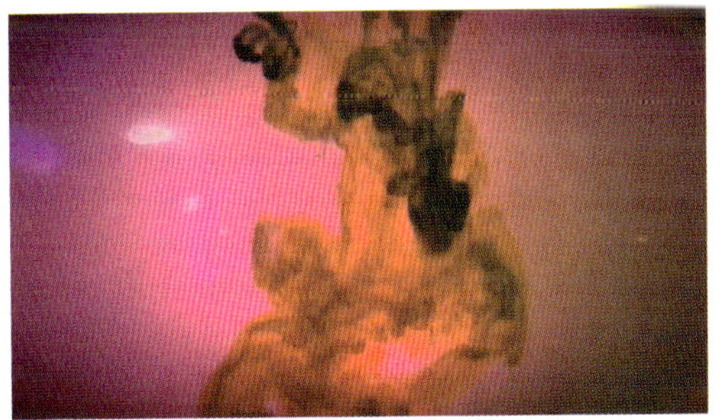
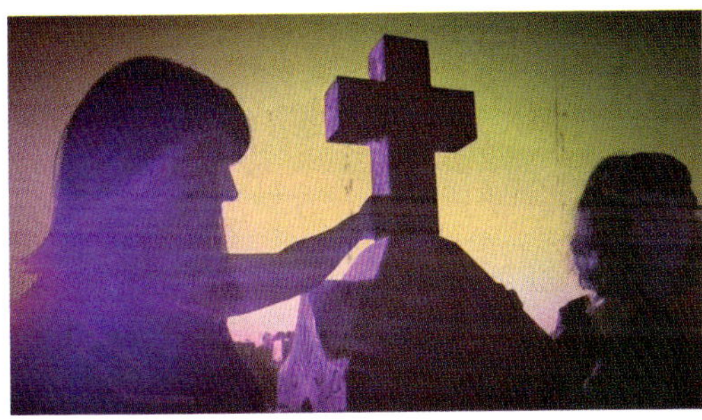
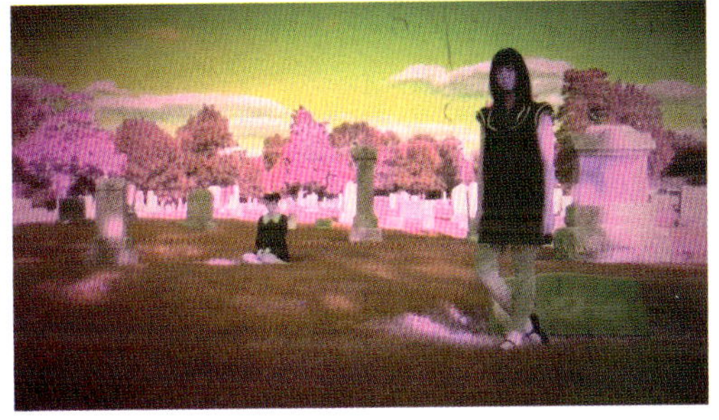

Image stills from *The Cemetery Girls*

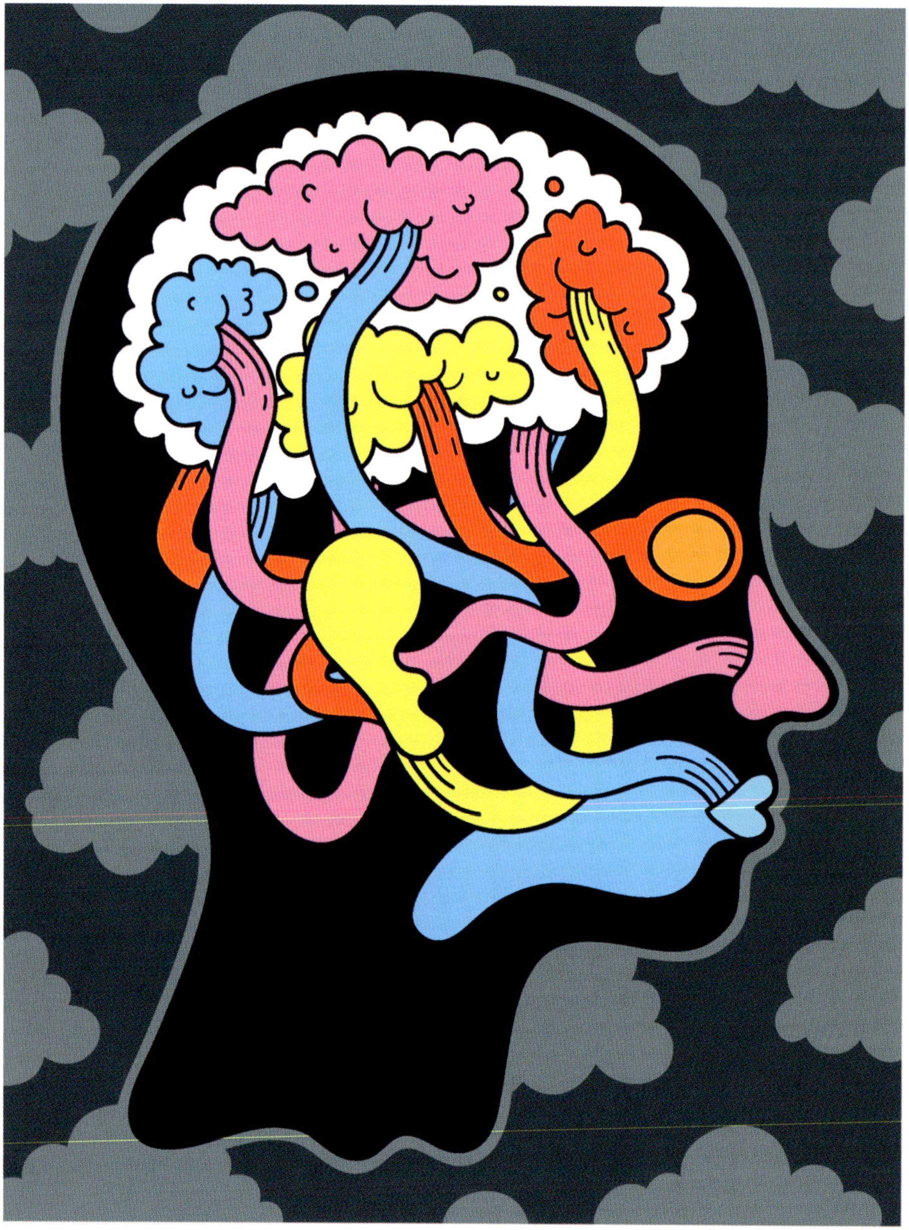

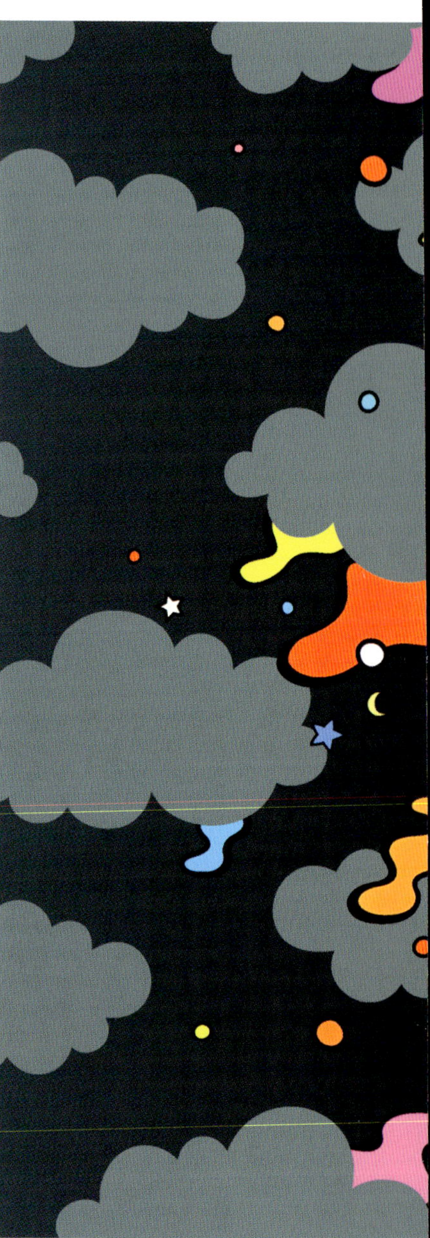

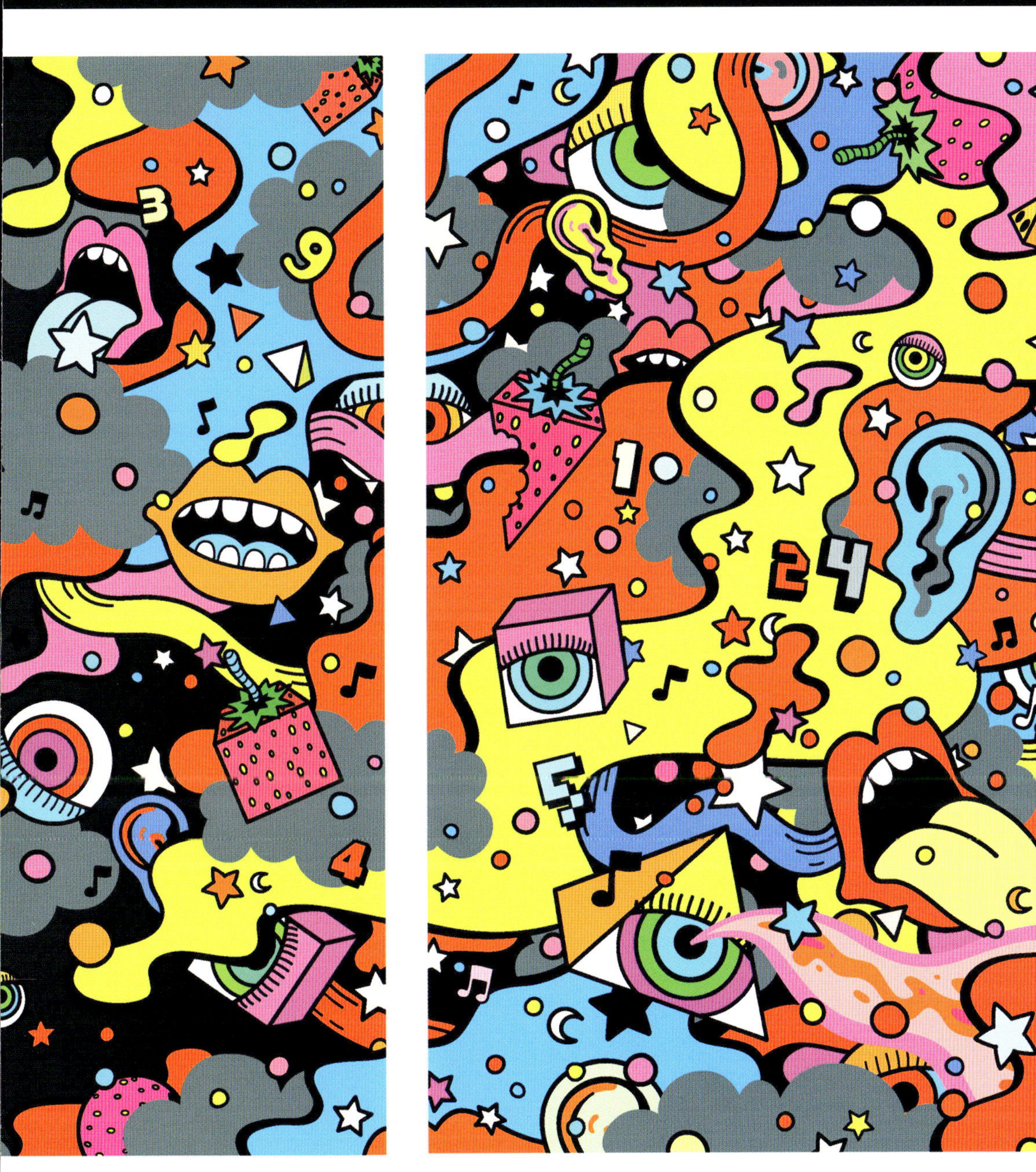

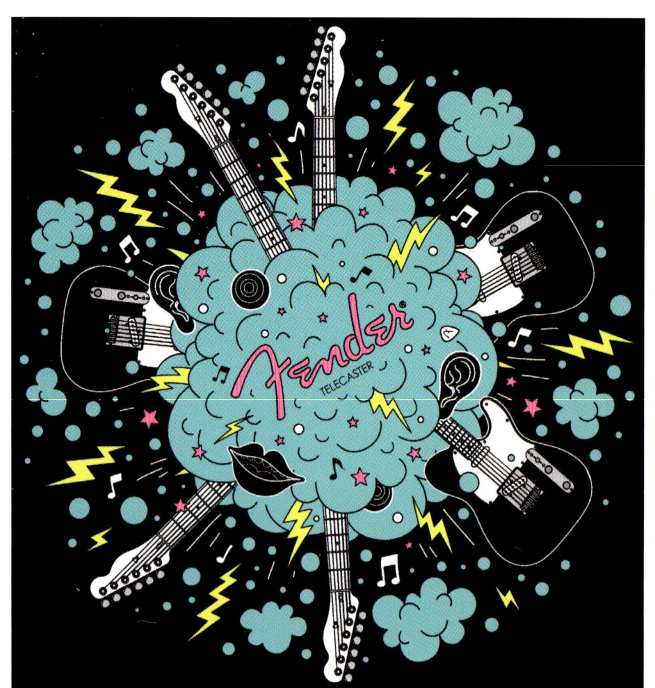

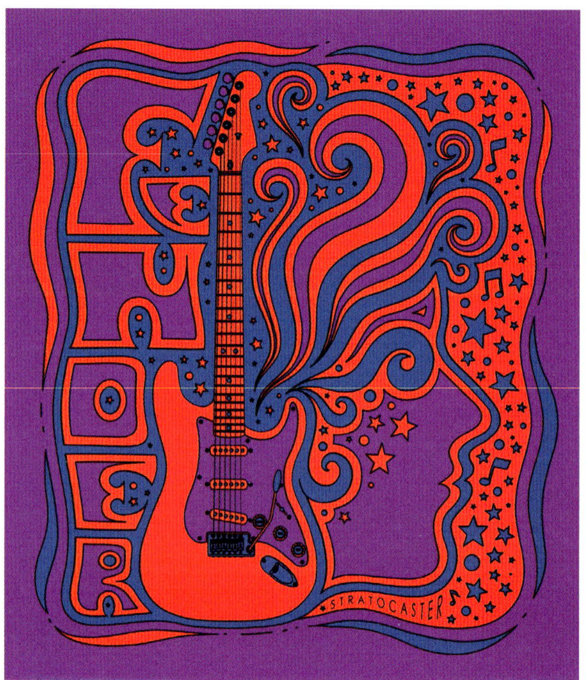

T-shirt graphics for Fender

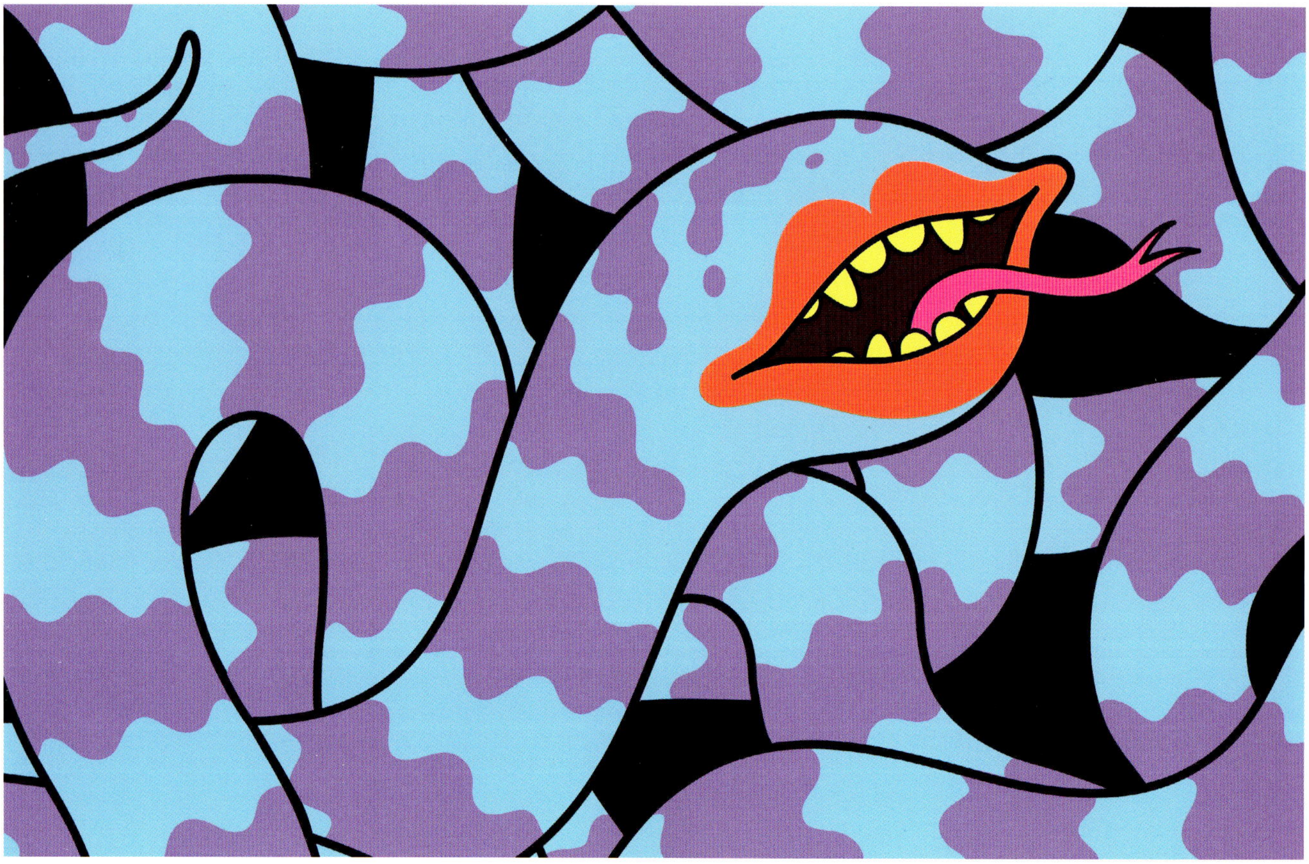

Moonrise Serpent

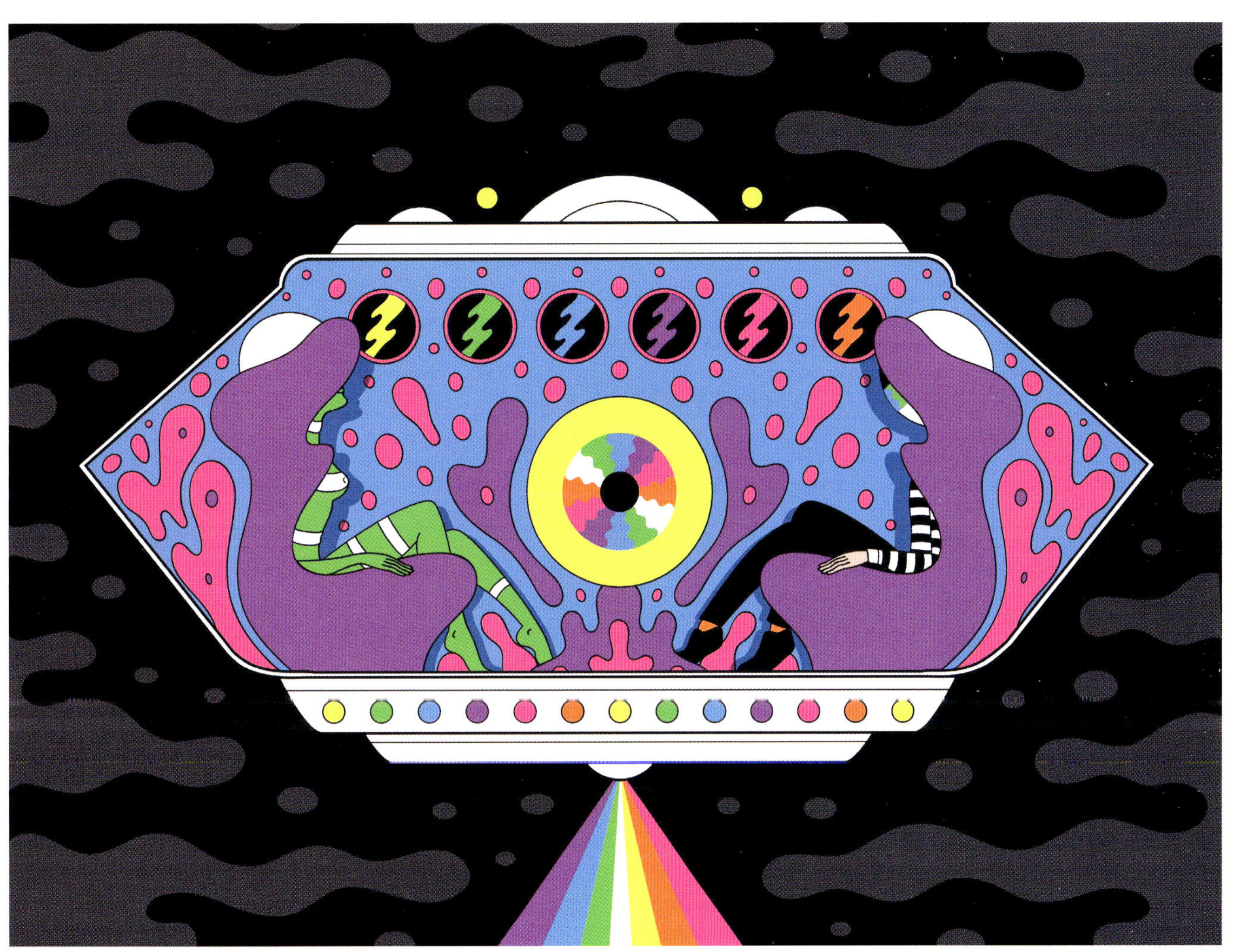

Editorial illustration for *Tribe* Magazine

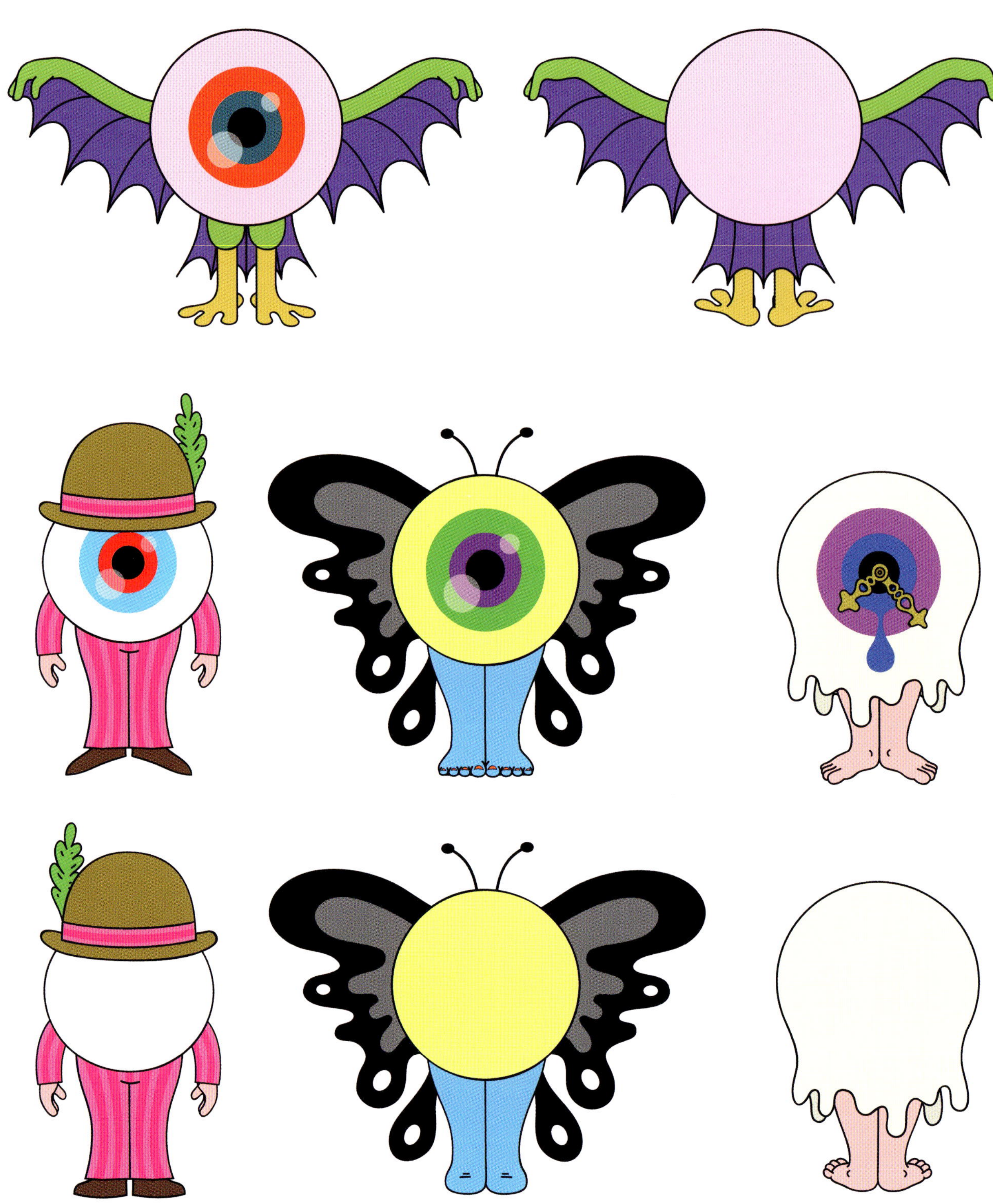

The Eye Guys character design

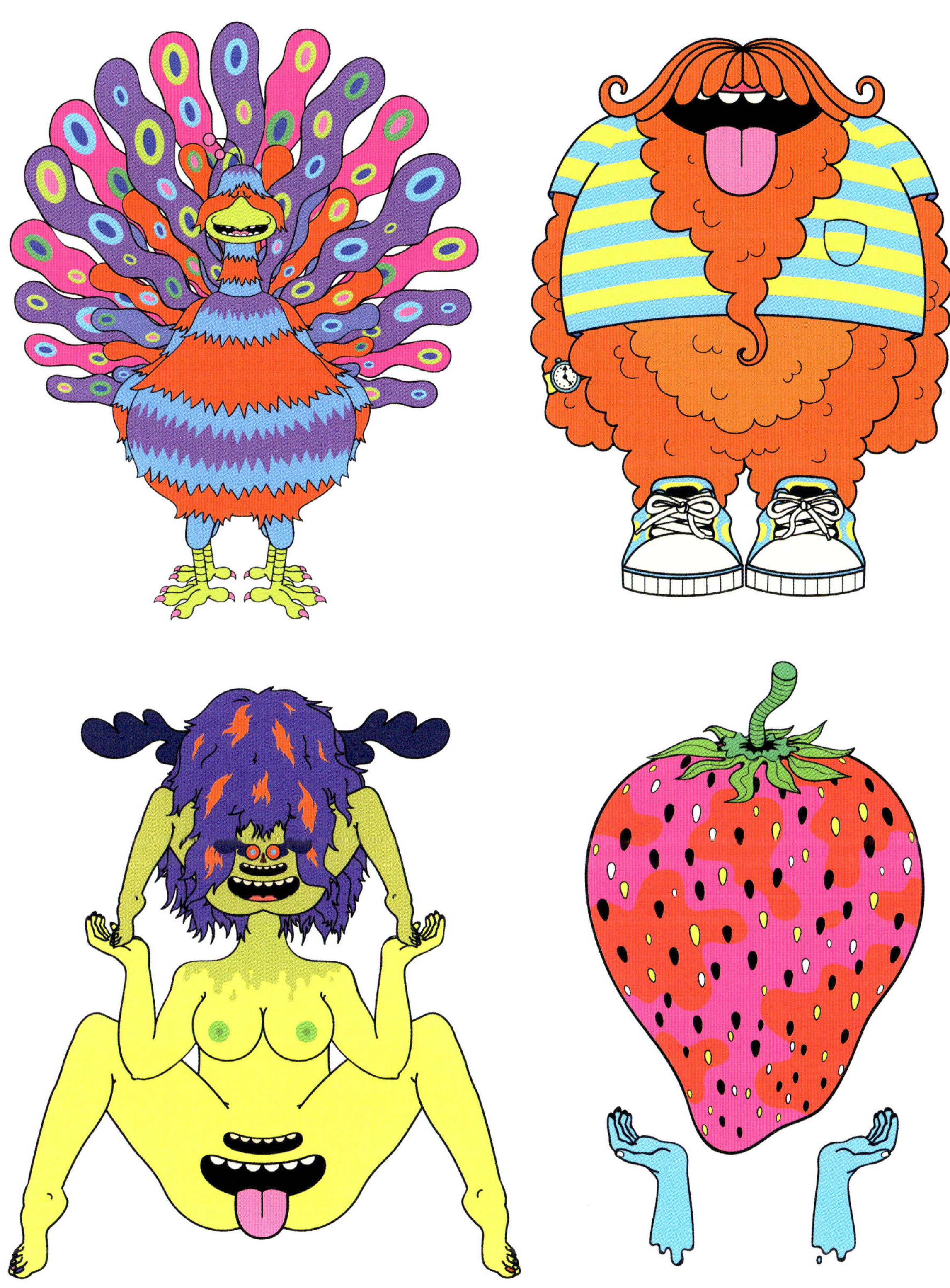

Illustration and character designs for London's Designer's Block festival

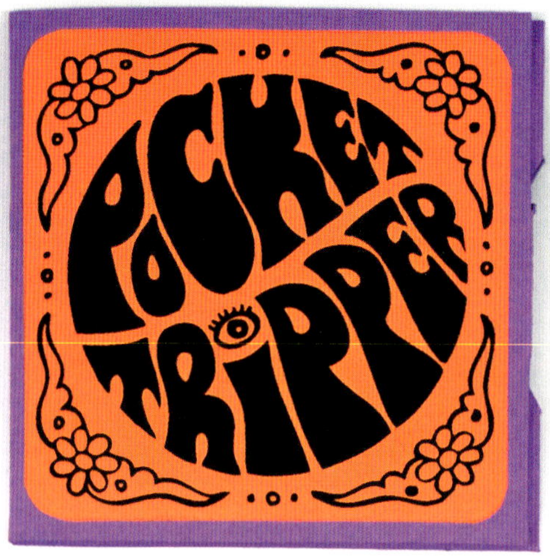

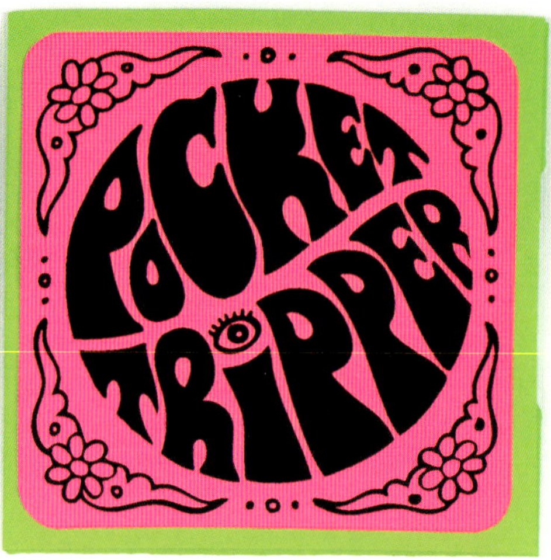

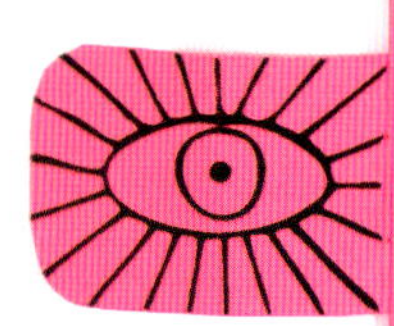
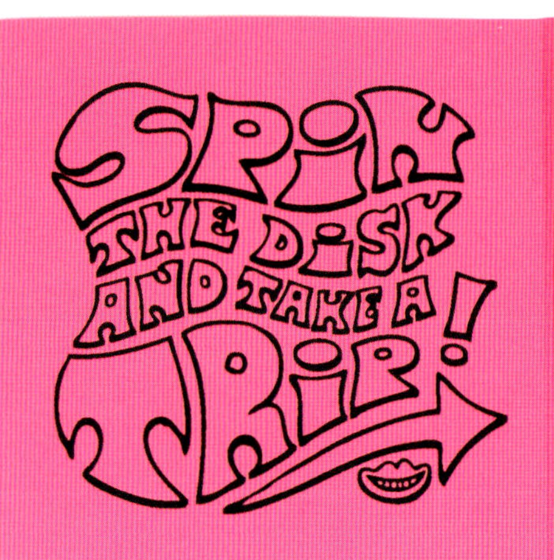

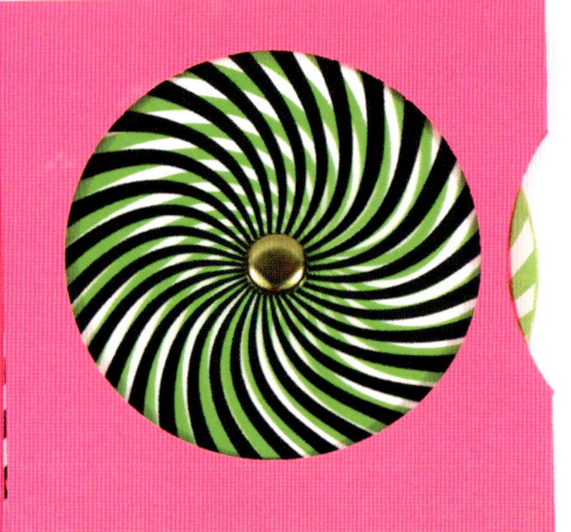
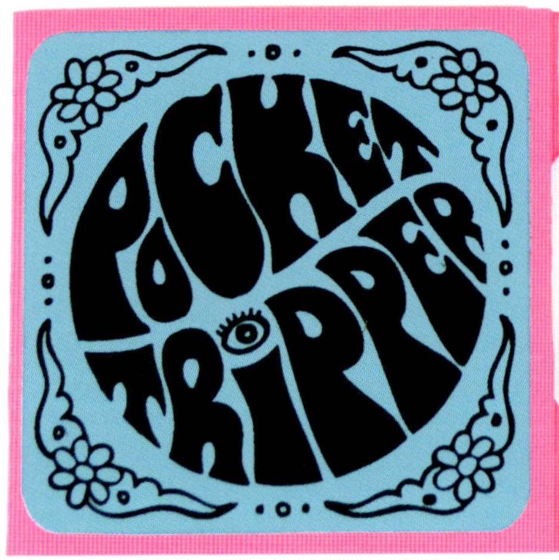

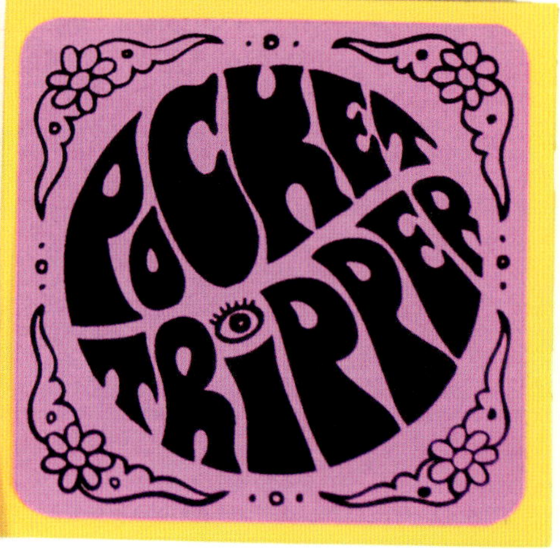

The Pocket Tripper

"A portable psychedelic interactive art toy for your pocket."

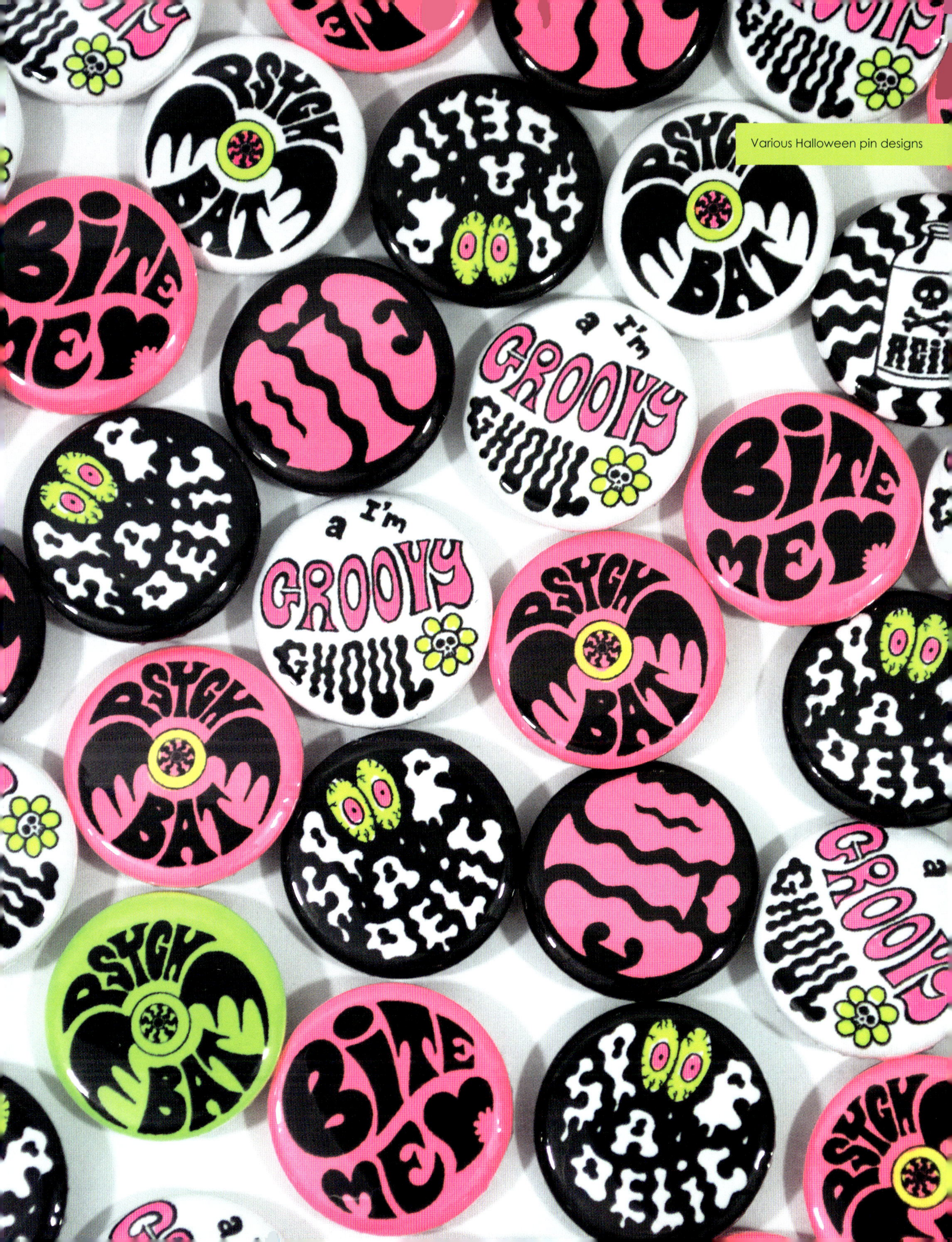

Various Halloween pin designs

Chapter Six:

The Artist in His Natural Habitat

I was raised as a Jehovah's Witness. I didn't celebrate my first birthday until I was twelve. By that time my mom was fellowshipped out of the religion. My parents were divorced and all the shit hit the fan, which was a good thing. My brother, sister, and I, all we knew was that religion. We weren't allowed to have worldly friends. That's why I'm okay being alone a lot, because we didn't have friends. Everybody was scary and evil to us, so we stayed home, making art and playing video games. That's helped mold me in a lot of ways, maybe most importantly growing up with everything being taboo, whether it's music, art, nudity, all that stuff. They would probably find the colors I'm using evil.

I have a few close people, but I don't feel like I'm part of a movement or any kind of group. To be honest with you, I don't know where I fit in, and I don't think a lot of other people know where I fit in. As far as understanding, I don't think that matters. I don't think people have a hard time appreciating or supporting my work, but I don't know if they really know what to make of it. I find that oftentimes people can't look away, but they also can't get too close because they don't really know how to deal with it. It's a weird place to be in. I appreciate all I've done and accomplished but there are parts that make you wonder how far it can go with this weird shit that I make. I think there's a natural balance, with me being the type of person that doesn't want to become stale, to have fluctuating interests, always pushing myself. Creativity and pushing yourself should always come first. Yes, you must feed yourself and your family, but that's personally why I have been an illustrator for over ten years. I've never done a commissioned painting and I never will, because painting is number one for me. If I die tomorrow and can only be remembered for one thing, that's the thing I want people to know. I don't want to be pressured with painting, I don't want to be persuaded. That's my universe and I don't want anyone to touch it. That's the one thing I have control over no matter what.

Oliver in his living room with *Death at First Sight*.

Oliver Hibert

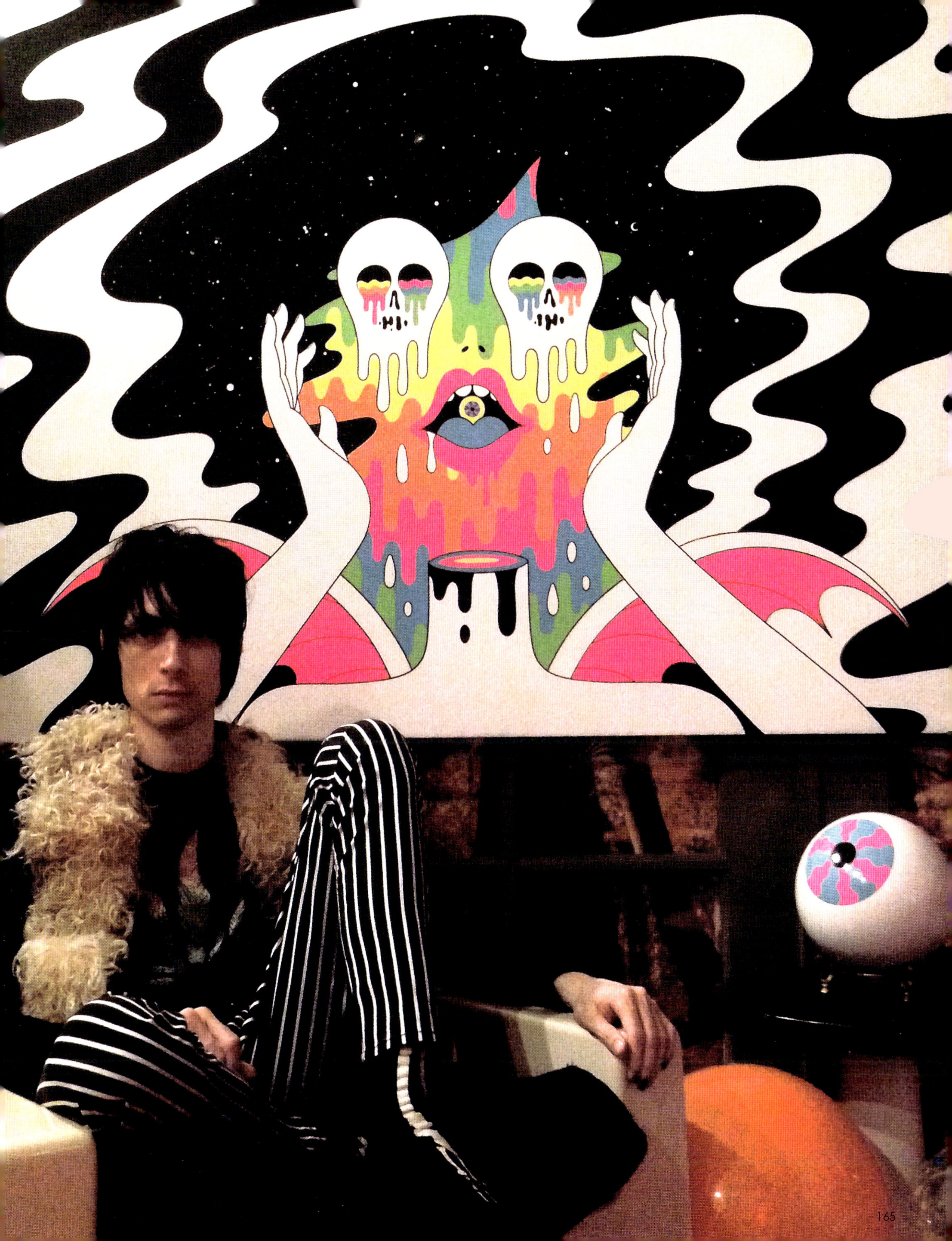

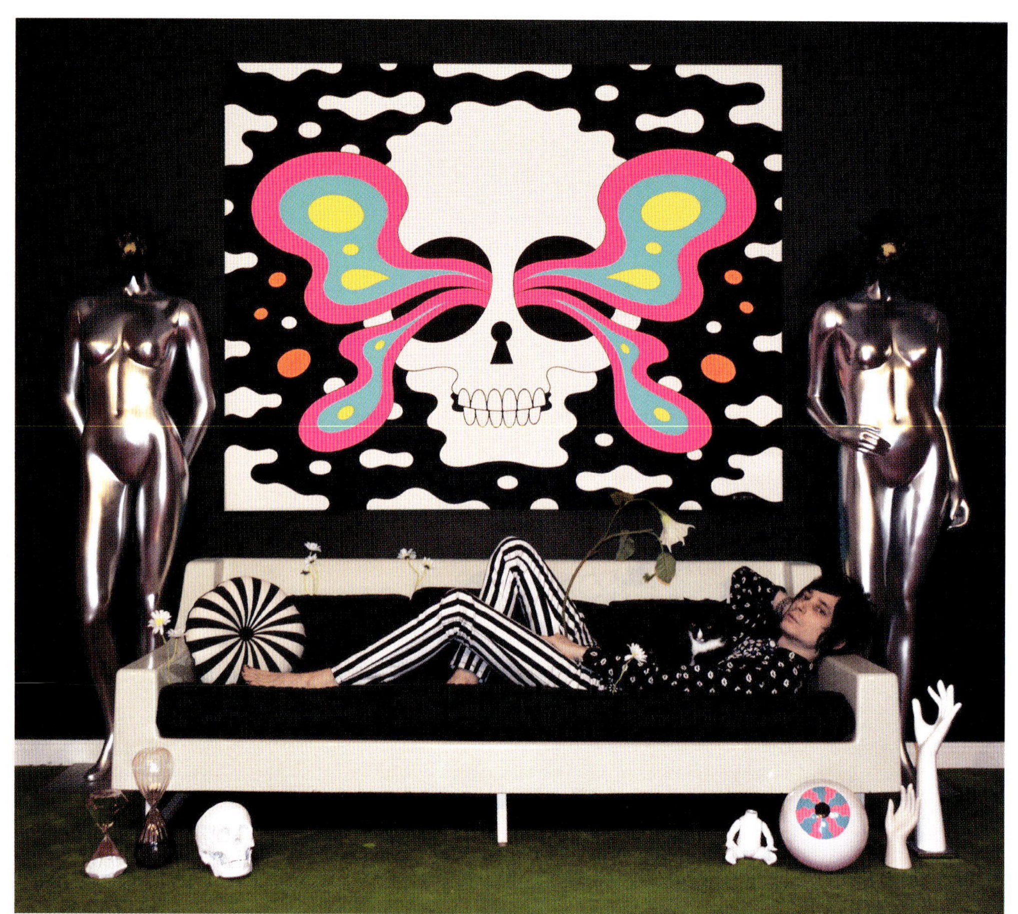

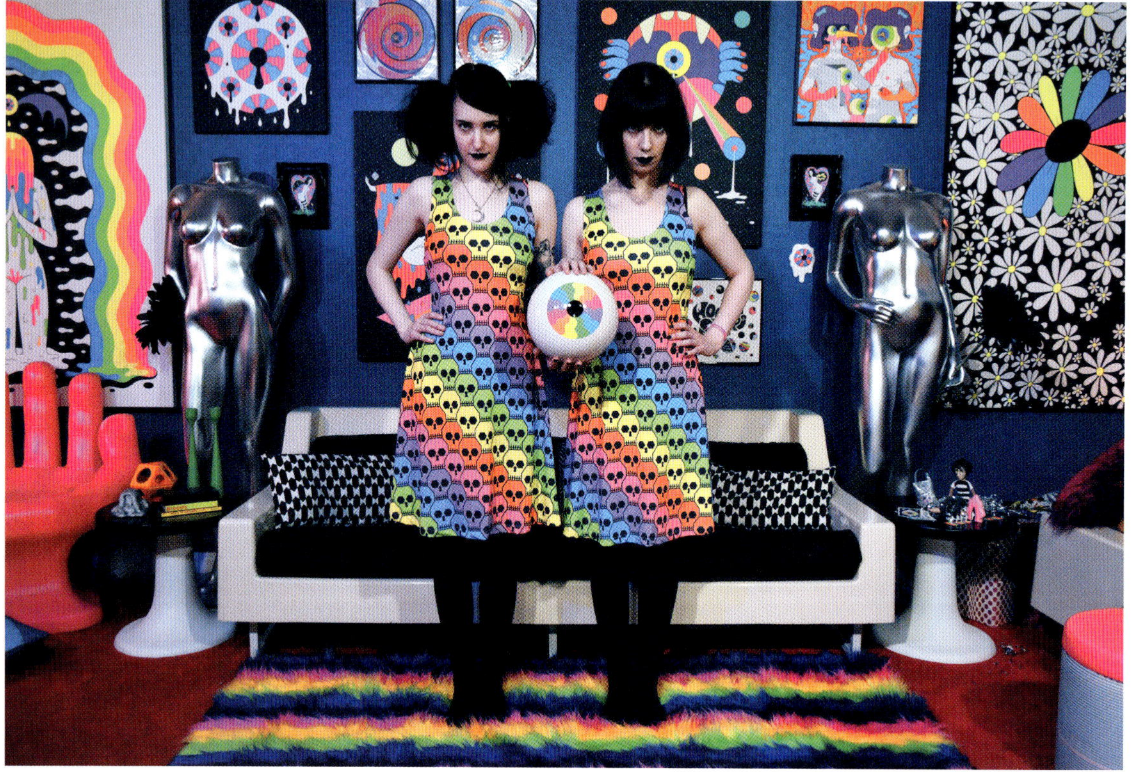

Jacqueline Denton and Danielle Hibert modeling Haunted Rainbow clothing designs

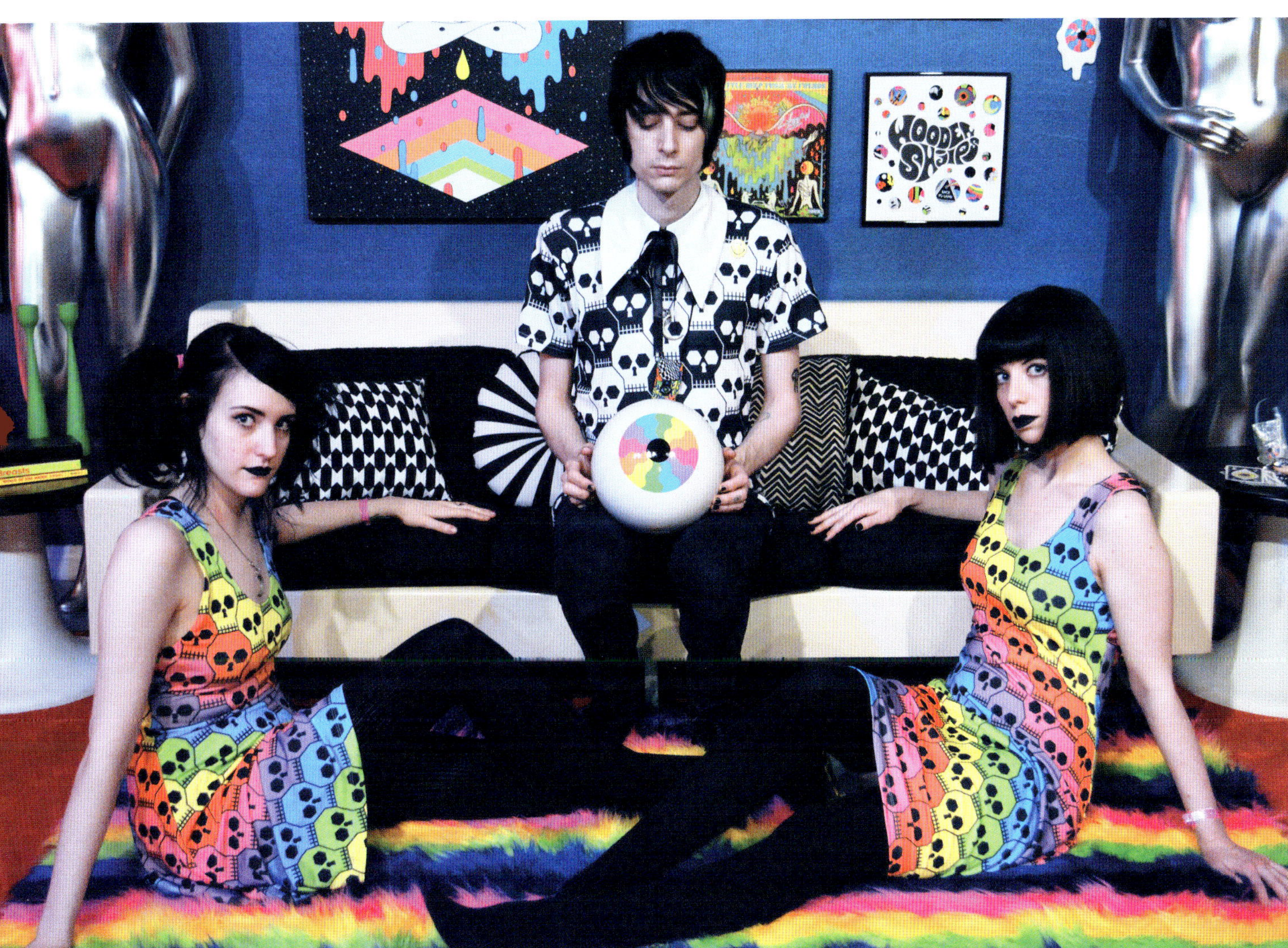

Haunted Rainbow clothing promo photo with Jacqueline Denton, Oliver Hibert, and Danielle Hibert

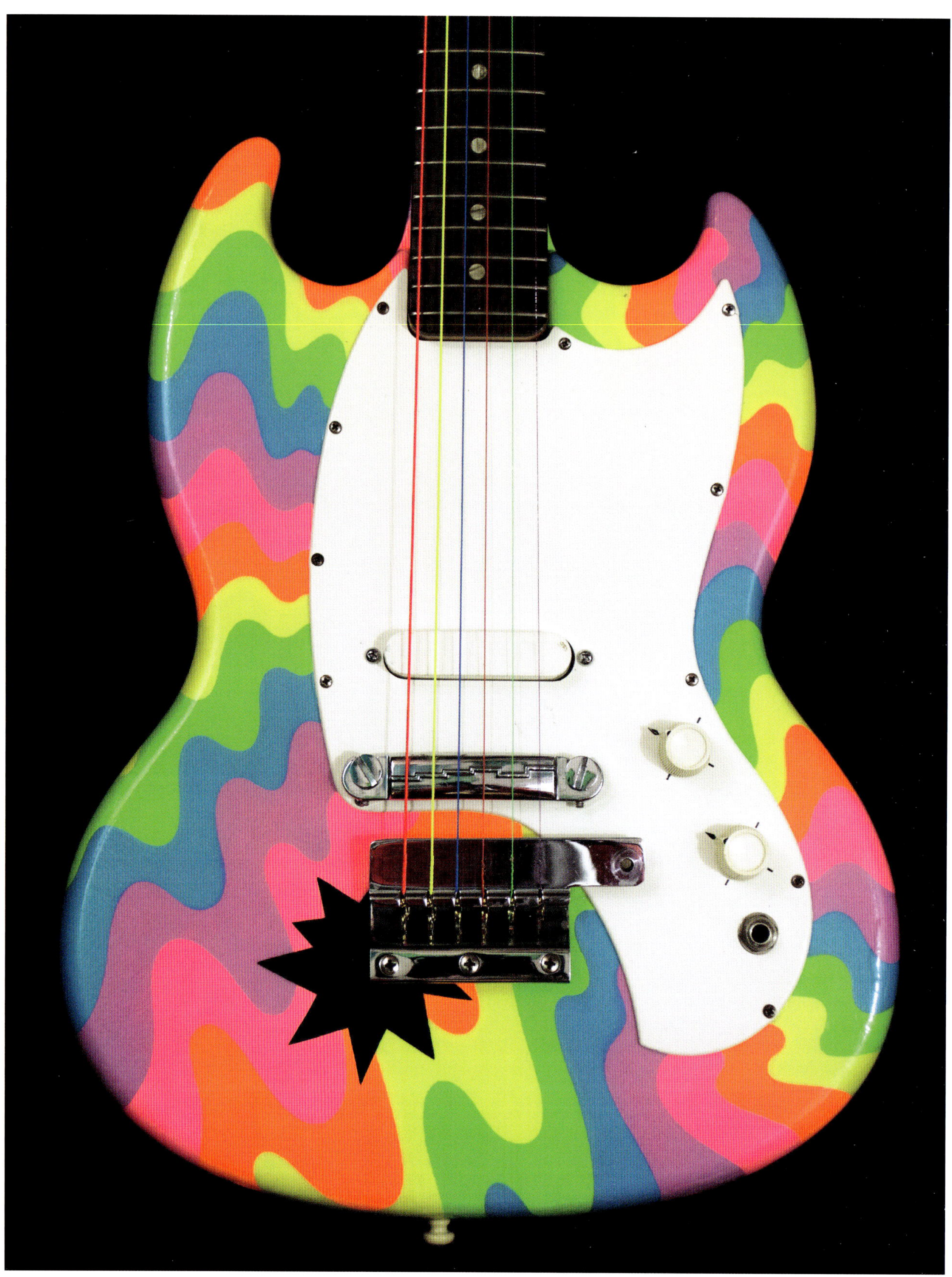

Psychedelic painted custom guitar

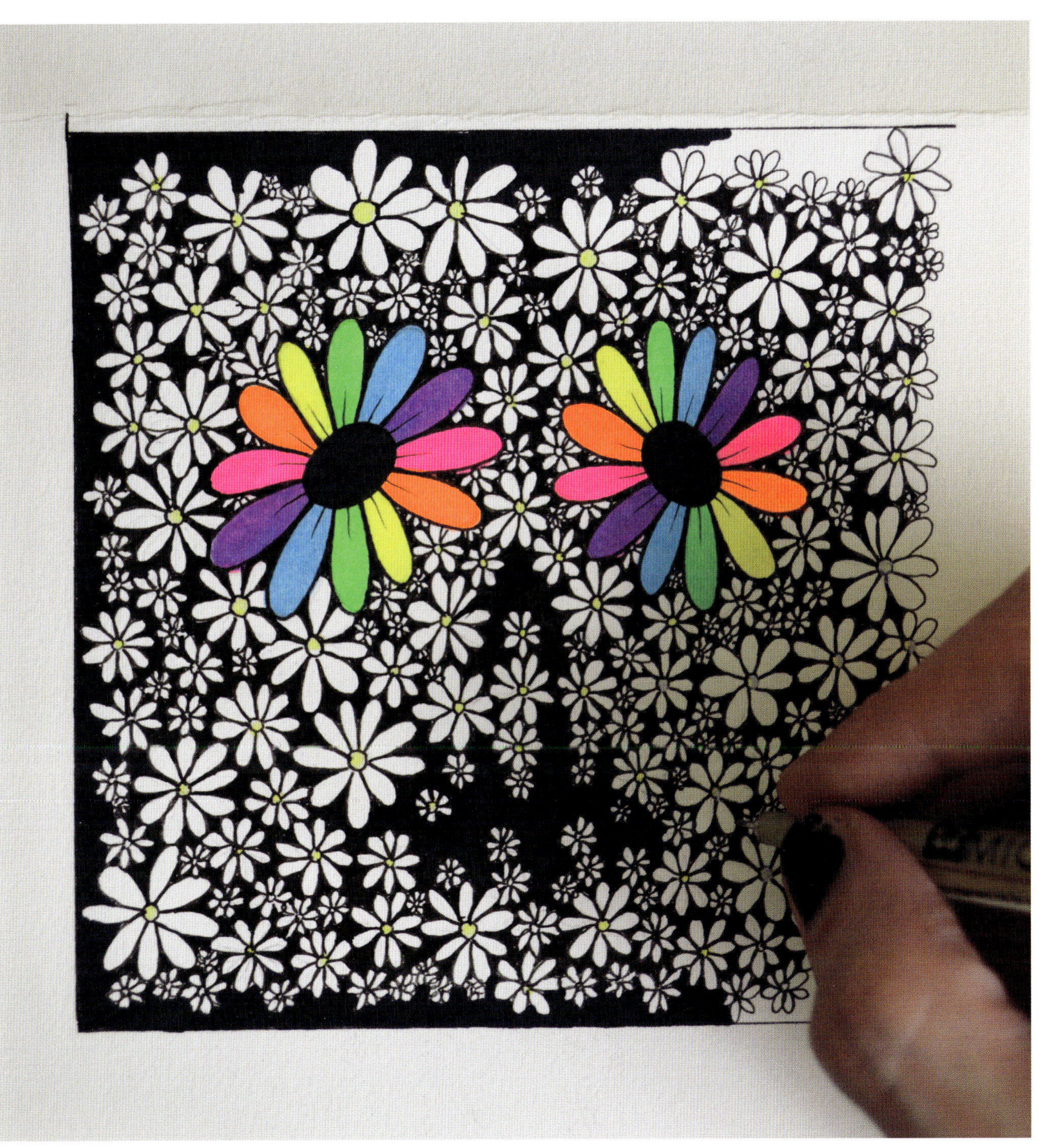

Drawing *Scream thy Last Scream*

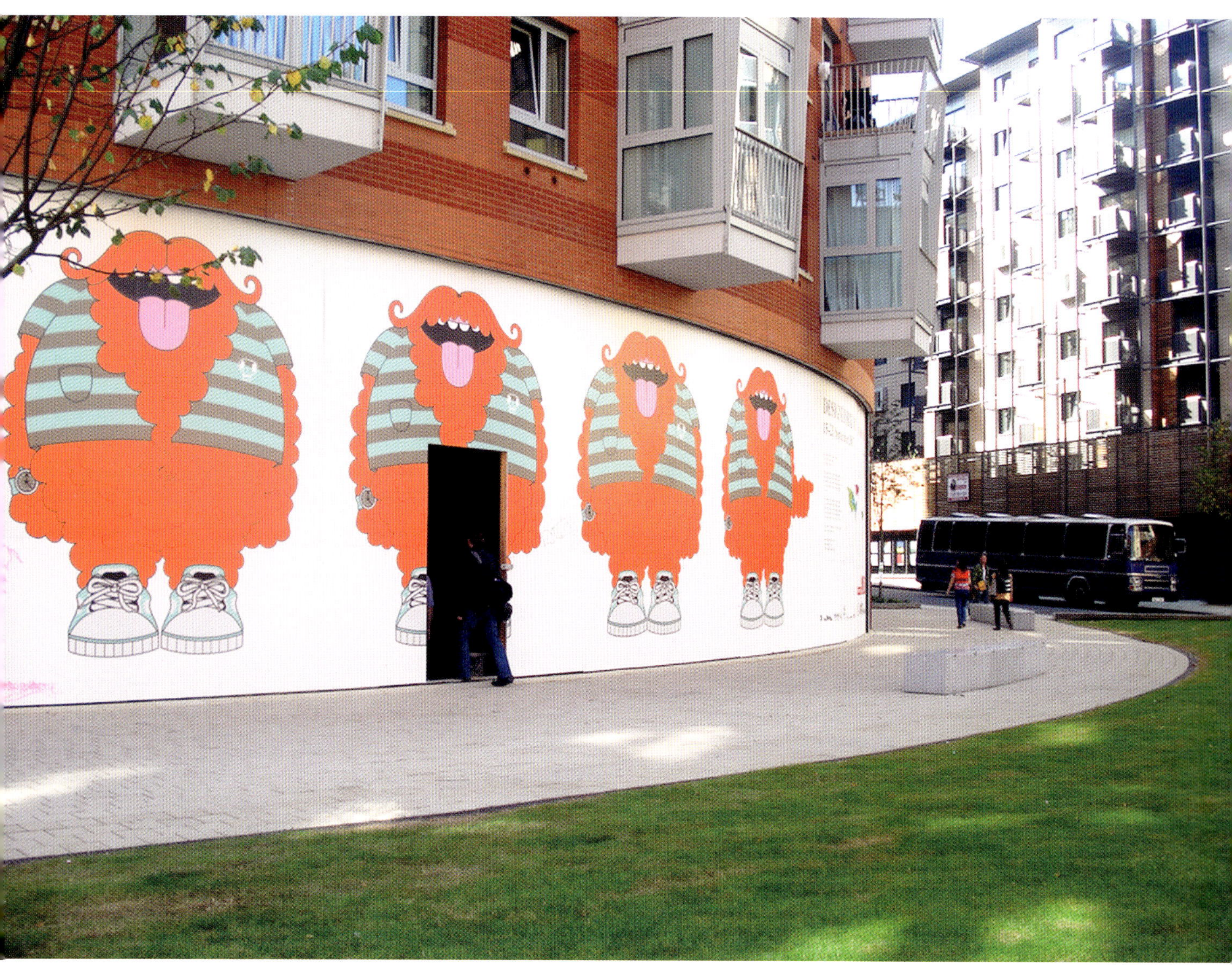

Character design for London's Designer's Block festival exterior installation

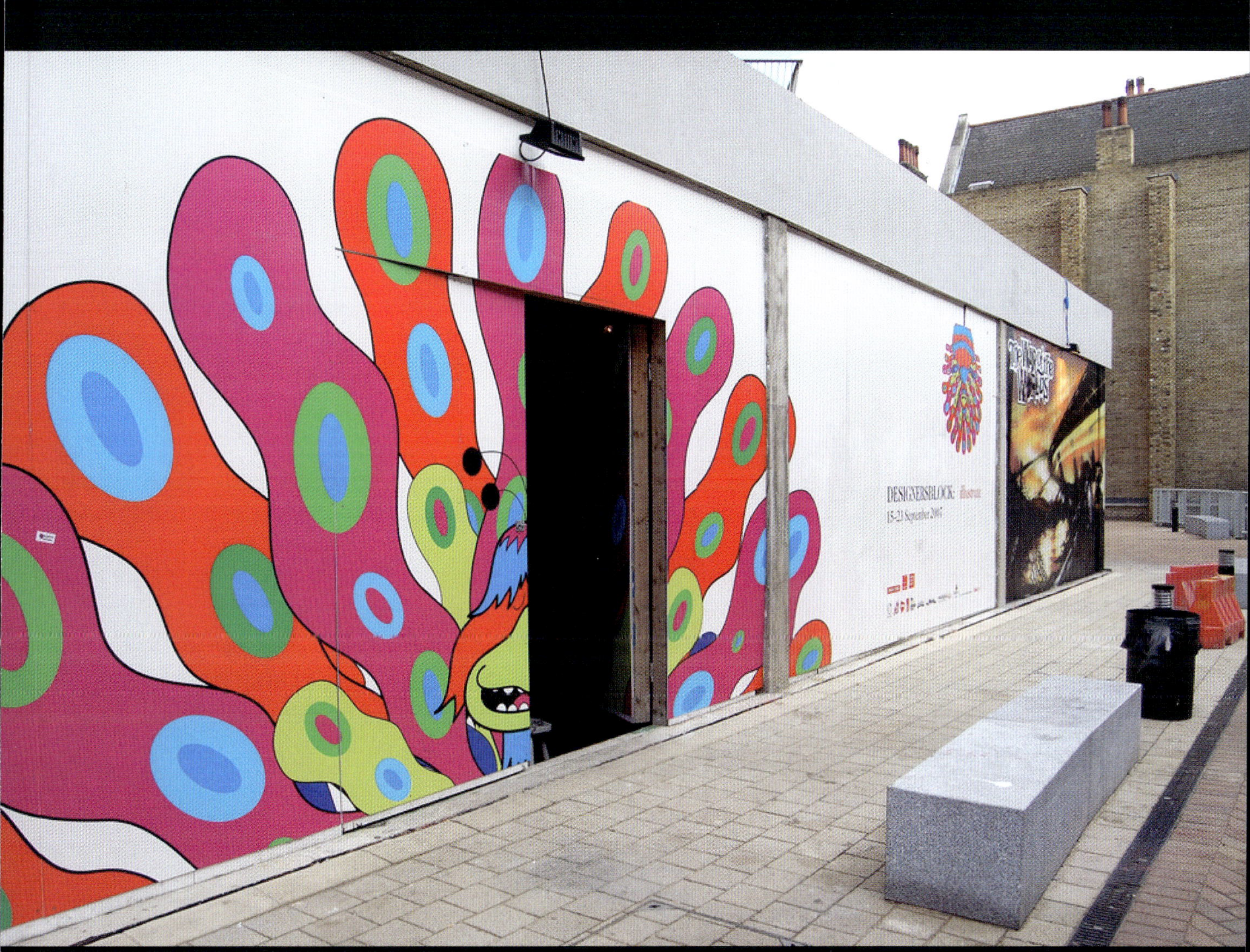
DESIGNERSBLOCK:

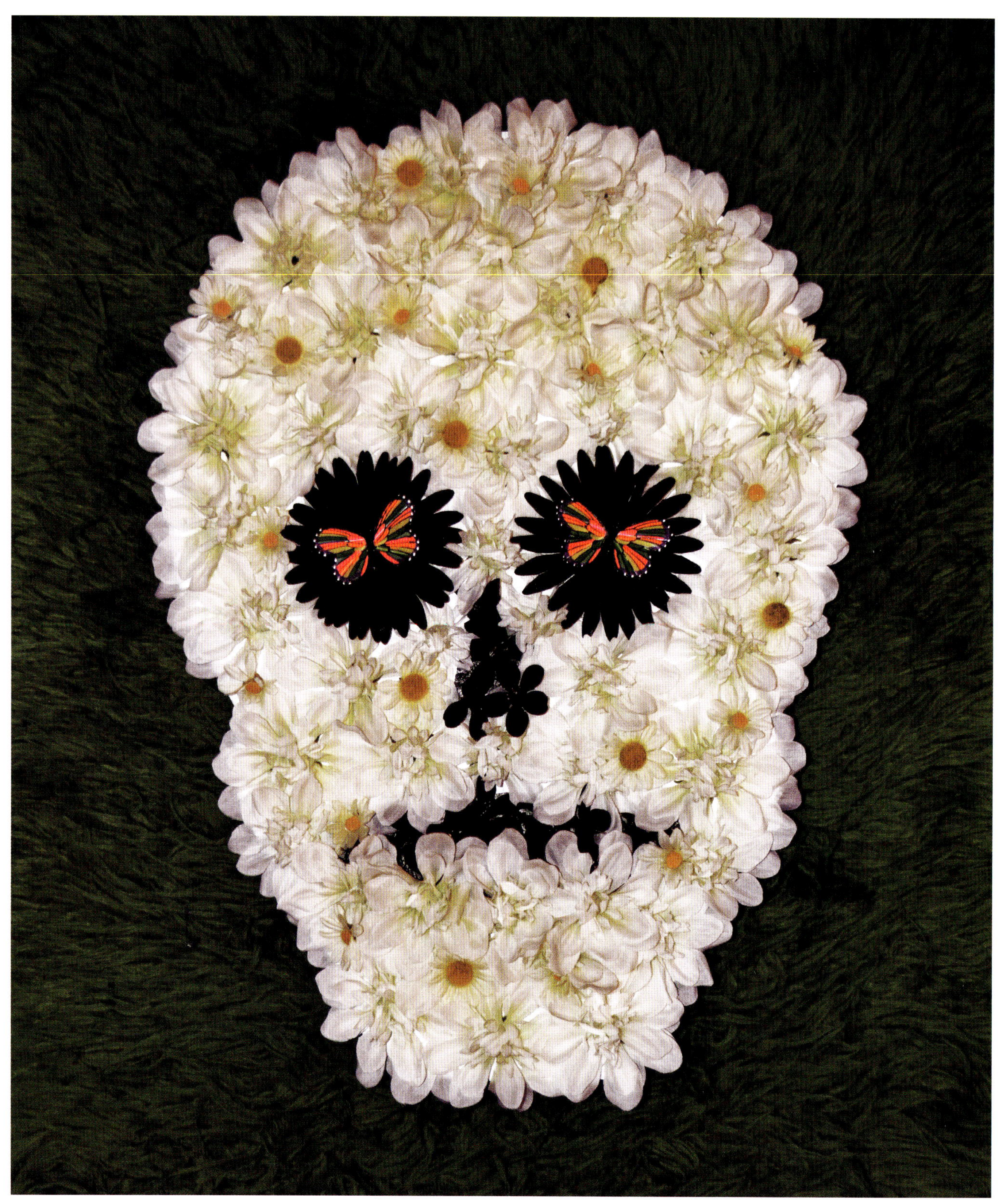

Flower skullpture

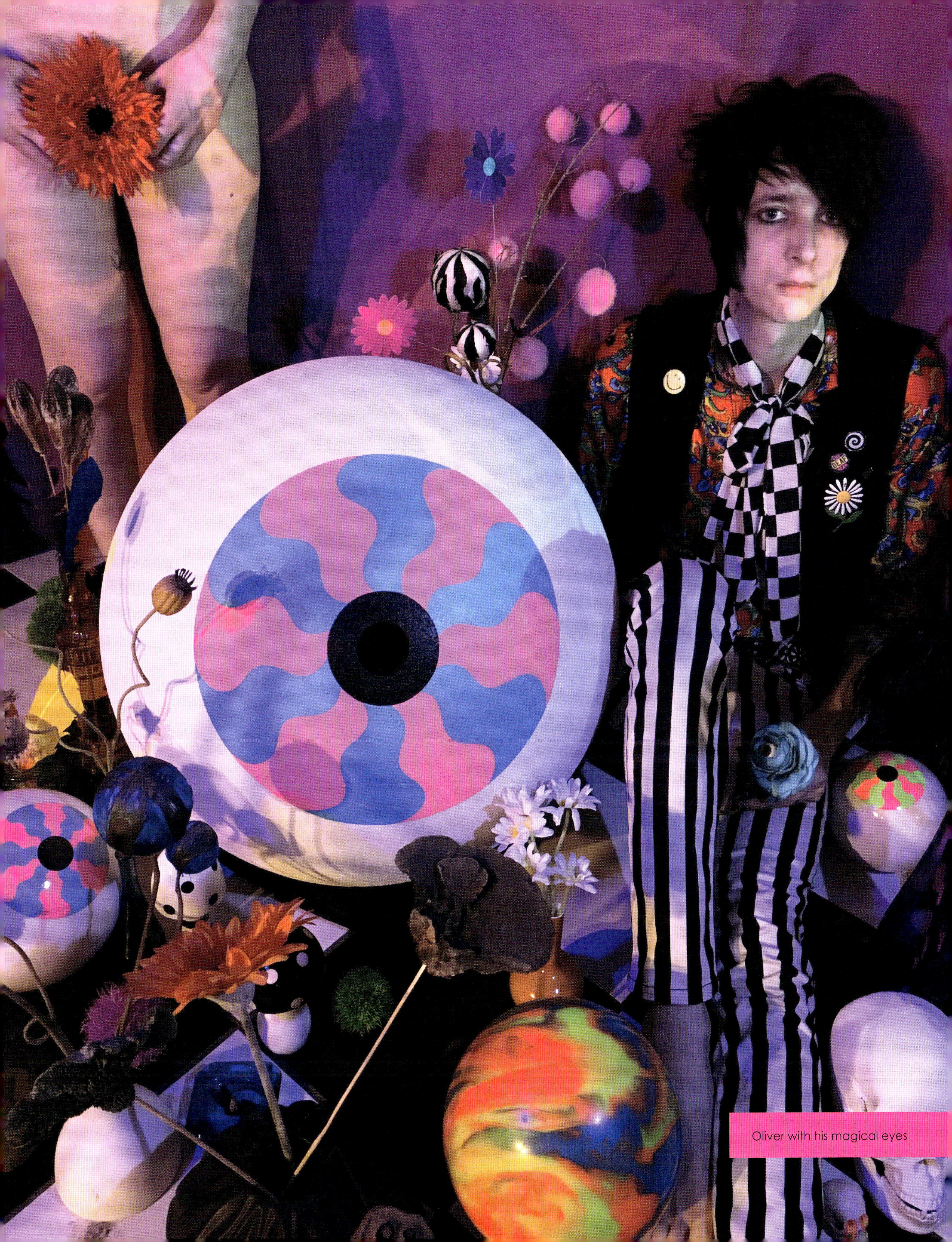

Oliver with his magical eyes

Photo by Seth Miranda

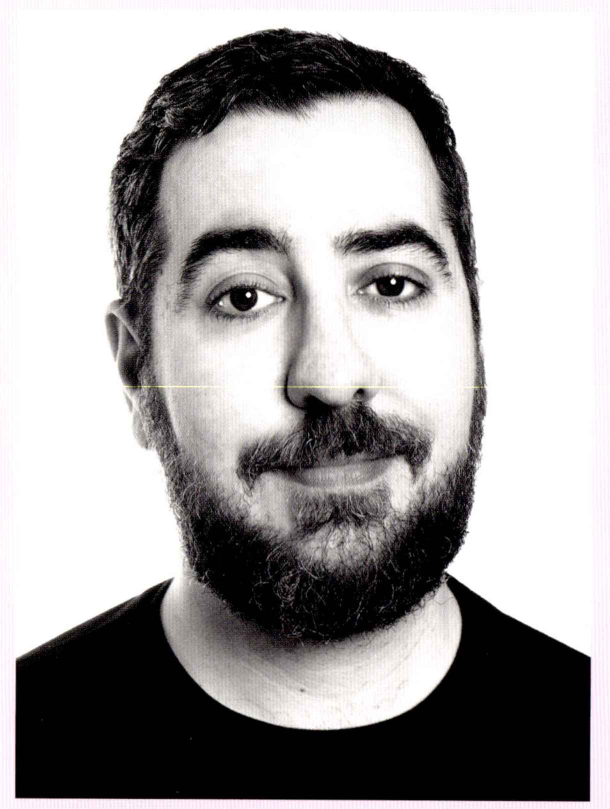

About the Author

Angelo Madrigale lives and works in New York City. He and his wife Lisa were the former owners and directors of the Metropolis Gallery, named one of the world's "Top 100 Galleries" by *Juxtapoz* Magazine in 2010. This is his first book.

About Oliver

Oliver Hibert works and lives in the deep valley desert of Arizona. Surrounded by a garden of peacocks, he fills the night with bright psychedelic fantasies of art in many mediums. Self taught and determined, Hibert entered the gallery scene when he was sixteen years old, and now has shown his work in galleries and museums across the globe—with only the stars in the sky being the limit.

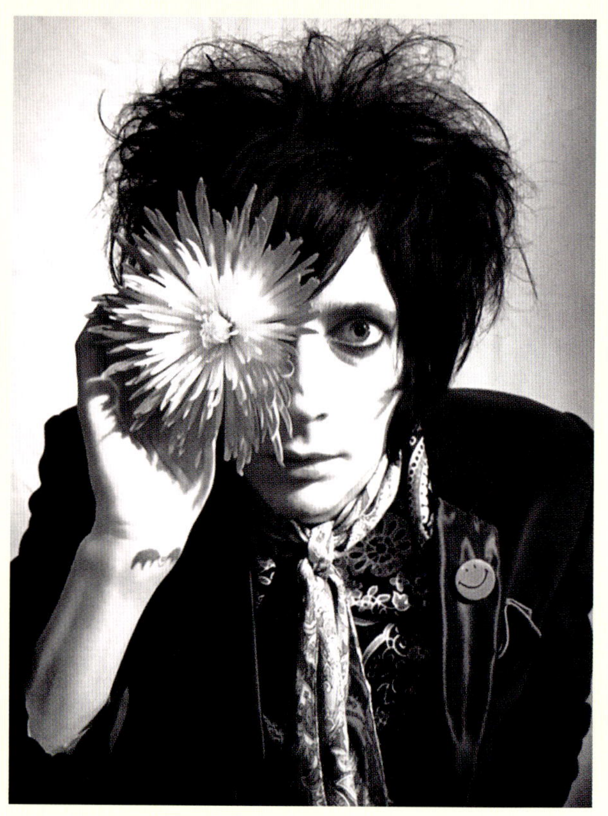

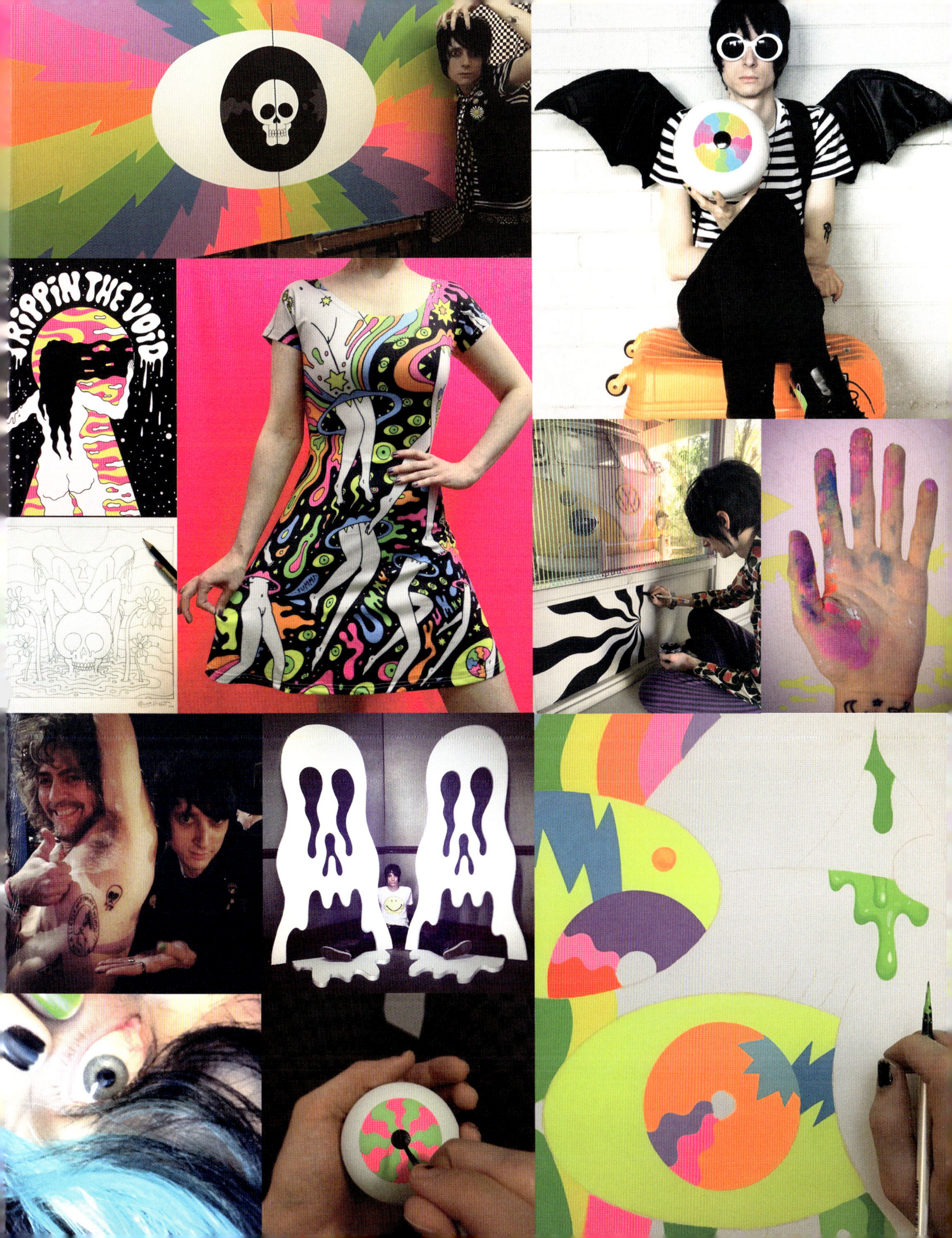
RIPPIN THE VOID

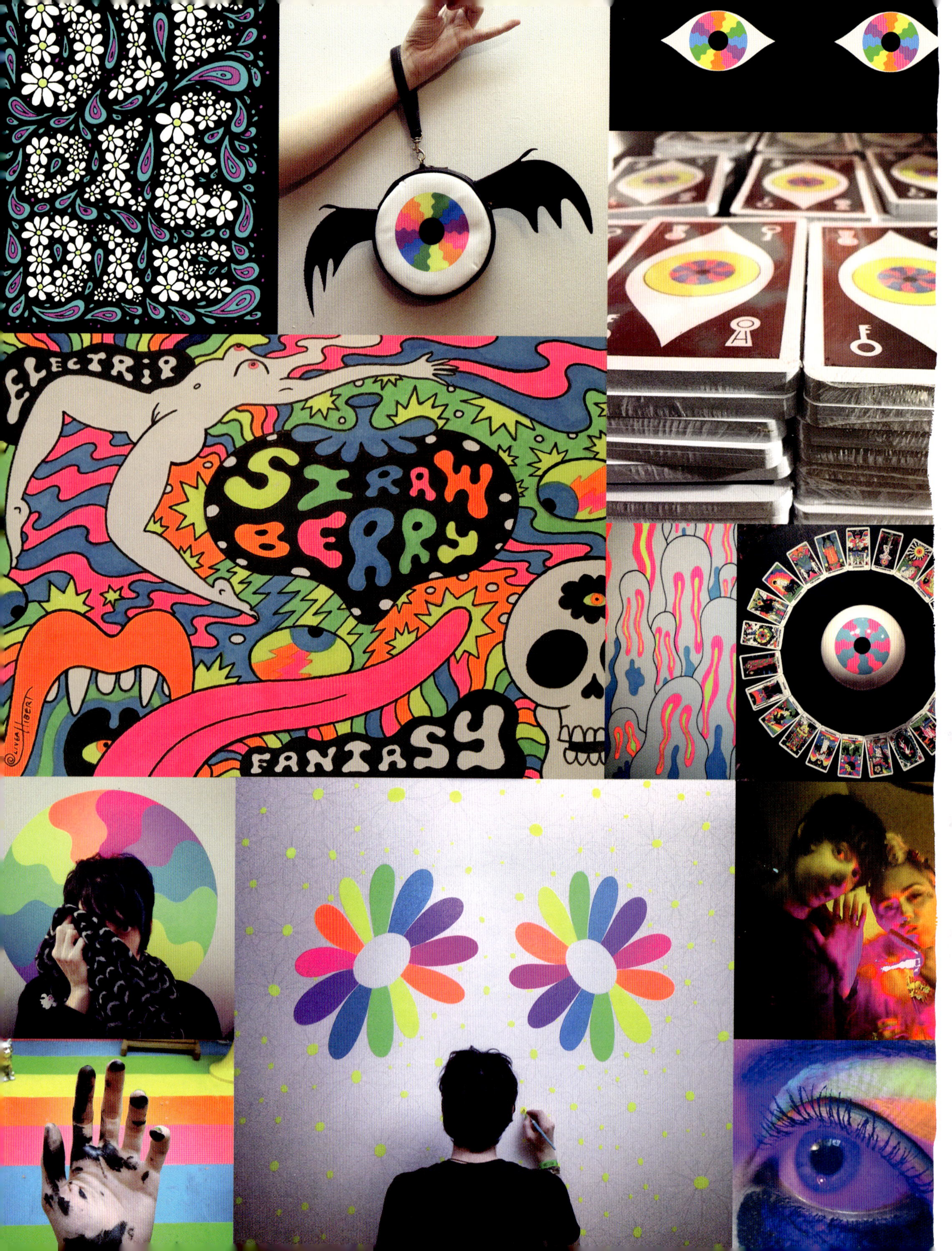
ELECTRIP
STRAW
BERRY
FANTASY

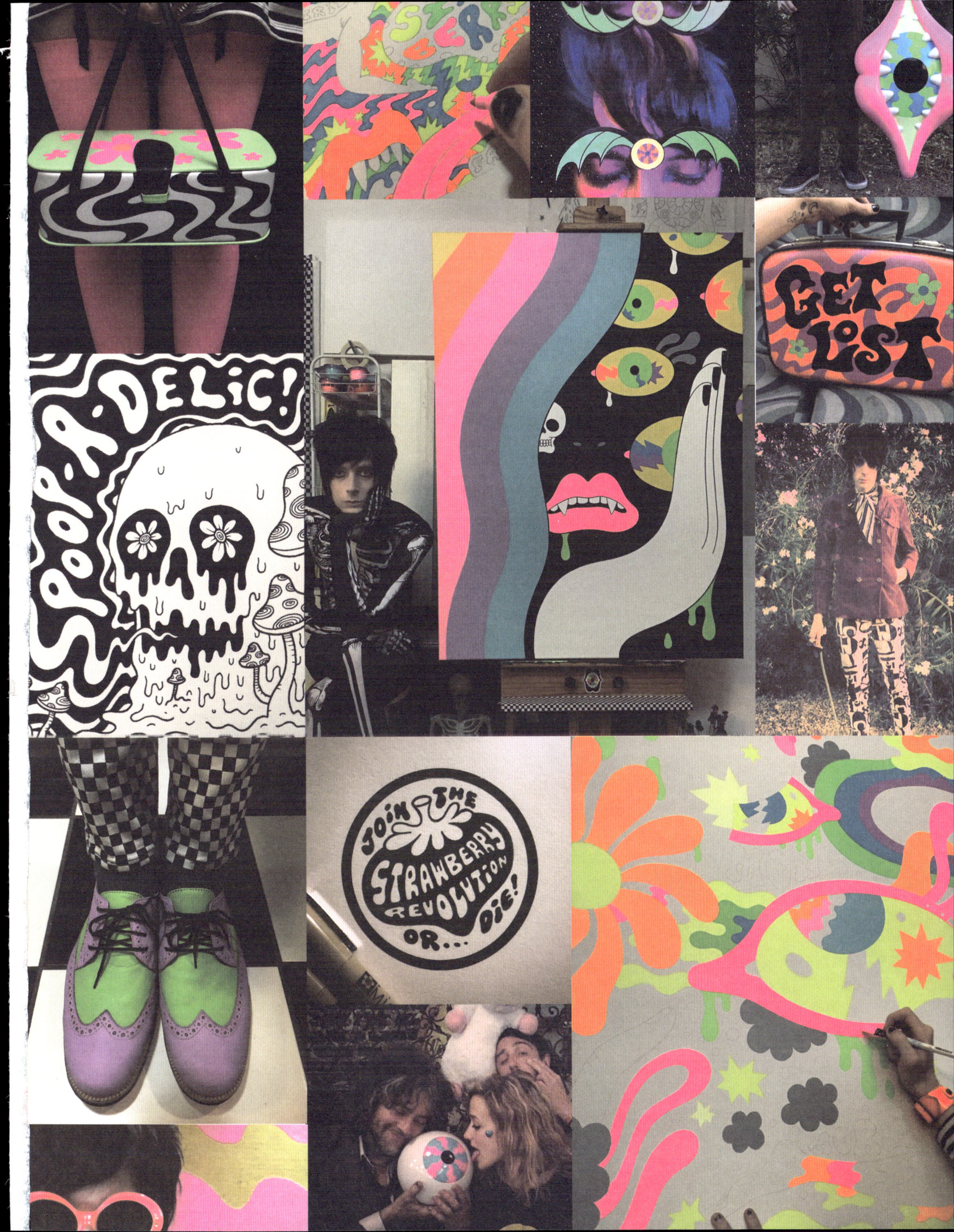
SPOOP-A-DELIC!
GET LOST
JOIN THE STRAWBERRY REVOLUTION OR... DIE!

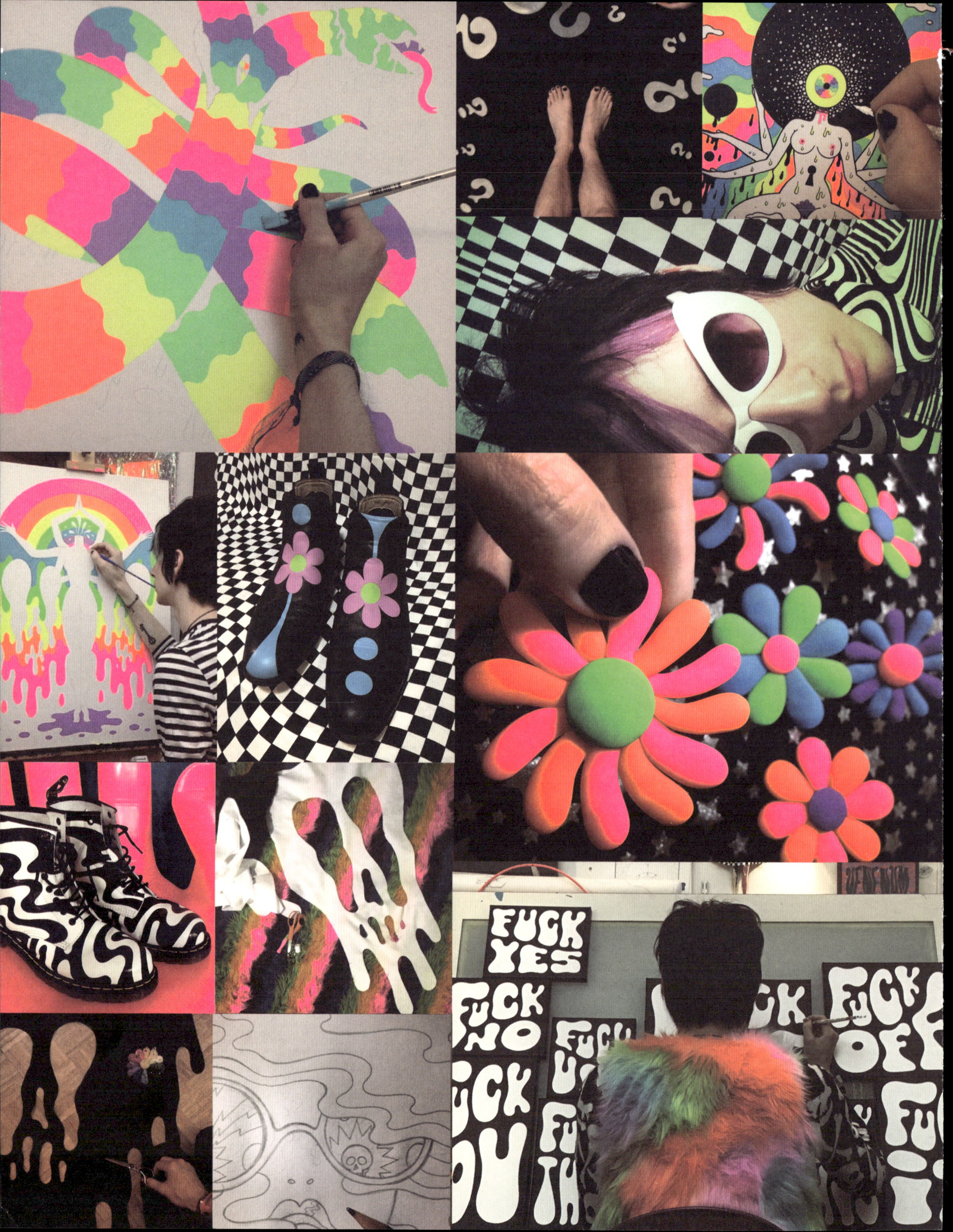
FUCK YES
FUCK NO